A Certain Magical Index

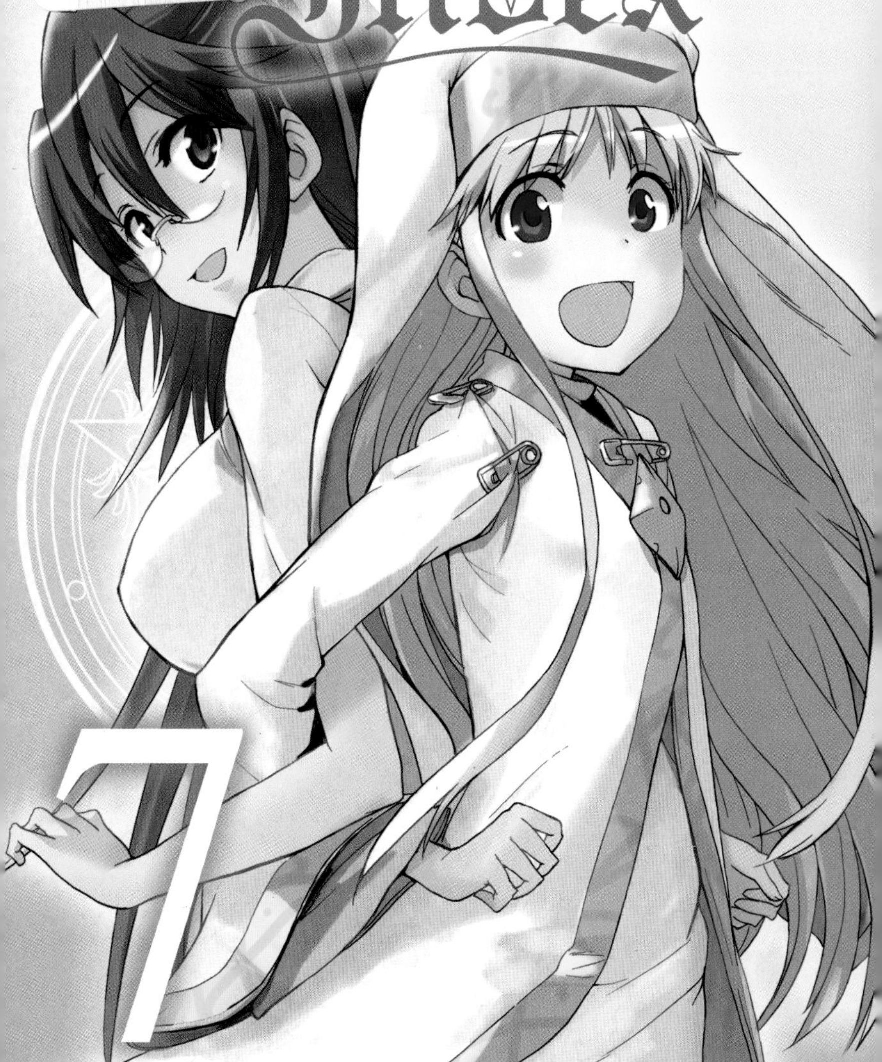

7

ORIGINAL STORY: KAZUMA KAMACHI

CHARACTER DESIGN: KIYOTAKA HAIMURA

CHUYA KOGINO

A CERTAIN MAGICAL INDEX **7** TABLE OF CONTENTS

Index Librorum Prohibitorum

#34 HYOUKA KAZAKIRI

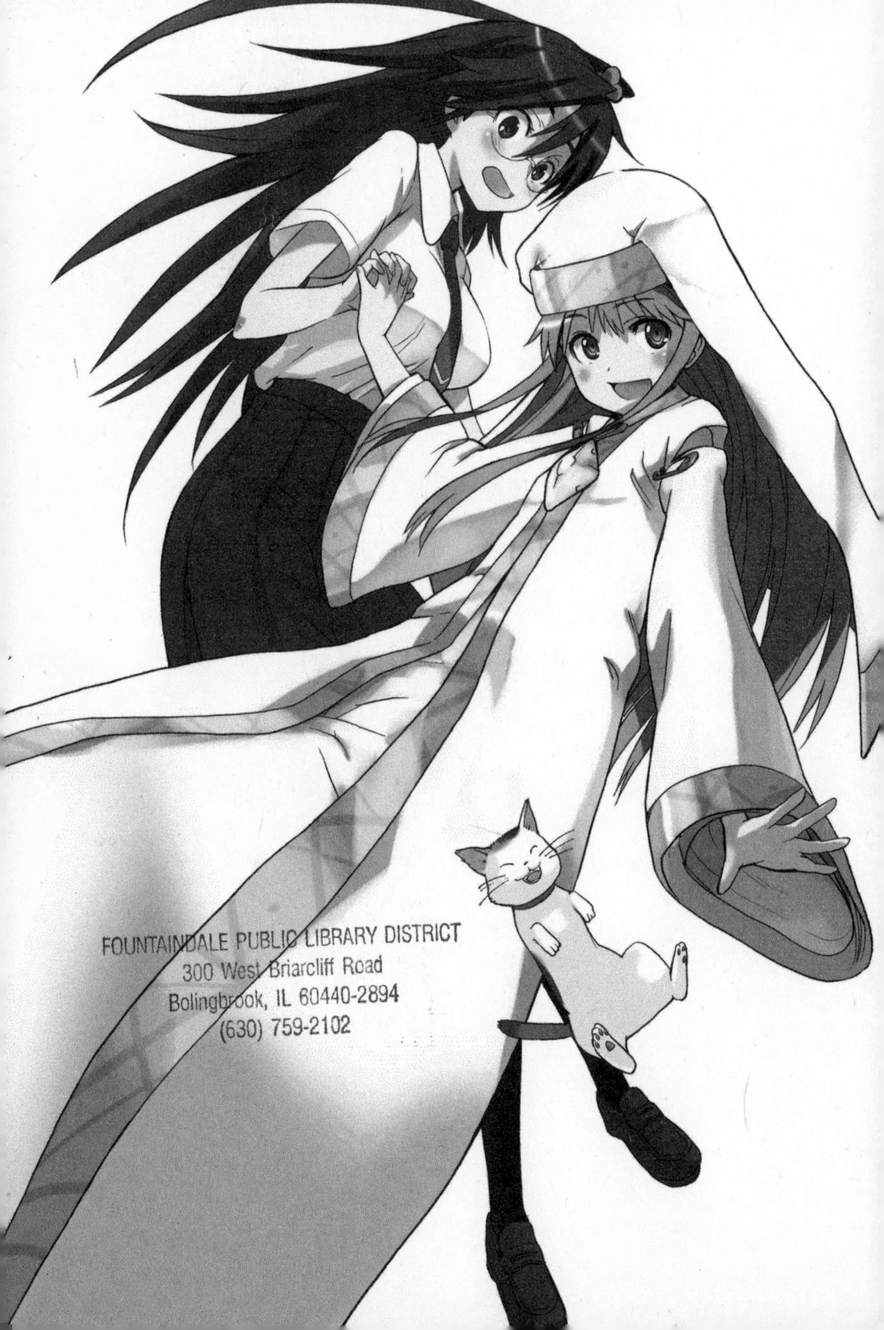

A Certain Magical Index

AN URBAN LEGEND RELATED TO ACADEMY CITY.

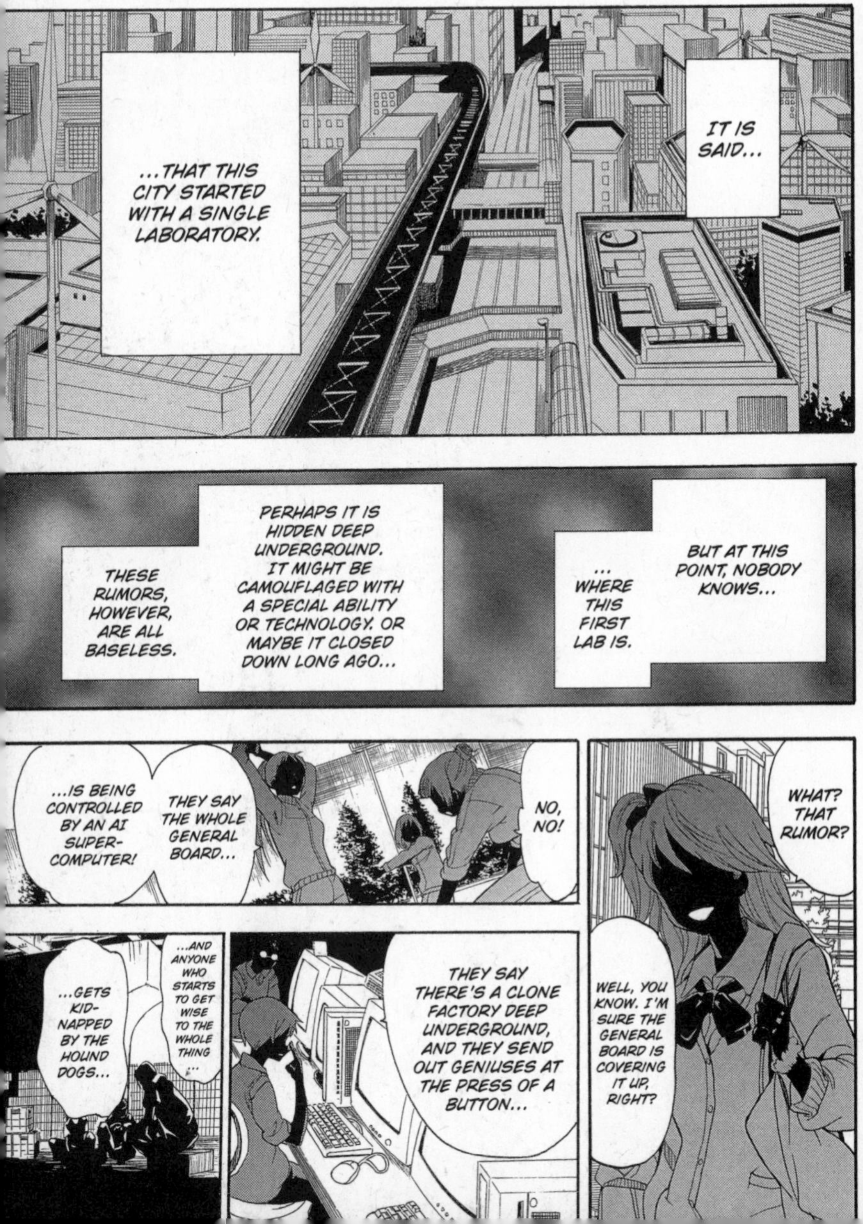
IT IS SAID...
...THAT THIS CITY STARTED WITH A SINGLE LABORATORY.
BUT AT THIS POINT, NOBODY KNOWS...
... WHERE THIS FIRST LAB IS.
PERHAPS IT IS HIDDEN DEEP UNDERGROUND. IT MIGHT BE CAMOUFLAGED WITH A SPECIAL ABILITY OR TECHNOLOGY. OR MAYBE IT CLOSED DOWN LONG AGO...
THESE RUMORS, HOWEVER, ARE ALL BASELESS.
WHAT? THAT RUMOR?
WELL, YOU KNOW. I'M SURE THE GENERAL BOARD IS COVERING IT UP, RIGHT?
NO, NO!
THEY SAY THE WHOLE GENERAL BOARD...
...IS BEING CONTROLLED BY AN AI SUPER-COMPUTER!
THEY SAY THERE'S A CLONE FACTORY DEEP UNDERGROUND, AND THEY SEND OUT GENIUSES AT THE PRESS OF A BUTTON...
...AND ANYONE WHO STARTS TO GET WISE TO THE WHOLE THING...
...GETS KID-NAPPED BY THE HOUND DOGS...

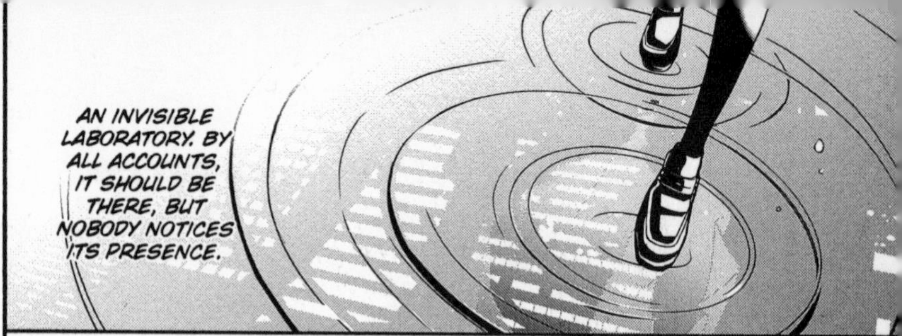
AN INVISIBLE LABORATORY. BY ALL ACCOUNTS, IT SHOULD BE THERE, BUT NOBODY NOTICES ITS PRESENCE.

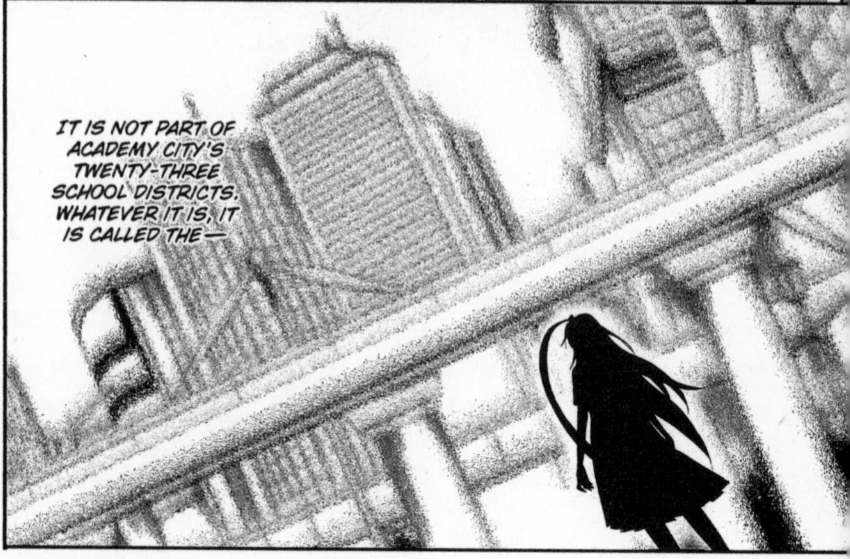
IT IS NOT PART OF ACADEMY CITY'S TWENTY-THREE SCHOOL DISTRICTS. WHATEVER IT IS, IT IS CALLED THE—

FIVE ELEMENTS SOCIETY, IN THE ITH (IMAGINARY NUMBER) SCHOOL DISTRICT.

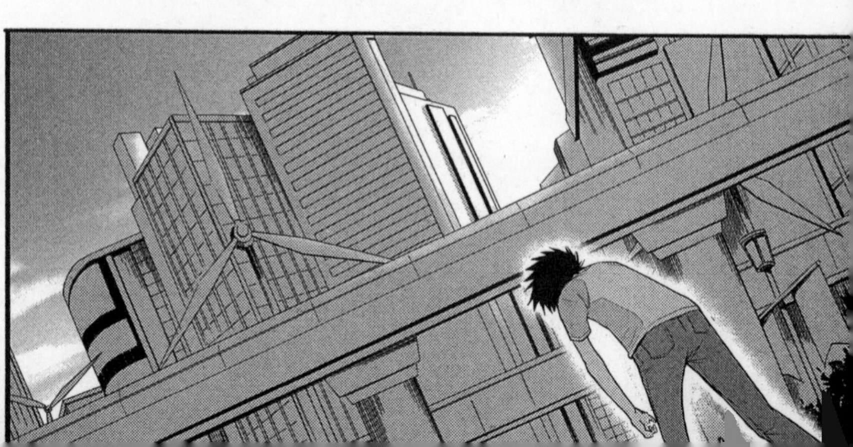

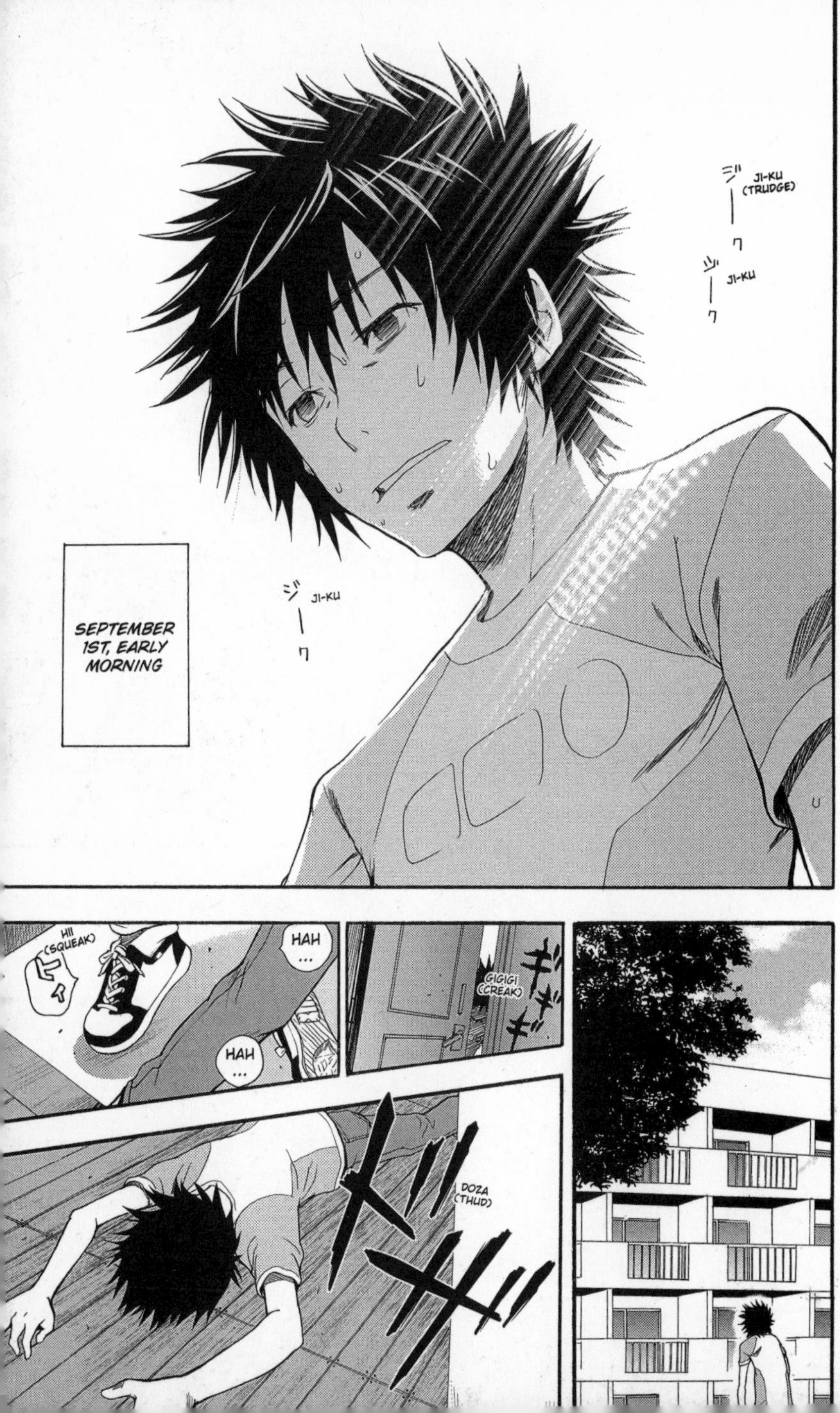

JI-KU (TRUDGE)
JI-KU
JI-KU
SEPTEMBER 1ST, EARLY MORNING
GIGIGI (CREAK)
HAH ...
HII (SQUEAK)
HAH ...
DOZA (THUD)

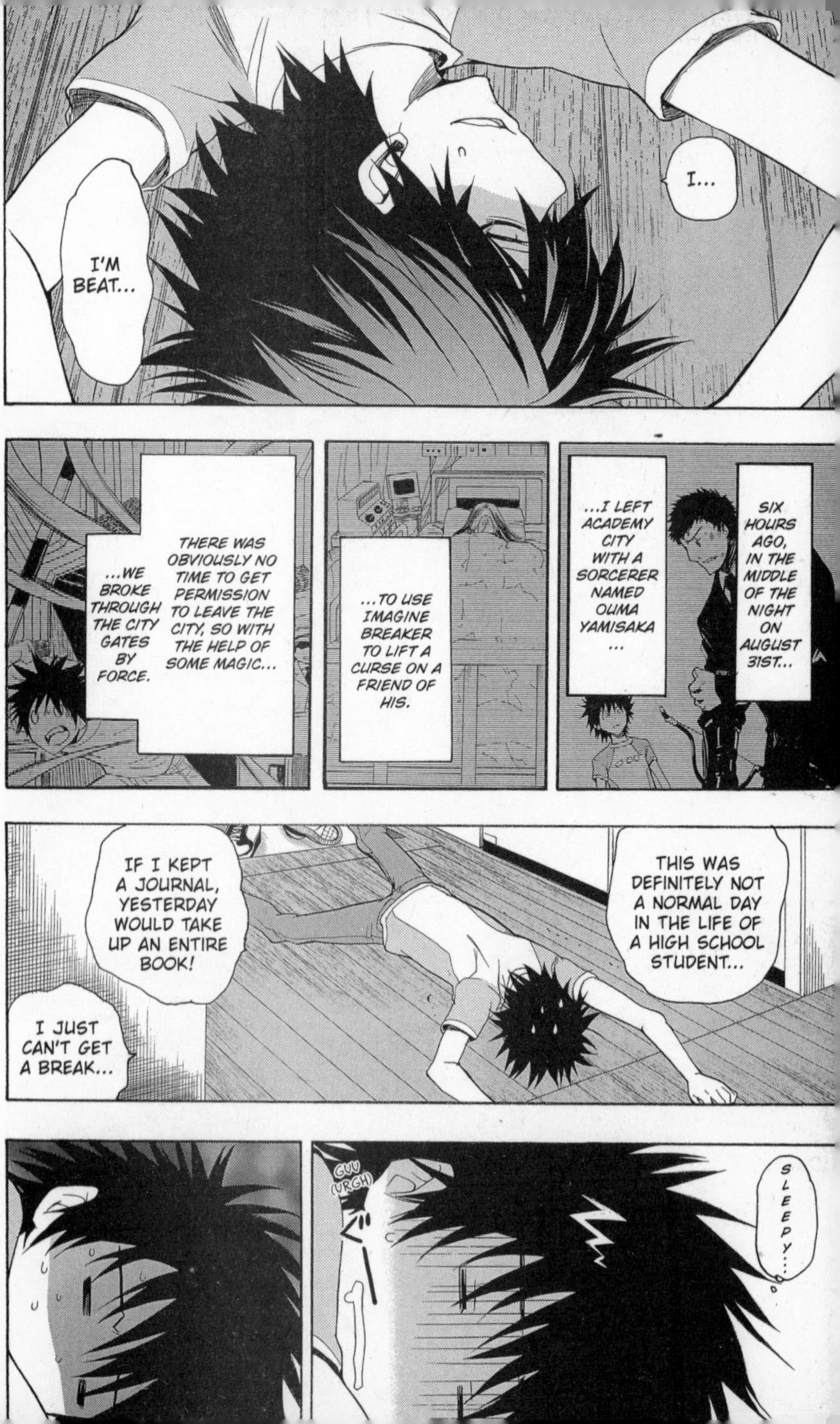
I...
I'M BEAT...
SIX HOURS AGO, IN THE MIDDLE OF THE NIGHT ON AUGUST 31ST...
...I LEFT ACADEMY CITY WITH A SORCERER NAMED OUMA YAMISAKA...
...TO USE IMAGINE BREAKER TO LIFT A CURSE ON A FRIEND OF HIS.
THERE WAS OBVIOUSLY NO TIME TO GET PERMISSION TO LEAVE THE CITY, SO WITH THE HELP OF SOME MAGIC...
...WE BROKE THROUGH THE CITY GATES BY FORCE.
THIS WAS DEFINITELY NOT A NORMAL DAY IN THE LIFE OF A HIGH SCHOOL STUDENT...
IF I KEPT A JOURNAL, YESTERDAY WOULD TAKE UP AN ENTIRE BOOK!
I JUST CAN'T GET A BREAK...
SLEEPY...
GUU (URGH)

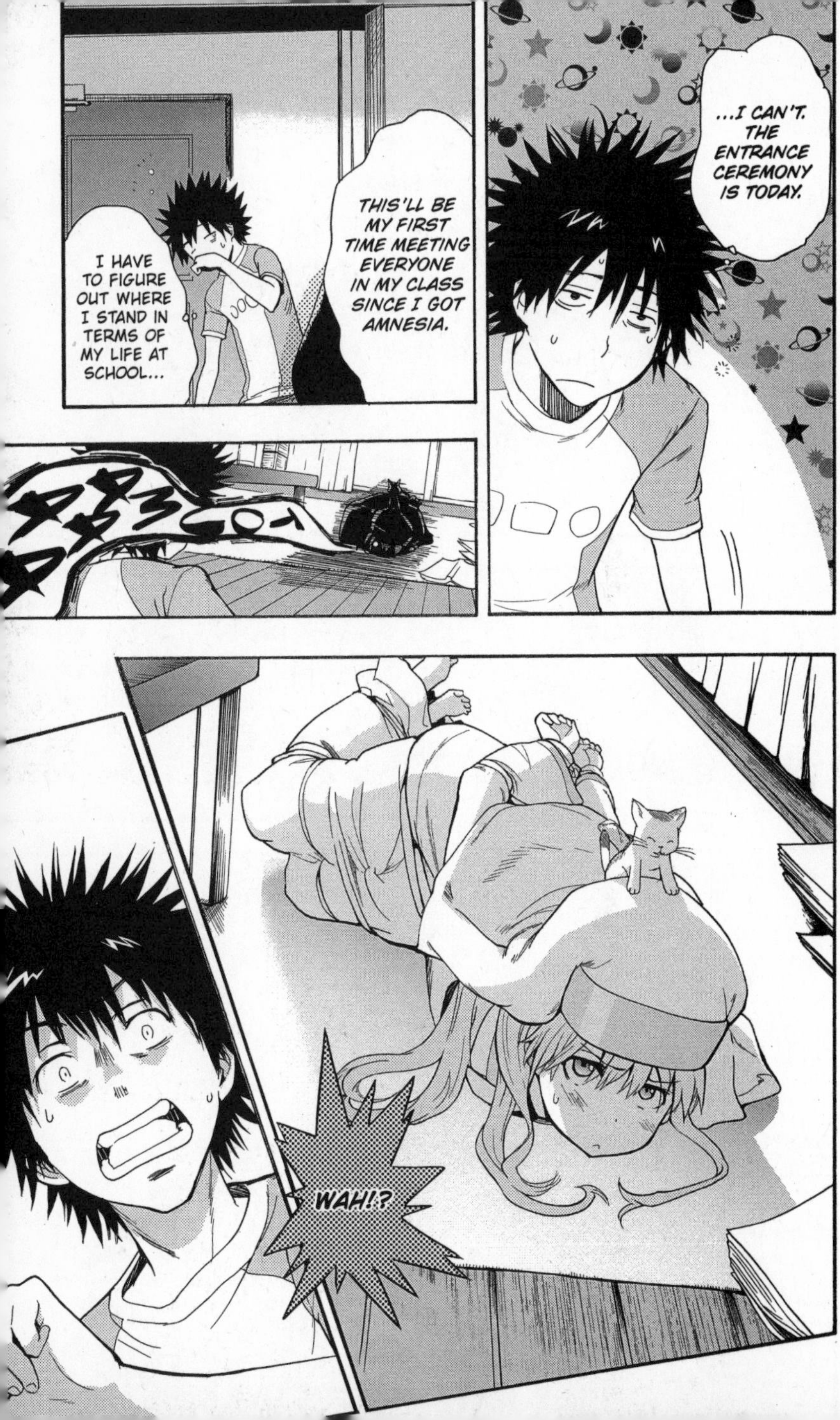
...I CAN'T. THE ENTRANCE CEREMONY IS TODAY.
THIS'LL BE MY FIRST TIME MEETING EVERYONE IN MY CLASS SINCE I GOT AMNESIA.
I HAVE TO FIGURE OUT WHERE I STAND IN TERMS OF MY LIFE AT SCHOOL...
WAH!?

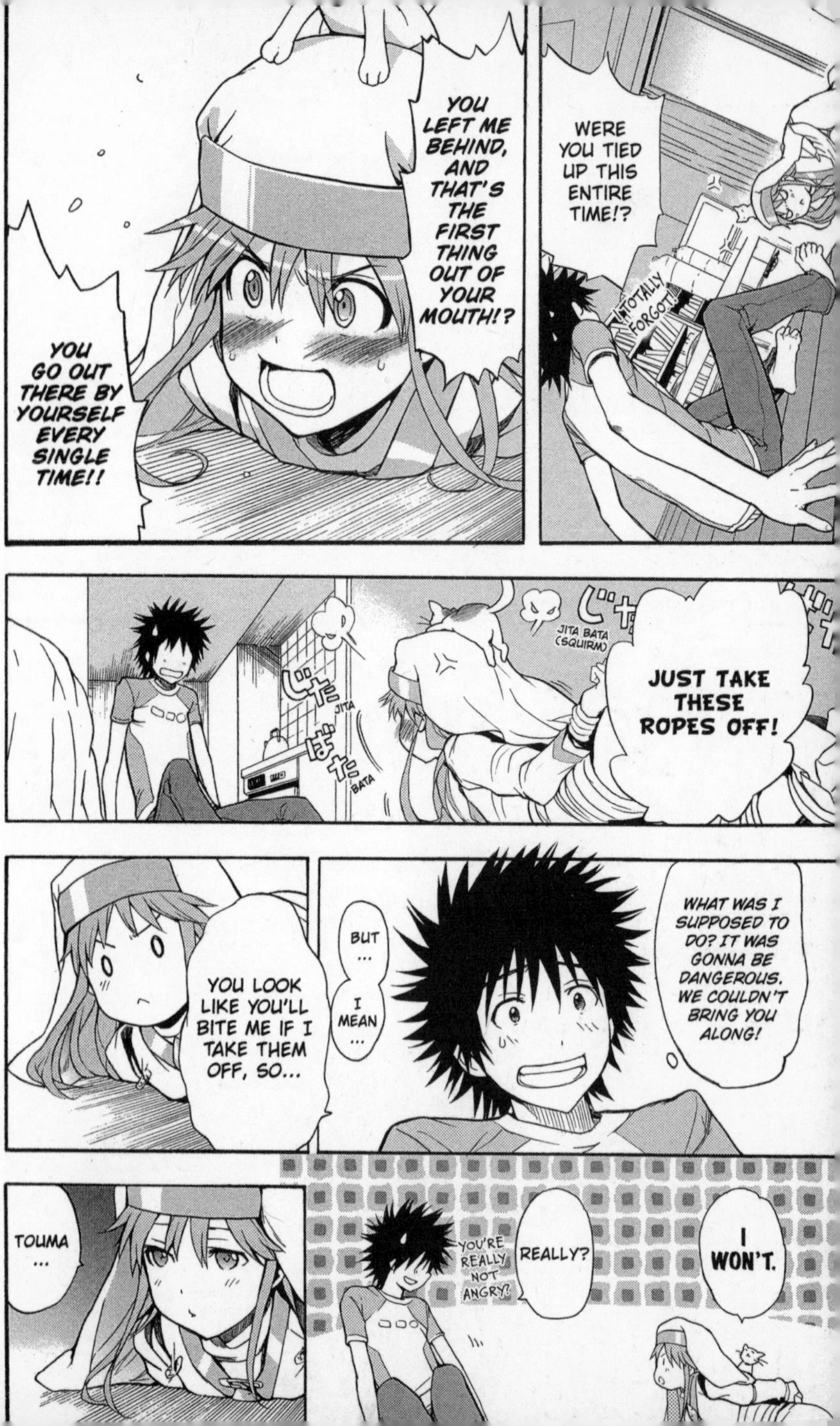
WERE YOU TIED UP THIS ENTIRE TIME!?
I TOTALLY FORGOT!
YOU LEFT ME BEHIND, AND THAT'S THE FIRST THING OUT OF YOUR MOUTH!?
YOU GO OUT THERE BY YOURSELF EVERY SINGLE TIME!!
JUST TAKE THESE ROPES OFF!
JITA BATA (SQUIRM)
JITA
BATA
WHAT WAS I SUPPOSED TO DO? IT WAS GONNA BE DANGEROUS. WE COULDN'T BRING YOU ALONG!
BUT ...
I MEAN ...
YOU LOOK LIKE YOU'LL BITE ME IF I TAKE THEM OFF, SO...
I WON'T.
REALLY?
YOU'RE REALLY NOT ANGRY?
TOUMA ...

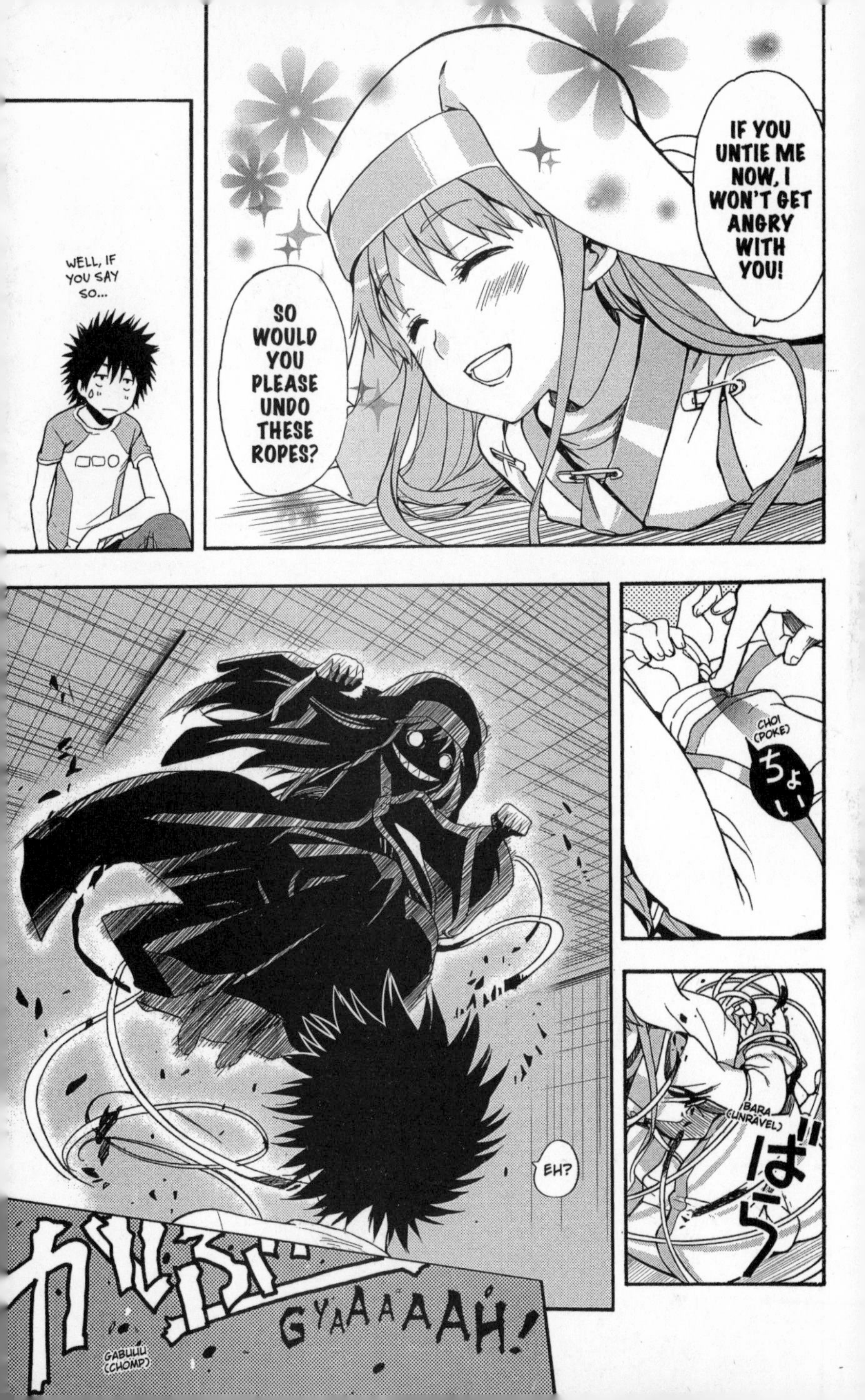
IF YOU UNTIE ME NOW, I WON'T GET ANGRY WITH YOU!
SO WOULD YOU PLEASE UNDO THESE ROPES?
WELL, IF YOU SAY SO...
CHOI (POKE)
ちょい
BARA (UNRAVEL)
ばら
EH?
GYAAAAAH!
GABUUU (CHOMP)

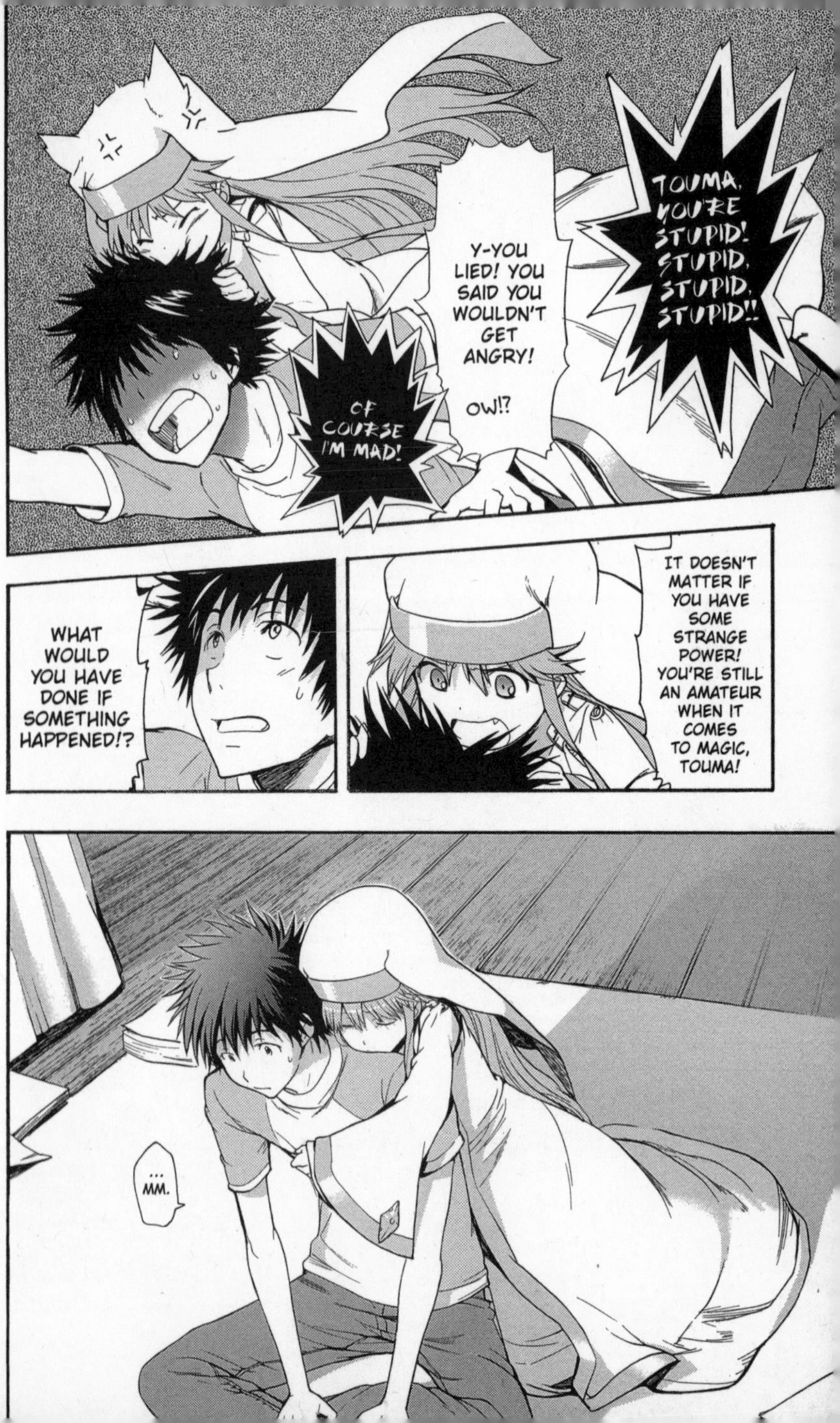
TOUMA, YOU'RE STUPID! STUPID, STUPID, STUPID!!
Y-YOU LIED! YOU SAID YOU WOULDN'T GET ANGRY!
OW!?
OF COURSE I'M MAD!
IT DOESN'T MATTER IF YOU HAVE SOME STRANGE POWER! YOU'RE STILL AN AMATEUR WHEN IT COMES TO MAGIC, TOUMA!
WHAT WOULD YOU HAVE DONE IF SOMETHING HAPPENED!?
... MM.

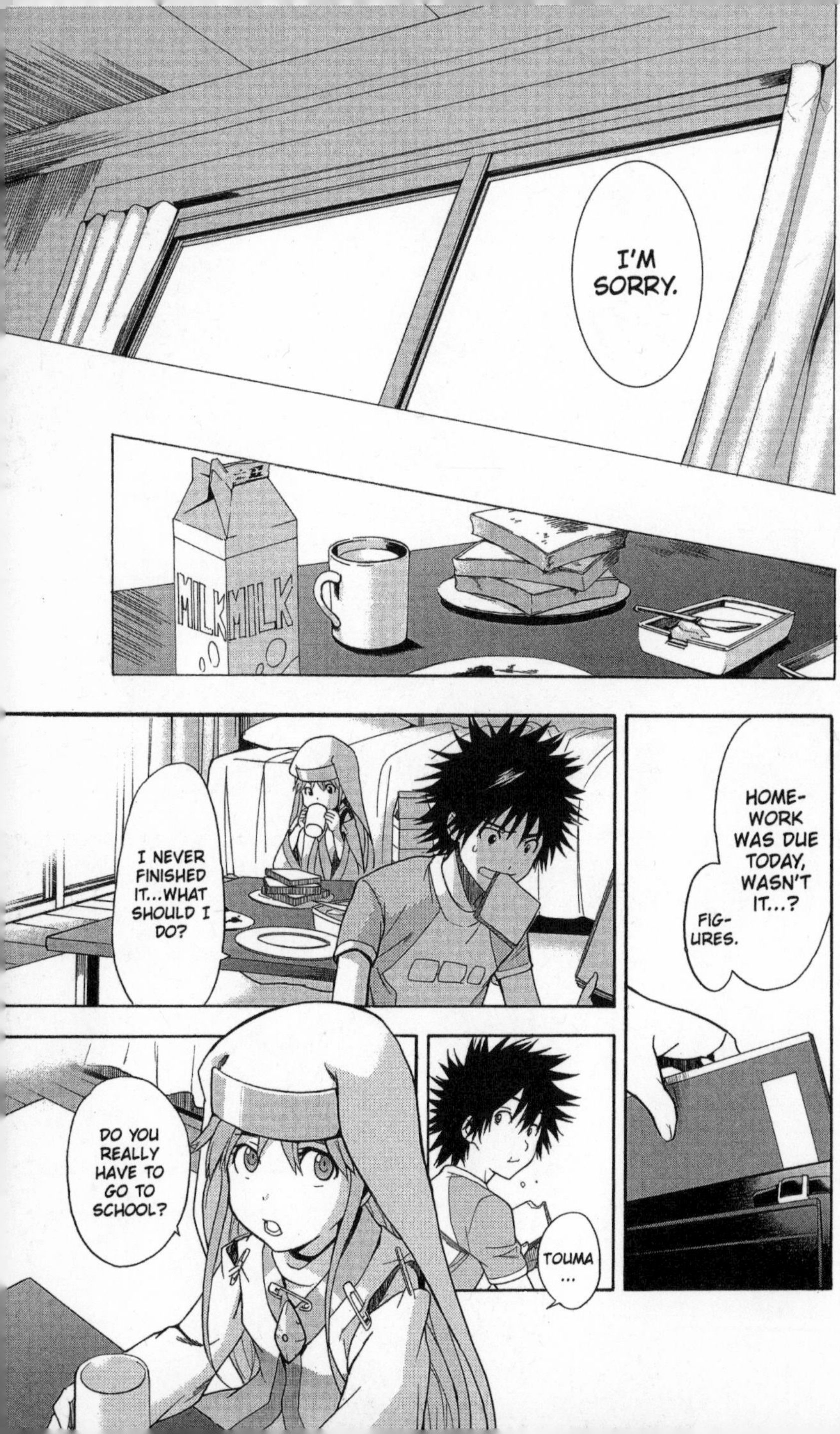

I'M SORRY.
MILK MILK
HOME-WORK WAS DUE TODAY, WASN'T IT...?
FIG-URES.
I NEVER FINISHED IT...WHAT SHOULD I DO?
TOUMA...
DO YOU REALLY HAVE TO GO TO SCHOOL?

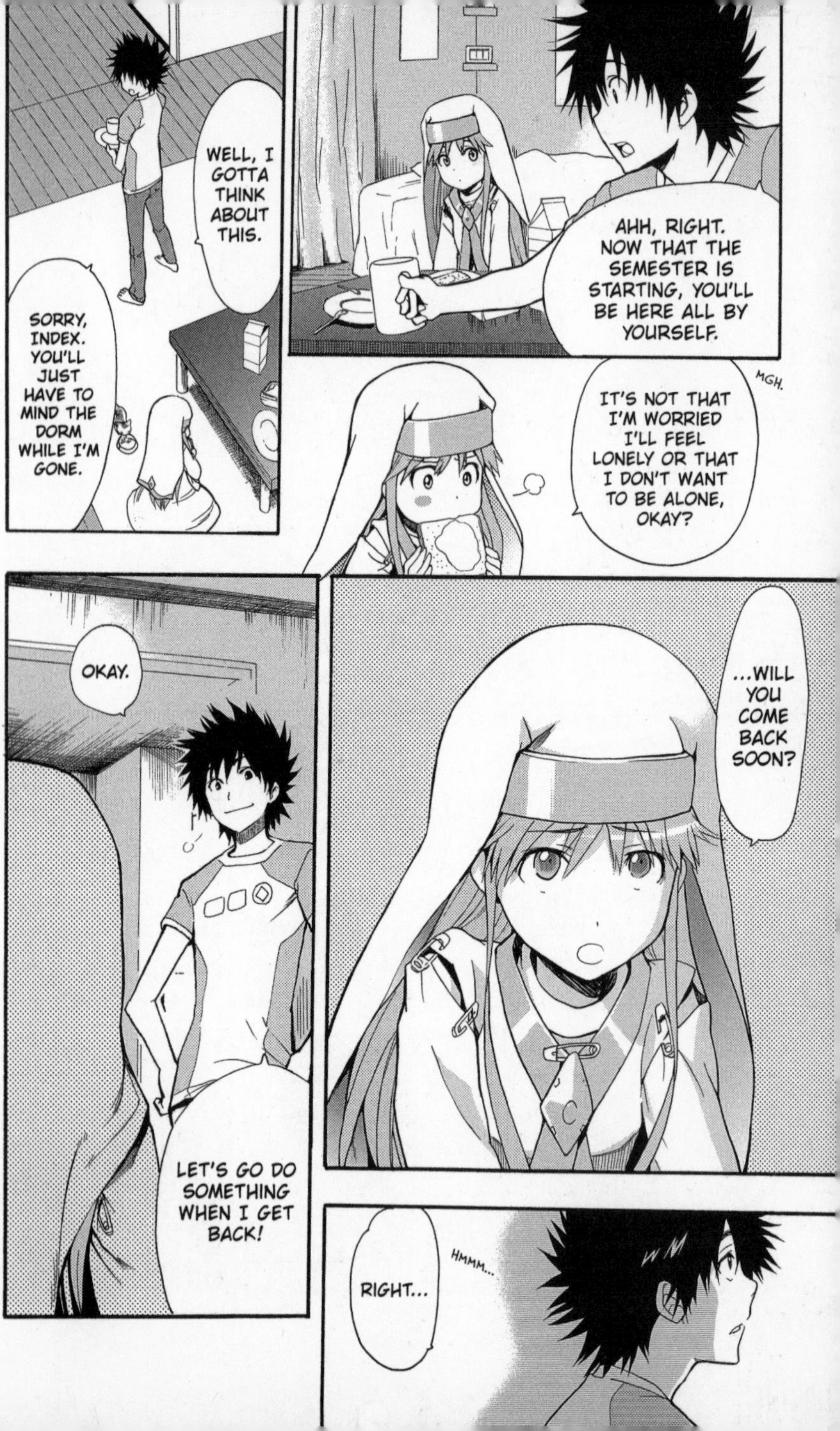
AHH, RIGHT. NOW THAT THE SEMESTER IS STARTING, YOU'LL BE HERE ALL BY YOURSELF.
WELL, I GOTTA THINK ABOUT THIS.
SORRY, INDEX. YOU'LL JUST HAVE TO MIND THE DORM WHILE I'M GONE.
MGH.
IT'S NOT THAT I'M WORRIED I'LL FEEL LONELY OR THAT I DON'T WANT TO BE ALONE, OKAY?
...WILL YOU COME BACK SOON?
OKAY.
LET'S GO DO SOMETHING WHEN I GET BACK!
HMMM...
RIGHT...

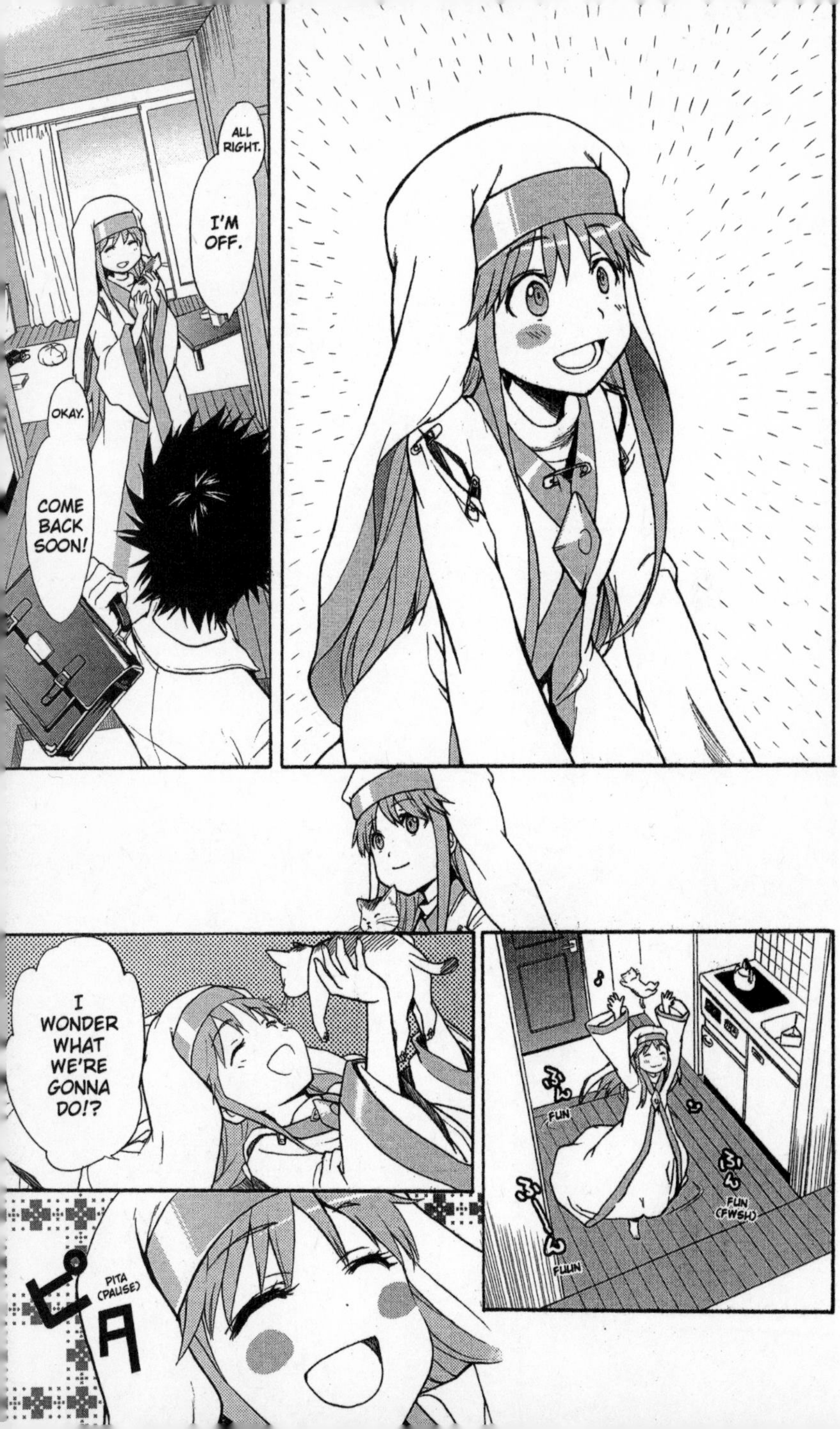
ALL RIGHT.
I'M OFF.
OKAY.
COME BACK SOON!
FUN (FWSH)
FUN
FUUN
I WONDER WHAT WE'RE GONNA DO!?
PITA (PAUSE)

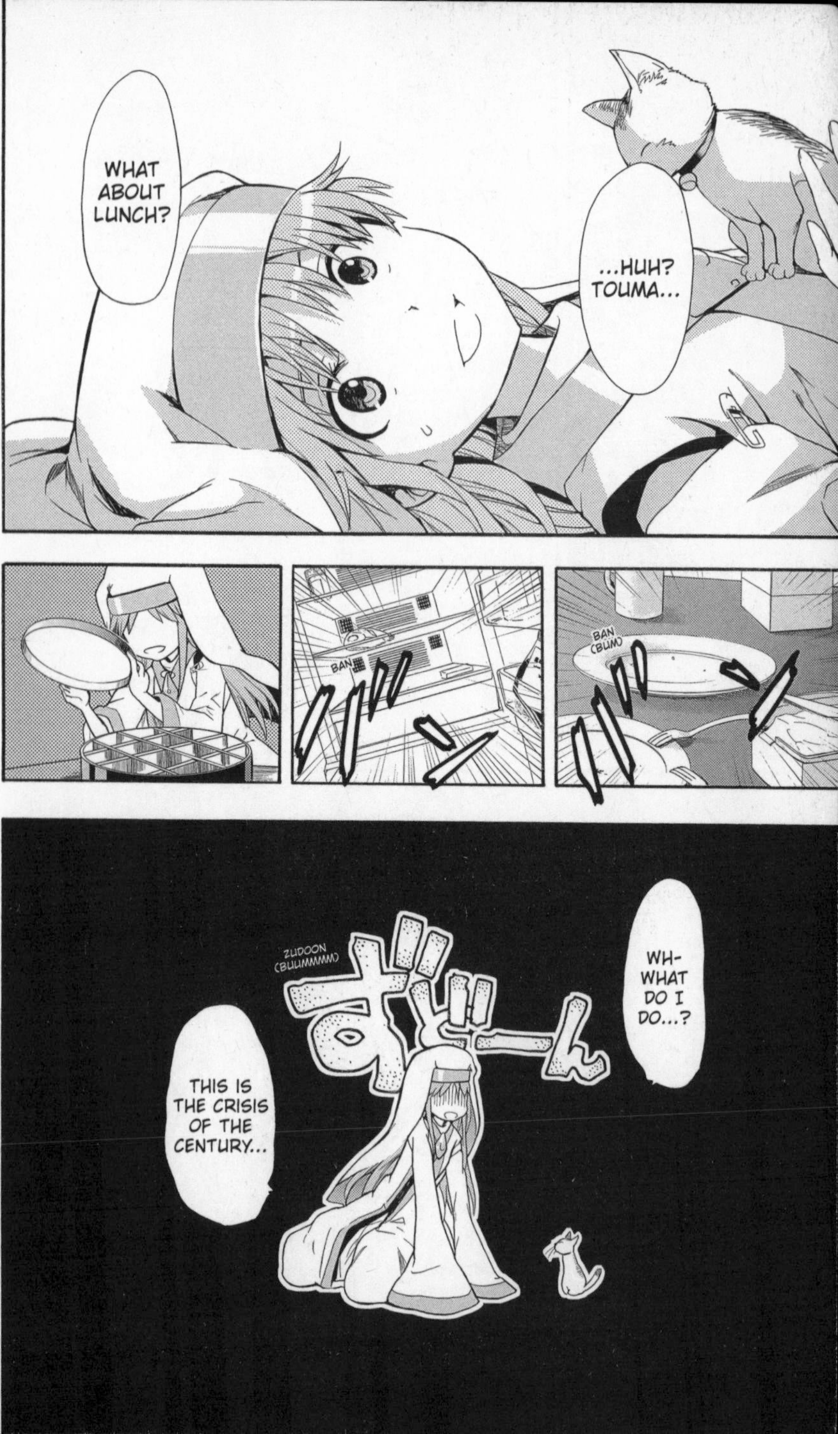
...HUH? TOUMA...
WHAT ABOUT LUNCH?
BAN (BUM)
BAN
WH- WHAT DO I DO...?
ZUDOON (BUUMMMMM)
THIS IS THE CRISIS OF THE CENTURY...

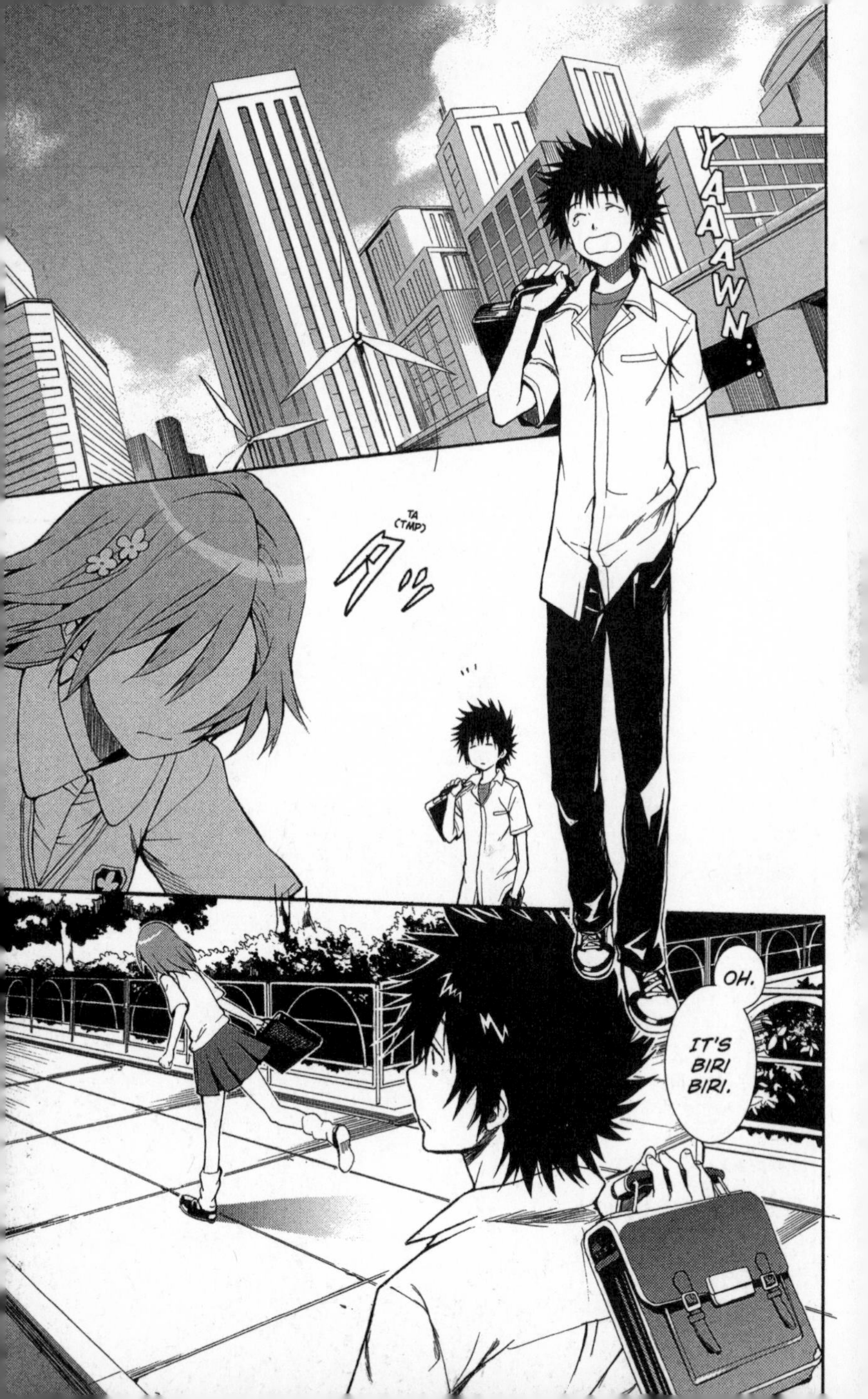
YAAAAWN...
TA (TMP)
OH.
IT'S BIRI BIRI.

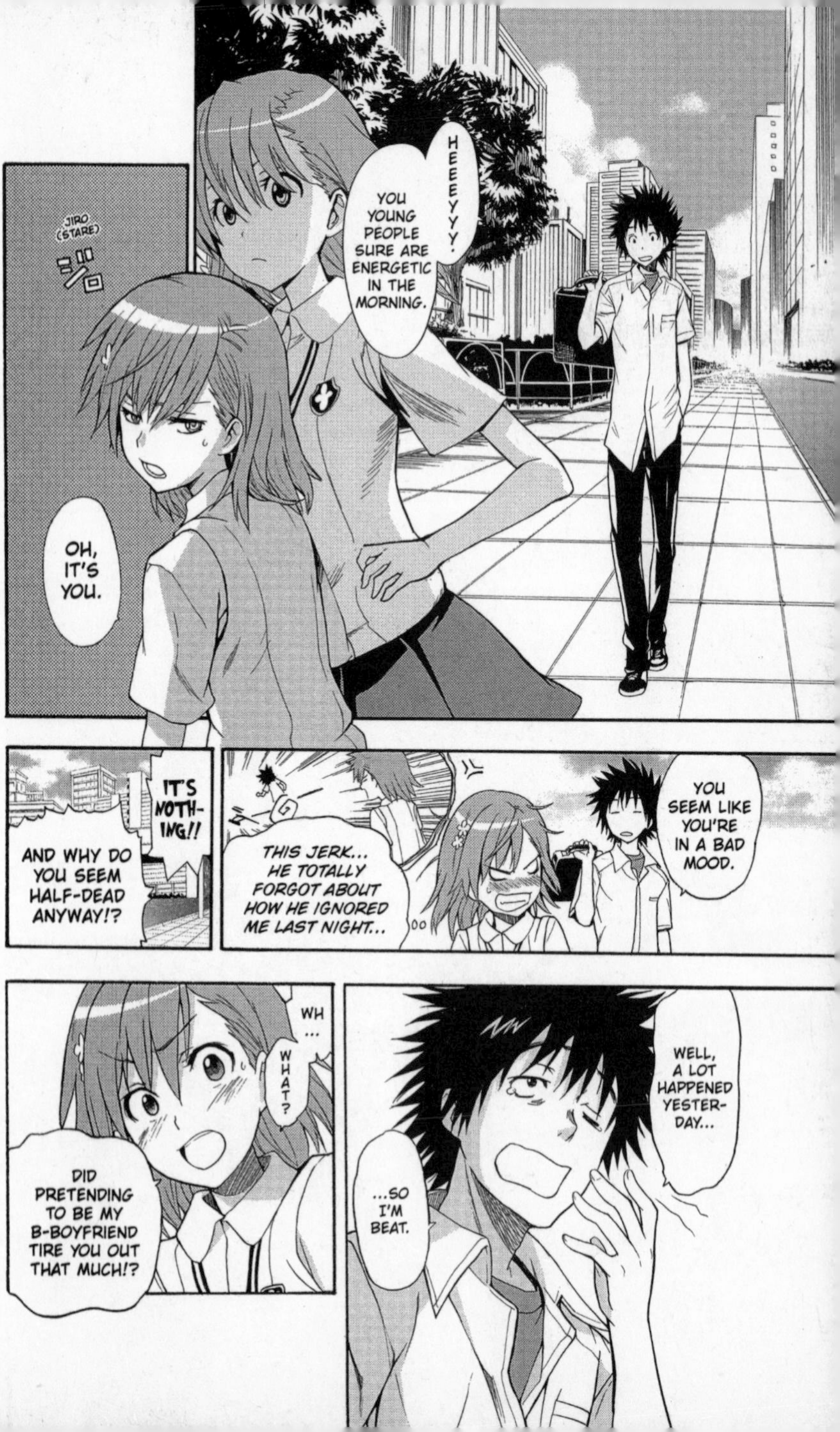
HEEEEYYY.
YOU YOUNG PEOPLE SURE ARE ENERGETIC IN THE MORNING.
JIRO (STARE)
OH, IT'S YOU.
YOU SEEM LIKE YOU'RE IN A BAD MOOD.
THIS JERK... HE TOTALLY FORGOT ABOUT HOW HE IGNORED ME LAST NIGHT...
IT'S NOTHING!!
AND WHY DO YOU SEEM HALF-DEAD ANYWAY!?
WELL, A LOT HAPPENED YESTERDAY...
...SO I'M BEAT.
WH... WHAT?
DID PRETENDING TO BE MY B-BOYFRIEND TIRE YOU OUT THAT MUCH!?

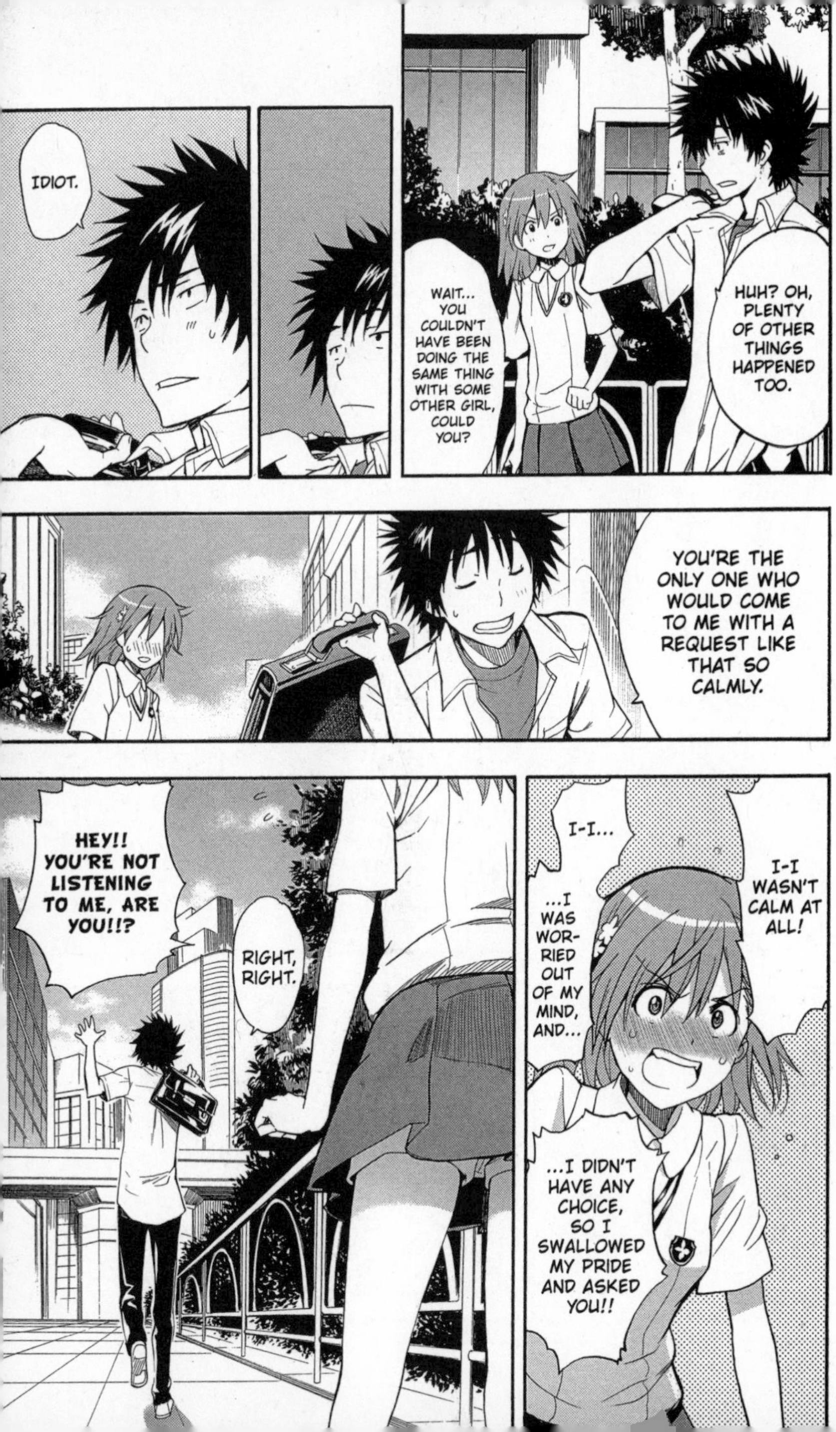
HUH? OH, PLENTY OF OTHER THINGS HAPPENED TOO.
WAIT... YOU COULDN'T HAVE BEEN DOING THE SAME THING WITH SOME OTHER GIRL, COULD YOU?
IDIOT.
YOU'RE THE ONLY ONE WHO WOULD COME TO ME WITH A REQUEST LIKE THAT SO CALMLY.
I-I WASN'T CALM AT ALL!
I-I...
...I WAS WORRIED OUT OF MY MIND, AND...
...I DIDN'T HAVE ANY CHOICE, SO I SWALLOWED MY PRIDE AND ASKED YOU!!
HEY!! YOU'RE NOT LISTENING TO ME, ARE YOU!!?
RIGHT, RIGHT.

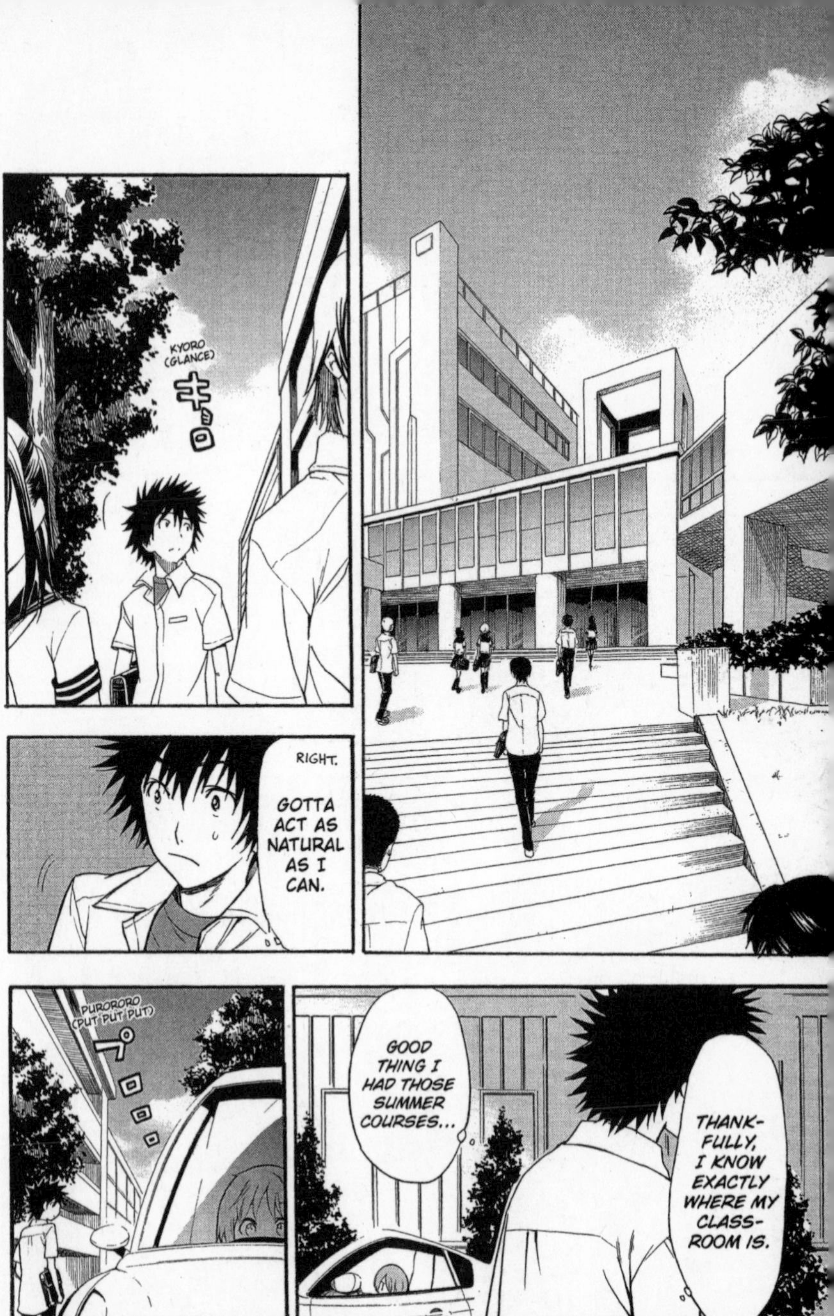
KYORO (GLANCE)
キョロ
RIGHT.
GOTTA ACT AS NATURAL AS I CAN.
THANK-FULLY, I KNOW EXACTLY WHERE MY CLASS-ROOM IS.
GOOD THING I HAD THOSE SUMMER COURSES...
PURORORO (PUT PUT PUT)
プロロロ

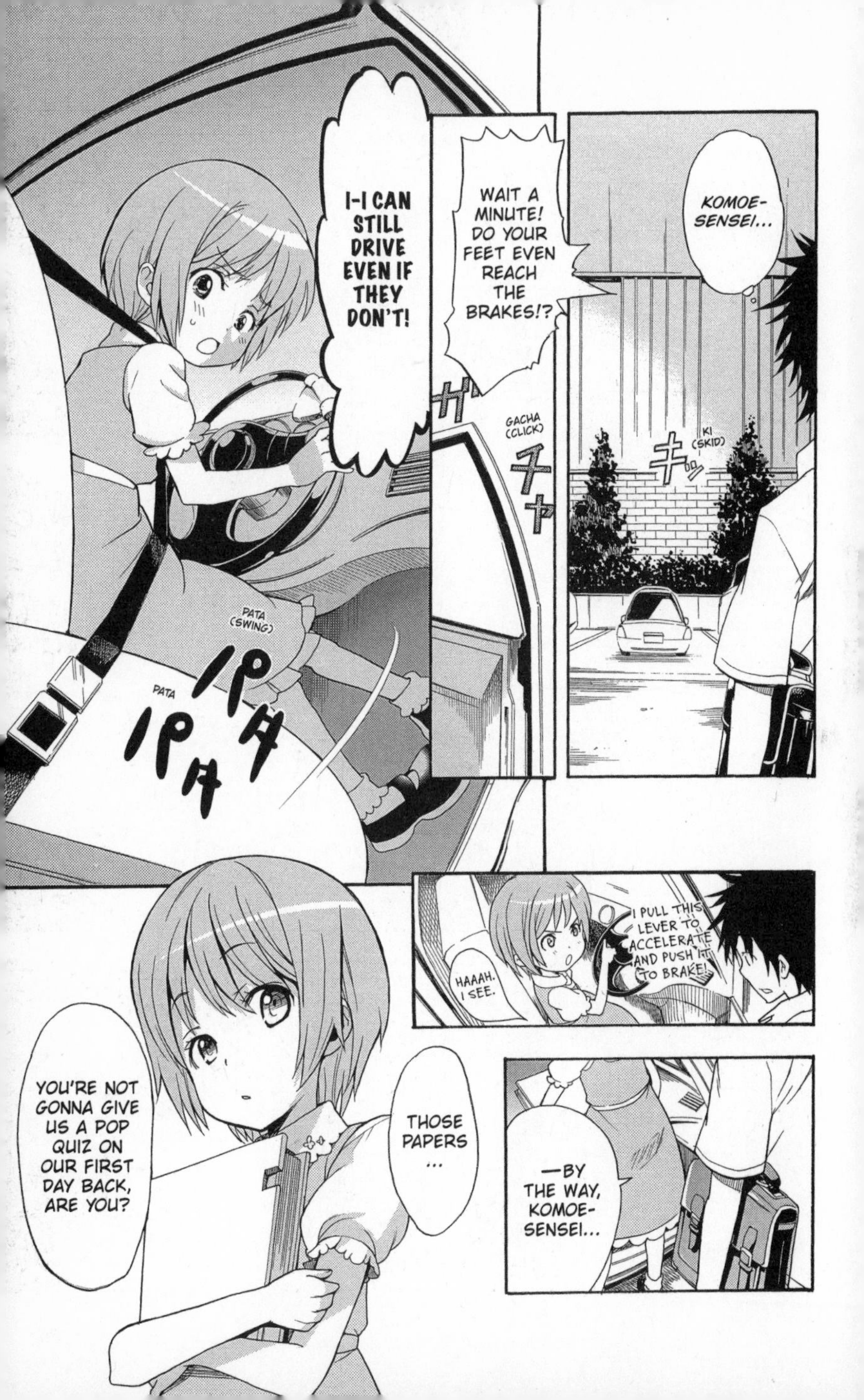

KOMOE-SENSEI...
KI (SKID)
キッ
WAIT A MINUTE! DO YOUR FEET EVEN REACH THE BRAKES!?
GACHA (CLICK)
ガチャ
I-I CAN STILL DRIVE EVEN IF THEY DON'T!
PATA (SWING)
PATA
パタパタ
I PULL THIS LEVER TO ACCELERATE AND PUSH IT TO BRAKE!
HAAAH. I SEE.
—BY THE WAY, KOMOE-SENSEI...
THOSE PAPERS...
YOU'RE NOT GONNA GIVE US A POP QUIZ ON OUR FIRST DAY BACK, ARE YOU?

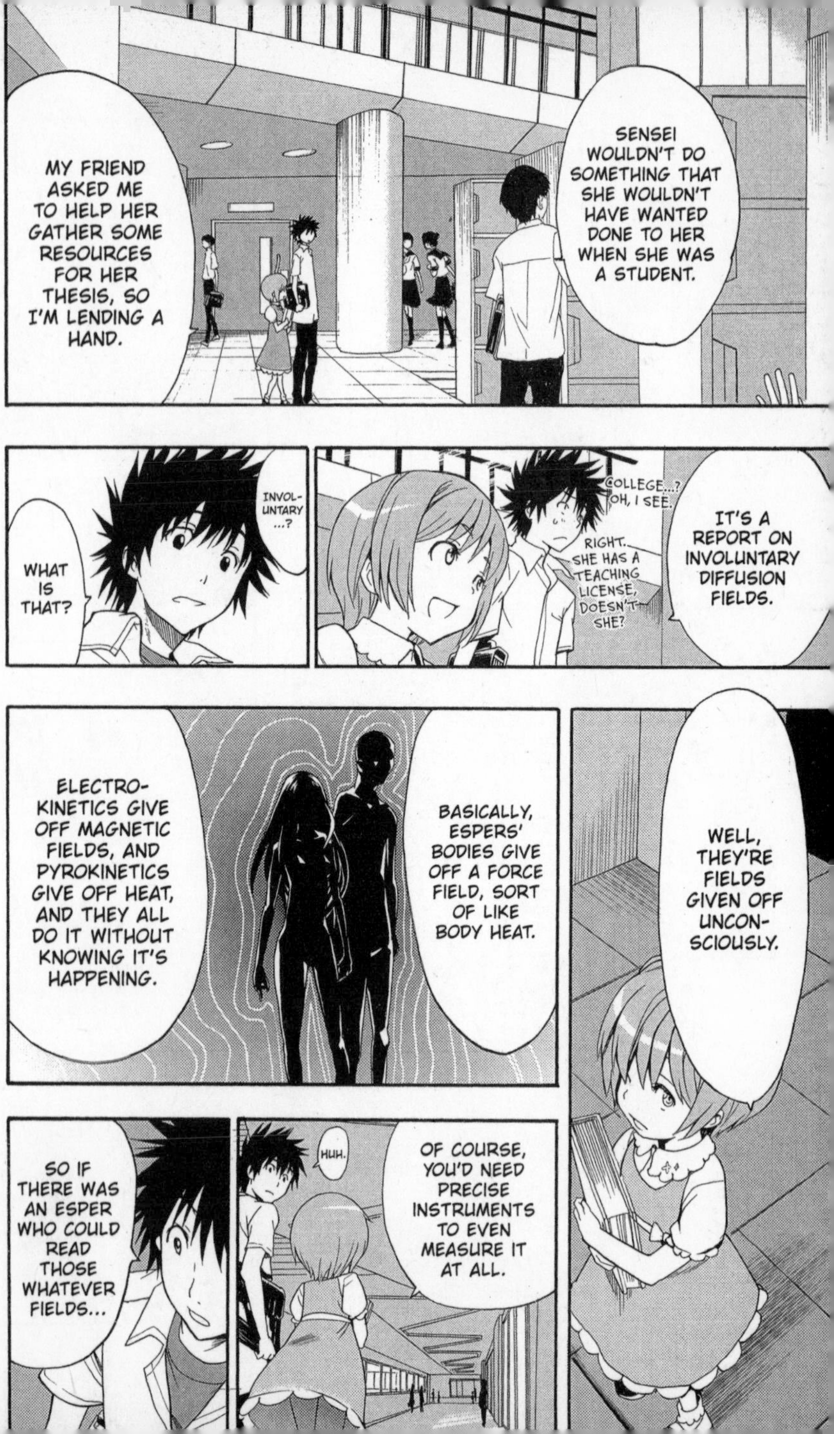
SENSEI WOULDN'T DO SOMETHING THAT SHE WOULDN'T HAVE WANTED DONE TO HER WHEN SHE WAS A STUDENT.
MY FRIEND ASKED ME TO HELP HER GATHER SOME RESOURCES FOR HER THESIS, SO I'M LENDING A HAND.
IT'S A REPORT ON INVOLUNTARY DIFFUSION FIELDS.
COLLEGE...? OH, I SEE.
RIGHT. SHE HAS A TEACHING LICENSE, DOESN'T SHE?
INVOLUNTARY...?
WHAT IS THAT?
WELL, THEY'RE FIELDS GIVEN OFF UNCONSCIOUSLY.
BASICALLY, ESPERS' BODIES GIVE OFF A FORCE FIELD, SORT OF LIKE BODY HEAT.
ELECTRO-KINETICS GIVE OFF MAGNETIC FIELDS, AND PYROKINETICS GIVE OFF HEAT, AND THEY ALL DO IT WITHOUT KNOWING IT'S HAPPENING.
OF COURSE, YOU'D NEED PRECISE INSTRUMENTS TO EVEN MEASURE IT AT ALL.
HUH.
SO IF THERE WAS AN ESPER WHO COULD READ THOSE WHATEVER FIELDS...

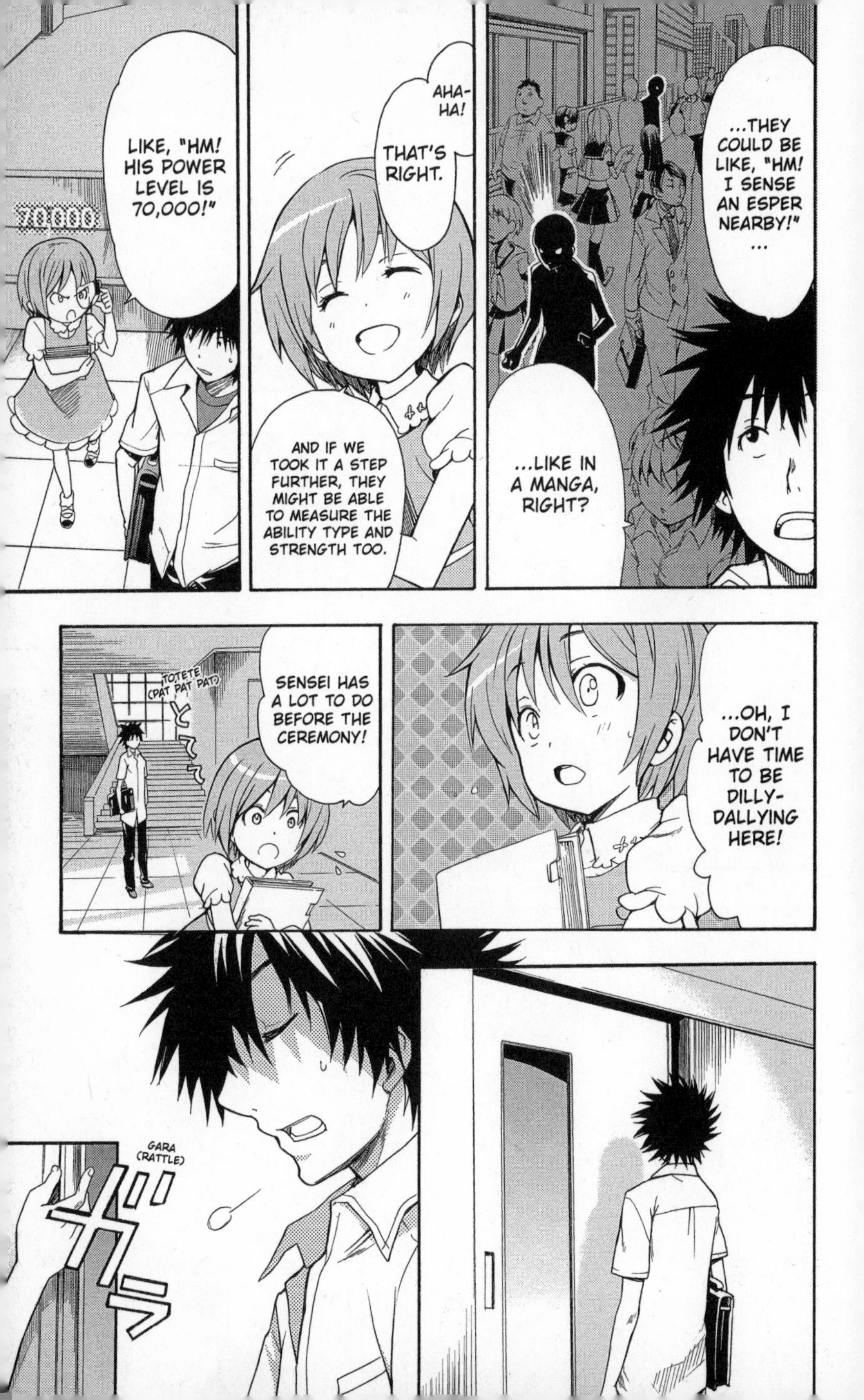
...THEY COULD BE LIKE, "HM! I SENSE AN ESPER NEARBY!" ...
...LIKE IN A MANGA, RIGHT?
AHA-HA!
THAT'S RIGHT.
AND IF WE TOOK IT A STEP FURTHER, THEY MIGHT BE ABLE TO MEASURE THE ABILITY TYPE AND STRENGTH TOO.
LIKE, "HM! HIS POWER LEVEL IS 70,000!"
70000
...OH, I DON'T HAVE TIME TO BE DILLY-DALLYING HERE!
SENSEI HAS A LOT TO DO BEFORE THE CEREMONY!
TOTETE (PAT PAT PAT)
GARA (RATTLE)

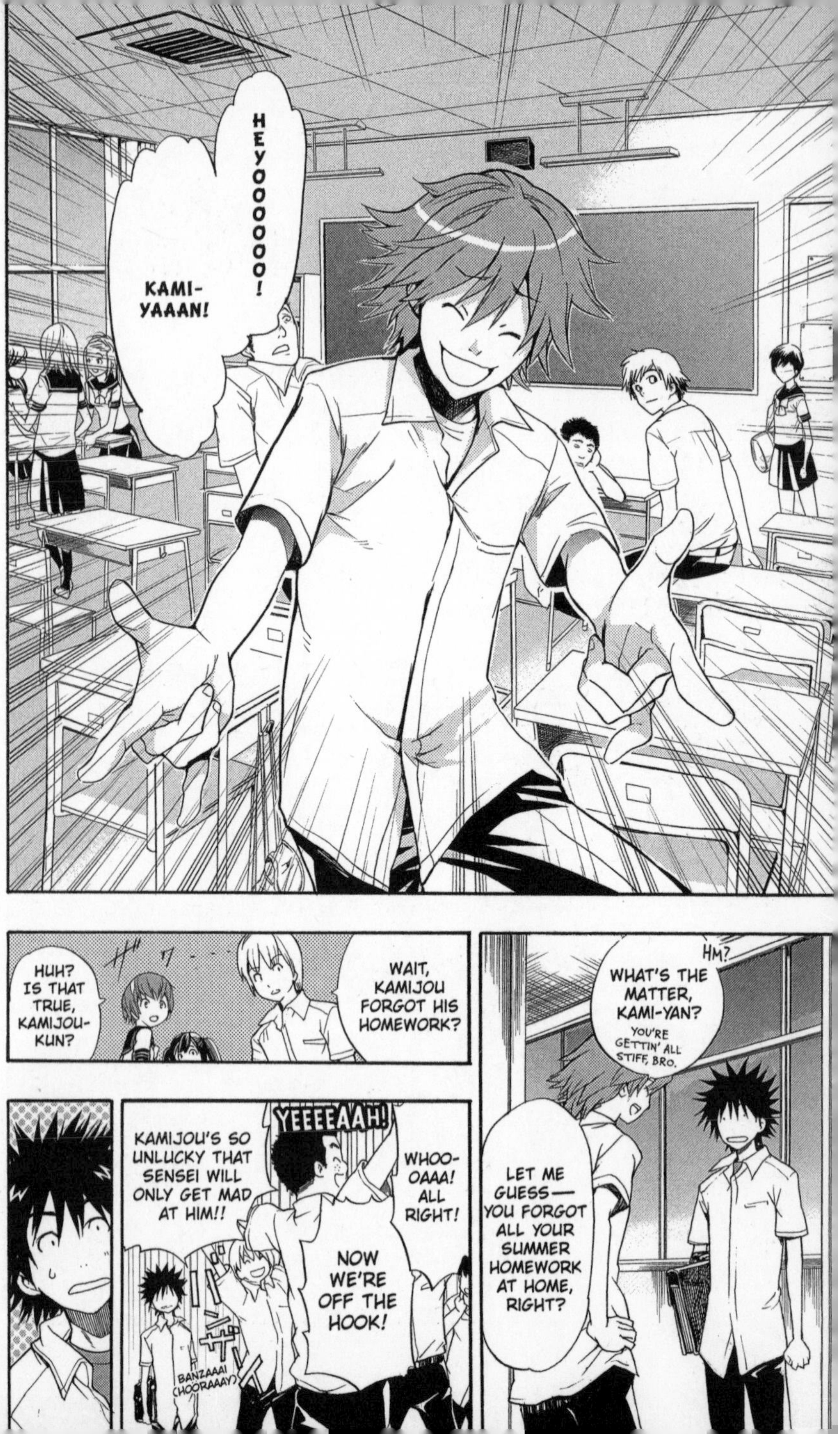
HEYOOOOOOO!
KAMI-YAAAN!
HM?
WHAT'S THE MATTER, KAMI-YAN?
YOU'RE GETTIN' ALL STIFF, BRO.
LET ME GUESS— YOU FORGOT ALL YOUR SUMMER HOMEWORK AT HOME, RIGHT?
WAIT, KAMIJOU FORGOT HIS HOMEWORK?
HUH? IS THAT TRUE, KAMIJOU-KUN?
YEEEEAAH!
WHOO-OAAA! ALL RIGHT!
KAMIJOU'S SO UNLUCKY THAT SENSEI WILL ONLY GET MAD AT HIM!!
NOW WE'RE OFF THE HOOK!
BANZAAAI (HOORAAAY)

YOU KNOW, DUDE, I FORGOT MINE ON PURPOSE SO THAT KOMOE-SENSEI WOULD GET ANGRY AT ME.

YOU'RE GONNA MAKE HER CRY...

ザワ ZAWA (CHATTER)

WAI (YAY)

ワイ

ザワ ZAWA

ザワ ZAWA

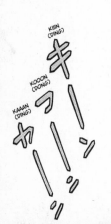

KIIN (DING)
キーン

KOOON (DONG)
コーン

KAAAN (DING)
カーン

ホ (SIGH)
ホー

THANK GOODNESS.

LOOKS LIKE A PRETTY EASY-GOING CLASS.

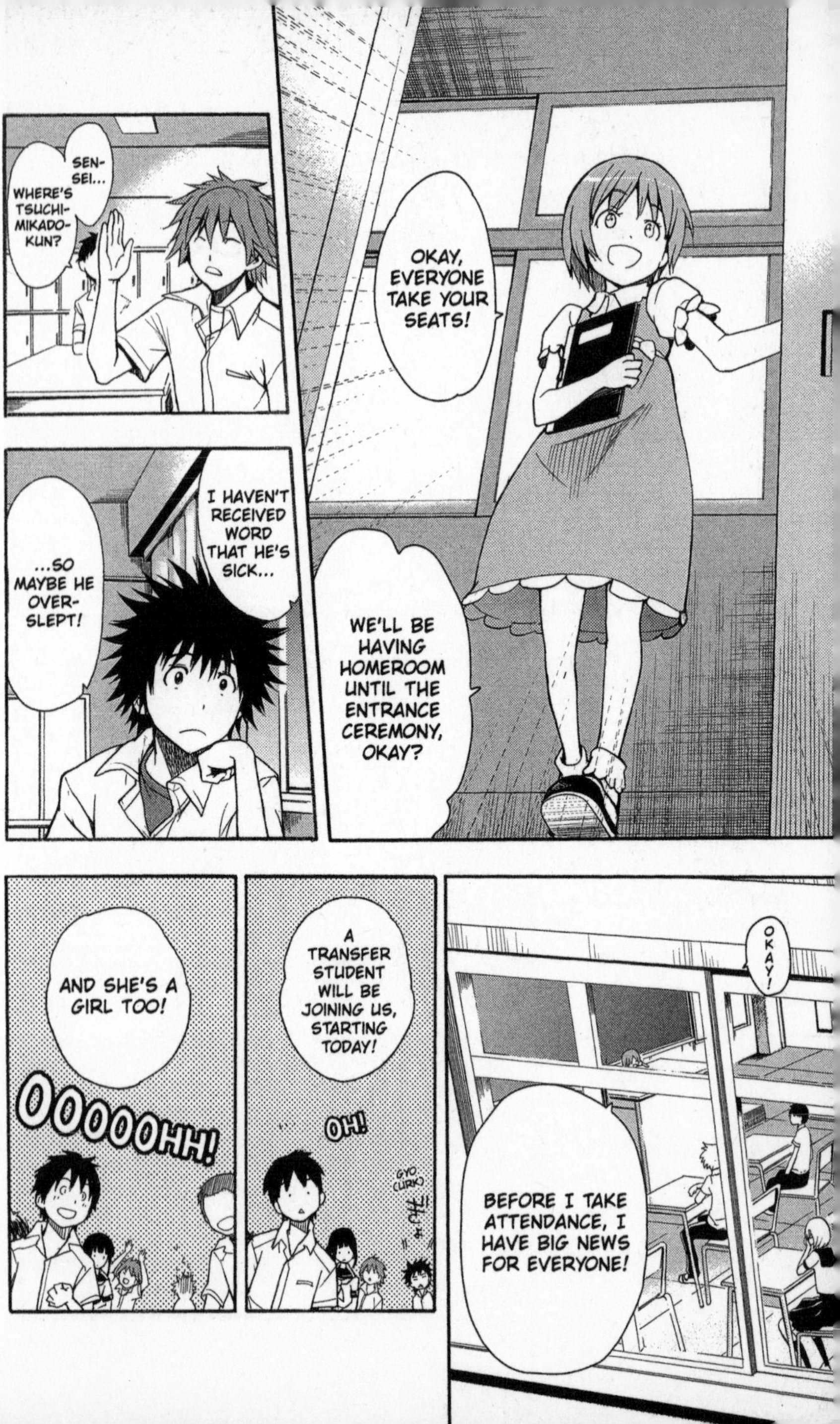
OKAY, EVERYONE TAKE YOUR SEATS!
WE'LL BE HAVING HOMEROOM UNTIL THE ENTRANCE CEREMONY, OKAY?
SEN-SEI... WHERE'S TSUCHI-MIKADO-KUN?
I HAVEN'T RECEIVED WORD THAT HE'S SICK...
...SO MAYBE HE OVER-SLEPT!
OKAY!
BEFORE I TAKE ATTENDANCE, I HAVE BIG NEWS FOR EVERYONE!
A TRANSFER STUDENT WILL BE JOINING US, STARTING TODAY!
OH!
GYO (URK)
AND SHE'S A GIRL TOO!
OOOOOHH!

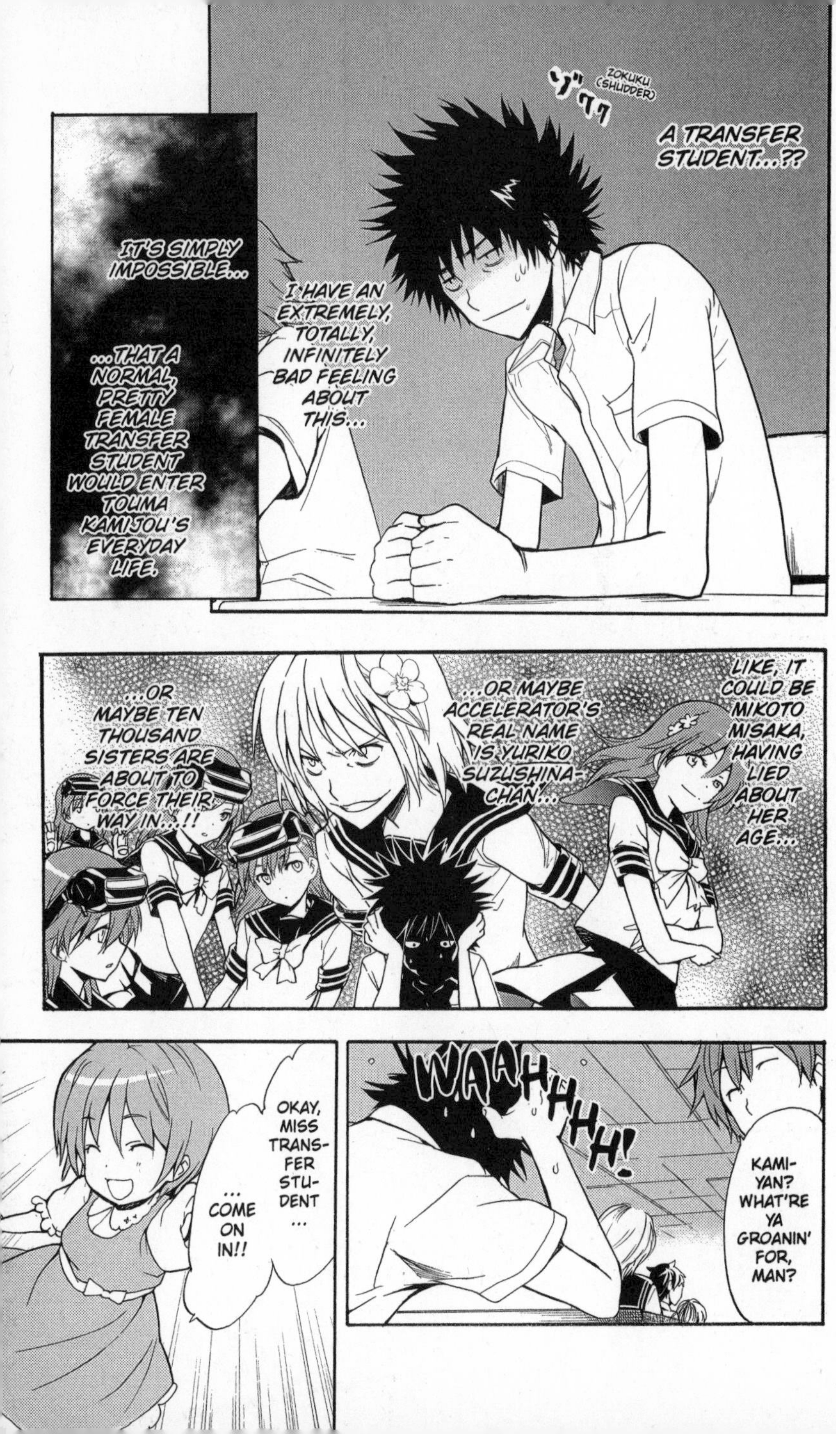
ゾクク
ZOKUKU (SHUDDER)
A TRANSFER STUDENT...??
I HAVE AN EXTREMELY, TOTALLY, INFINITELY BAD FEELING ABOUT THIS...
IT'S SIMPLY IMPOSSIBLE...
...THAT A NORMAL, PRETTY FEMALE TRANSFER STUDENT WOULD ENTER TOUMA KAMIJOU'S EVERYDAY LIFE.
LIKE, IT COULD BE MIKOTO MISAKA, HAVING LIED ABOUT HER AGE...
...OR MAYBE ACCELERATOR'S REAL NAME IS YURIKO SUZUSHINA-CHAN...
...OR MAYBE TEN THOUSAND SISTERS ARE ABOUT TO FORCE THEIR WAY IN...!!
WAAHHHHH!
KAMI-YAN? WHAT'RE YA GROANIN' FOR, MAN?
OKAY, MISS TRANS-FER STU-DENT...
...COME ON IN!!

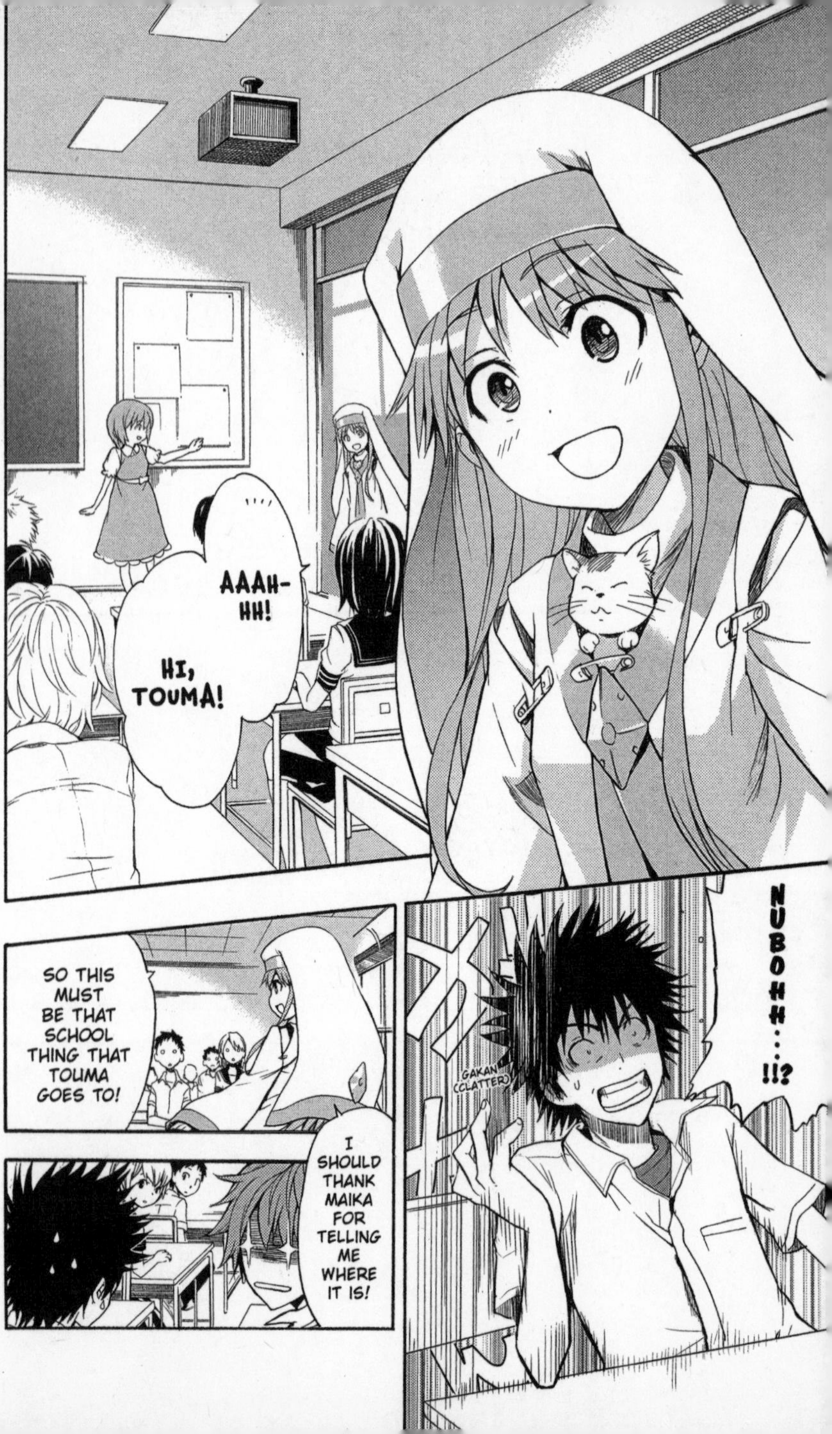
...
AAAH-HH!
HI, TOUMA!
NUBOHH...!!?
GAKAN (CLATTER)
SO THIS MUST BE THAT SCHOOL THING THAT TOUMA GOES TO!
I SHOULD THANK MAIKA FOR TELLING ME WHERE IT IS!

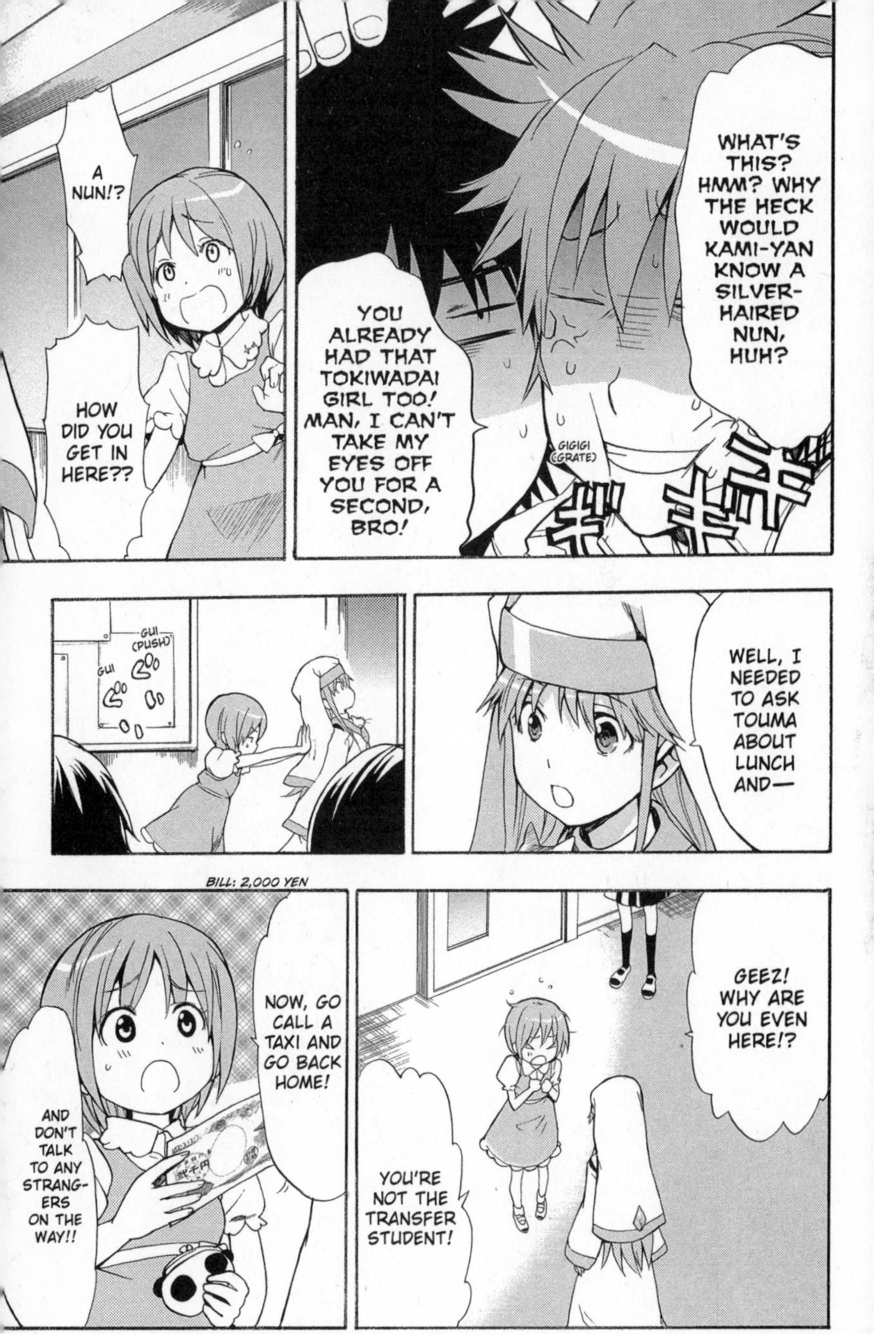
WHAT'S THIS? HMM? WHY THE HECK WOULD KAMI-YAN KNOW A SILVER-HAIRED NUN, HUH?
YOU ALREADY HAD THAT TOKIWADAI GIRL TOO! MAN, I CAN'T TAKE MY EYES OFF YOU FOR A SECOND, BRO!
GIGIGI (GRATE)
A NUN!?
HOW DID YOU GET IN HERE??
WELL, I NEEDED TO ASK TOUMA ABOUT LUNCH AND—
GUI (PUSH)
GUI
GEEZ! WHY ARE YOU EVEN HERE!?
YOU'RE NOT THE TRANSFER STUDENT!
BILL: 2,000 YEN
NOW, GO CALL A TAXI AND GO BACK HOME!
AND DON'T TALK TO ANY STRANGERS ON THE WAY!!

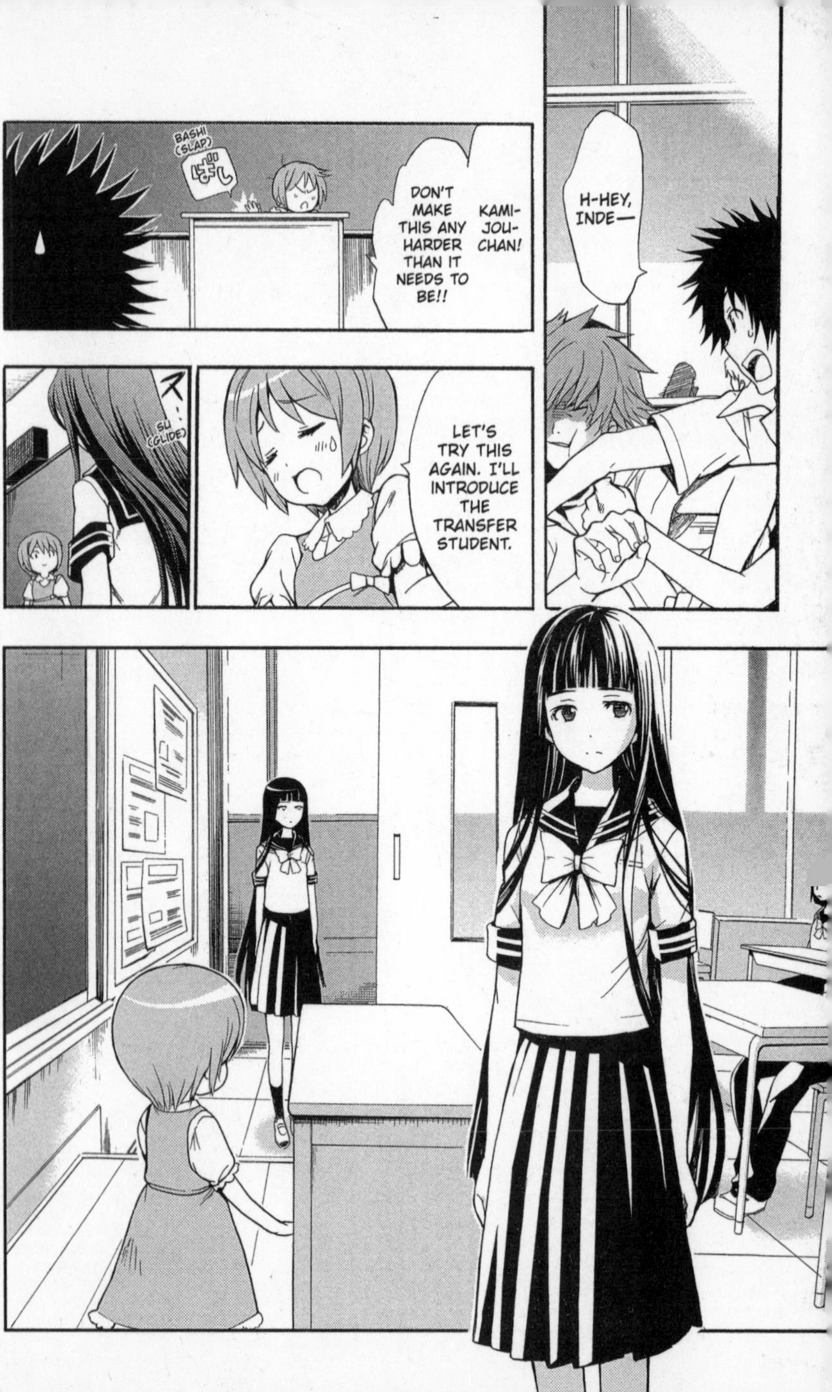
H-HEY, INDE—
KAMIJOU-CHAN! DON'T MAKE THIS ANY HARDER THAN IT NEEDS TO BE!!
BASHI (SLAP)
ばし
LET'S TRY THIS AGAIN. I'LL INTRODUCE THE TRANSFER STUDENT.
ス
SU (GLIDE)

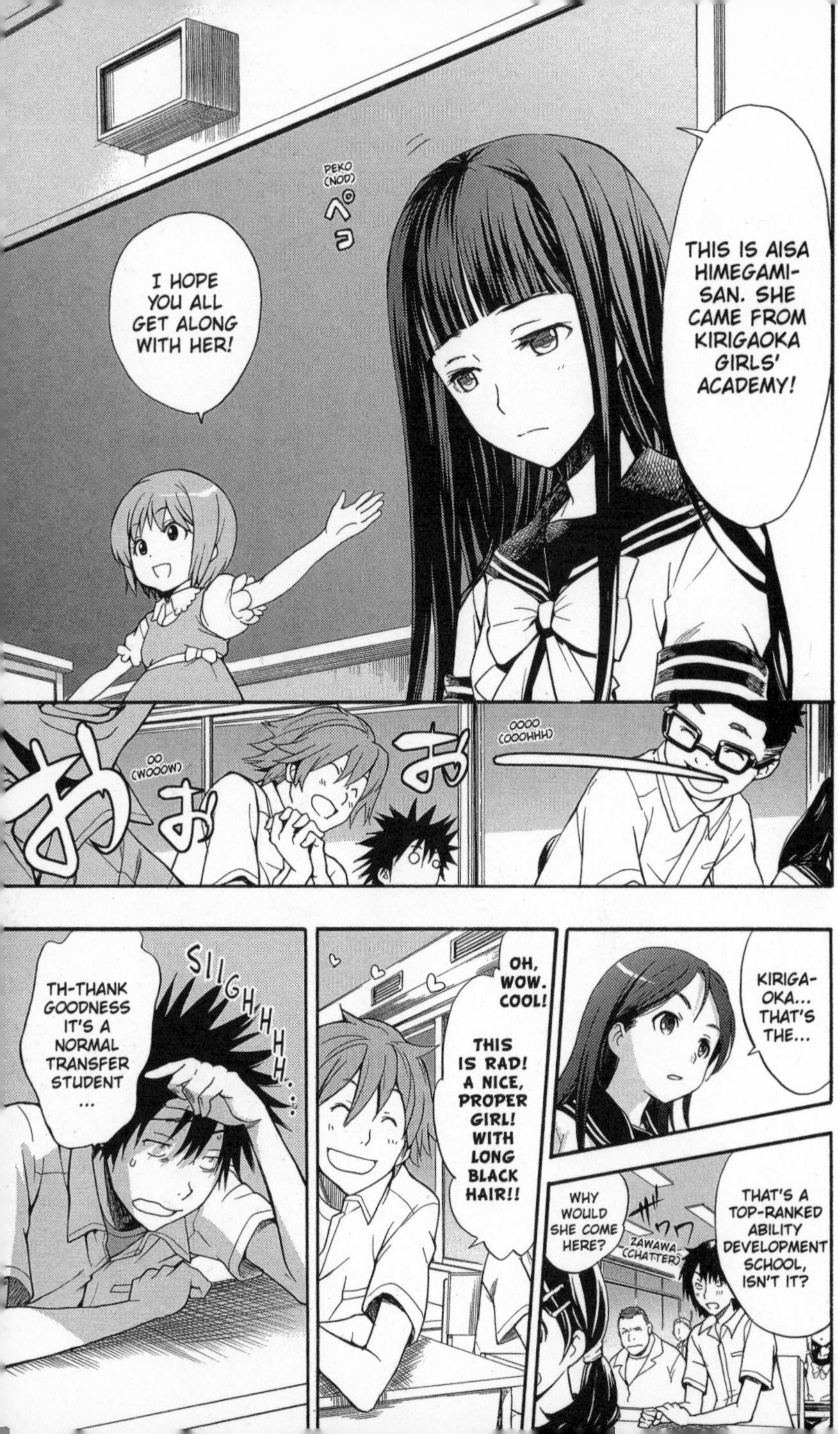
THIS IS AISA HIMEGAMI-SAN. SHE CAME FROM KIRIGAOKA GIRLS' ACADEMY!
PEKO (NOD)
ペコ
I HOPE YOU ALL GET ALONG WITH HER!
OOOO (OOOHHH)
お
OO (WOOOW)
おお
KIRIGA-OKA... THAT'S THE...
THAT'S A TOP-RANKED ABILITY DEVELOPMENT SCHOOL, ISN'T IT?
ZAWAWA (CHATTER)
WHY WOULD SHE COME HERE?
OH, WOW. COOL!
THIS IS RAD! A NICE, PROPER GIRL! WITH LONG BLACK HAIR!!
SIIGHHHH...
TH-THANK GOODNESS IT'S A NORMAL TRANSFER STUDENT ...

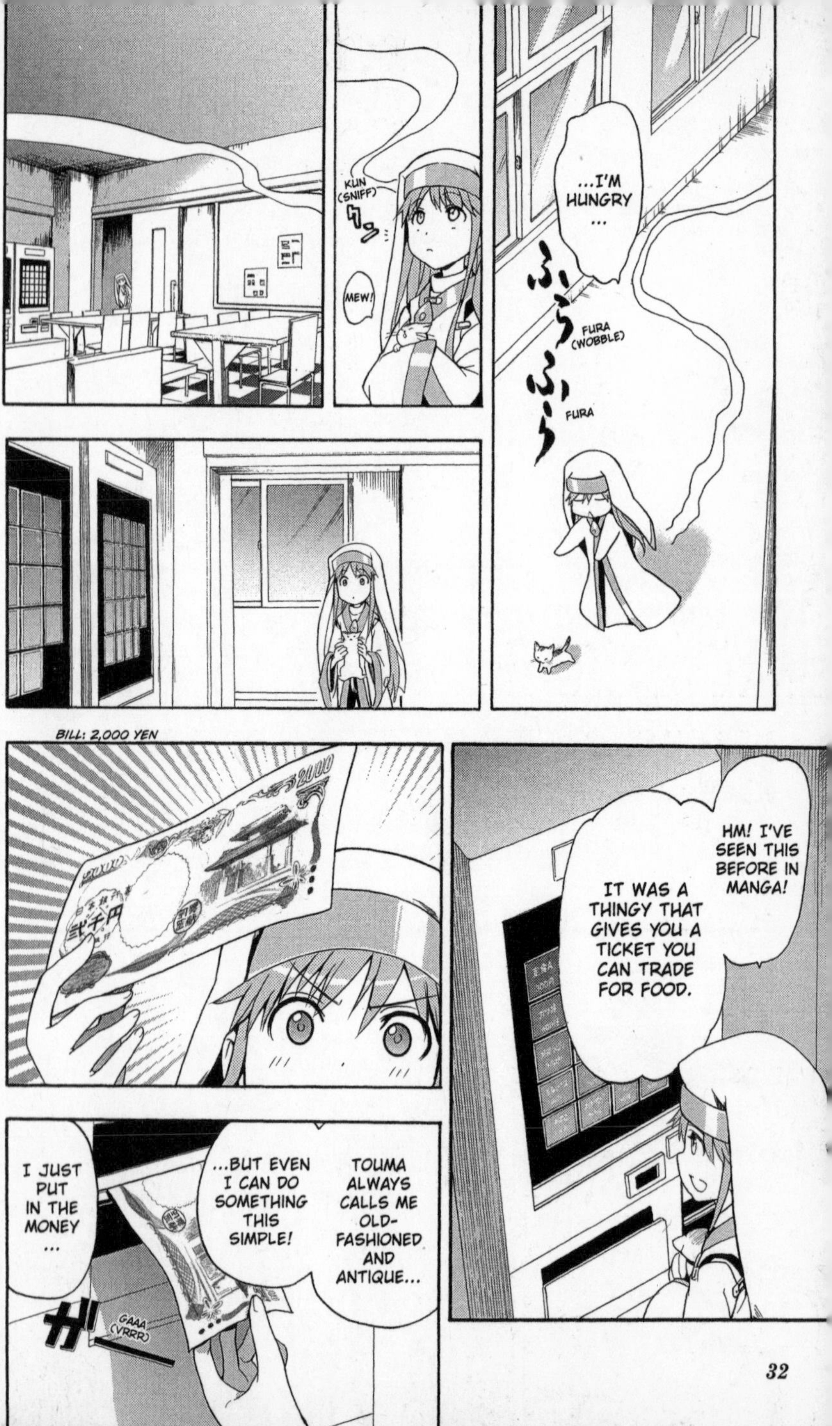
...I'M HUNGRY...
FURA (WOBBLE)
FURA
KUN (SNIFF)
MEW!
BILL: 2,000 YEN
HM! I'VE SEEN THIS BEFORE IN MANGA!
IT WAS A THINGY THAT GIVES YOU A TICKET YOU CAN TRADE FOR FOOD.
TOUMA ALWAYS CALLS ME OLD-FASHIONED AND ANTIQUE...
...BUT EVEN I CAN DO SOMETHING THIS SIMPLE!
I JUST PUT IN THE MONEY...
GAAA (VRRR)

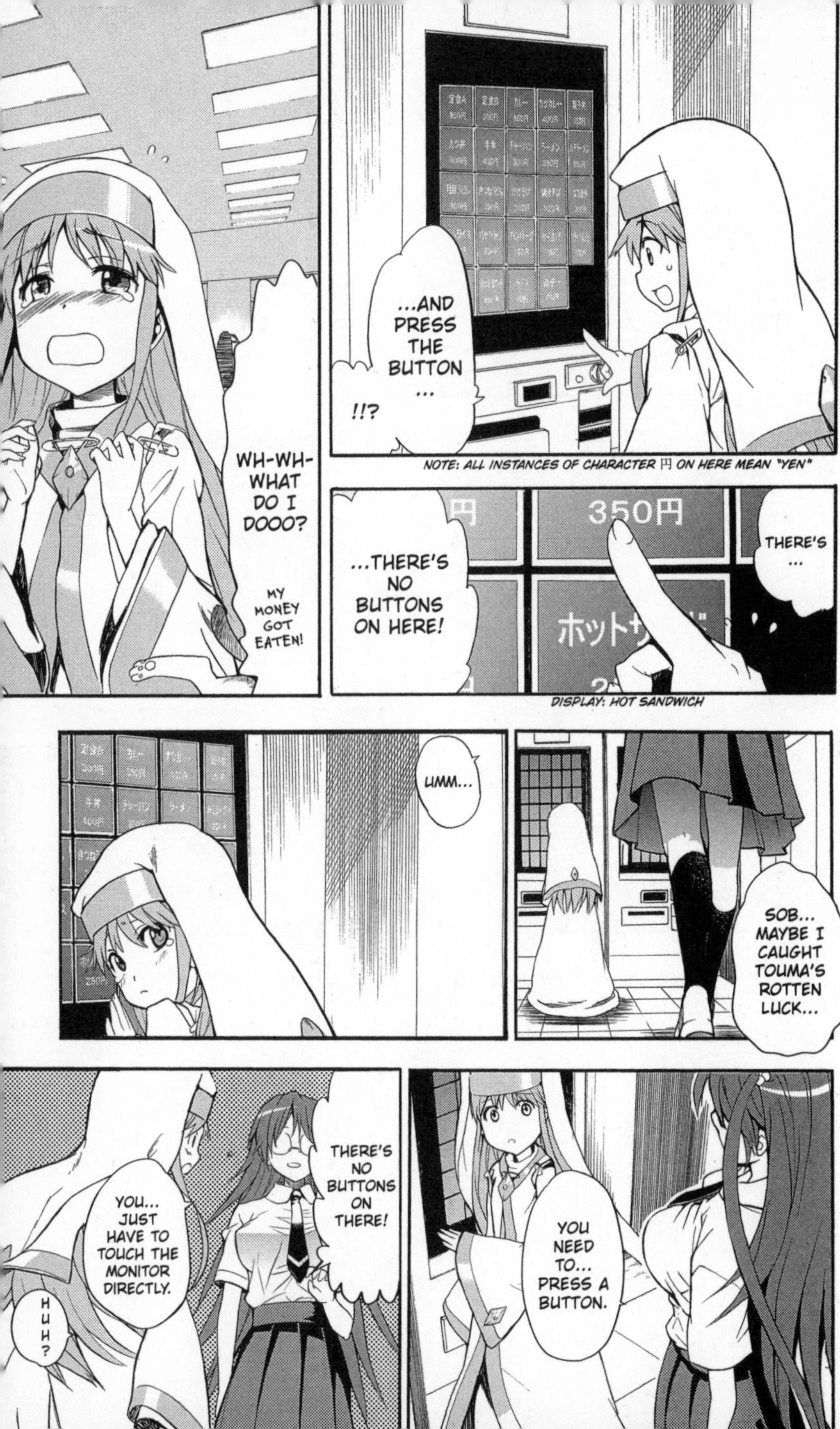
...AND PRESS THE BUTTON ...
!!?
NOTE: ALL INSTANCES OF CHARACTER 円 ON HERE MEAN "YEN"
350円
ホットサ
THERE'S ...
...THERE'S NO BUTTONS ON HERE!
DISPLAY: HOT SANDWICH
WH-WH-WHAT DO I DOOOO?
MY MONEY GOT EATEN!
SOB... MAYBE I CAUGHT TOUMA'S ROTTEN LUCK...
UMM...
YOU NEED TO... PRESS A BUTTON.
THERE'S NO BUTTONS ON THERE!
YOU... JUST HAVE TO TOUCH THE MONITOR DIRECTLY.
HUH?

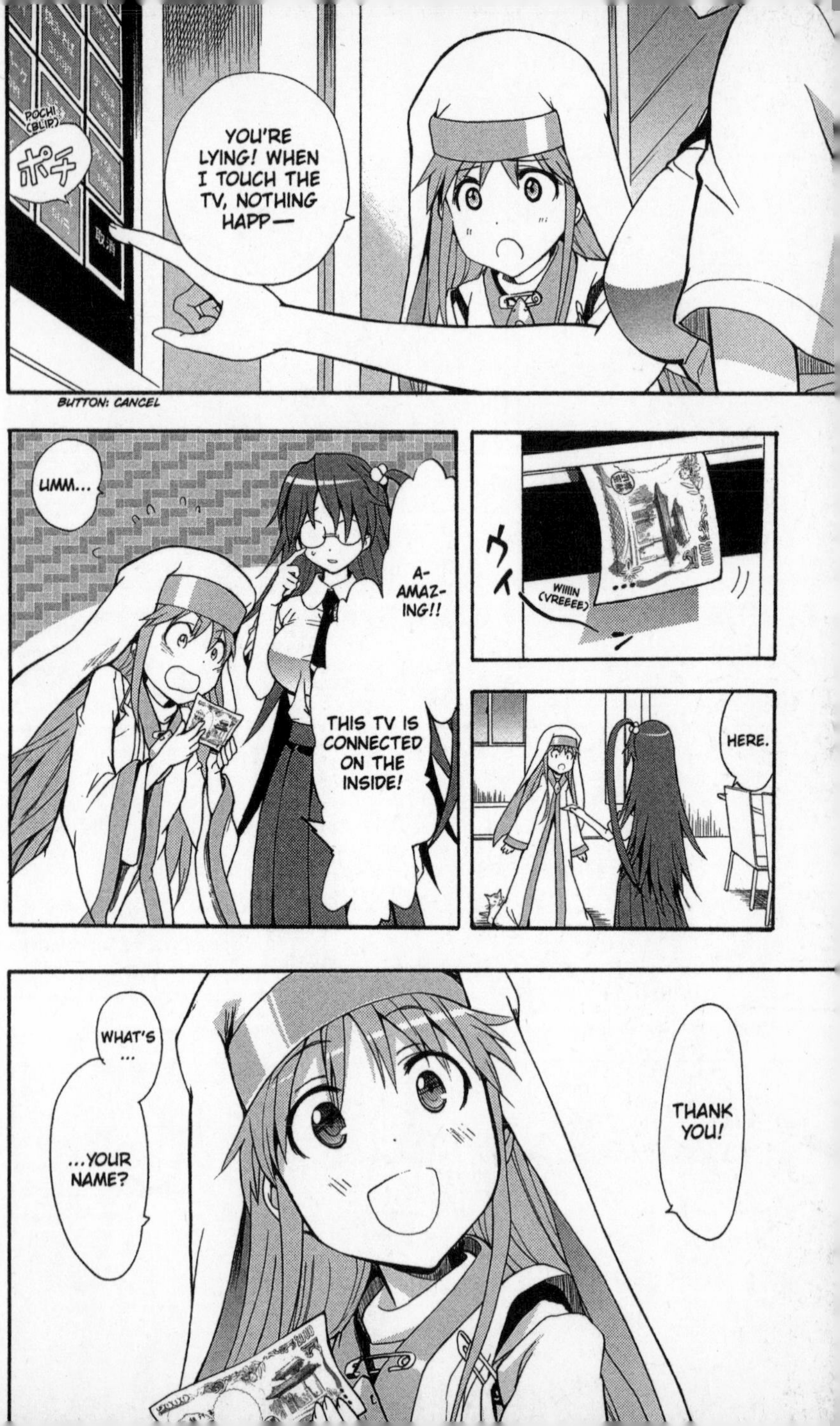
YOU'RE LYING! WHEN I TOUCH THE TV, NOTHING HAPP—
ポチ
POCHI (BLIP)
BUTTON: CANCEL
ウィ
WIIIN (VREEEE)
HERE.
A-AMAZING!!
THIS TV IS CONNECTED ON THE INSIDE!
UMM...
THANK YOU!
WHAT'S ...
...YOUR NAME?

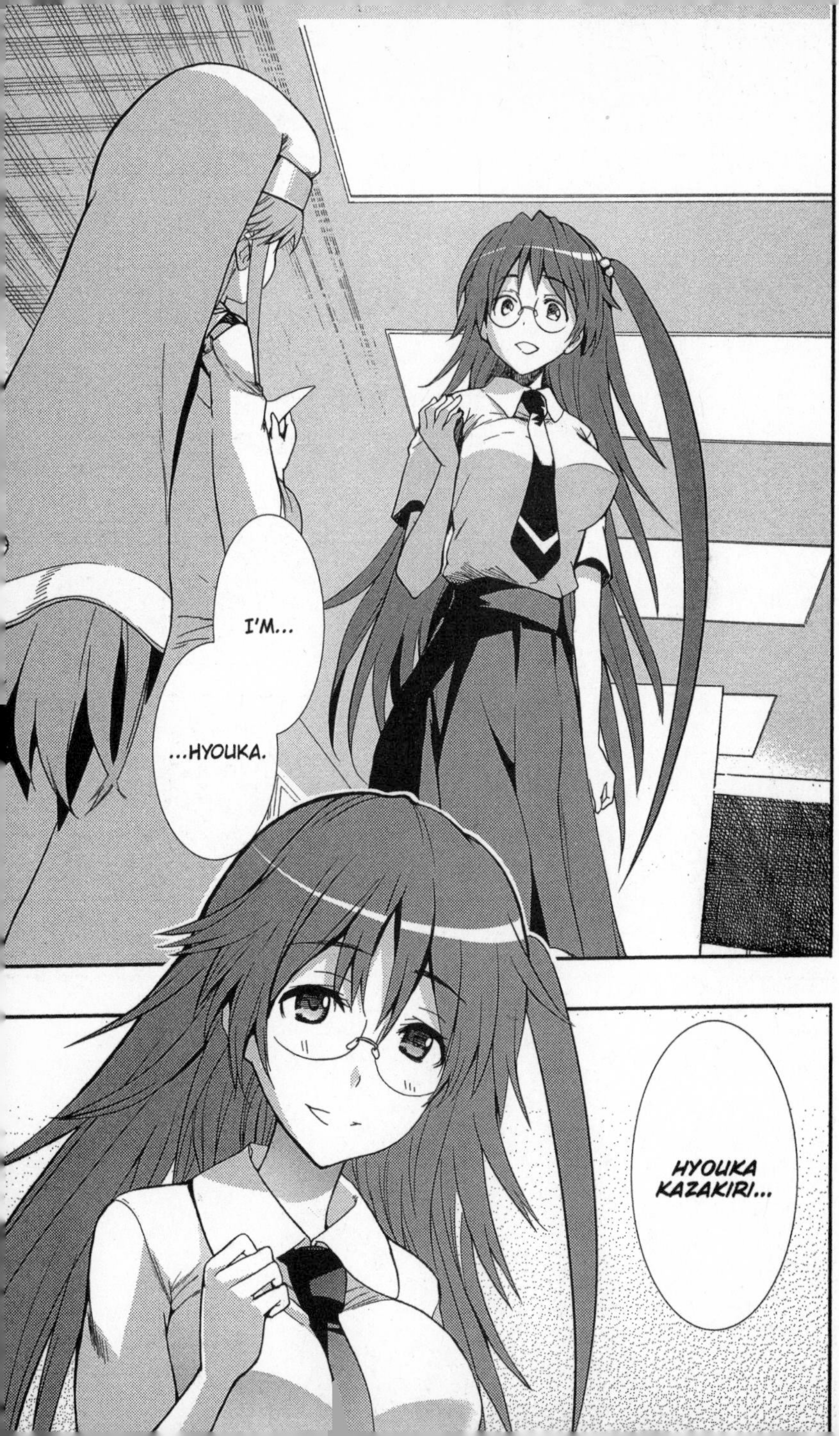
I'M...
...HYOUKA.
HYOUKA KAZAKIRI...

A Certain Magical Index

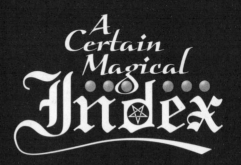

GOUIN
(VRRRR)
ゴウン
ブ・ウン
GOUN

ACADEMY
CITY GATE

BURORO
(VROOM)

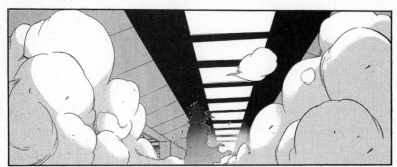

HM?

MONITOR: UNKNOWN

未認証

STOP

PIPI
(BEEP)

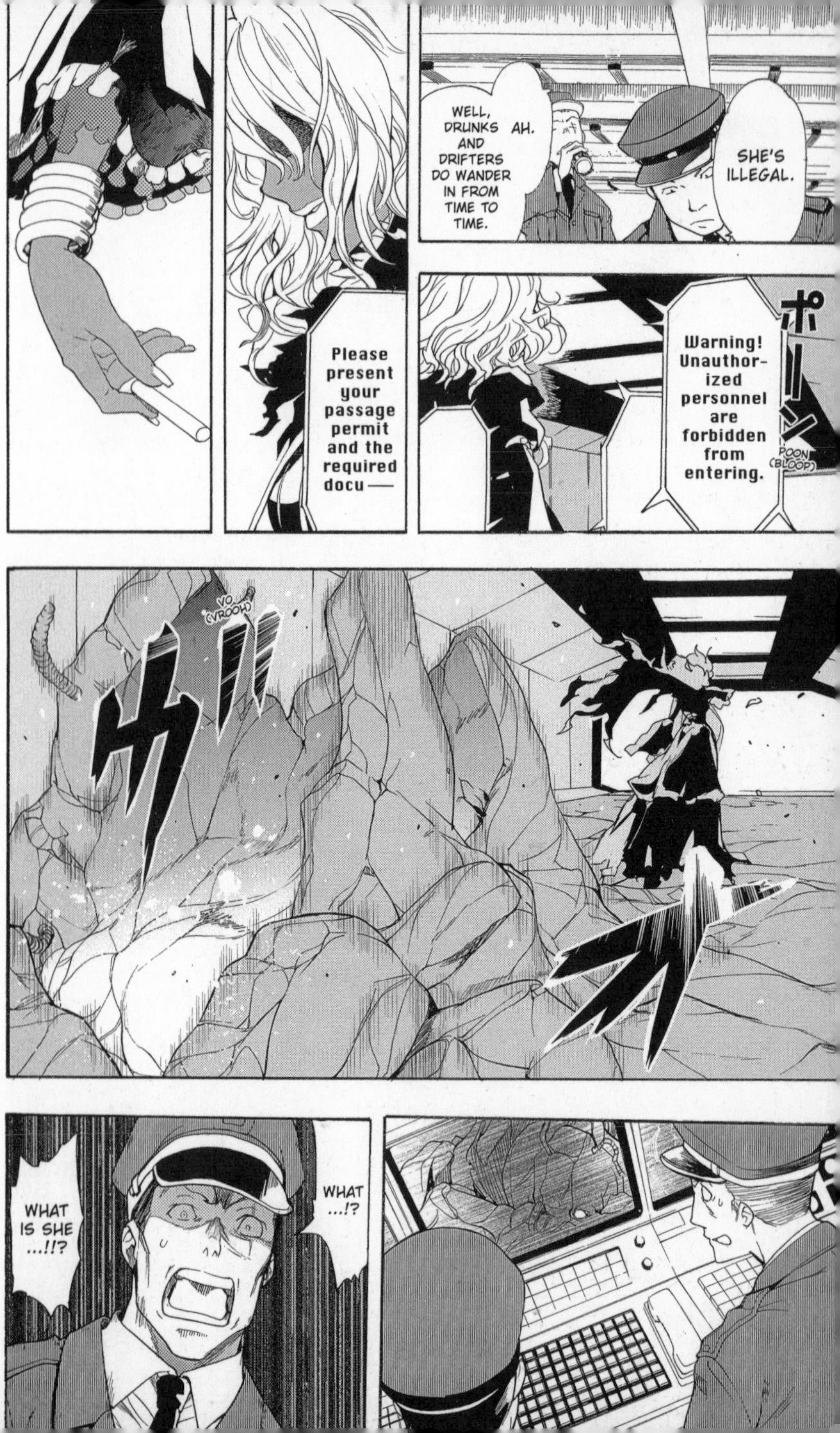
SHE'S ILLEGAL.
AH.
WELL, DRUNKS AND DRIFTERS DO WANDER IN FROM TIME TO TIME.
ポーン
POON (BLOOP)
Warning! Unauthorized personnel are forbidden from entering.
Please present your passage permit and the required docu—
VO (VROOH)
WHAT ...!?
WHAT IS SHE ...!!?

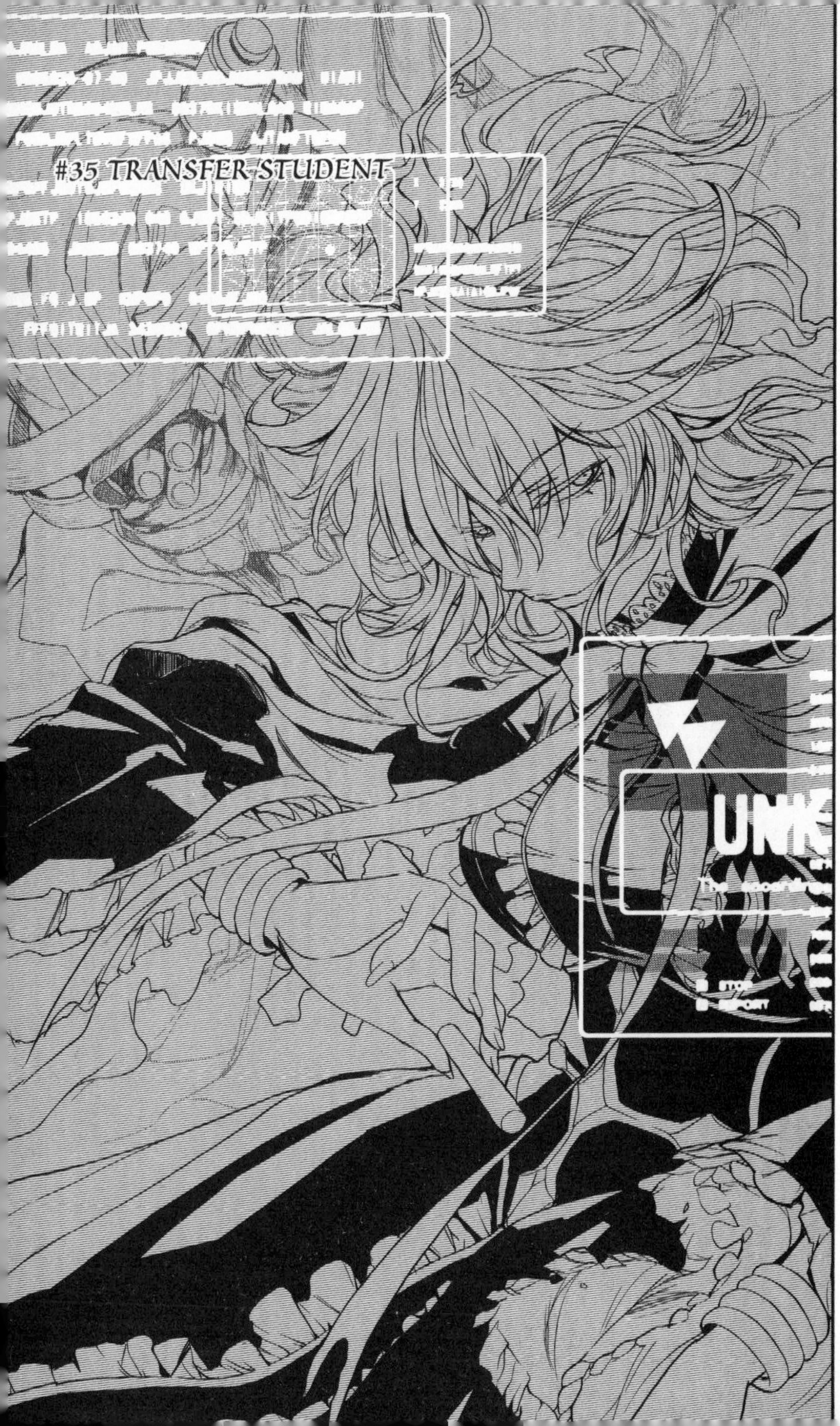
#35 TRANSFER STUDENT

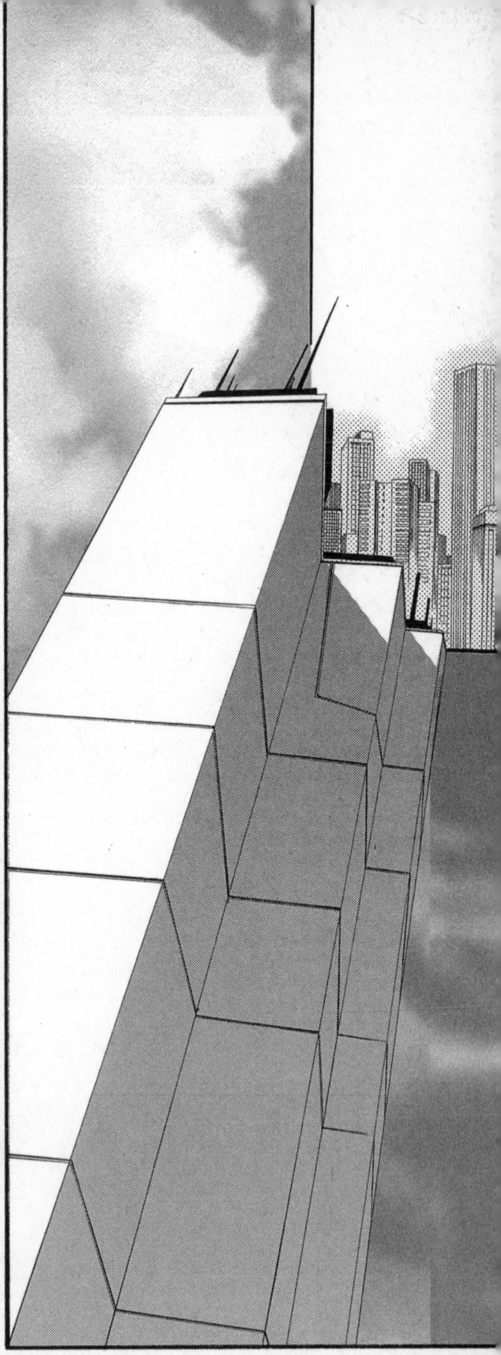

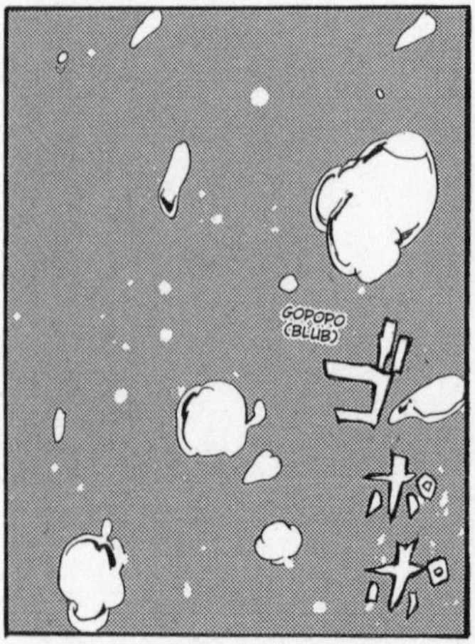
GOPOPO
(BLUB)

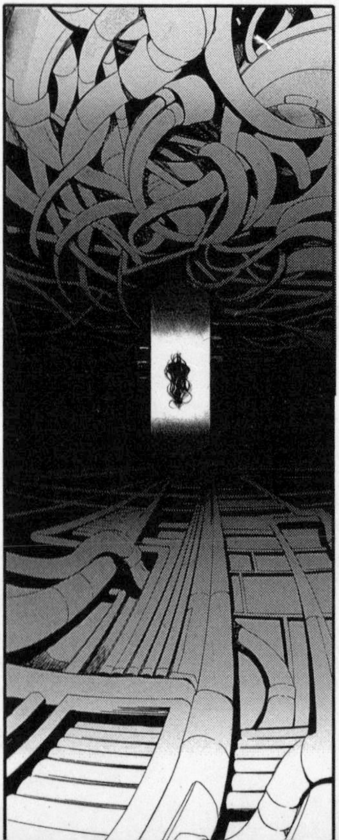

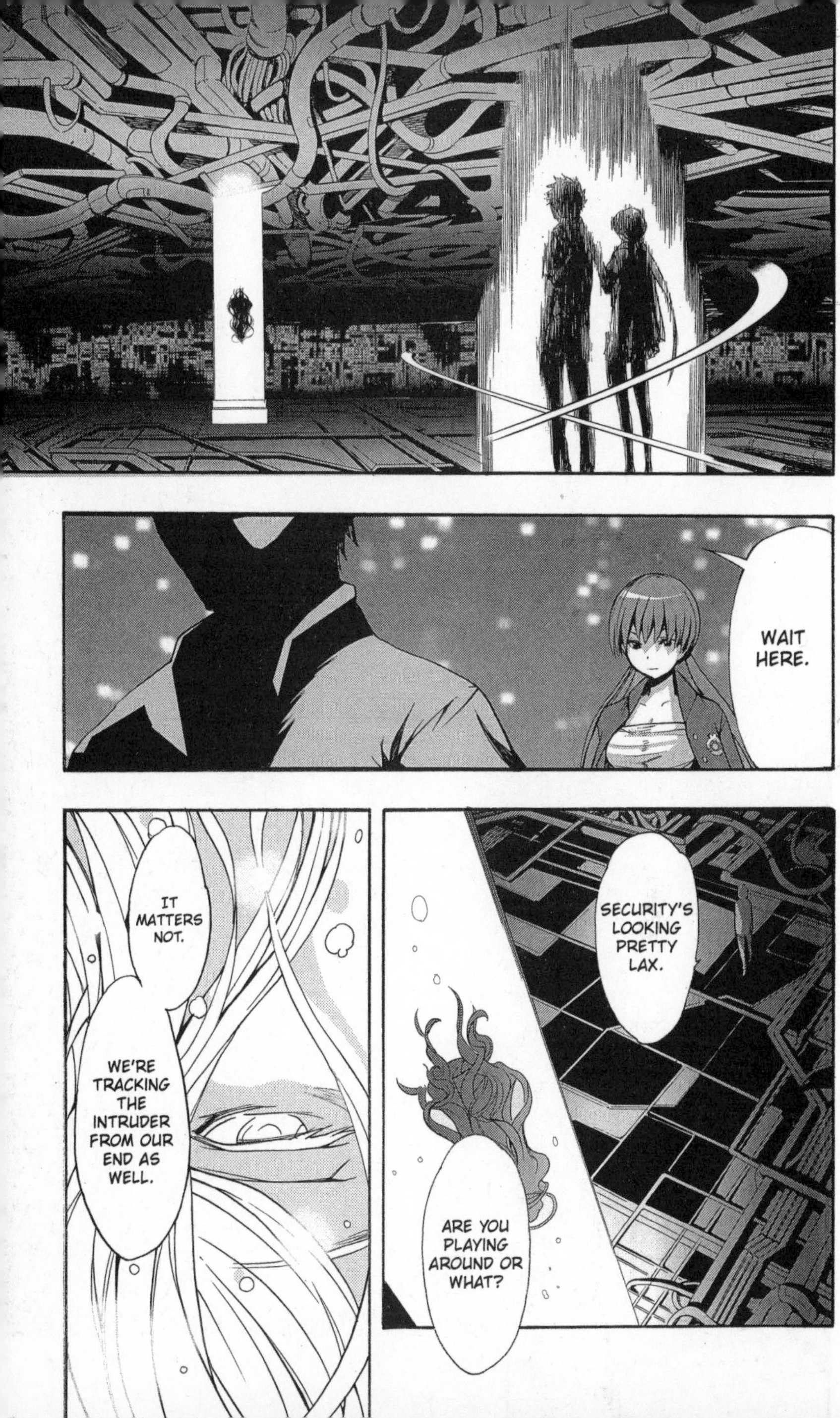
WAIT HERE.
SECURITY'S LOOKING PRETTY LAX.
ARE YOU PLAYING AROUND OR WHAT?
IT MATTERS NOT.
WE'RE TRACKING THE INTRUDER FROM OUR END AS WELL.

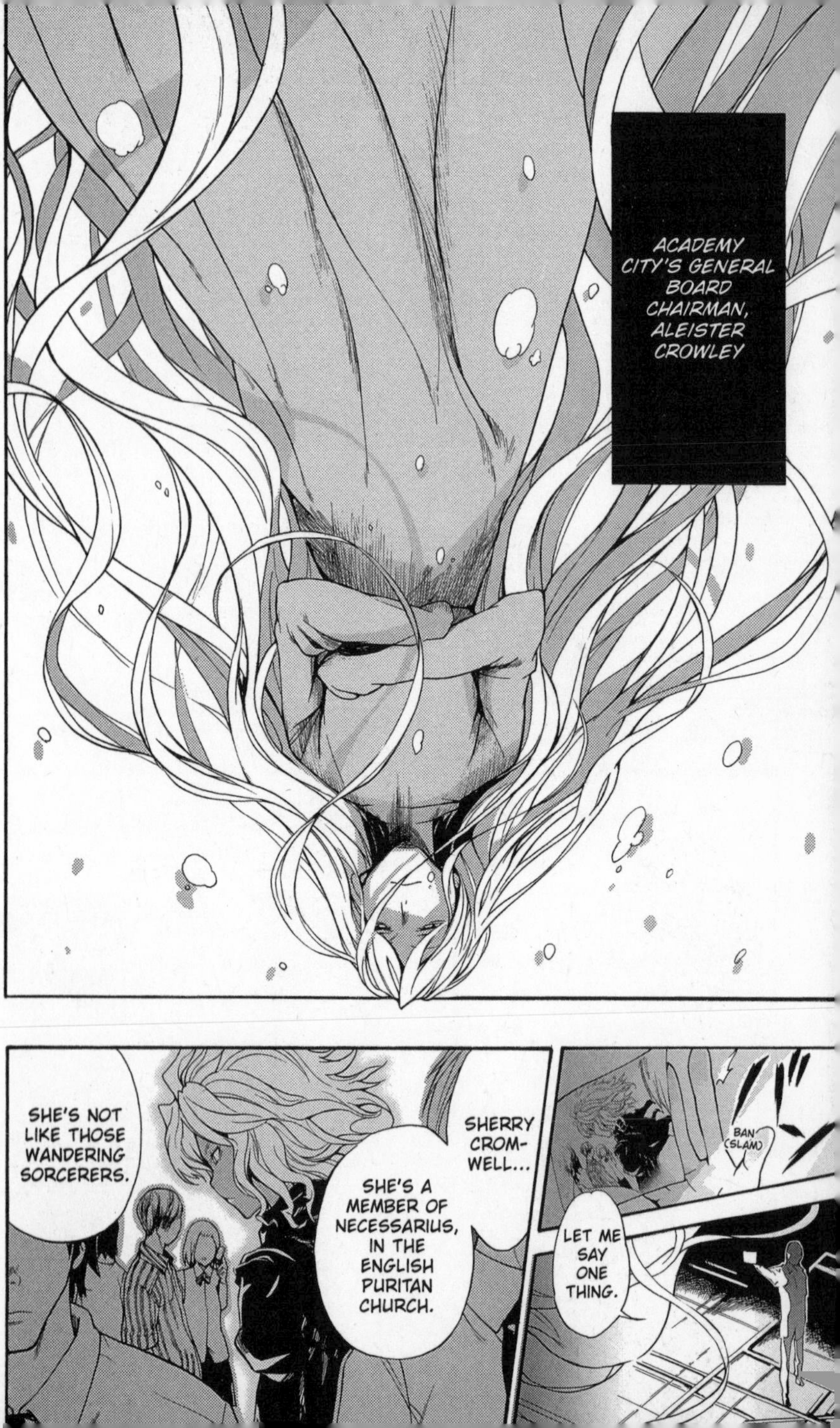
ACADEMY CITY'S GENERAL BOARD CHAIRMAN, ALEISTER CROWLEY
BAN (SLAM)
LET ME SAY ONE THING.
SHERRY CROM-WELL...
SHE'S A MEMBER OF NECESSARIUS, IN THE ENGLISH PURITAN CHURCH.
SHE'S NOT LIKE THOSE WANDERING SORCERERS.

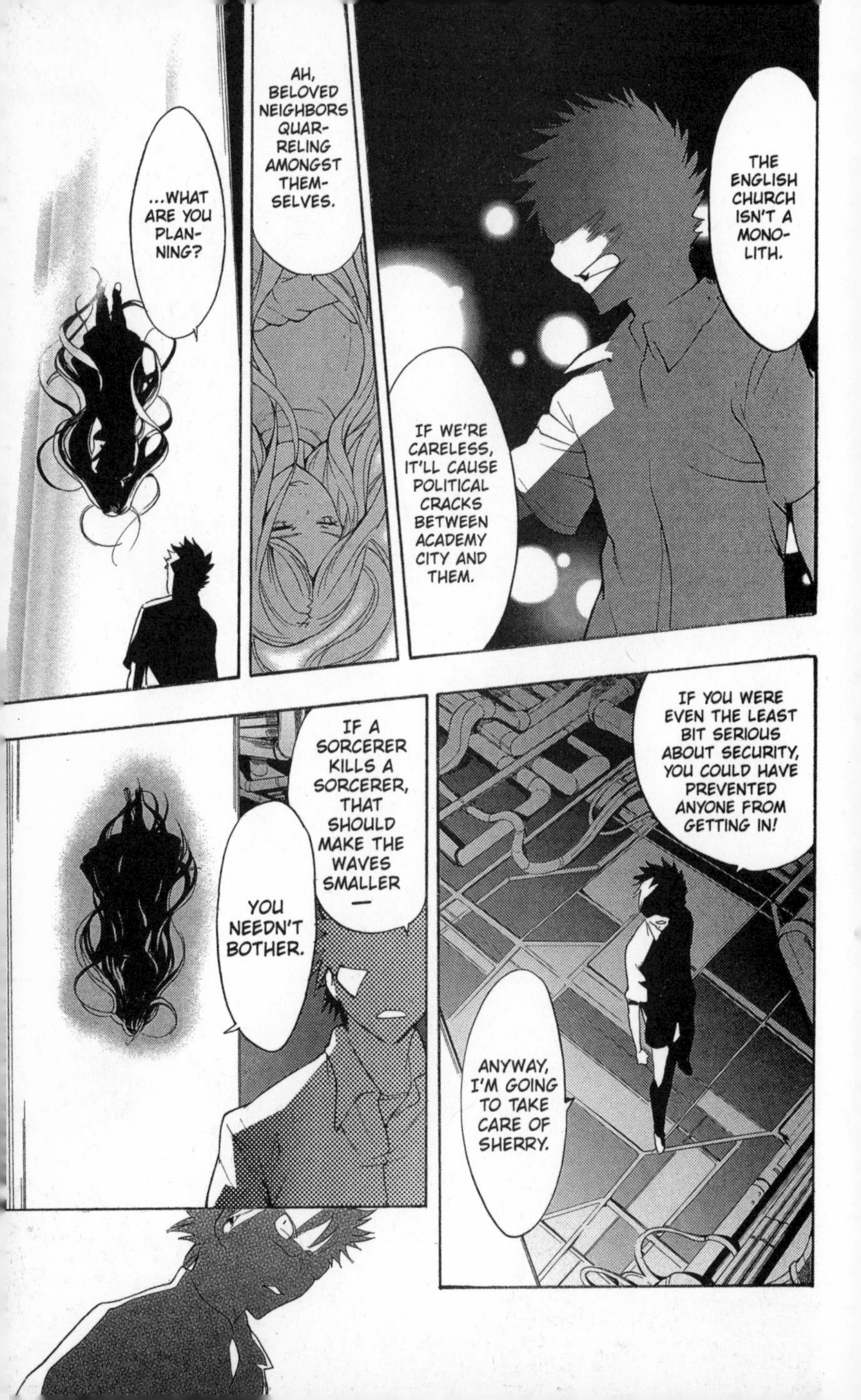
THE ENGLISH CHURCH ISN'T A MONOLITH.
IF WE'RE CARELESS, IT'LL CAUSE POLITICAL CRACKS BETWEEN ACADEMY CITY AND THEM.
AH, BELOVED NEIGHBORS QUARRELING AMONGST THEMSELVES.
...WHAT ARE YOU PLANNING?
IF YOU WERE EVEN THE LEAST BIT SERIOUS ABOUT SECURITY, YOU COULD HAVE PREVENTED ANYONE FROM GETTING IN!
ANYWAY, I'M GOING TO TAKE CARE OF SHERRY.
IF A SORCERER KILLS A SORCERER, THAT SHOULD MAKE THE WAVES SMALLER —
YOU NEEDN'T BOTHER.

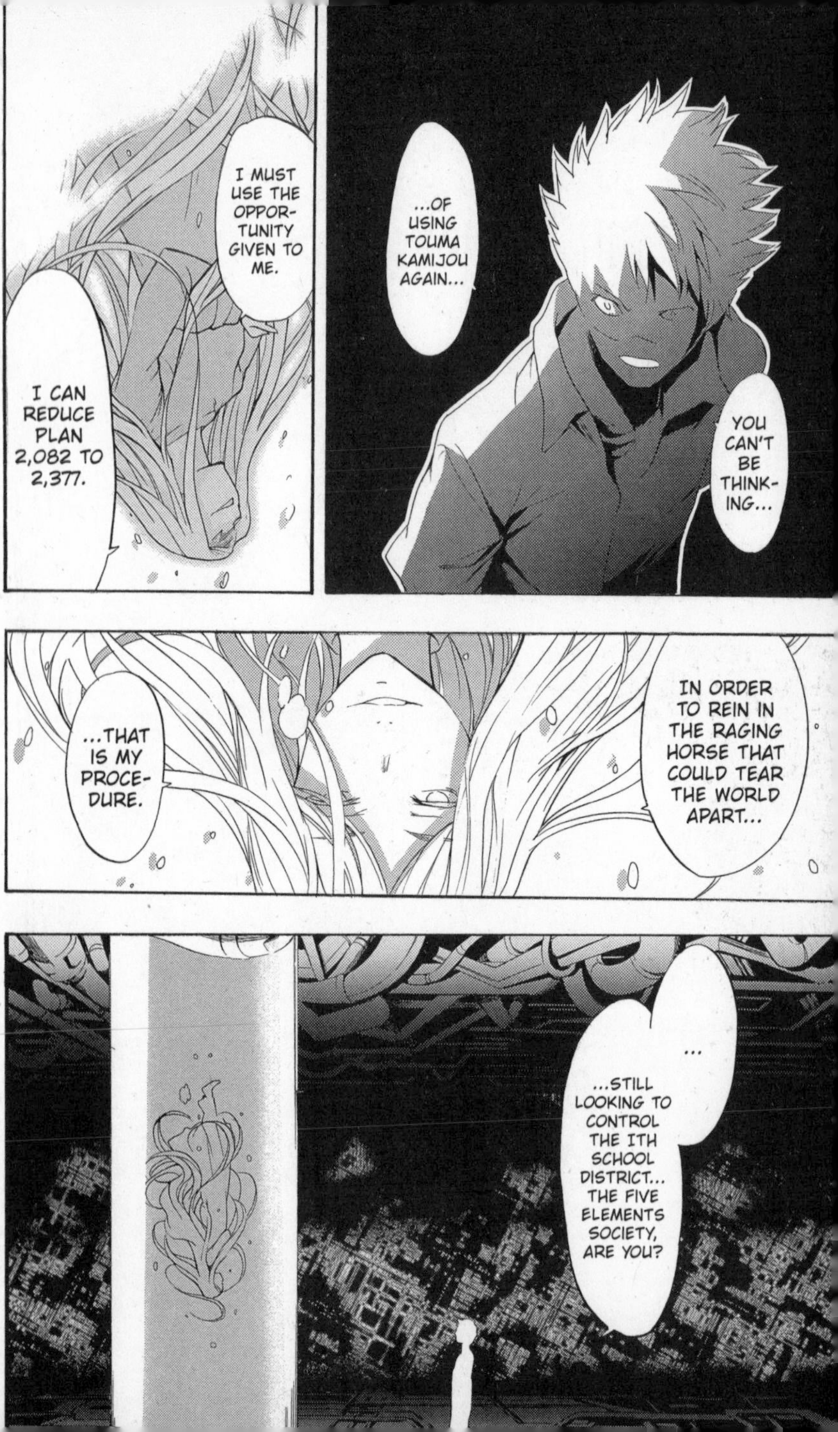
YOU CAN'T BE THINKING...
...OF USING TOUMA KAMIJOU AGAIN...
I MUST USE THE OPPORTUNITY GIVEN TO ME.
I CAN REDUCE PLAN 2,082 TO 2,377.
IN ORDER TO REIN IN THE RAGING HORSE THAT COULD TEAR THE WORLD APART...
...THAT IS MY PROCEDURE.
...
...STILL LOOKING TO CONTROL THE ITH SCHOOL DISTRICT... THE FIVE ELEMENTS SOCIETY, ARE YOU?

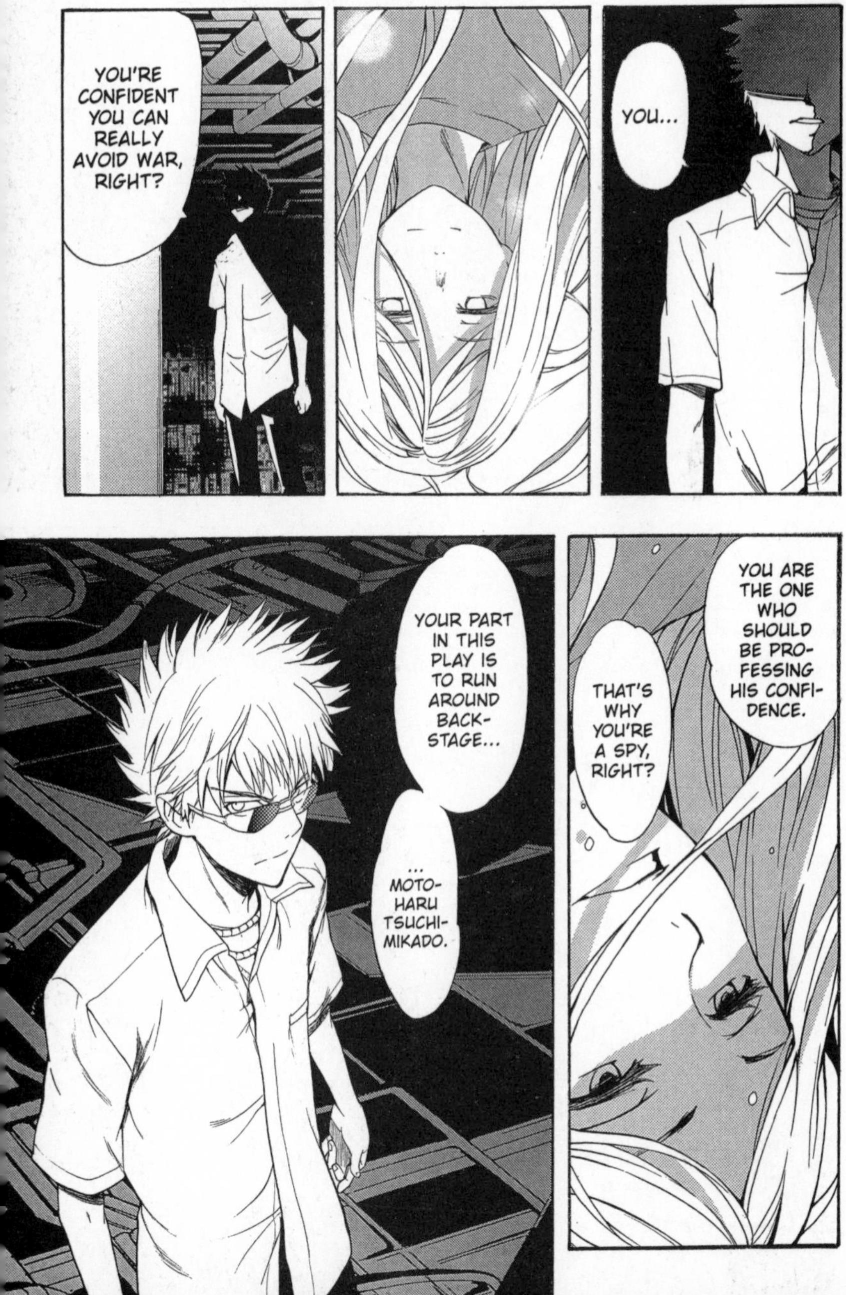
YOU...
YOU'RE CONFIDENT YOU CAN REALLY AVOID WAR, RIGHT?
YOU ARE THE ONE WHO SHOULD BE PRO-FESSING HIS CONFI-DENCE.
THAT'S WHY YOU'RE A SPY, RIGHT?
YOUR PART IN THIS PLAY IS TO RUN AROUND BACK-STAGE...
...MOTO-HARU TSUCHI-MIKADO.

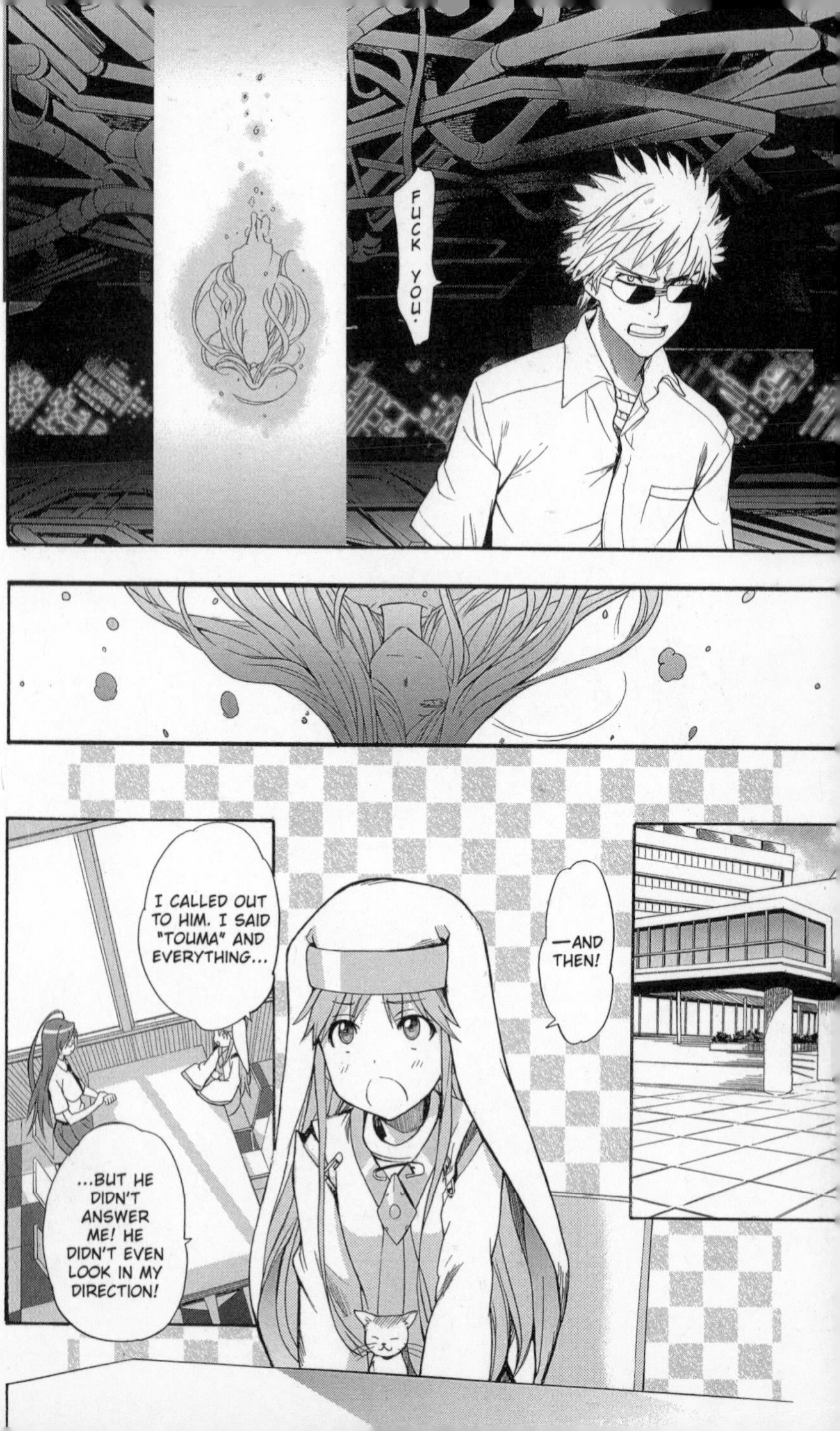
FUCK YOU.
—AND THEN!
I CALLED OUT TO HIM. I SAID "TOUMA" AND EVERYTHING...
...BUT HE DIDN'T ANSWER ME! HE DIDN'T EVEN LOOK IN MY DIRECTION!

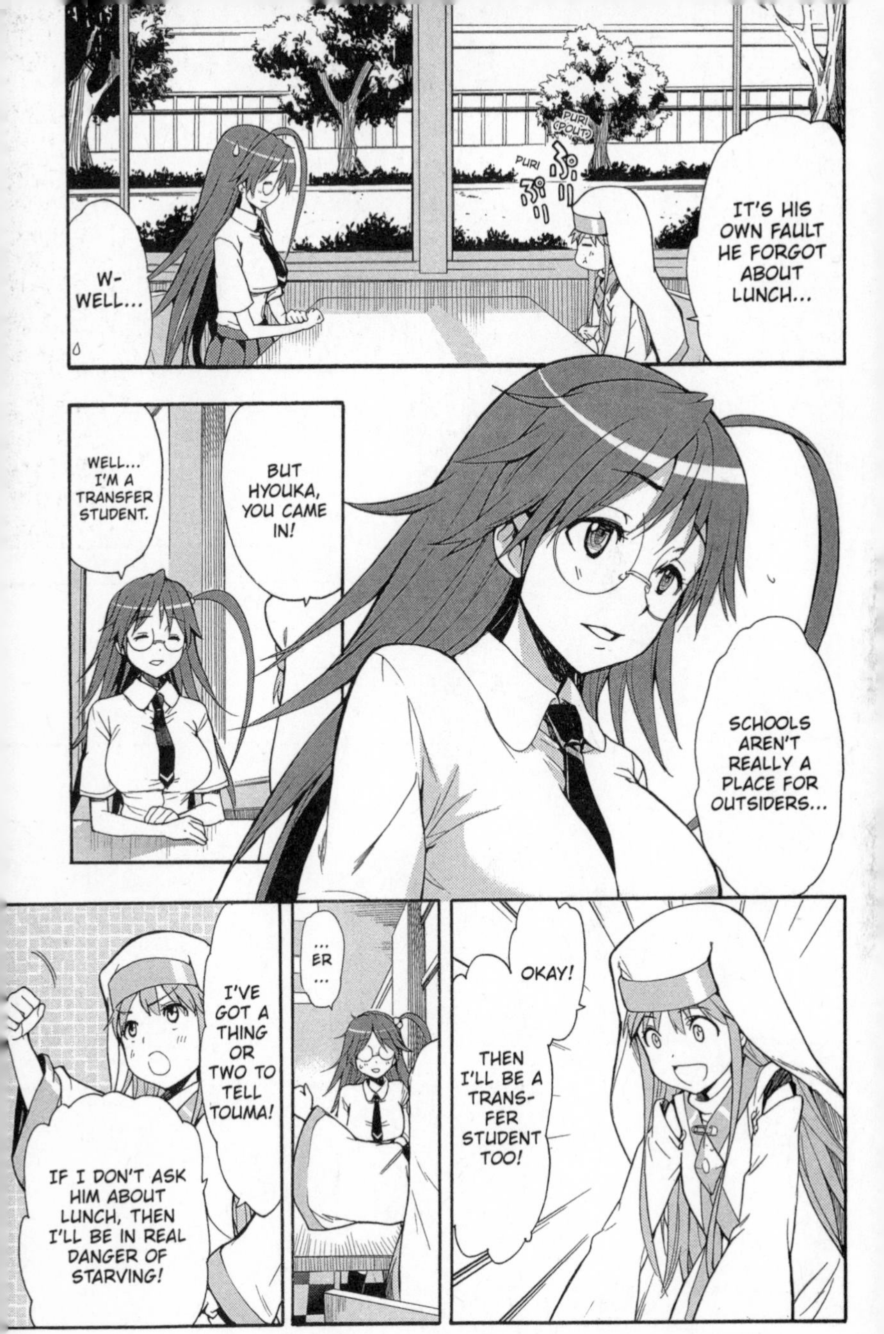
IT'S HIS OWN FAULT HE FORGOT ABOUT LUNCH...
PURI (POUT)
PURI
W-WELL...
SCHOOLS AREN'T REALLY A PLACE FOR OUTSIDERS...
BUT HYOUKA, YOU CAME IN!
WELL... I'M A TRANSFER STUDENT.
OKAY!
THEN I'LL BE A TRANS-FER STUDENT TOO!
... ER ...
I'VE GOT A THING OR TWO TO TELL TOUMA!
IF I DON'T ASK HIM ABOUT LUNCH, THEN I'LL BE IN REAL DANGER OF STARVING!

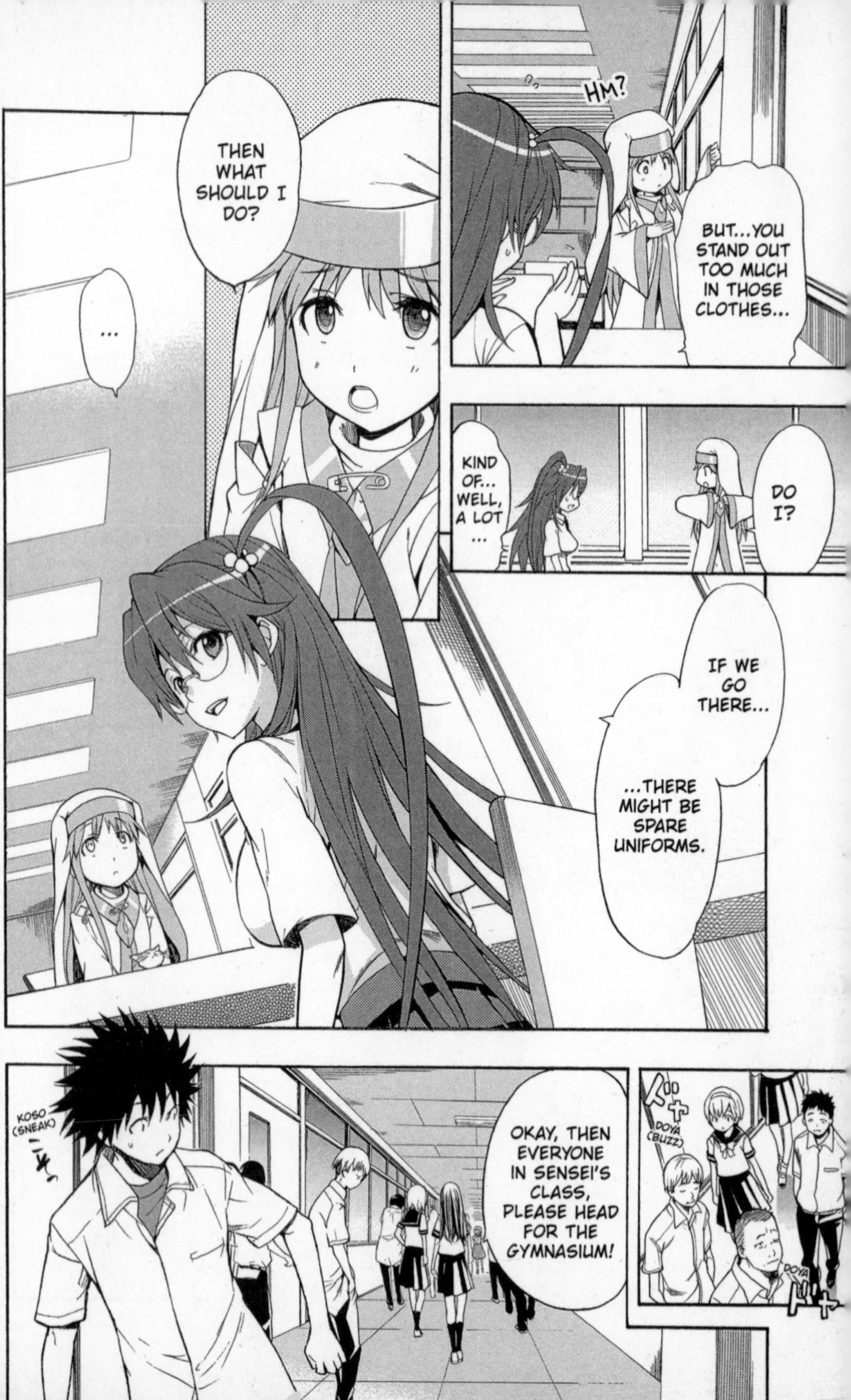
HM?
BUT...YOU STAND OUT TOO MUCH IN THOSE CLOTHES...
DO I?
KIND OF... WELL, A LOT...
THEN WHAT SHOULD I DO?
...
IF WE GO THERE...
...THERE MIGHT BE SPARE UNIFORMS.
DOYA (BUZZ)
DOYA
OKAY, THEN EVERYONE IN SENSEI'S CLASS, PLEASE HEAD FOR THE GYMNASIUM!
KOSO (SNEAK)

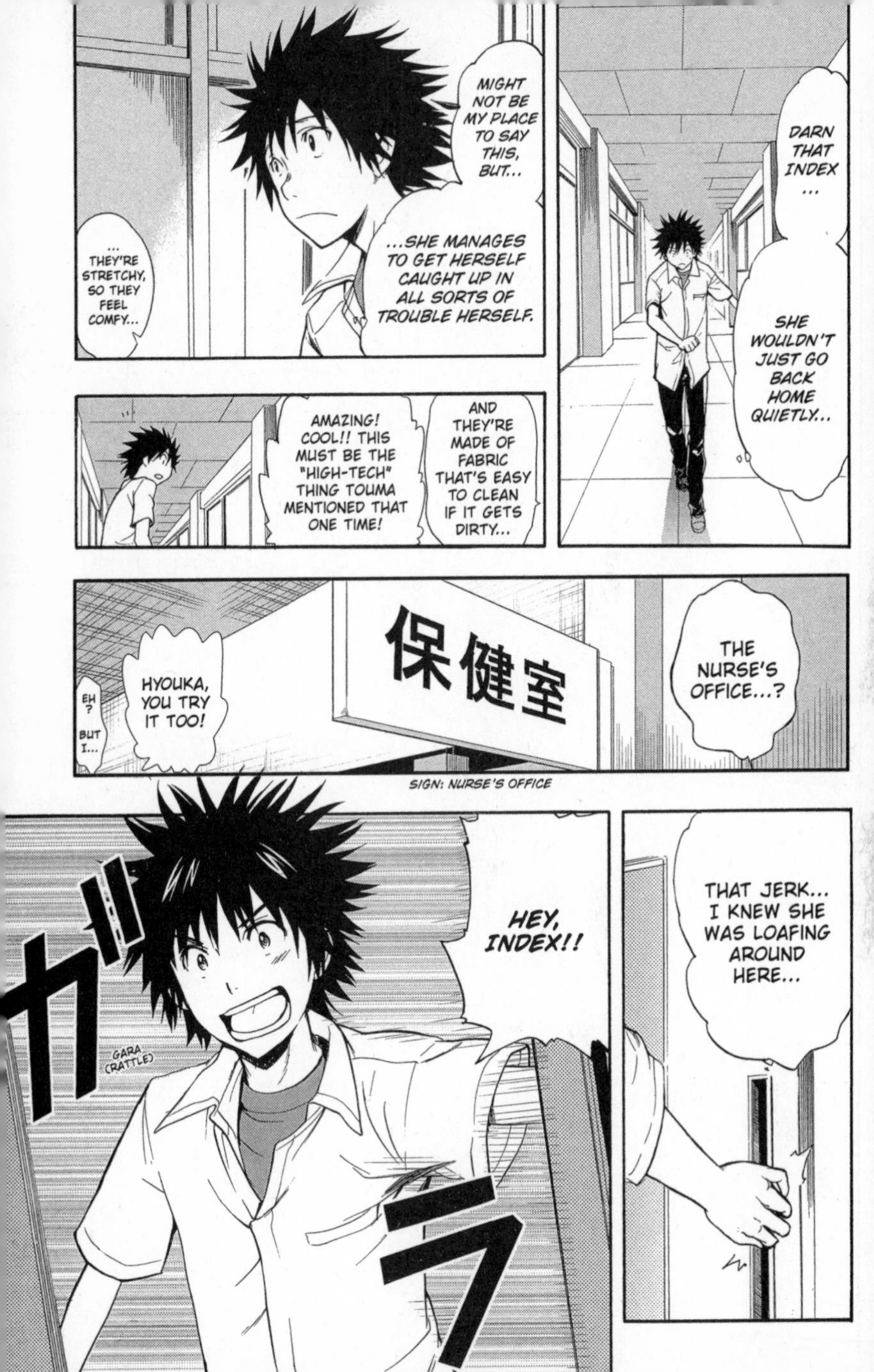
DARN THAT INDEX ...
SHE WOULDN'T JUST GO BACK HOME QUIETLY...
MIGHT NOT BE MY PLACE TO SAY THIS, BUT...
...SHE MANAGES TO GET HERSELF CAUGHT UP IN ALL SORTS OF TROUBLE HERSELF.
... THEY'RE STRETCHY, SO THEY FEEL COMFY...
AND THEY'RE MADE OF FABRIC THAT'S EASY TO CLEAN IF IT GETS DIRTY...
AMAZING! COOL!! THIS MUST BE THE "HIGH-TECH" THING TOUMA MENTIONED THAT ONE TIME!
THE NURSE'S OFFICE...?
保健室
HYOUKA, YOU TRY IT TOO!
EH? BUT I...
SIGN: NURSE'S OFFICE
THAT JERK... I KNEW SHE WAS LOAFING AROUND HERE...
HEY, INDEX!!
ガラ
GARA (RATTLE)

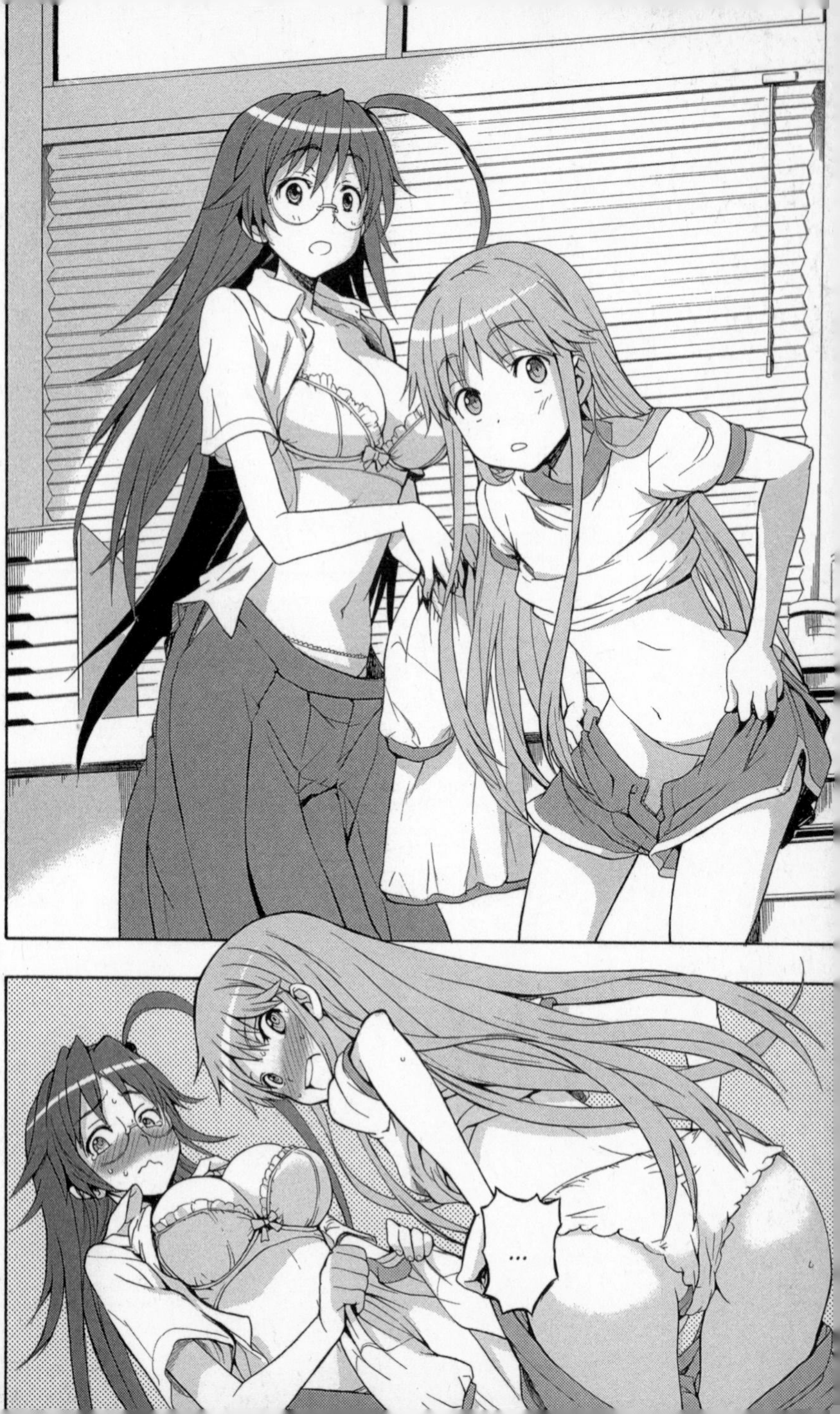
...

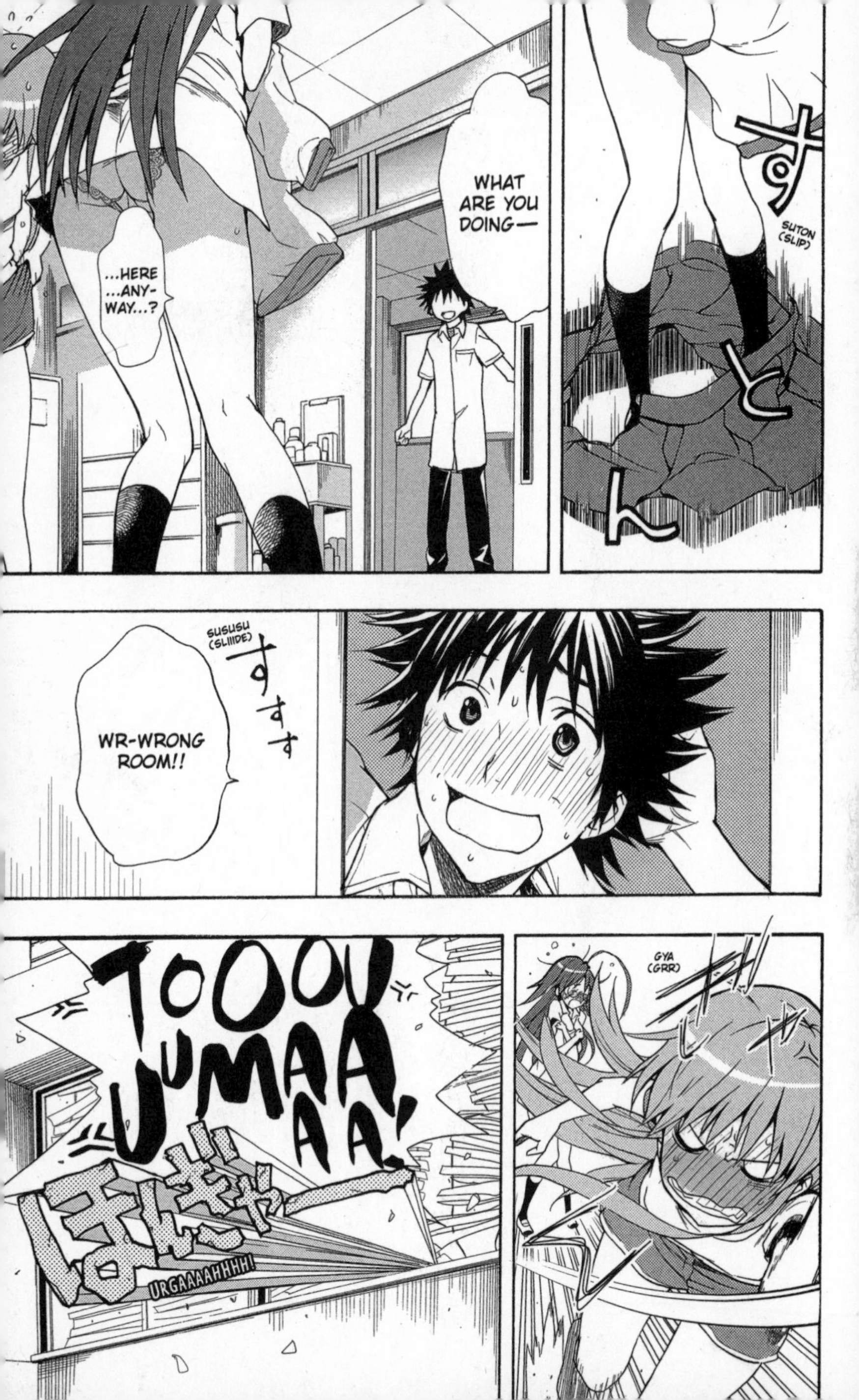
すとん
SUTON (SLIP)
WHAT ARE YOU DOING—
...HERE ...ANY-WAY...?
SUSUSU (SLIIIDE)
すすす
WR-WRONG ROOM!!
GYA (GRR)
TOOOUUMAAAA
URGAAAAHHHH!

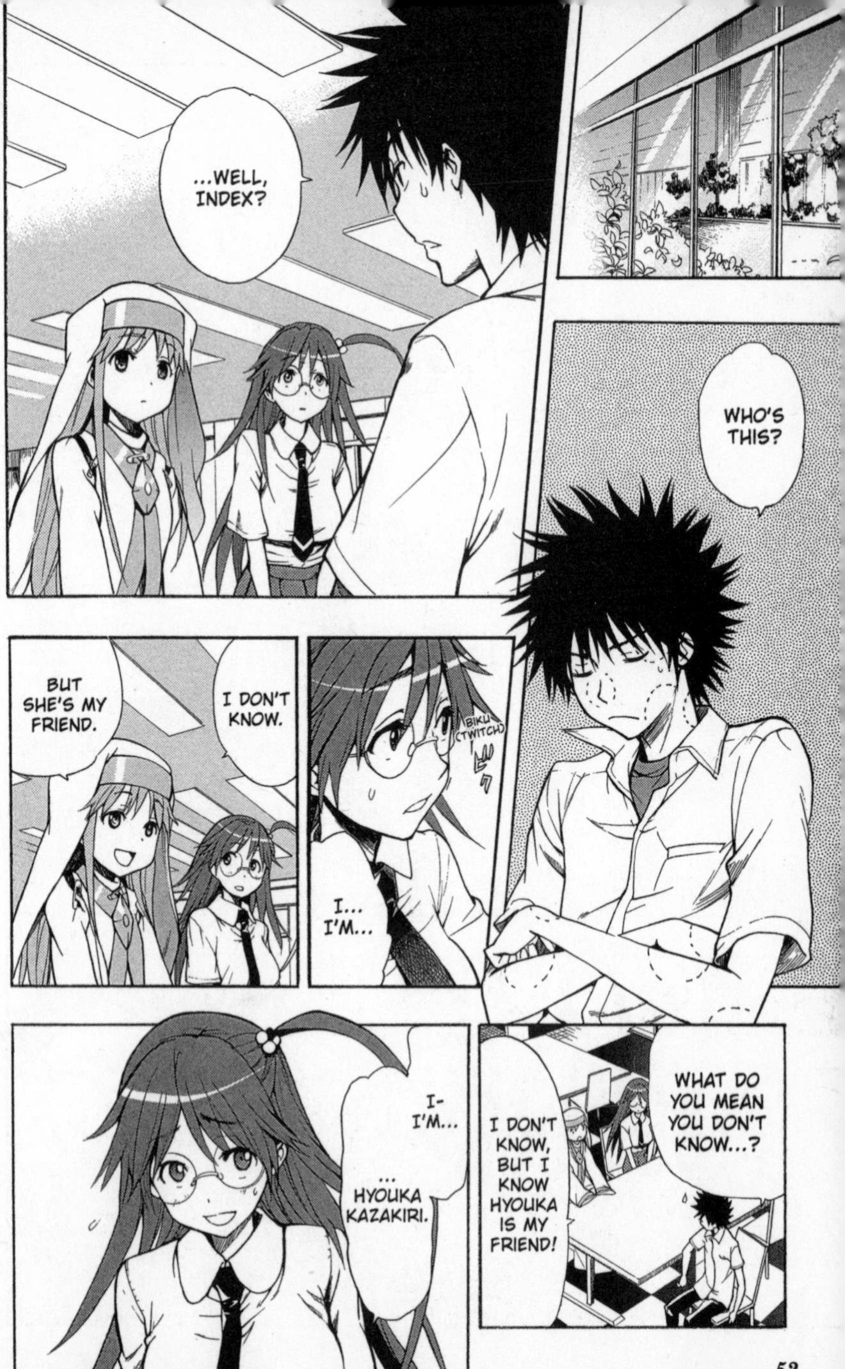
...WELL, INDEX?
WHO'S THIS?
BIKU (TWITCH)
I... I'M...
I DON'T KNOW.
BUT SHE'S MY FRIEND.
WHAT DO YOU MEAN YOU DON'T KNOW...?
I DON'T KNOW, BUT I KNOW HYOUKA IS MY FRIEND!
I- I'M...
... HYOUKA KAZAKIRI.

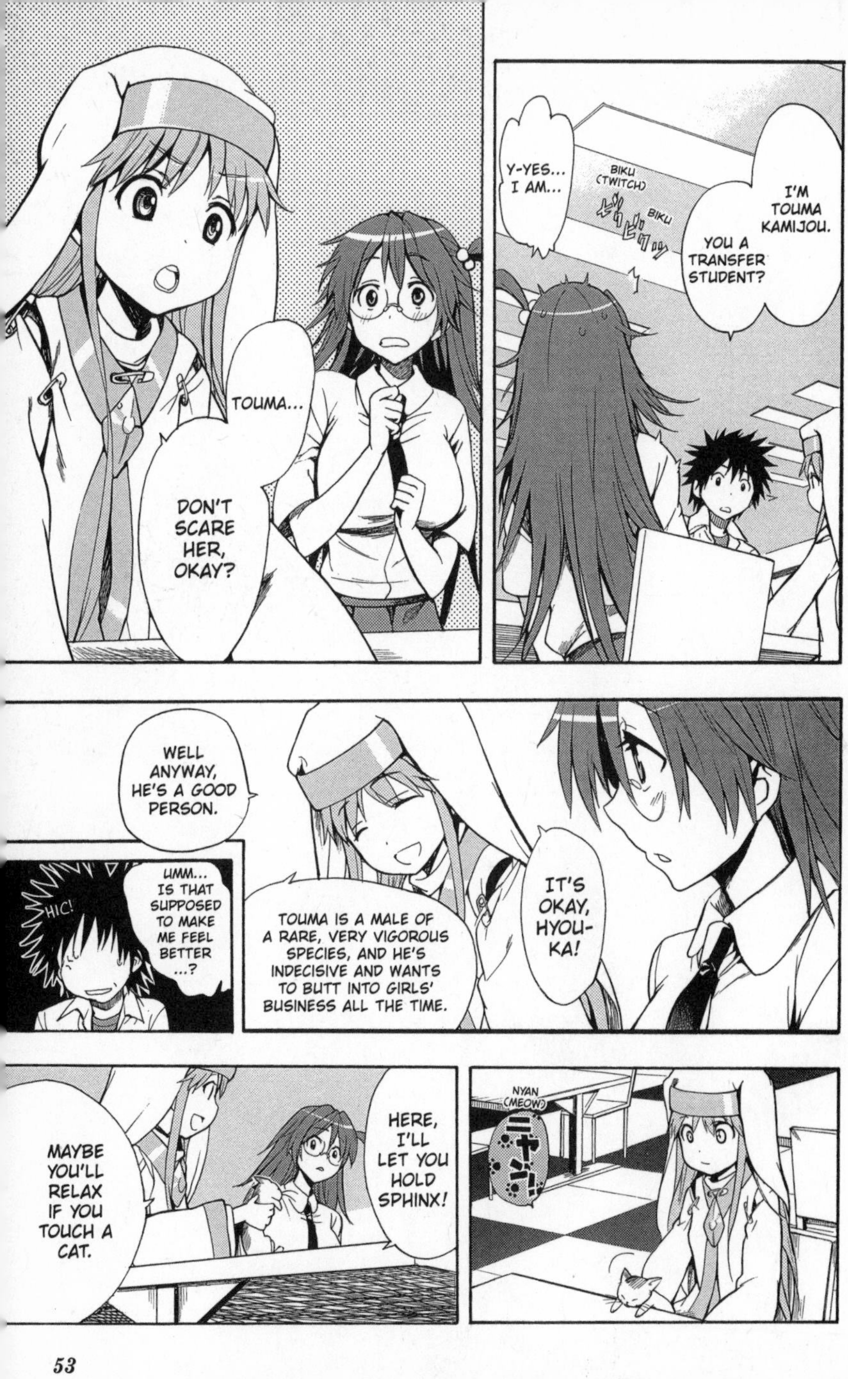
I'M TOUMA KAMIJOU.
YOU A TRANSFER STUDENT?
BIKU (TWITCH)
BIKU
Y-YES... I AM...
TOUMA...
DON'T SCARE HER, OKAY?
IT'S OKAY, HYOU-KA!
WELL ANYWAY, HE'S A GOOD PERSON.
TOUMA IS A MALE OF A RARE, VERY VIGOROUS SPECIES, AND HE'S INDECISIVE AND WANTS TO BUTT INTO GIRLS' BUSINESS ALL THE TIME.
HIC!
UMM... IS THAT SUPPOSED TO MAKE ME FEEL BETTER ...?
NYAN (MEOW)
HERE, I'LL LET YOU HOLD SPHINX!
MAYBE YOU'LL RELAX IF YOU TOUCH A CAT.

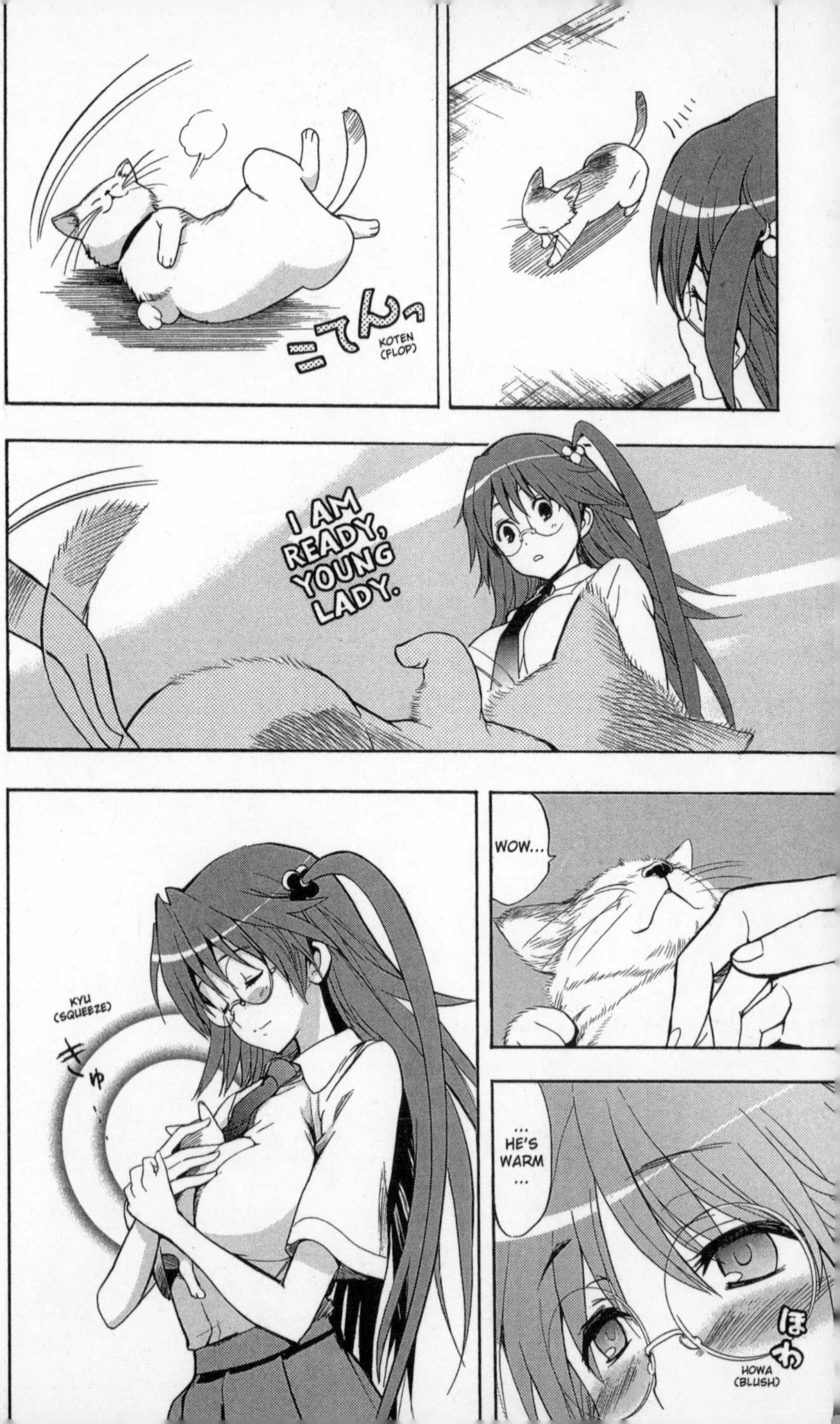
こてんっ
KOTEN (FLOP)
I AM READY, YOUNG LADY.
WOW...
... HE'S WARM ...
ほわ
HOWA (BLUSH)
きゅ
KYU (SQUEEZE)

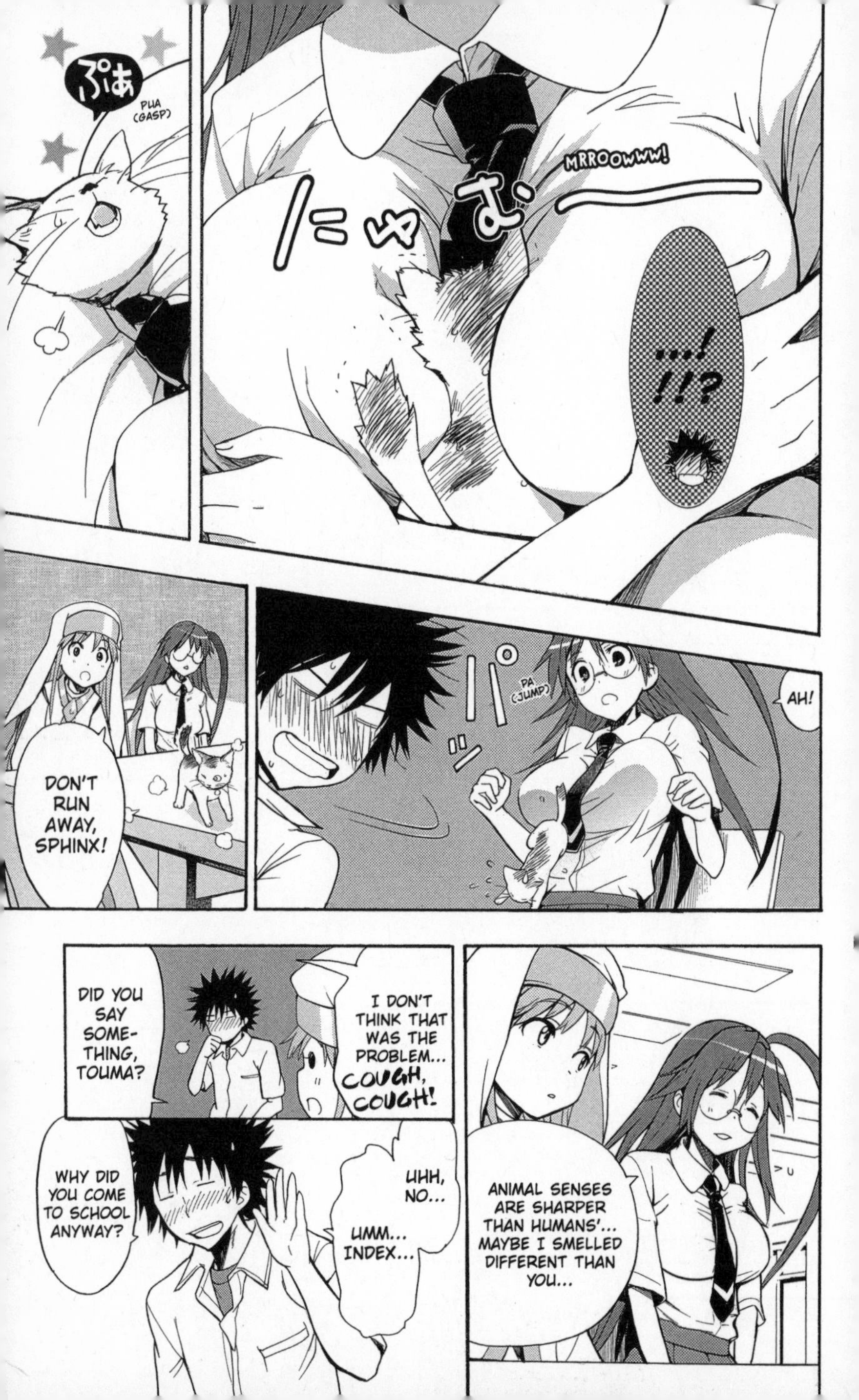
MRROOWWW!
...!
!!?
ぷあ
PUA (GASP)
パッ
PA (JUMP)
AH!
DON'T RUN AWAY, SPHINX!
ANIMAL SENSES ARE SHARPER THAN HUMANS'... MAYBE I SMELLED DIFFERENT THAN YOU...
I DON'T THINK THAT WAS THE PROBLEM... COUGH, COUGH!
DID YOU SAY SOMETHING, TOUMA?
UHH, NO...
UMM... INDEX...
WHY DID YOU COME TO SCHOOL ANYWAY?

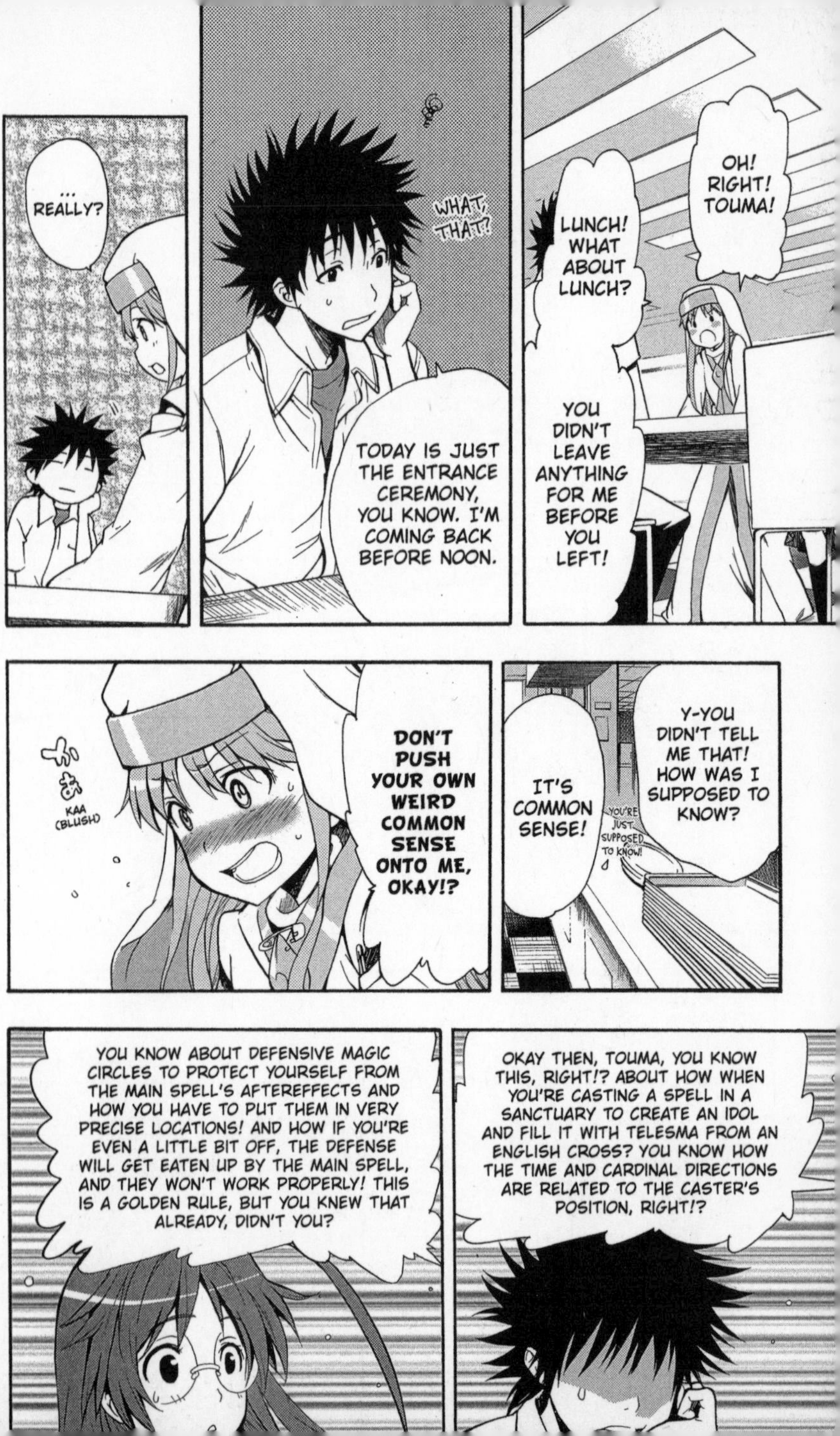
OH! RIGHT! TOUMA!
LUNCH! WHAT ABOUT LUNCH?
YOU DIDN'T LEAVE ANYTHING FOR ME BEFORE YOU LEFT!
WHAT, THAT?
TODAY IS JUST THE ENTRANCE CEREMONY, YOU KNOW. I'M COMING BACK BEFORE NOON.
... REALLY?
Y-YOU DIDN'T TELL ME THAT! HOW WAS I SUPPOSED TO KNOW?
IT'S COMMON SENSE!
YOU'RE JUST SUPPOSED TO KNOW!
KAA (BLUSH)
DON'T PUSH YOUR OWN WEIRD COMMON SENSE ONTO ME, OKAY!?
OKAY THEN, TOUMA, YOU KNOW THIS, RIGHT!? ABOUT HOW WHEN YOU'RE CASTING A SPELL IN A SANCTUARY TO CREATE AN IDOL AND FILL IT WITH TELESMA FROM AN ENGLISH CROSS? YOU KNOW HOW THE TIME AND CARDINAL DIRECTIONS ARE RELATED TO THE CASTER'S POSITION, RIGHT!?
YOU KNOW ABOUT DEFENSIVE MAGIC CIRCLES TO PROTECT YOURSELF FROM THE MAIN SPELL'S AFTEREFFECTS AND HOW YOU HAVE TO PUT THEM IN VERY PRECISE LOCATIONS! AND HOW IF YOU'RE EVEN A LITTLE BIT OFF, THE DEFENSE WILL GET EATEN UP BY THE MAIN SPELL, AND THEY WON'T WORK PROPERLY! THIS IS A GOLDEN RULE, BUT YOU KNEW THAT ALREADY, DIDN'T YOU?

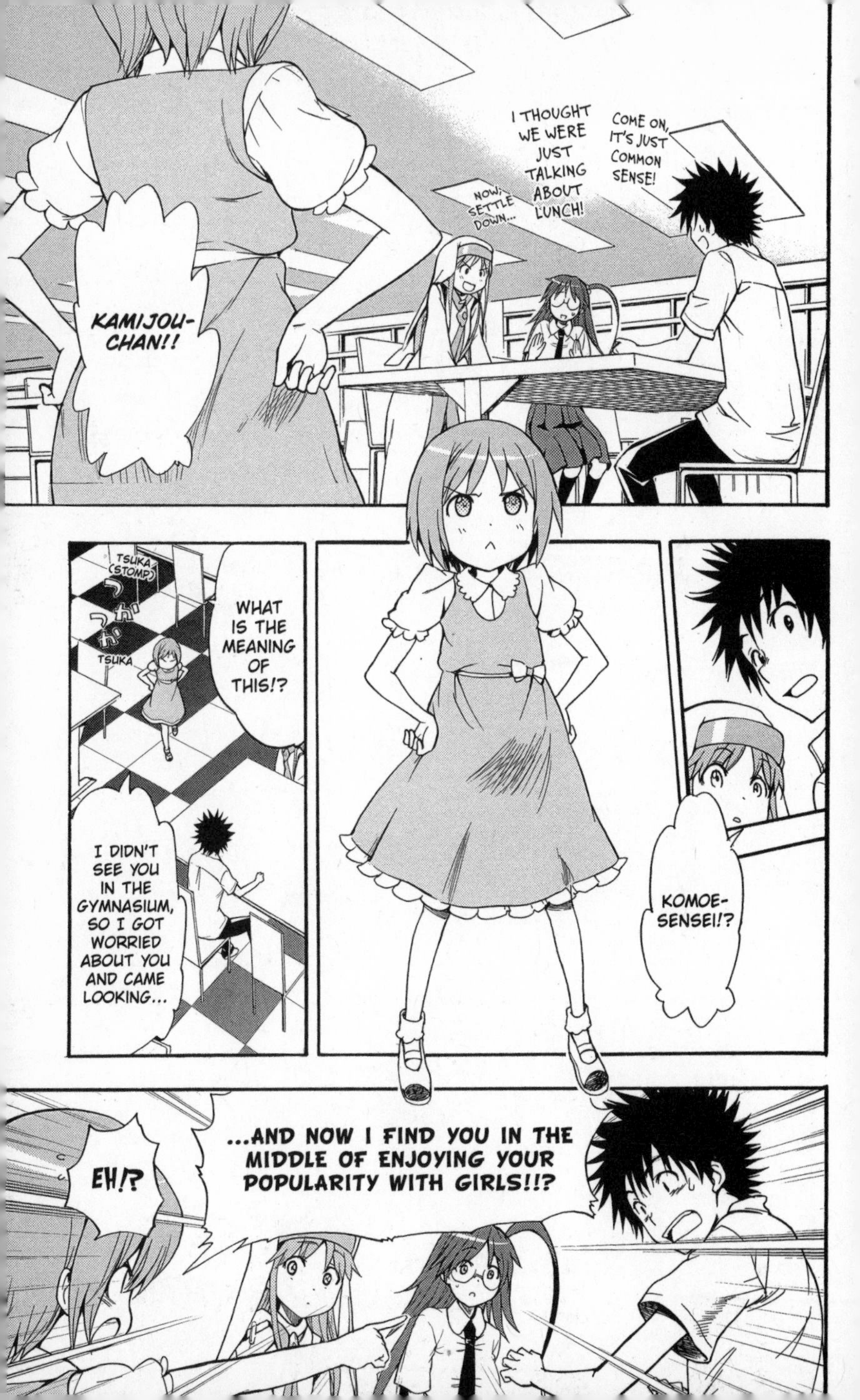
COME ON, IT'S JUST COMMON SENSE!
I THOUGHT WE WERE JUST TALKING ABOUT LUNCH!
NOW, SETTLE DOWN...
KAMIJOU-CHAN!!
KOMOE-SENSEI!?
WHAT IS THE MEANING OF THIS!?
TSUKA (STOMP)
つか つか
TSUKA
I DIDN'T SEE YOU IN THE GYMNASIUM, SO I GOT WORRIED ABOUT YOU AND CAME LOOKING...
...AND NOW I FIND YOU IN THE MIDDLE OF ENJOYING YOUR POPULARITY WITH GIRLS!!?
EH!?

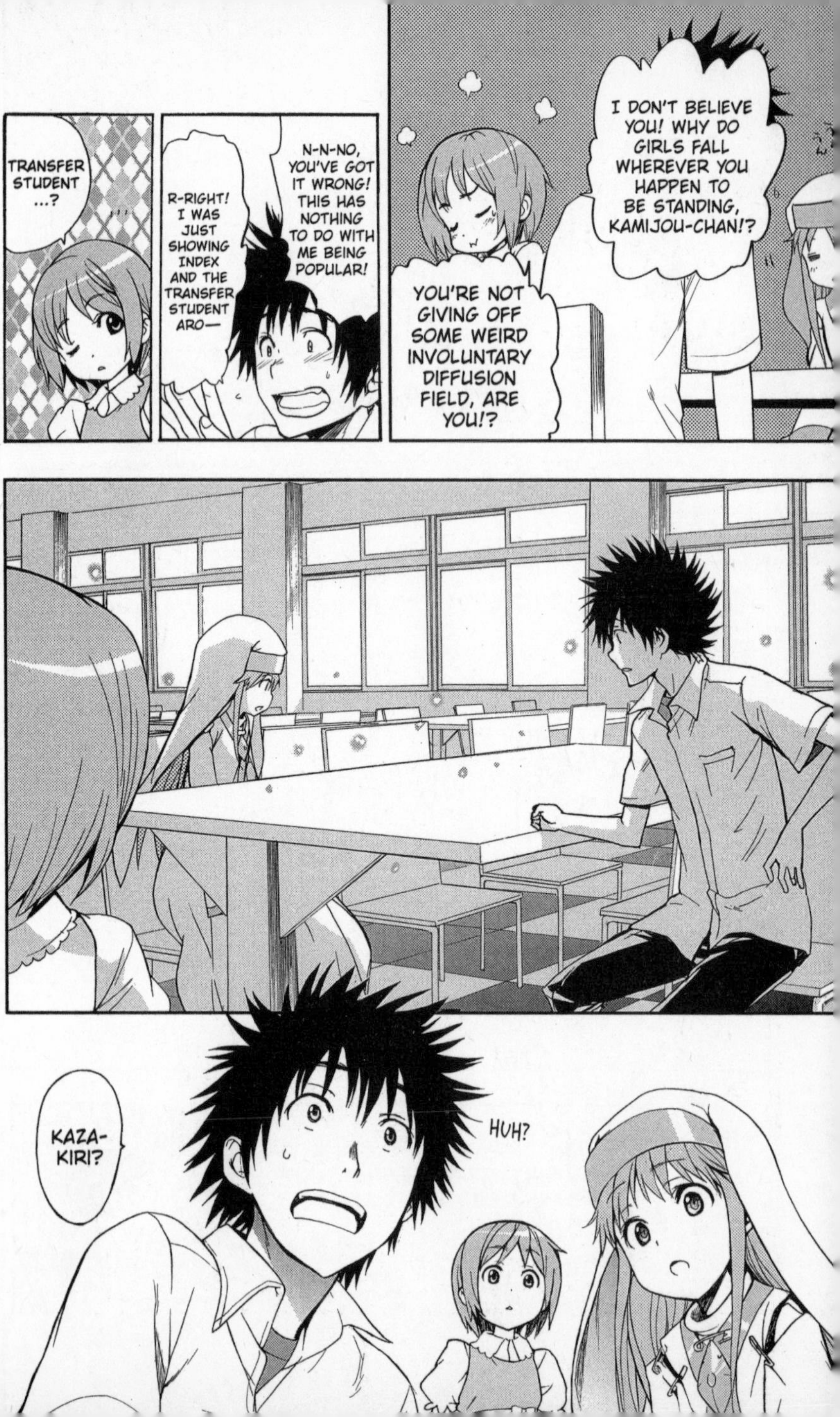
I DON'T BELIEVE YOU! WHY DO GIRLS FALL WHEREVER YOU HAPPEN TO BE STANDING, KAMIJOU-CHAN!?
YOU'RE NOT GIVING OFF SOME WEIRD INVOLUNTARY DIFFUSION FIELD, ARE YOU!?
N-N-NO, YOU'VE GOT IT WRONG! THIS HAS NOTHING TO DO WITH ME BEING POPULAR!
R-RIGHT! I WAS JUST SHOWING INDEX AND THE TRANSFER STUDENT ARO—
TRANSFER STUDENT ...?
HUH?
KAZA-KIRI?

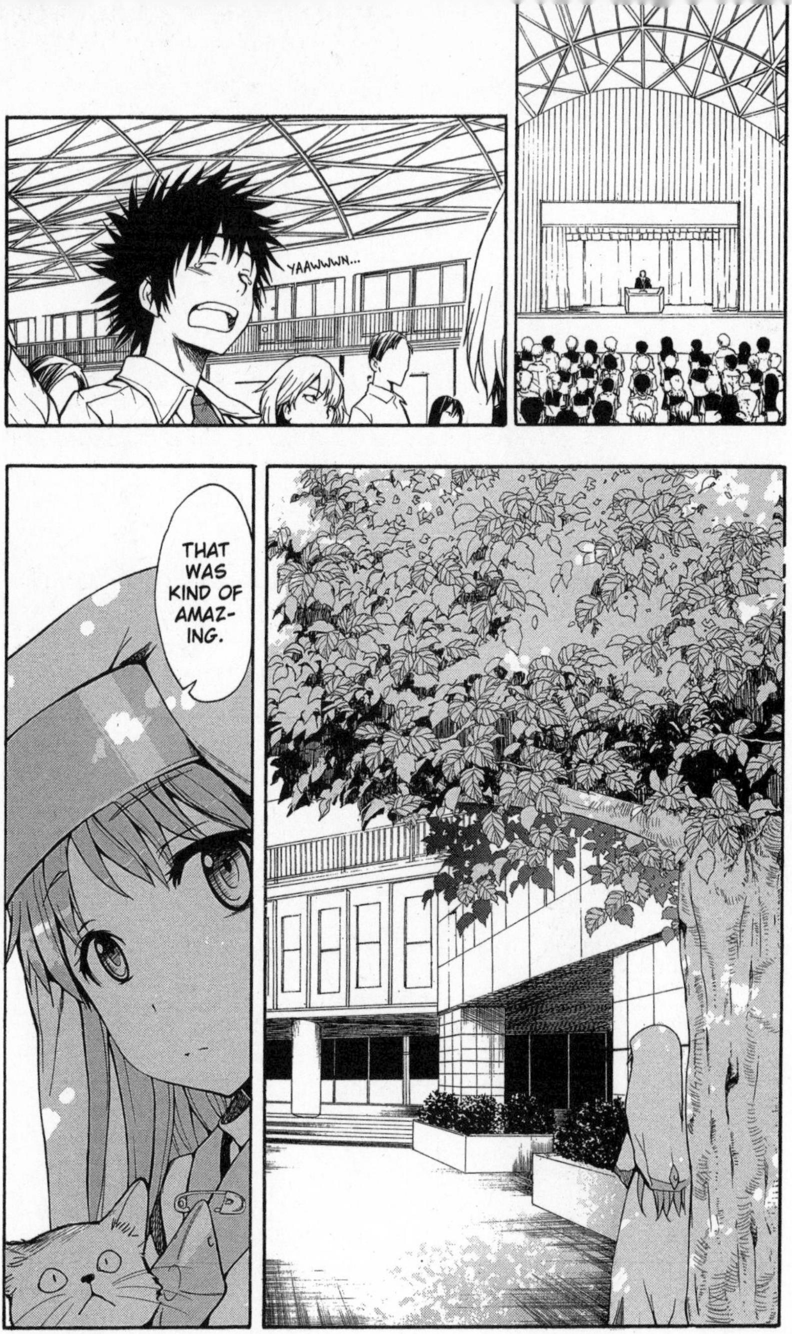
YAAWWWN...
THAT WAS KIND OF AMAZ-ING.

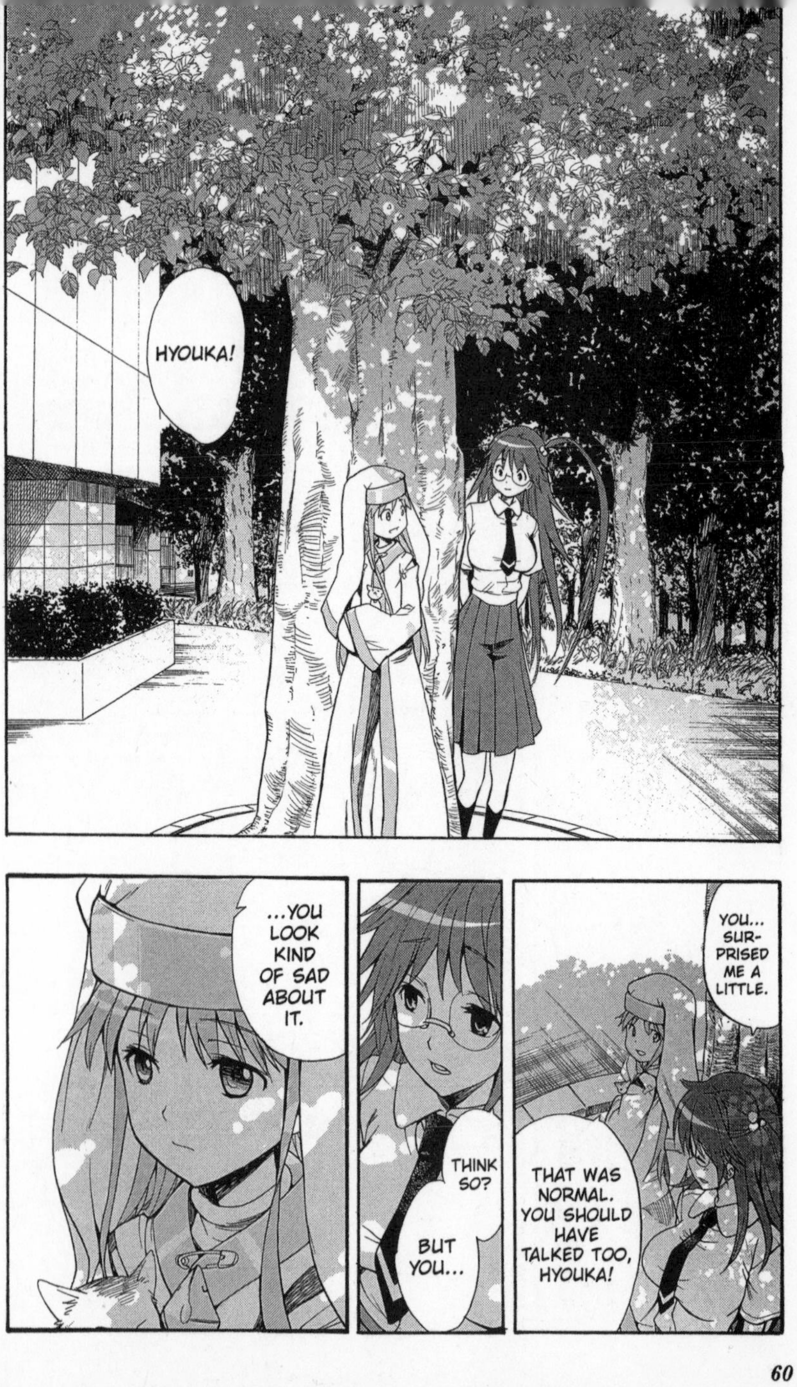
HYOUKA!
YOU... SURPRISED ME A LITTLE.
THAT WAS NORMAL. YOU SHOULD HAVE TALKED TOO, HYOUKA!
THINK SO?
BUT YOU...
...YOU LOOK KIND OF SAD ABOUT IT.

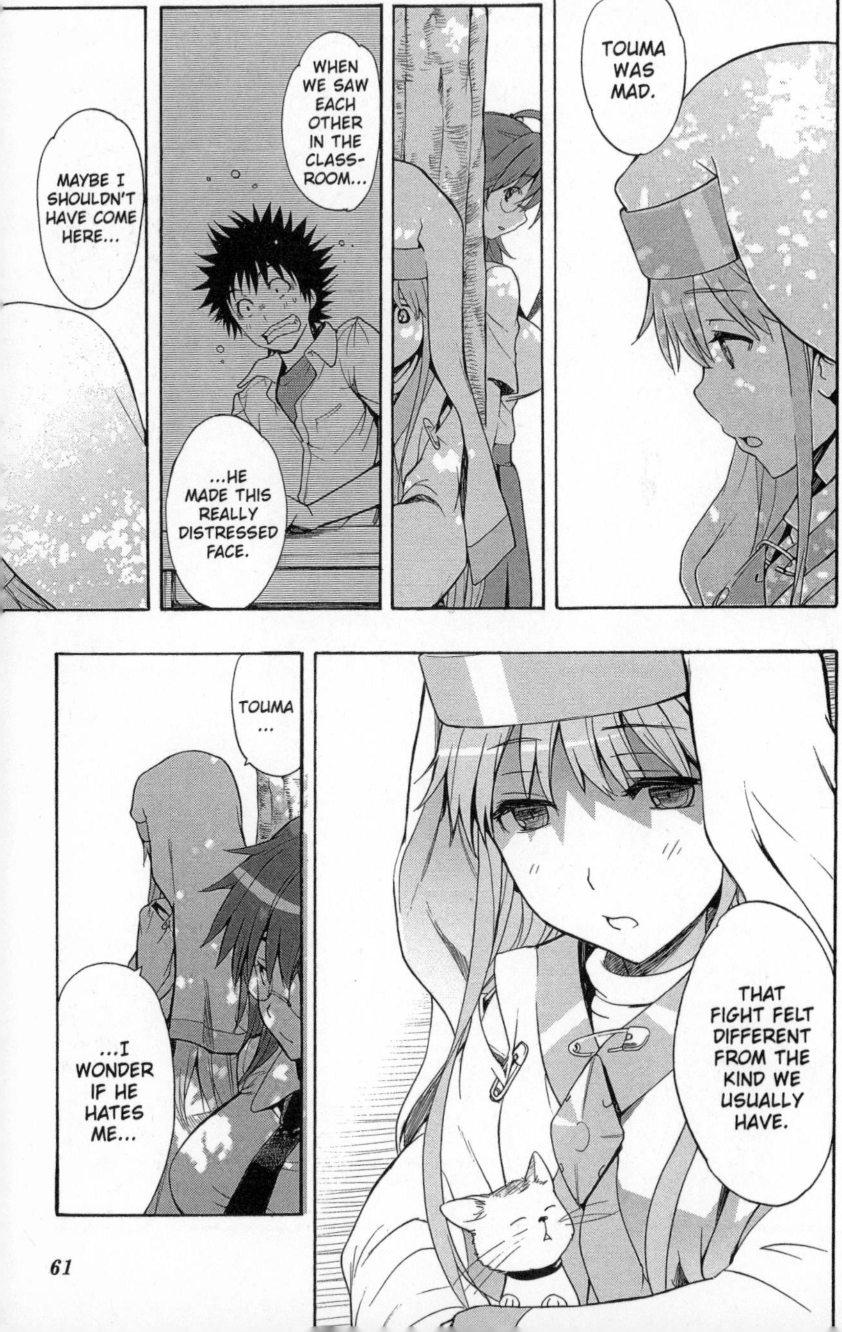
TOUMA WAS MAD.
WHEN WE SAW EACH OTHER IN THE CLASSROOM...
...HE MADE THIS REALLY DISTRESSED FACE.
MAYBE I SHOULDN'T HAVE COME HERE...
THAT FIGHT FELT DIFFERENT FROM THE KIND WE USUALLY HAVE.
TOUMA ...
...I WONDER IF HE HATES ME...

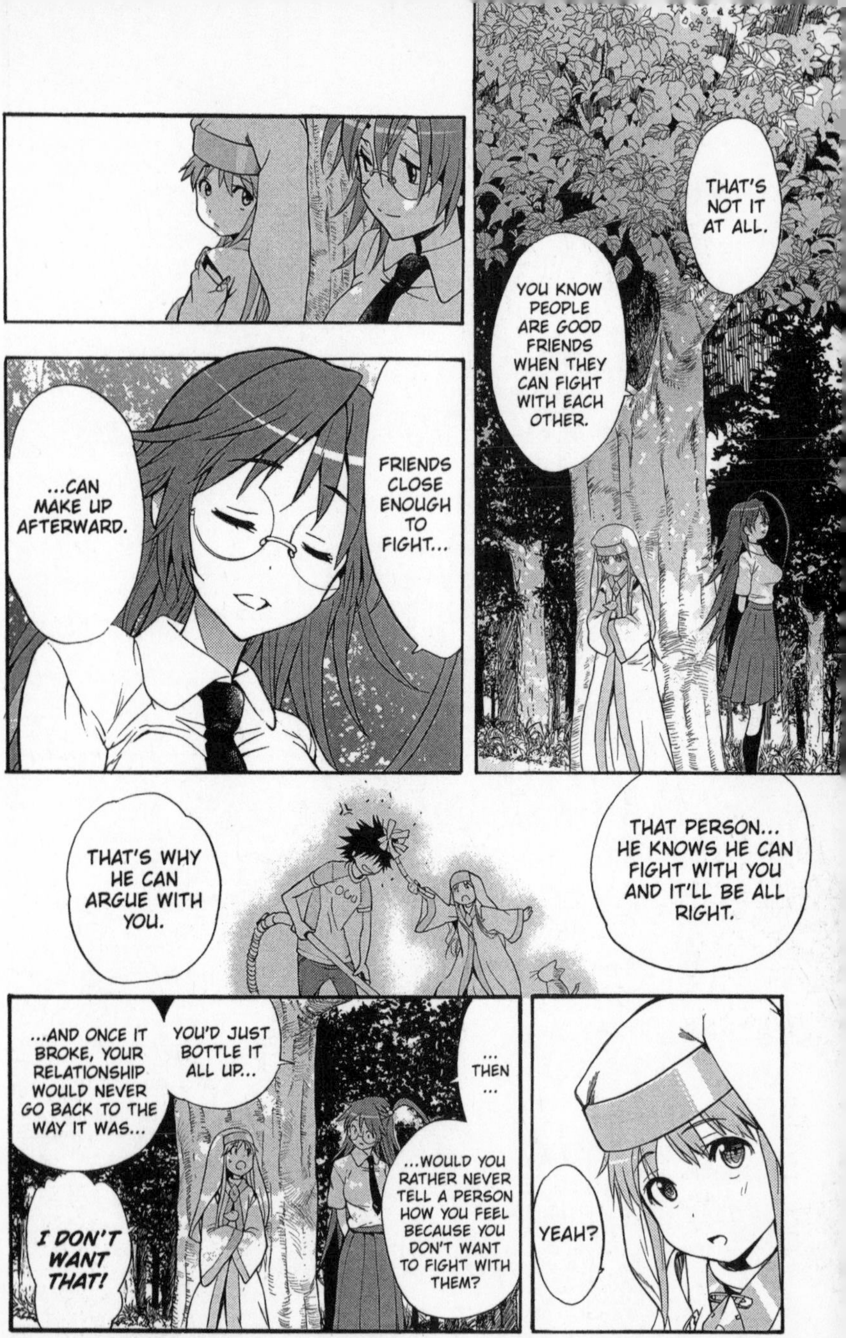
THAT'S NOT IT AT ALL.
YOU KNOW PEOPLE ARE GOOD FRIENDS WHEN THEY CAN FIGHT WITH EACH OTHER.
FRIENDS CLOSE ENOUGH TO FIGHT...
...CAN MAKE UP AFTERWARD.
THAT PERSON... HE KNOWS HE CAN FIGHT WITH YOU AND IT'LL BE ALL RIGHT.
THAT'S WHY HE CAN ARGUE WITH YOU.
YEAH?
...THEN...
...WOULD YOU RATHER NEVER TELL A PERSON HOW YOU FEEL BECAUSE YOU DON'T WANT TO FIGHT WITH THEM?
YOU'D JUST BOTTLE IT ALL UP...
...AND ONCE IT BROKE, YOUR RELATIONSHIP WOULD NEVER GO BACK TO THE WAY IT WAS...
I DON'T WANT THAT!

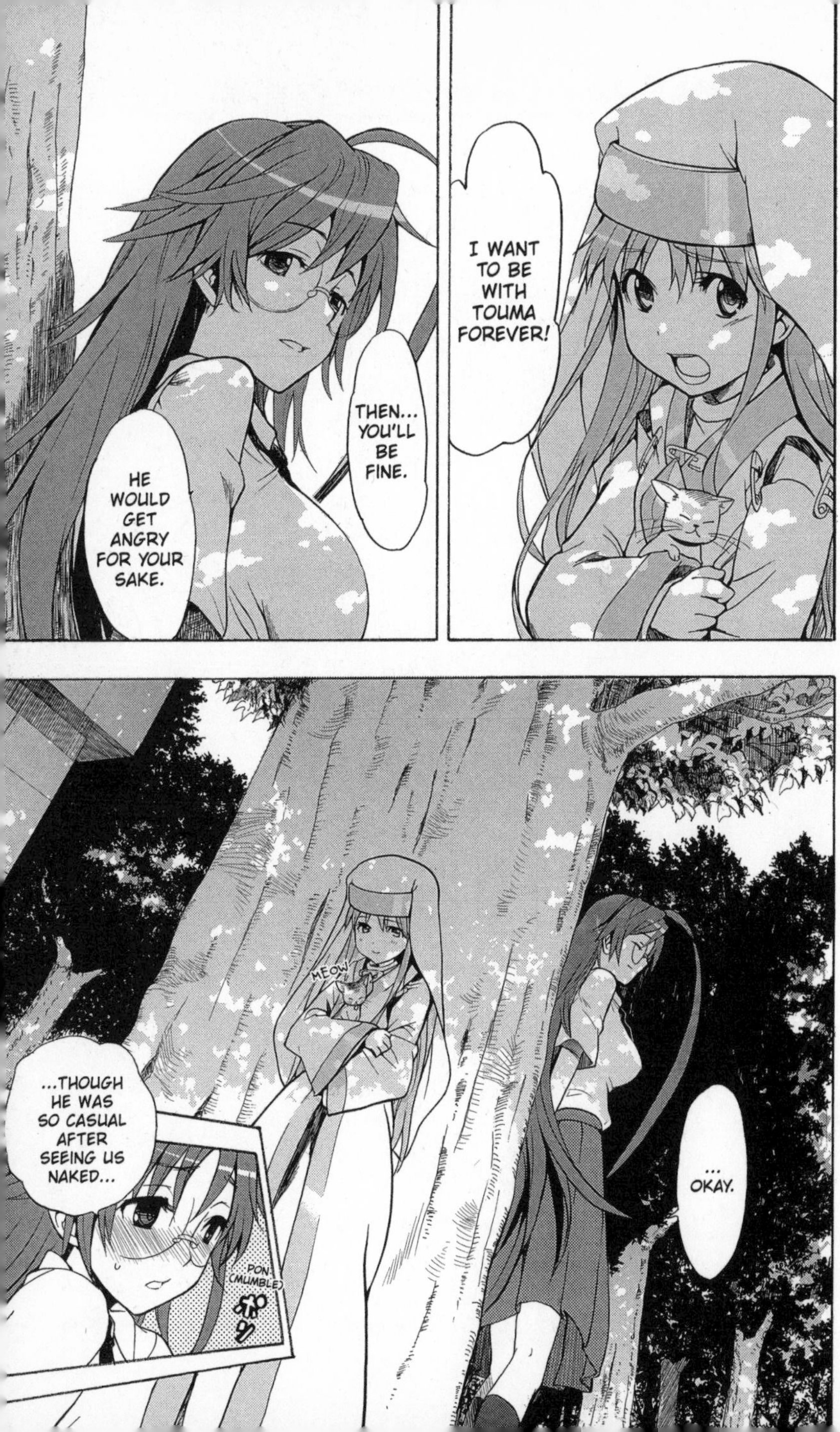
I WANT TO BE WITH TOUMA FOREVER!
THEN... YOU'LL BE FINE.
HE WOULD GET ANGRY FOR YOUR SAKE.
... OKAY.
MEOW
...THOUGH HE WAS SO CASUAL AFTER SEEING US NAKED...
PON (MUMBLE)

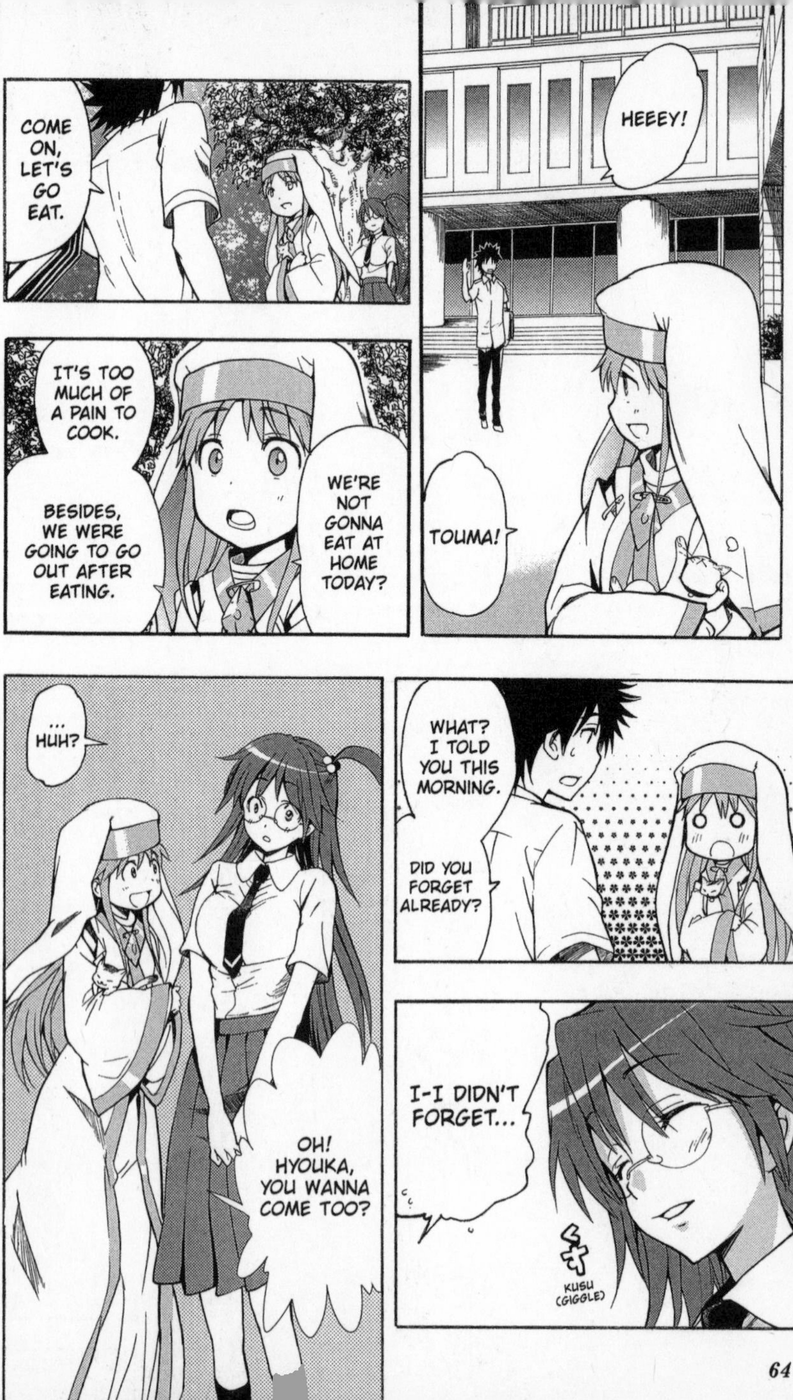
HEEEY!
TOUMA!
COME ON, LET'S GO EAT.
WE'RE NOT GONNA EAT AT HOME TODAY?
IT'S TOO MUCH OF A PAIN TO COOK.
BESIDES, WE WERE GOING TO GO OUT AFTER EATING.
WHAT? I TOLD YOU THIS MORNING.
DID YOU FORGET ALREADY?
I-I DIDN'T FORGET...
KUSU (GIGGLE)
OH! HYOUKA, YOU WANNA COME TOO?
... HUH?

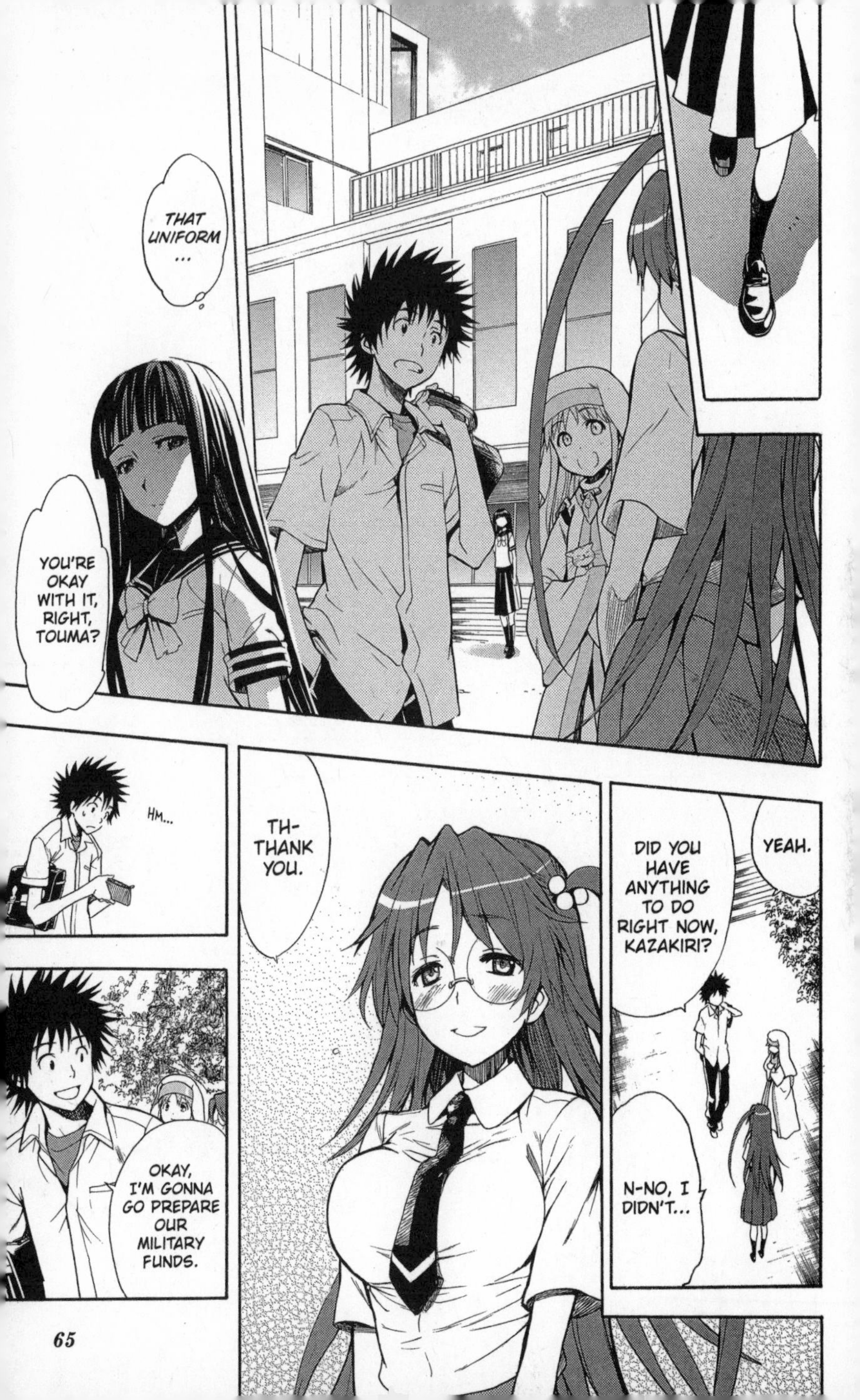
THAT UNIFORM...
YOU'RE OKAY WITH IT, RIGHT, TOUMA?
YEAH.
DID YOU HAVE ANYTHING TO DO RIGHT NOW, KAZAKIRI?
N-NO, I DIDN'T...
TH-THANK YOU.
HM...
OKAY, I'M GONNA GO PREPARE OUR MILITARY FUNDS.

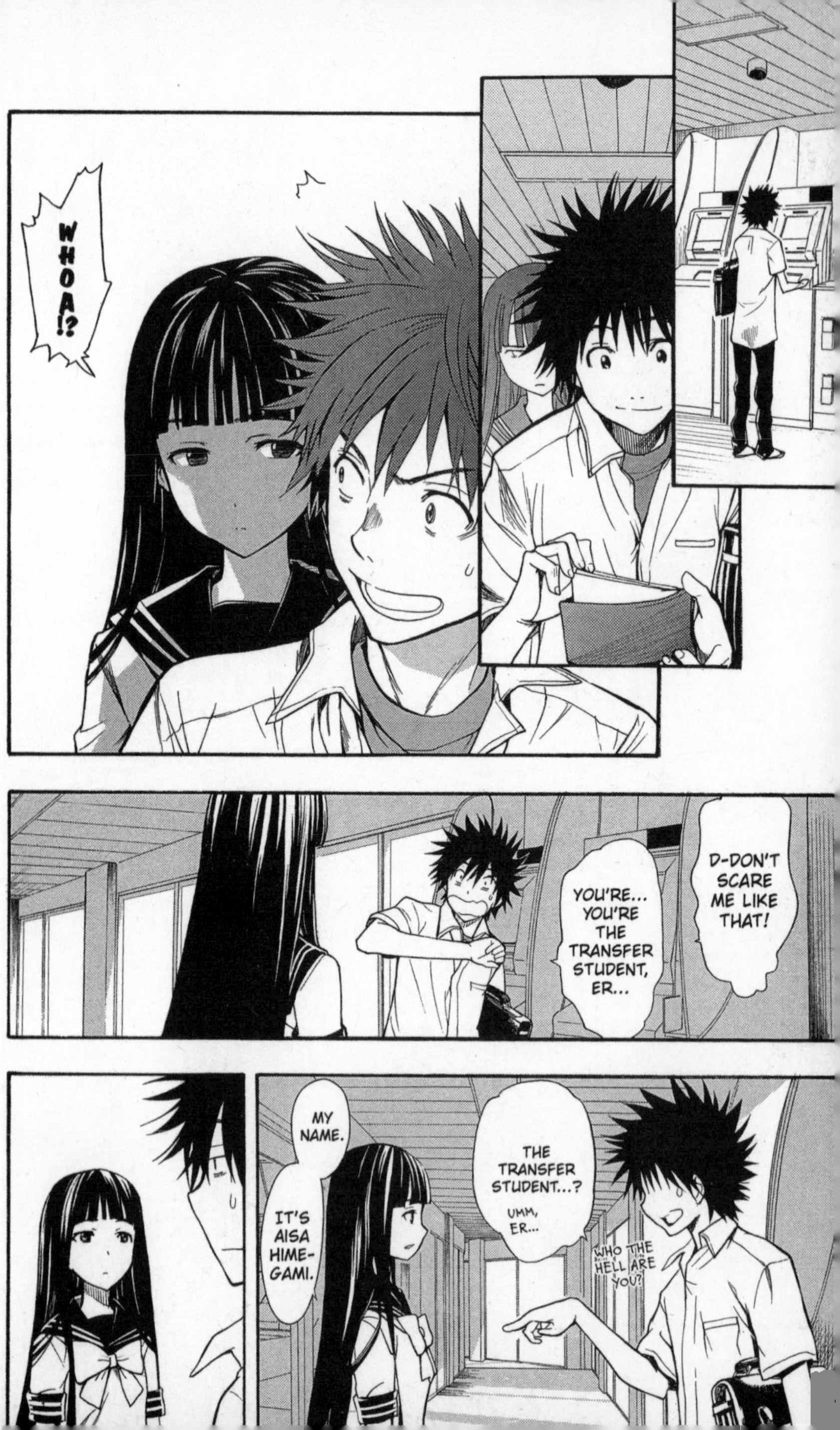
WHOA!?
D-DON'T SCARE ME LIKE THAT!
YOU'RE... YOU'RE THE TRANSFER STUDENT, ER...
THE TRANSFER STUDENT...?
UMM, ER...
WHO THE HELL ARE YOU?
MY NAME.
IT'S AISA HIME-GAMI.

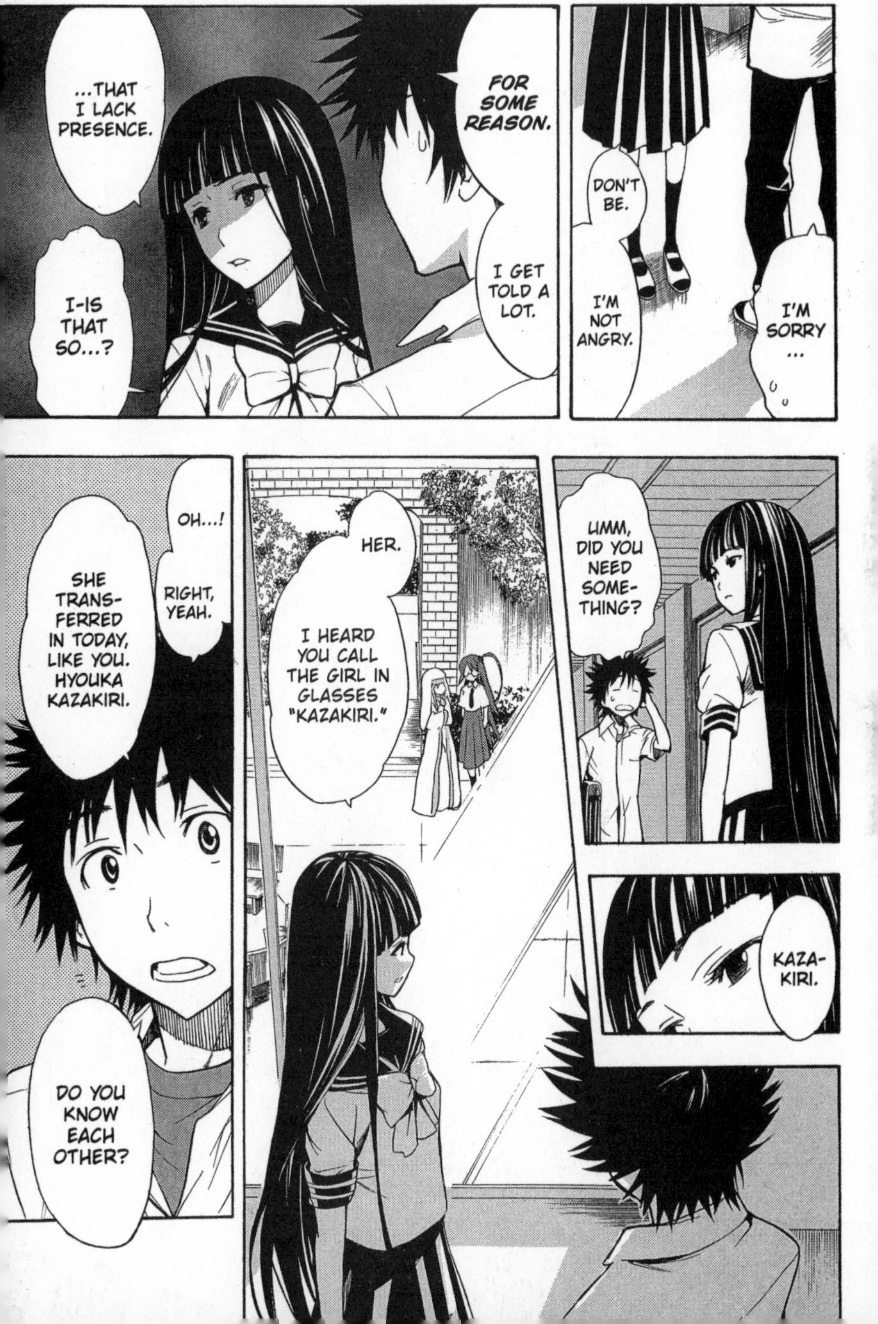
I'M SORRY...
DON'T BE.
I'M NOT ANGRY.
FOR SOME REASON.
I GET TOLD A LOT.
...THAT I LACK PRESENCE.
I-IS THAT SO...?
UMM, DID YOU NEED SOME-THING?
KAZA-KIRI.
HER.
I HEARD YOU CALL THE GIRL IN GLASSES "KAZAKIRI."
OH...!
RIGHT, YEAH.
SHE TRANS-FERRED IN TODAY, LIKE YOU. HYOUKA KAZAKIRI.
DO YOU KNOW EACH OTHER?

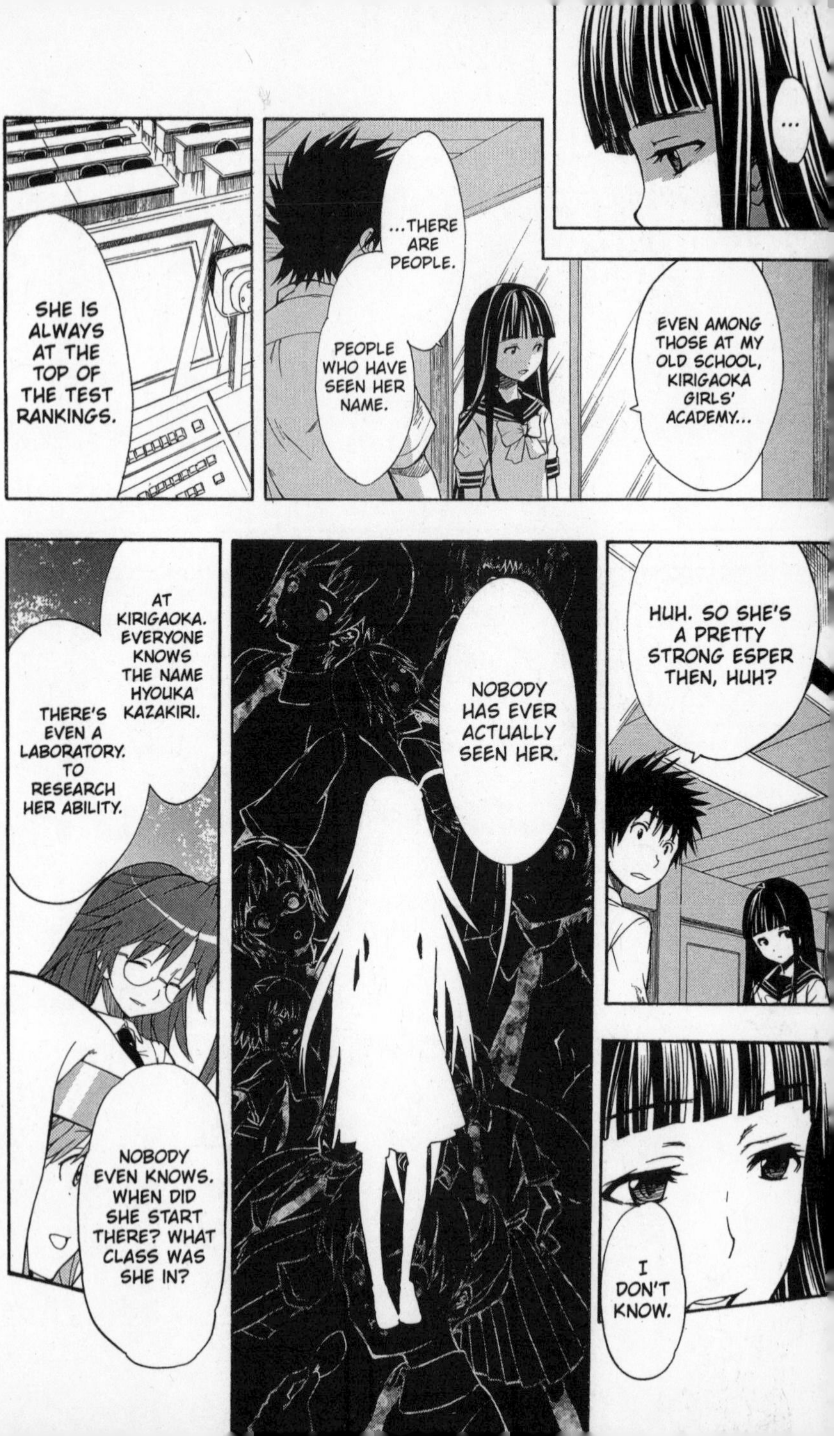
...
EVEN AMONG THOSE AT MY OLD SCHOOL, KIRIGAOKA GIRLS' ACADEMY...
...THERE ARE PEOPLE.
PEOPLE WHO HAVE SEEN HER NAME.
SHE IS ALWAYS AT THE TOP OF THE TEST RANKINGS.
HUH. SO SHE'S A PRETTY STRONG ESPER THEN, HUH?
I DON'T KNOW.
NOBODY HAS EVER ACTUALLY SEEN HER.
AT KIRIGAOKA. EVERYONE KNOWS THE NAME HYOUKA KAZAKIRI.
THERE'S EVEN A LABORATORY. TO RESEARCH HER ABILITY.
NOBODY EVEN KNOWS. WHEN DID SHE START THERE? WHAT CLASS WAS SHE IN?

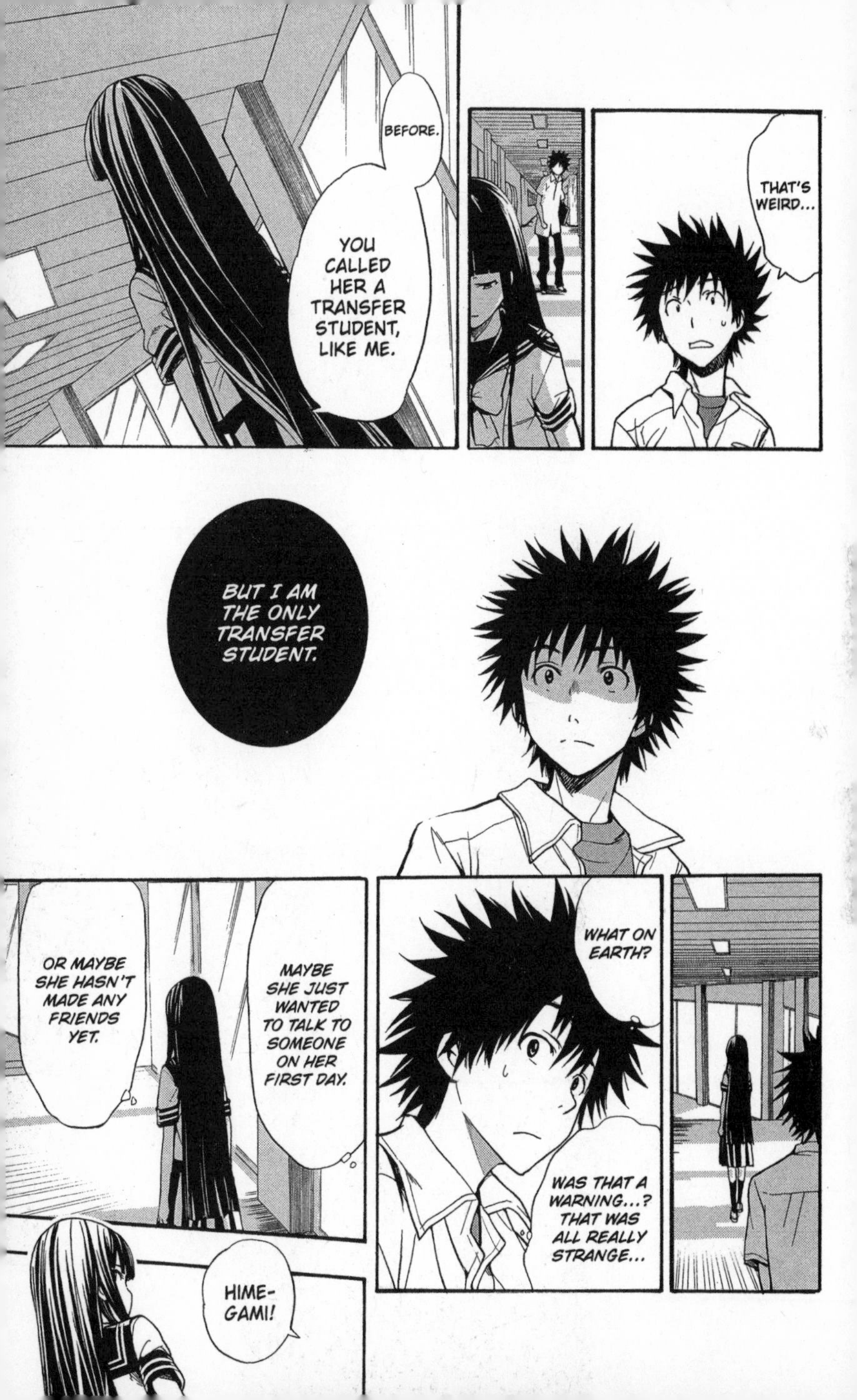

THAT'S WEIRD...
BEFORE.
YOU CALLED HER A TRANSFER STUDENT, LIKE ME.
BUT I AM THE ONLY TRANSFER STUDENT.
WHAT ON EARTH?
WAS THAT A WARNING...? THAT WAS ALL REALLY STRANGE...
MAYBE SHE JUST WANTED TO TALK TO SOMEONE ON HER FIRST DAY.
OR MAYBE SHE HASN'T MADE ANY FRIENDS YET.
HIME-GAMI!

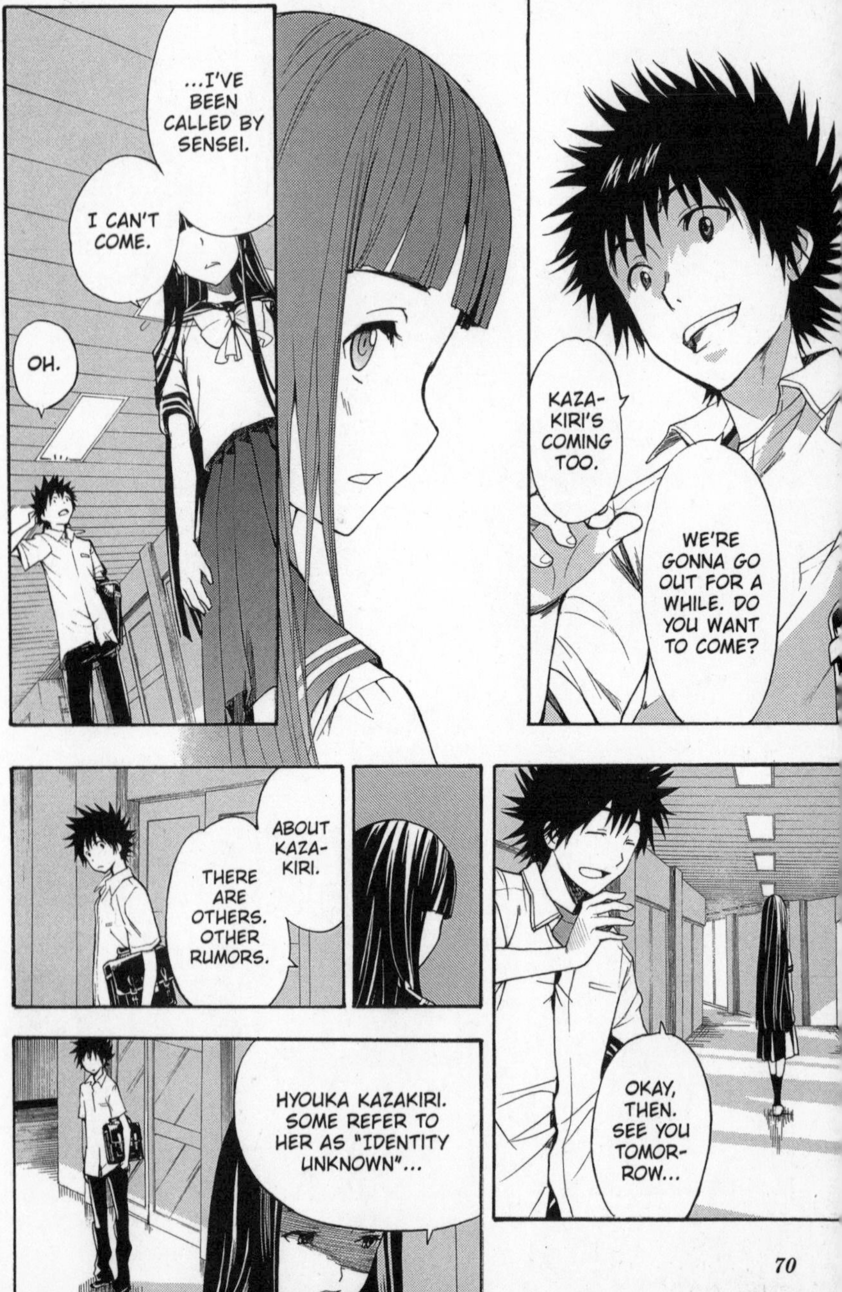
KAZA-KIRI'S COMING TOO.
WE'RE GONNA GO OUT FOR A WHILE. DO YOU WANT TO COME?
...I'VE BEEN CALLED BY SENSEI.
I CAN'T COME.
OH.
OKAY, THEN. SEE YOU TOMOR-ROW...
ABOUT KAZA-KIRI.
THERE ARE OTHERS. OTHER RUMORS.
HYOUKA KAZAKIRI. SOME REFER TO HER AS "IDENTITY UNKNOWN"...

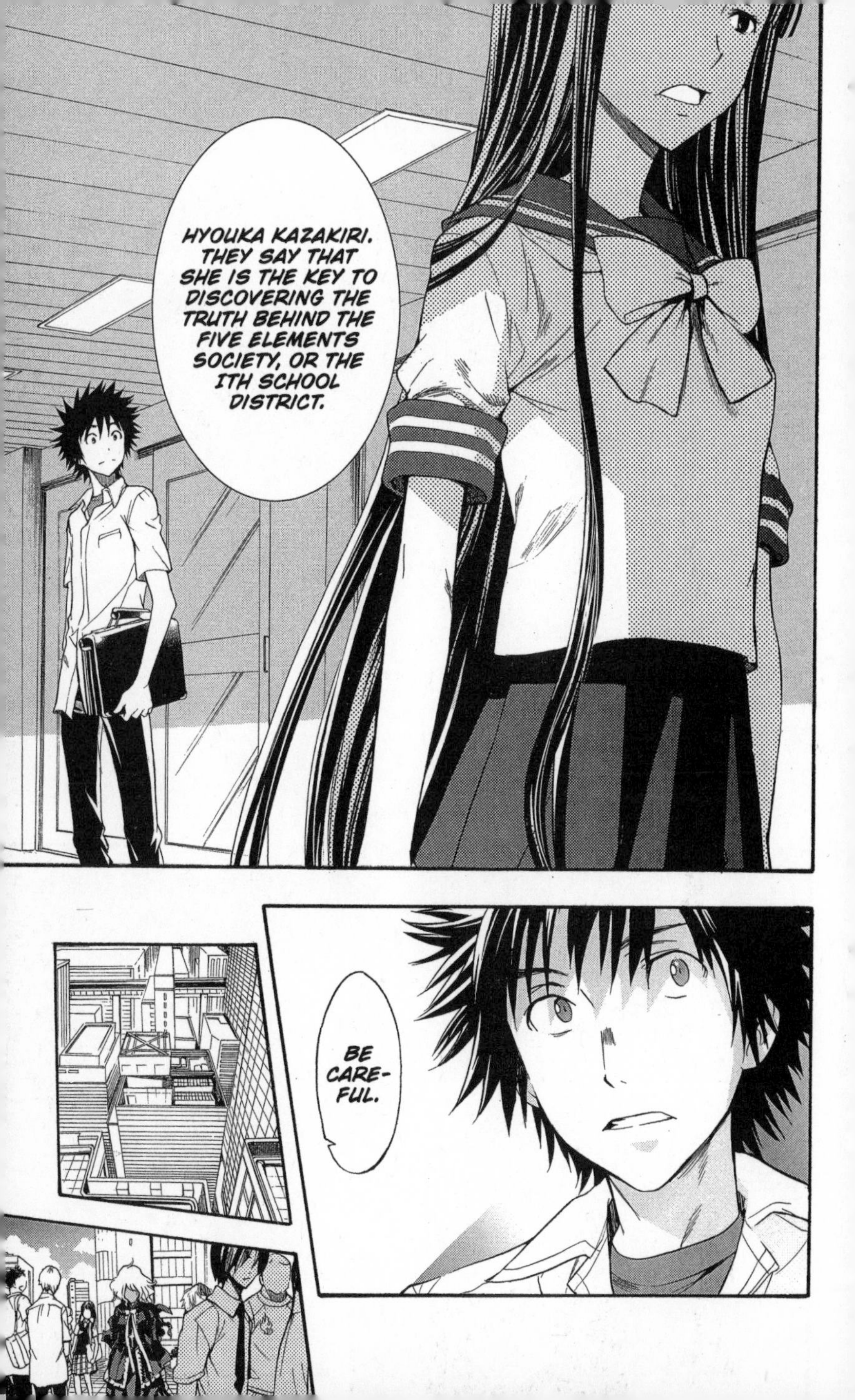
HYOUKA KAZAKIRI. THEY SAY THAT SHE IS THE KEY TO DISCOVERING THE TRUTH BEHIND THE FIVE ELEMENTS SOCIETY, OR THE ITH SCHOOL DISTRICT.
BE CARE-FUL.

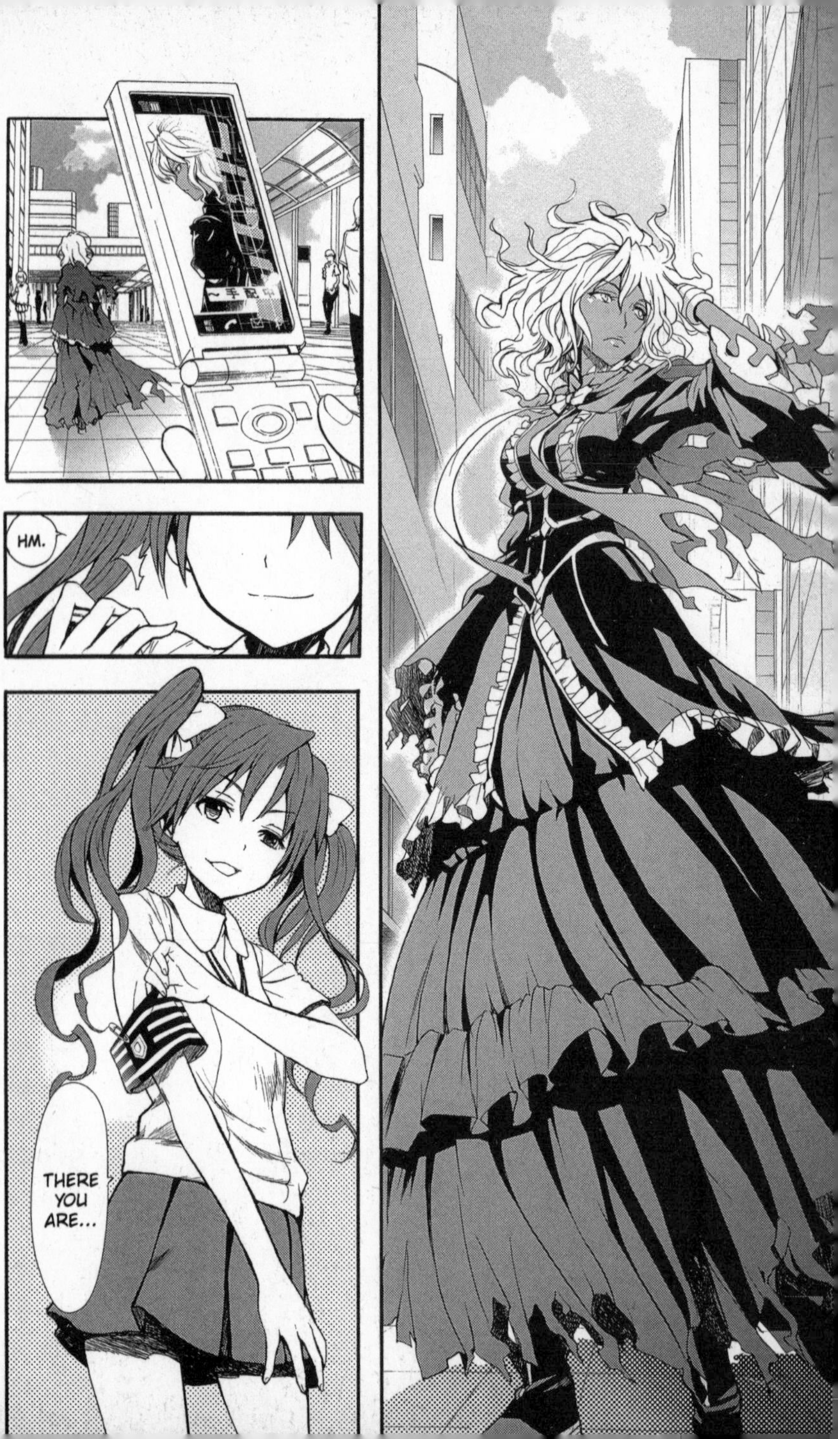
HM.
THERE YOU ARE...

A Certain Magical Index

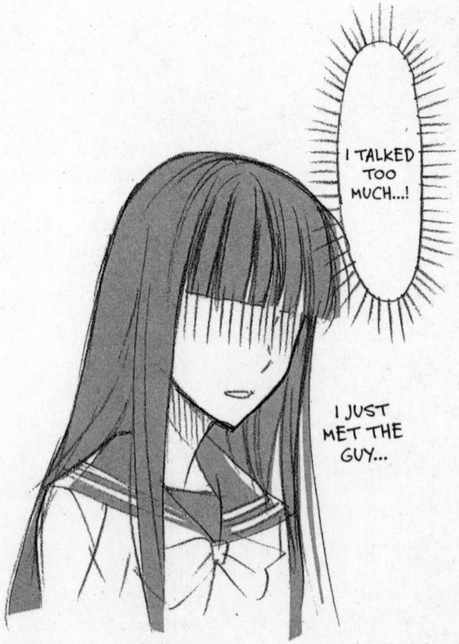
I TALKED TOO MUCH...!
I JUST MET THE GUY...

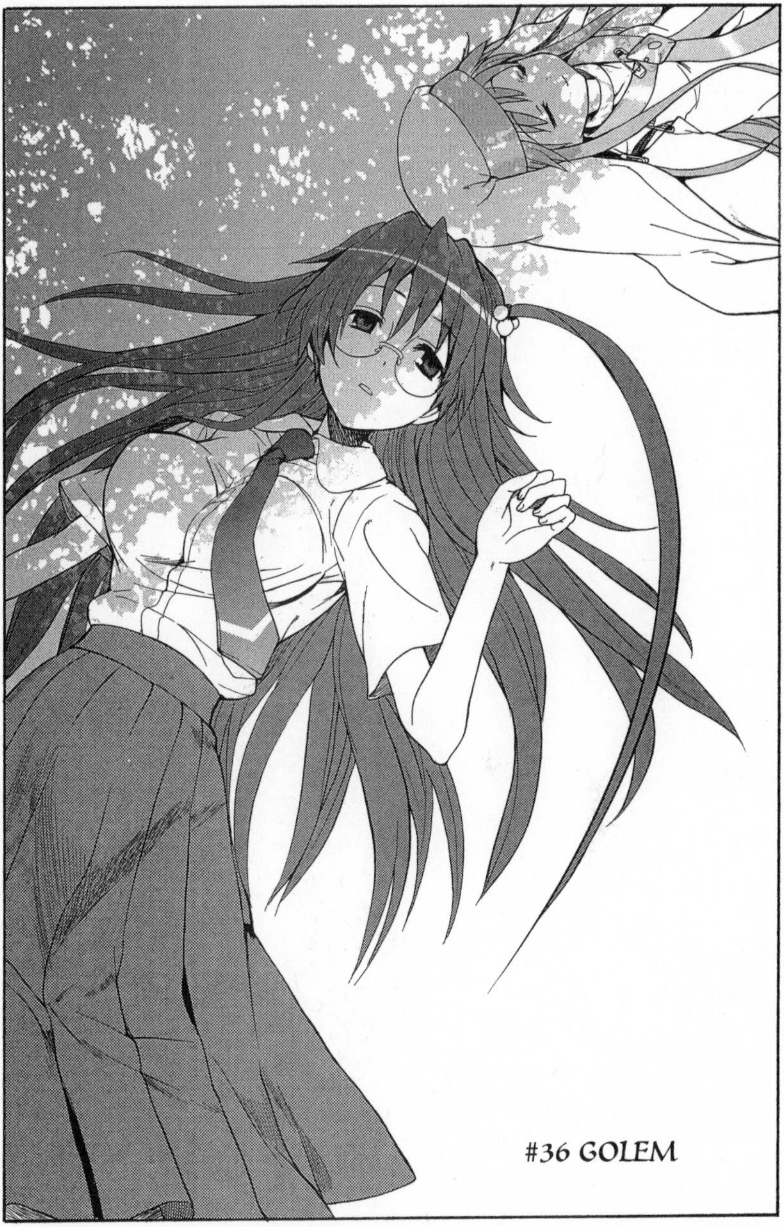
#36 GOLEM

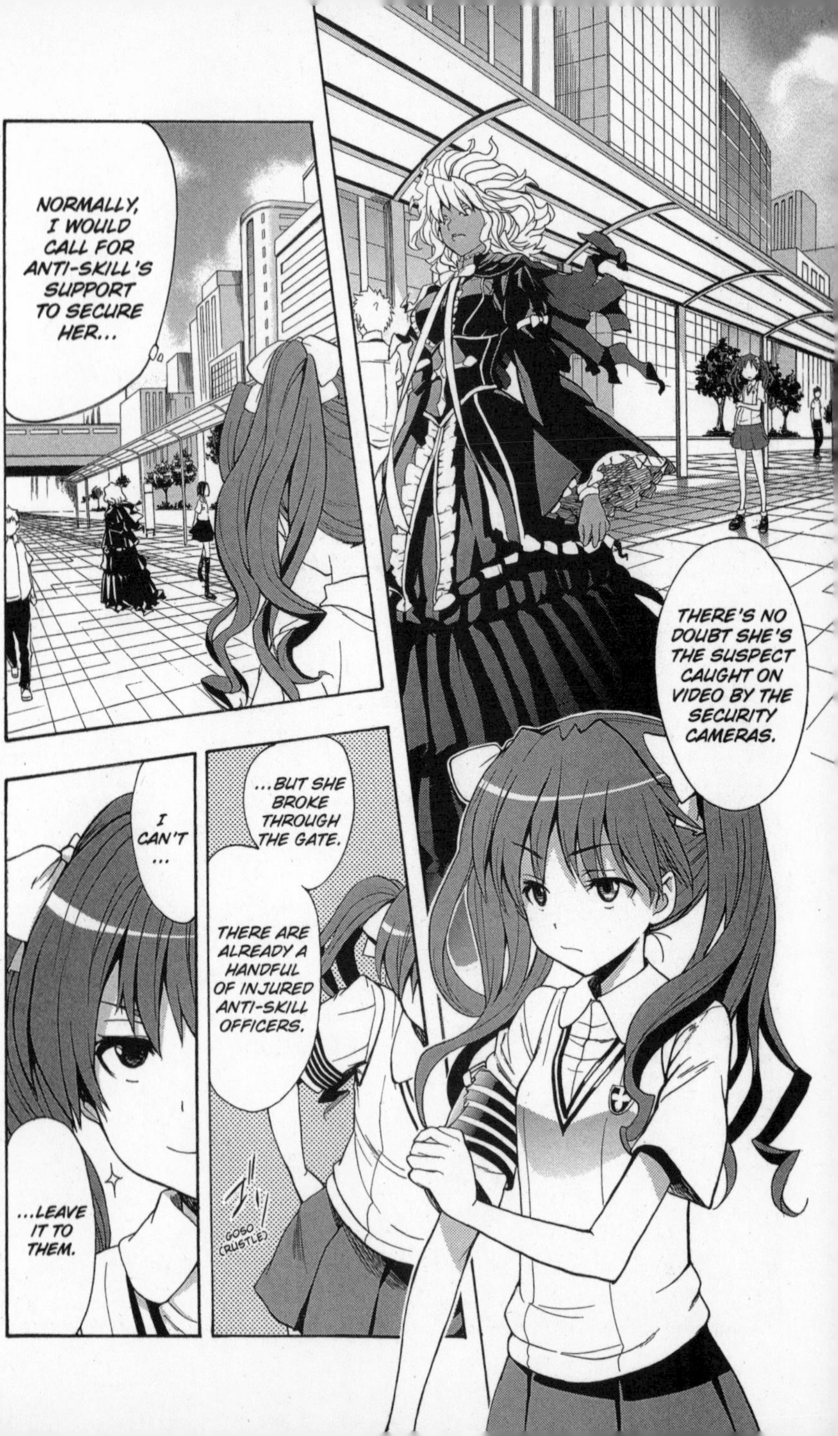
THERE'S NO DOUBT SHE'S THE SUSPECT CAUGHT ON VIDEO BY THE SECURITY CAMERAS.
NORMALLY, I WOULD CALL FOR ANTI-SKILL'S SUPPORT TO SECURE HER...
...BUT SHE BROKE THROUGH THE GATE.
THERE ARE ALREADY A HANDFUL OF INJURED ANTI-SKILL OFFICERS.
GOSO (RUSTLE)
I CAN'T...
...LEAVE IT TO THEM.

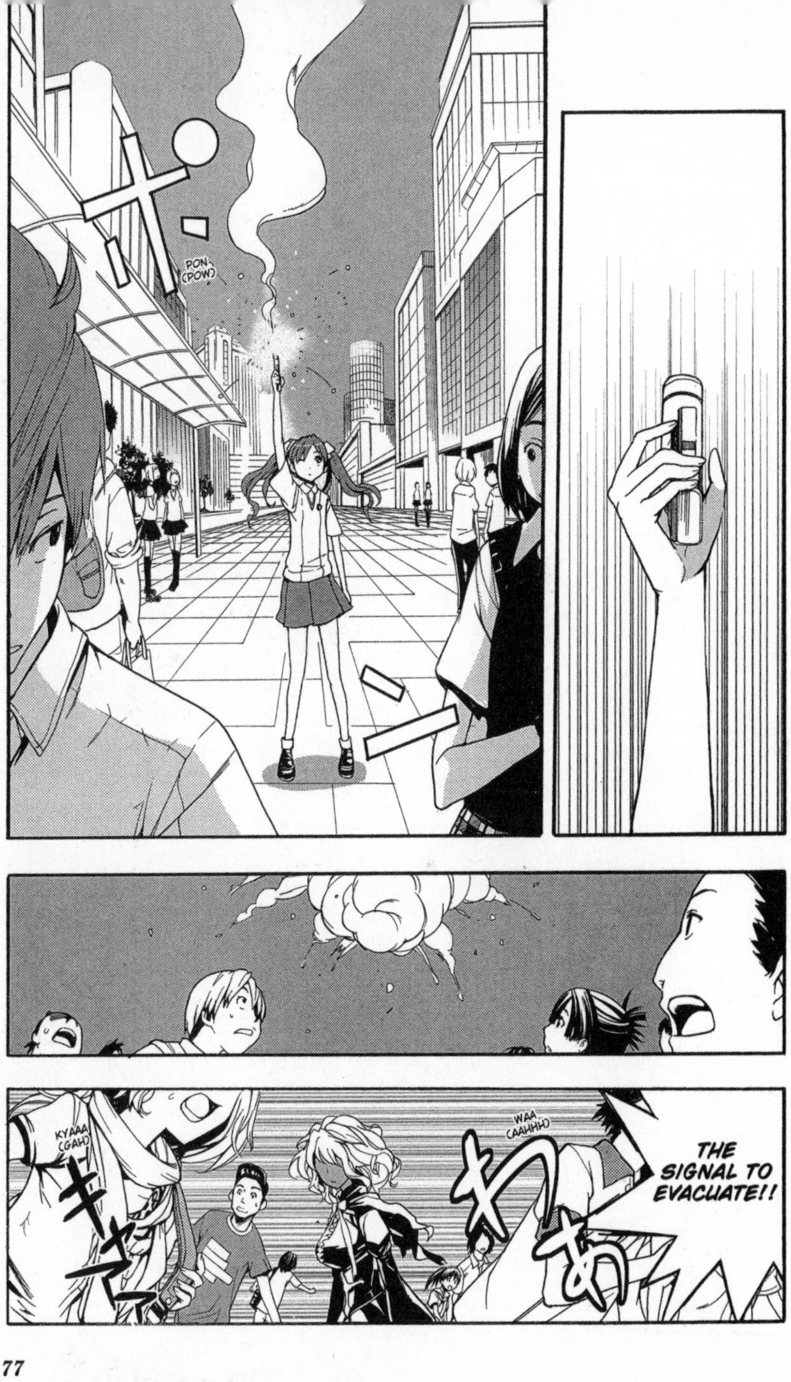
PON (POW)
THE SIGNAL TO EVACUATE!!
WAA (AAHHH)
わあ
KYAAA (GAH)

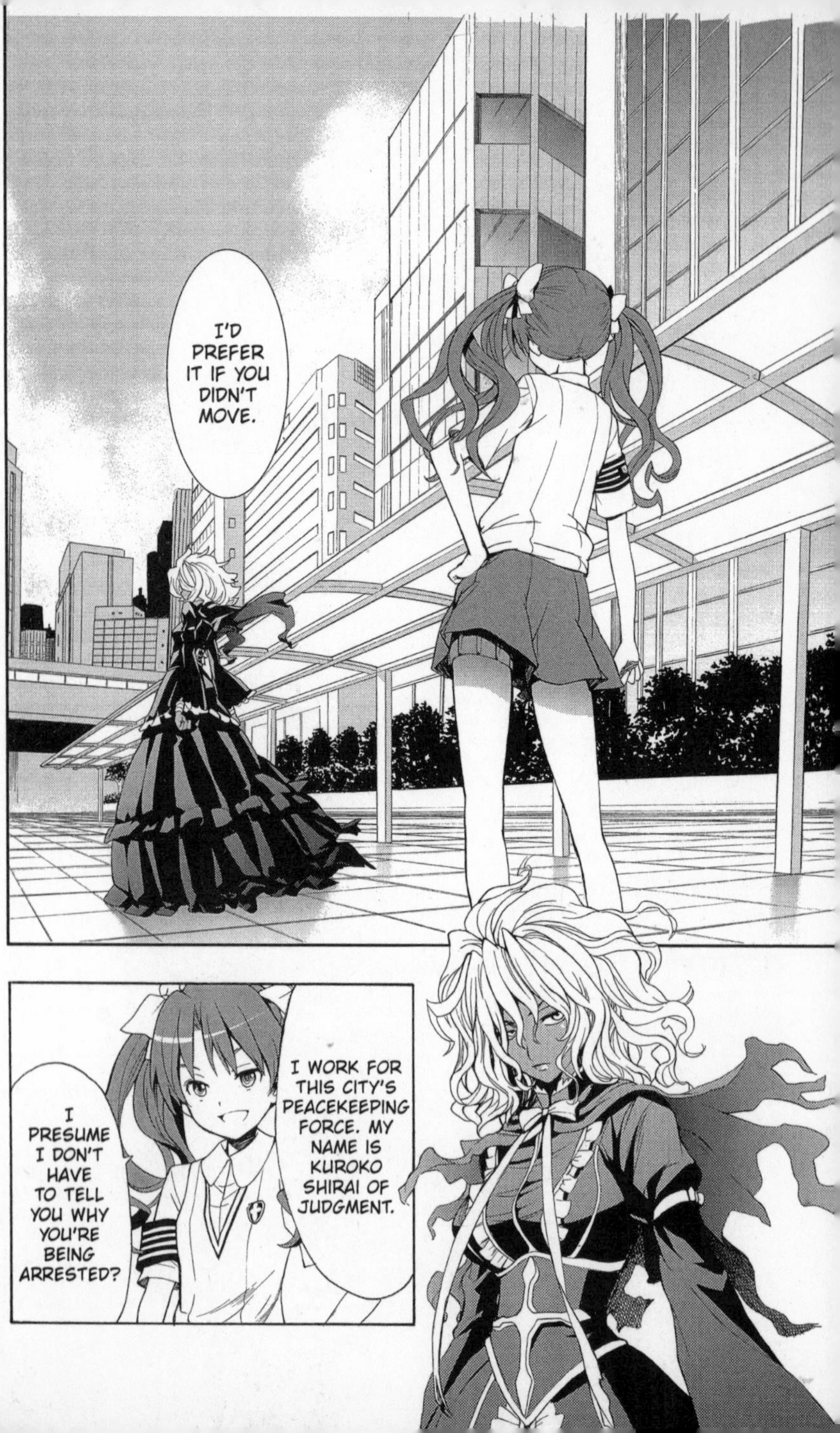
I'D PREFER IT IF YOU DIDN'T MOVE.
I WORK FOR THIS CITY'S PEACEKEEPING FORCE. MY NAME IS KUROKO SHIRAI OF JUDGMENT.
I PRESUME I DON'T HAVE TO TELL YOU WHY YOU'RE BEING ARRESTED?

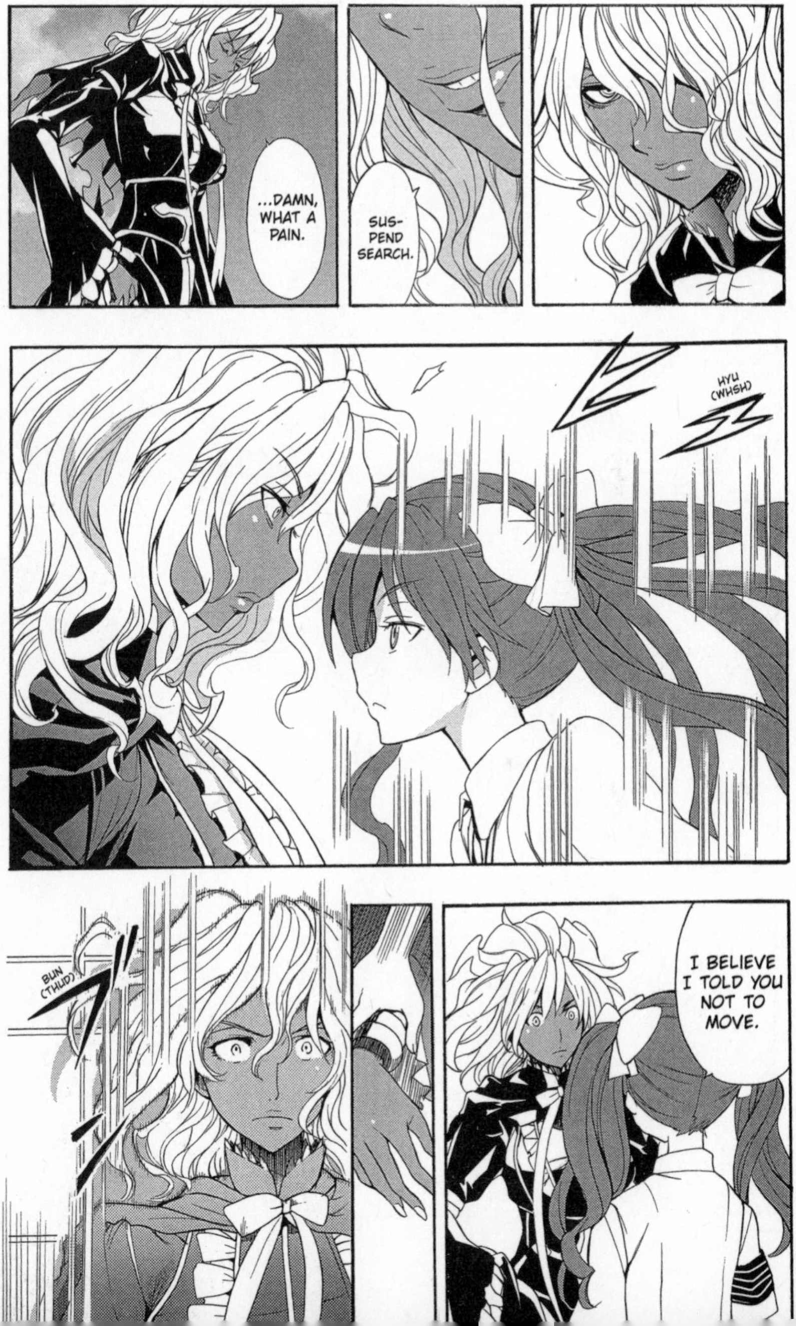
SUS-PEND SEARCH.
...DAMN, WHAT A PAIN.
HYU (WHSH)
I BELIEVE I TOLD YOU NOT TO MOVE.
BUN (THUD)

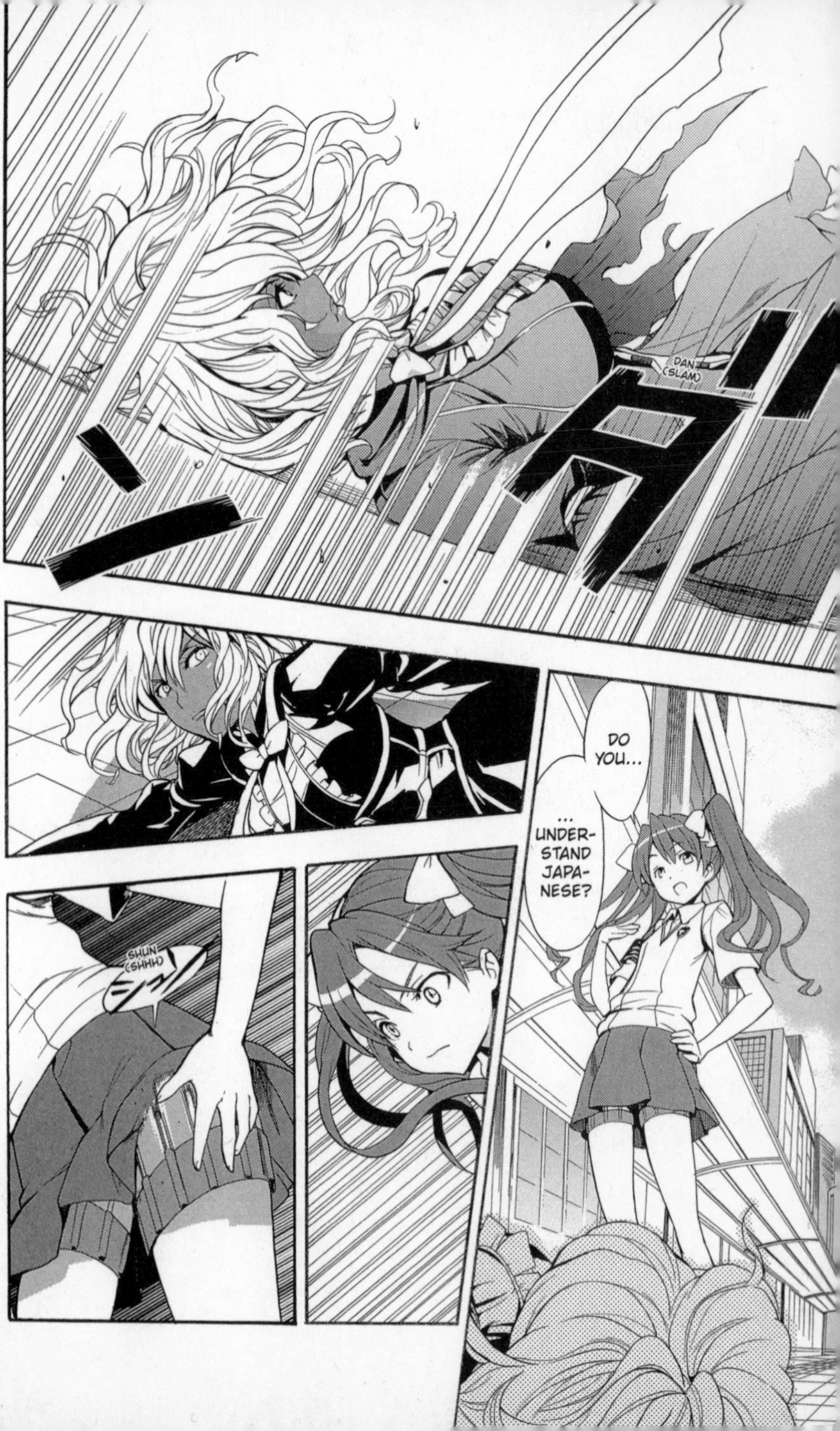
DAN (SLAM)
DO YOU...
...UNDERSTAND JAPANESE?
SHUN (SHHH)

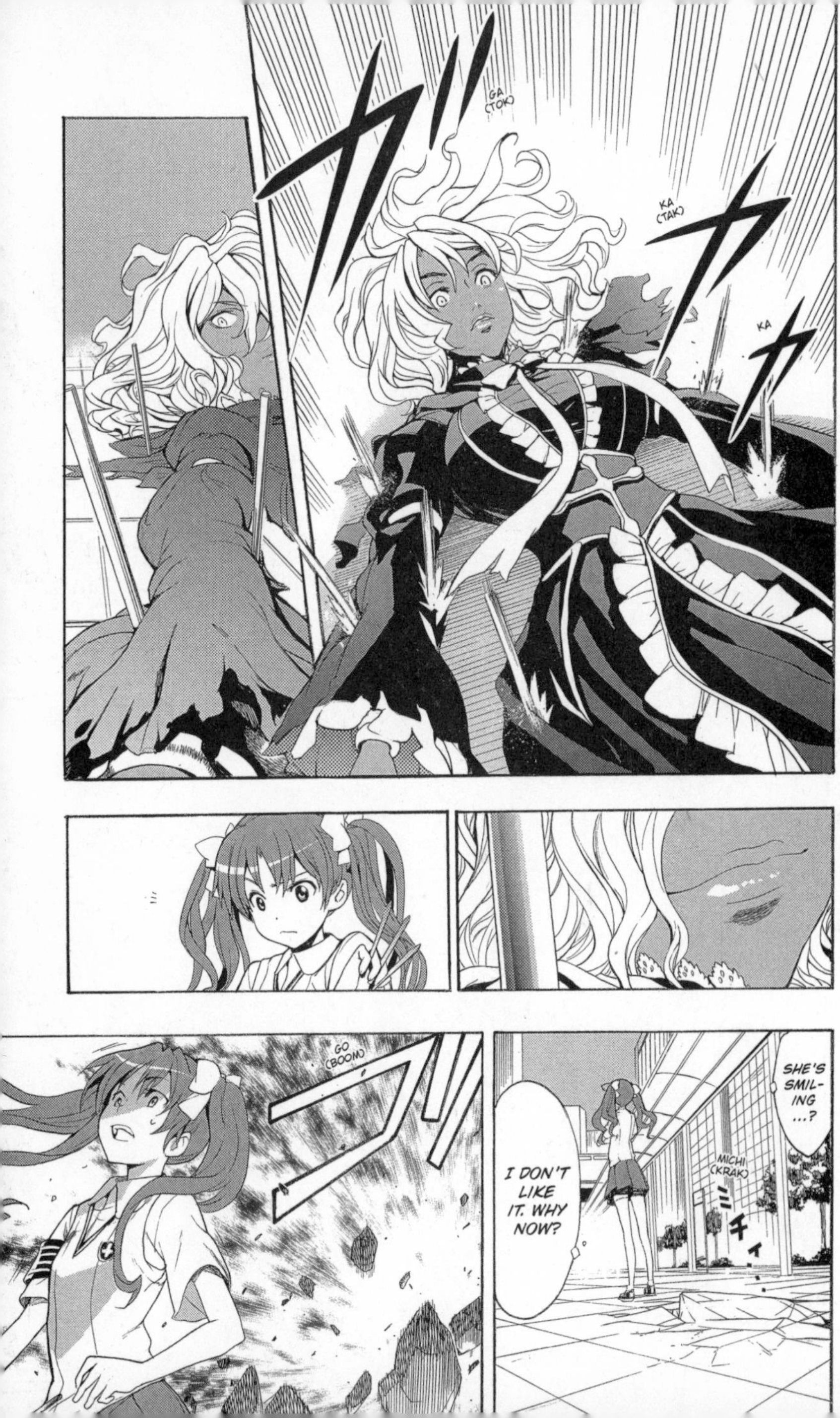
GA (TOK)
KA (TAK)
KA
SHE'S SMIL-ING ...?
I DON'T LIKE IT. WHY NOW?
MICHI (KRAK)
GO (BOOM)

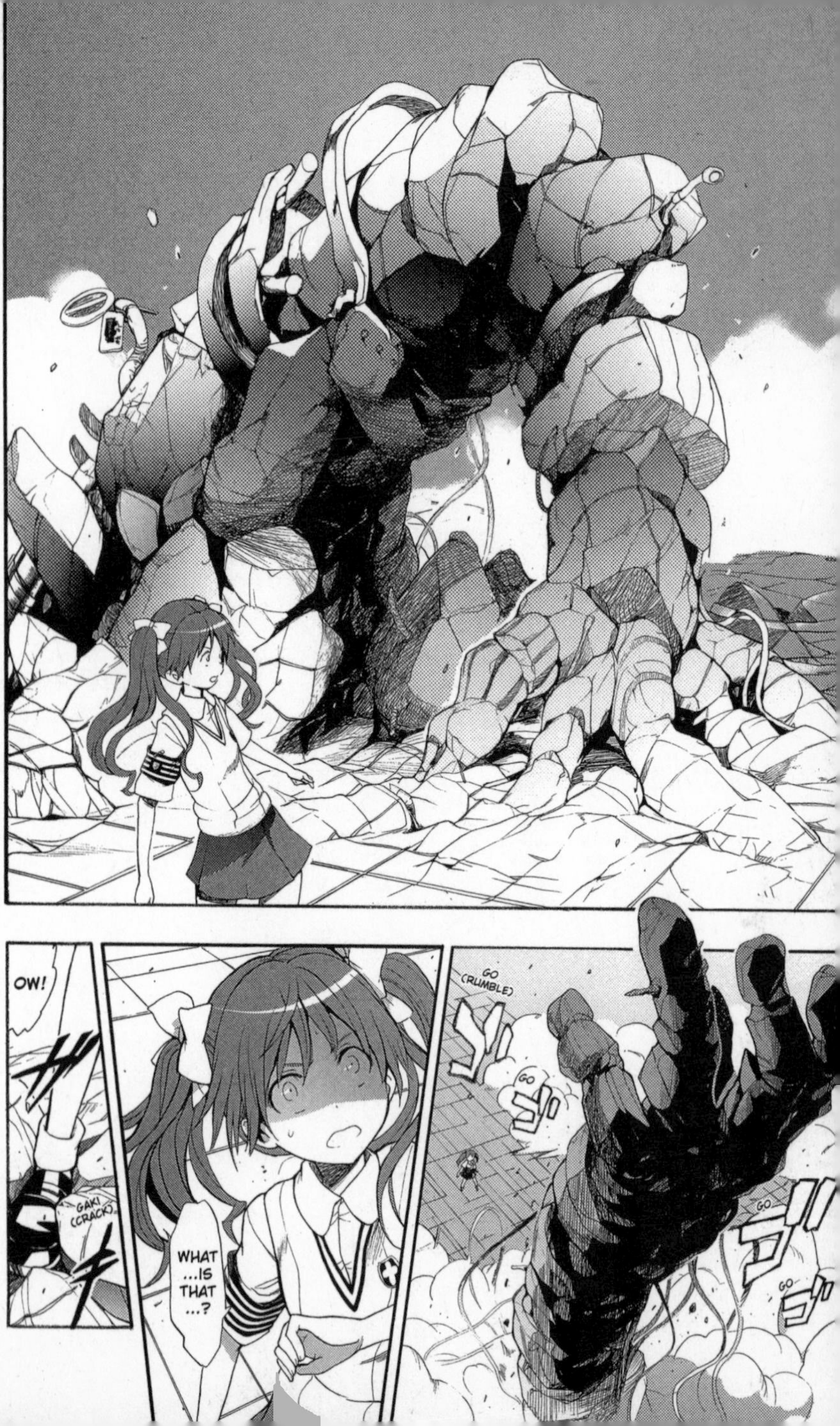
GO
(RUMBLE)
GO
GO
GO
WHAT
...IS
THAT
...?
OW!
GAKI
(CRACK)

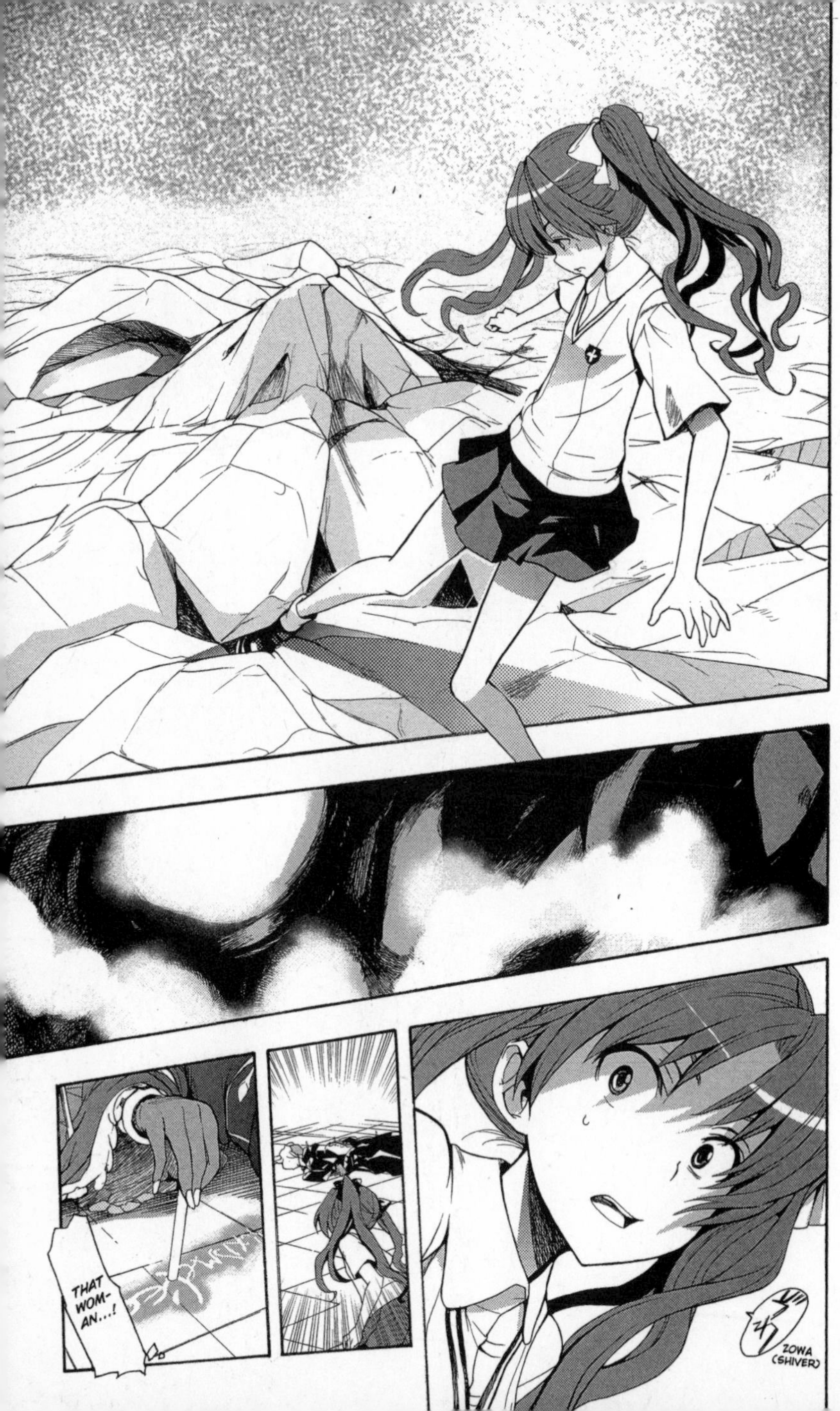
ZOWA (SHIVER)
THAT WOM- AN...!

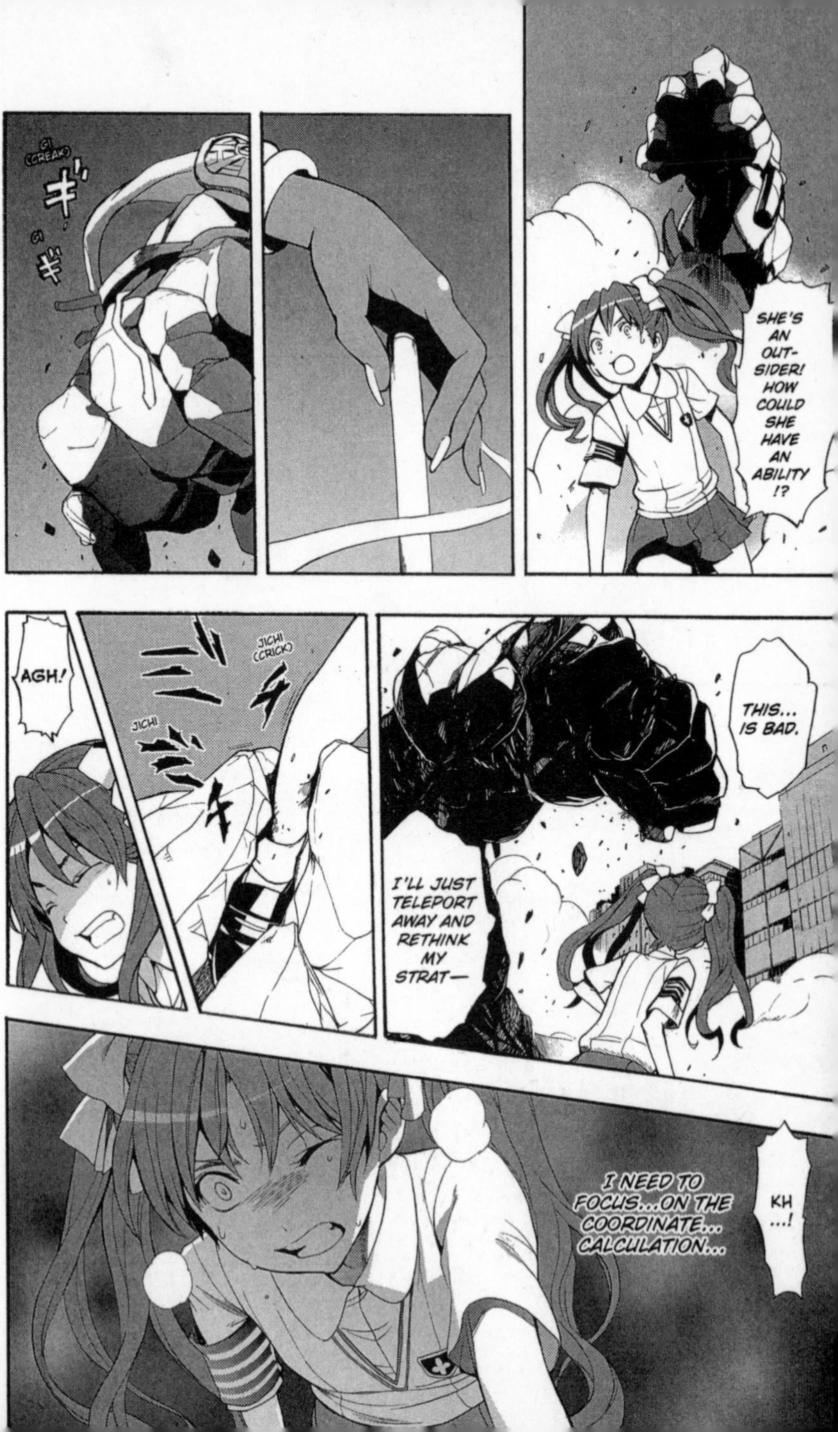
SHE'S AN OUTSIDER! HOW COULD SHE HAVE AN ABILITY!?
GI (CREAK)
ギ
GI
ギ
THIS... IS BAD.
I'LL JUST TELEPORT AWAY AND RETHINK MY STRAT—
JICHI (CRICK)
JICHI
AGH!
KH...!
I NEED TO FOCUS...ON THE COORDINATE... CALCULATION...

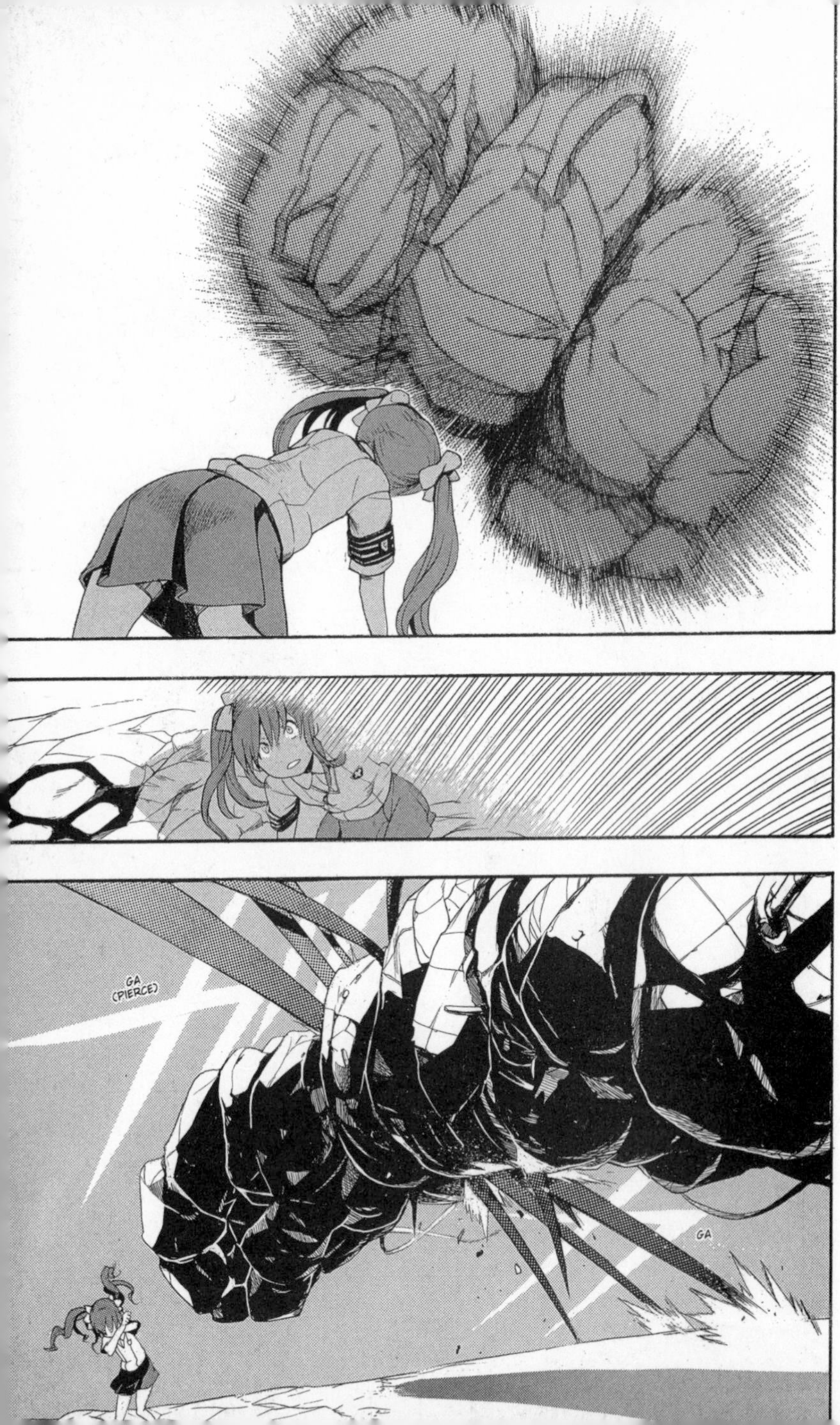
GA
GA
(PIERCE)

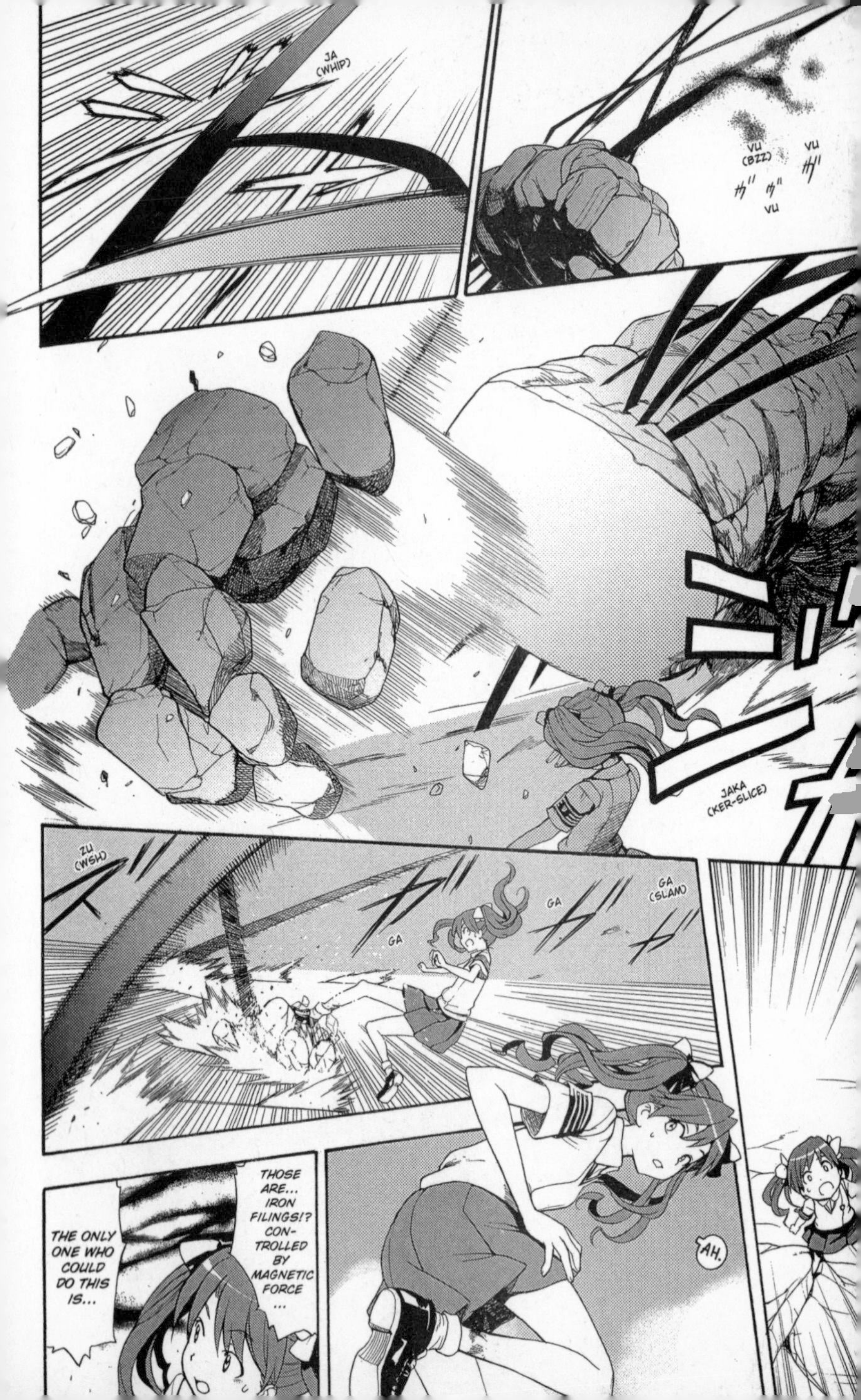
VU
(BZZ)
VU
VU
JA
(WHIP)
JAKA
(KER-SLICE)
GA
(SLAM)
GA
GA
ZU
(WSH)
AH.
THOSE ARE... IRON FILINGS!? CON-TROLLED BY MAGNETIC FORCE...
THE ONLY ONE WHO COULD DO THIS IS...

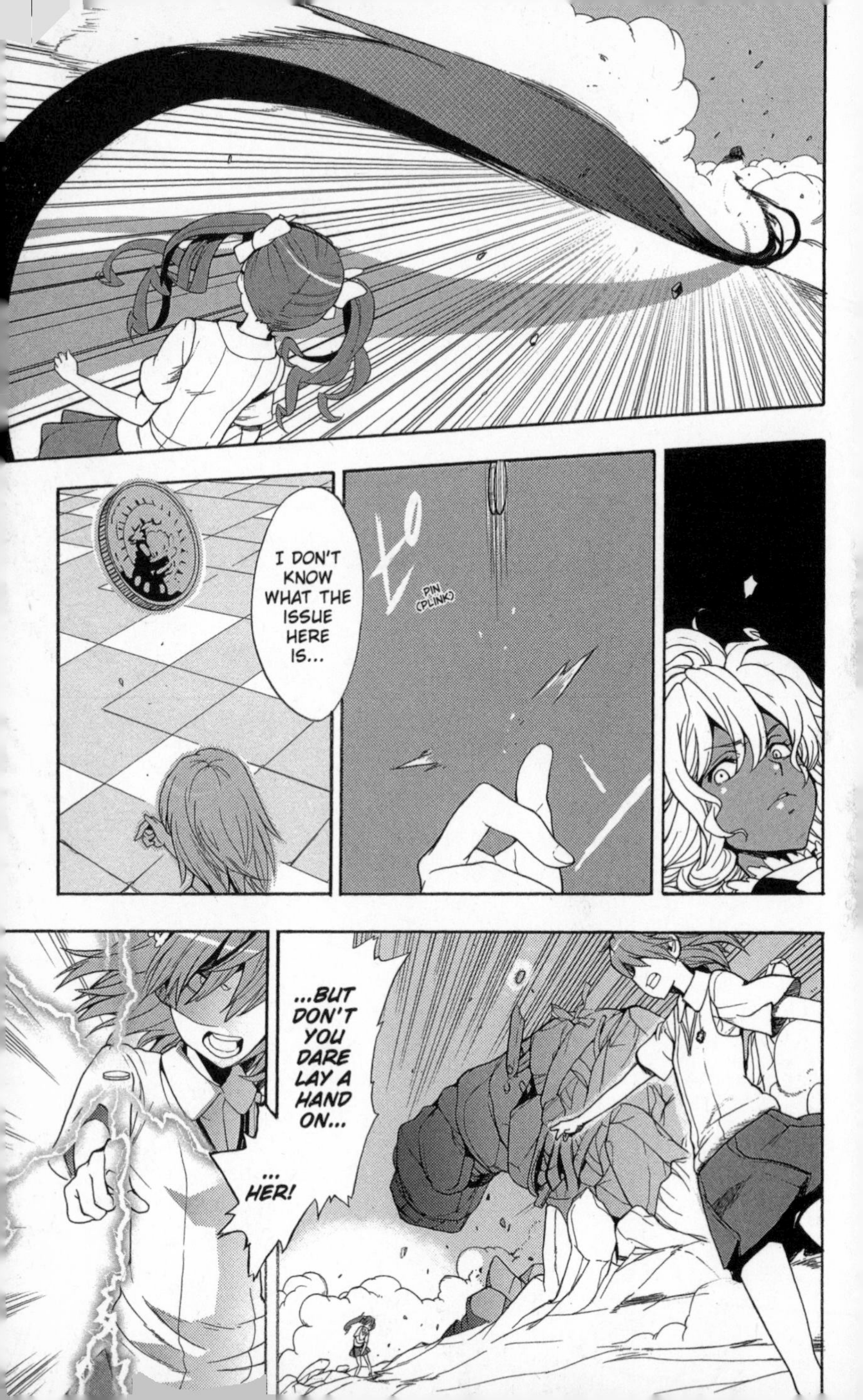
PIN (PLINK)
I DON'T KNOW WHAT THE ISSUE HERE IS...
...BUT DON'T YOU DARE LAY A HAND ON...
...HER!

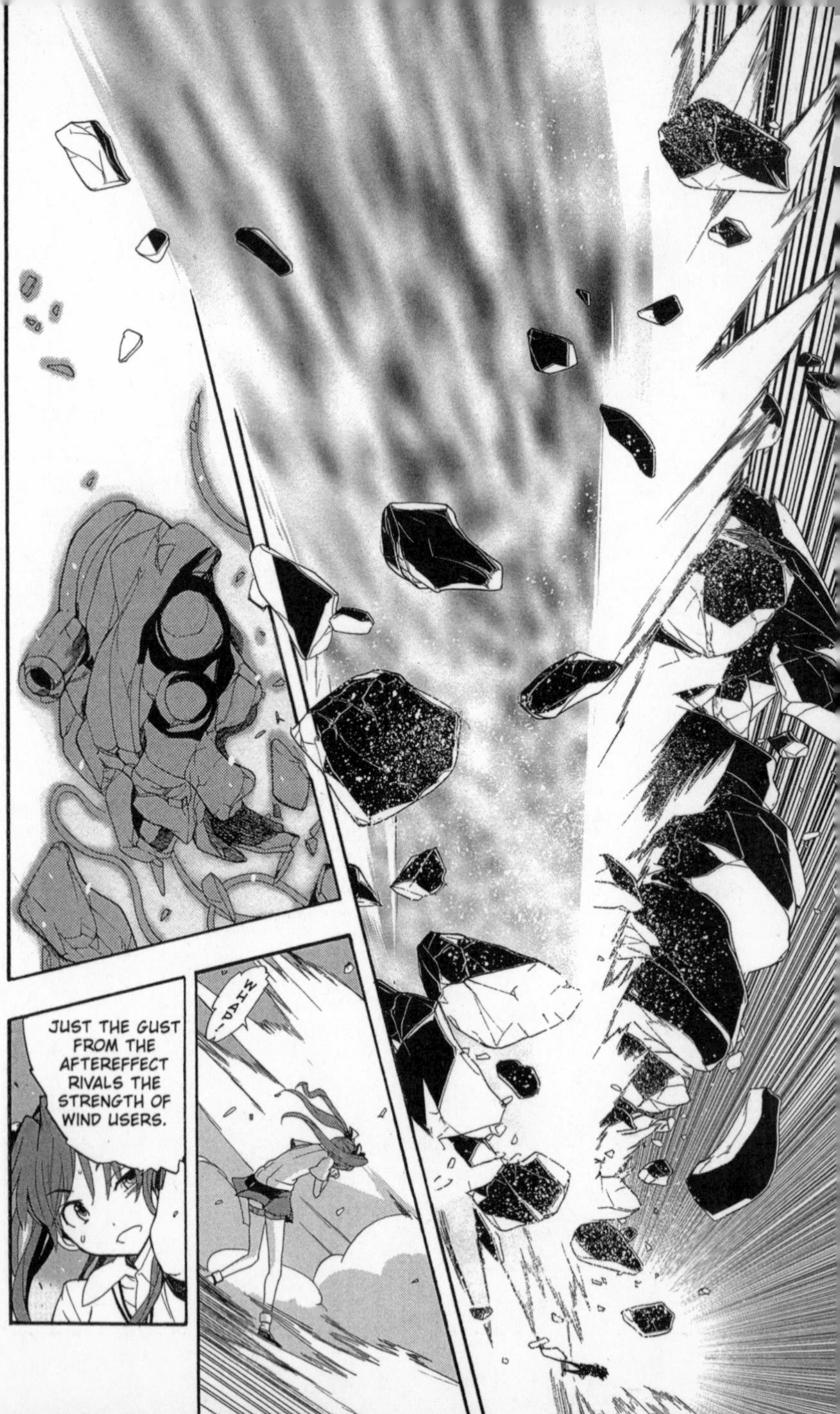
WHAP—!
JUST THE GUST FROM THE AFTEREFFECT RIVALS THE STRENGTH OF WIND USERS.

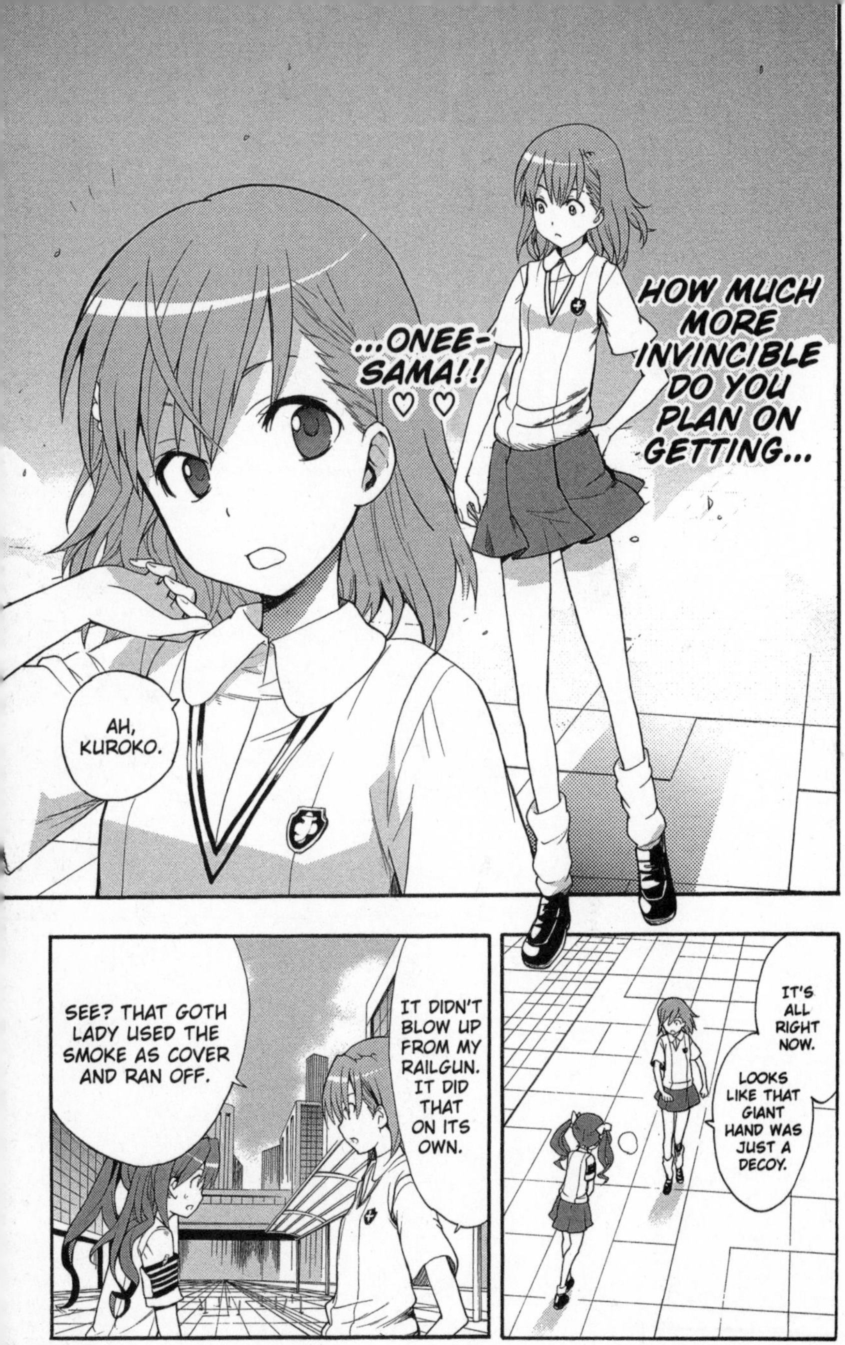
HOW MUCH MORE INVINCIBLE DO YOU PLAN ON GETTING...
...ONEE-SAMA!! ♡ ♡
AH, KUROKO.
IT'S ALL RIGHT NOW.
LOOKS LIKE THAT GIANT HAND WAS JUST A DECOY.
IT DIDN'T BLOW UP FROM MY RAILGUN. IT DID THAT ON ITS OWN.
SEE? THAT GOTH LADY USED THE SMOKE AS COVER AND RAN OFF.

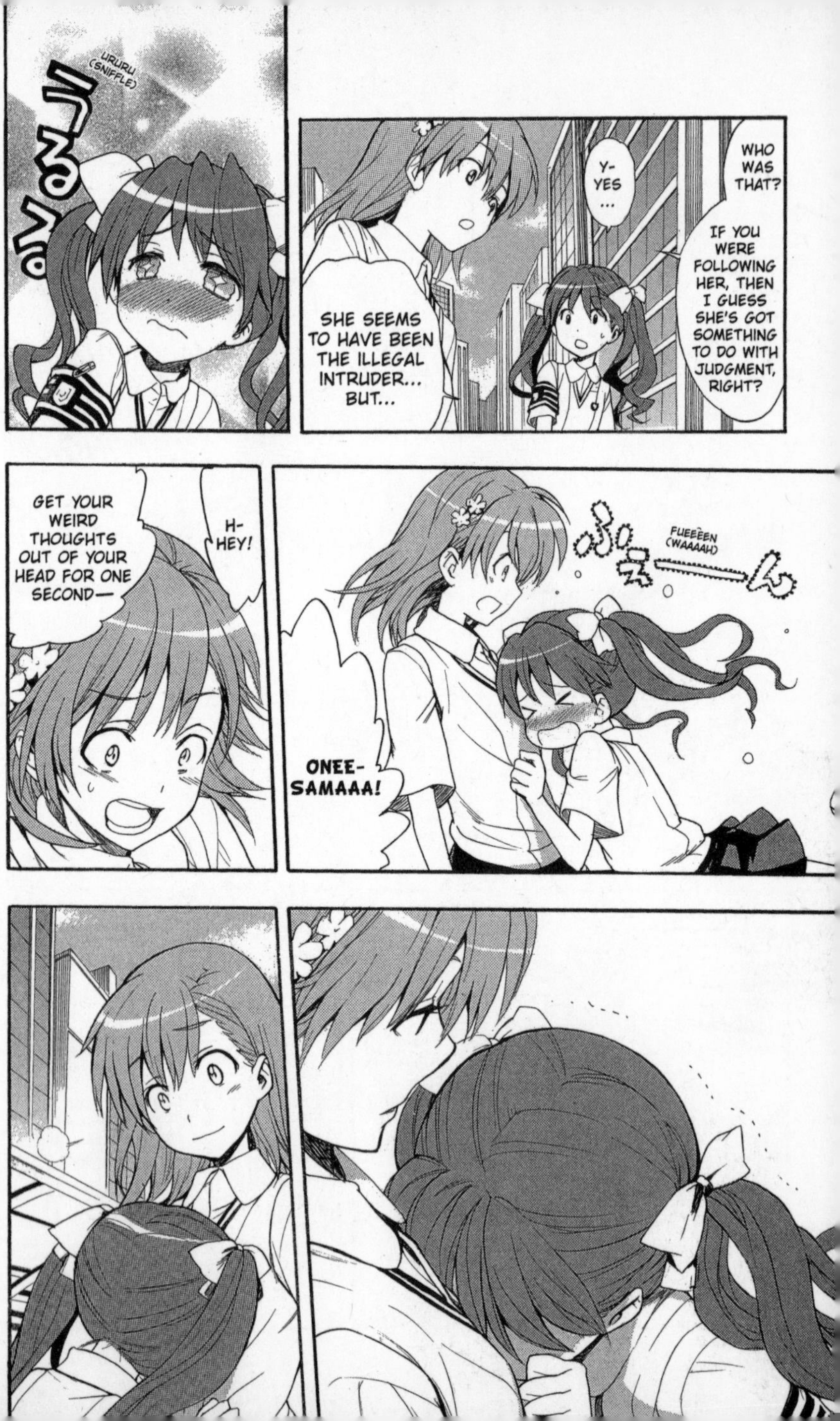
WHO WAS THAT?
IF YOU WERE FOLLOWING HER, THEN I GUESS SHE'S GOT SOMETHING TO DO WITH JUDGMENT, RIGHT?
Y-YES...
SHE SEEMS TO HAVE BEEN THE ILLEGAL INTRUDER... BUT...
うるる
URURU (SNIFFLE)
ふえーーーん
FUEEEEN (WAAAAH)
ONEE-SAMAAA!
H-HEY!
GET YOUR WEIRD THOUGHTS OUT OF YOUR HEAD FOR ONE SECOND—

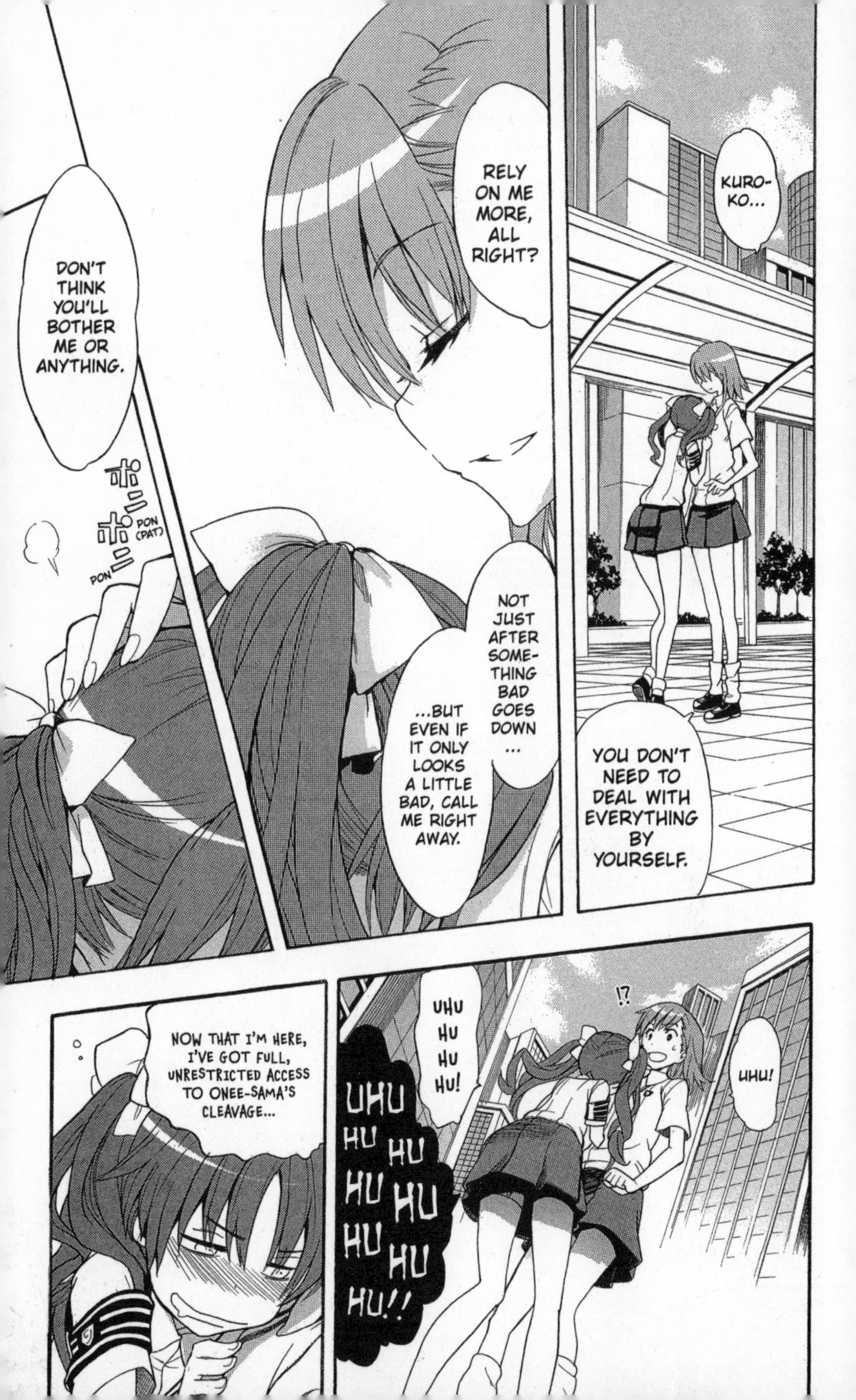
KURO-KO...
YOU DON'T NEED TO DEAL WITH EVERYTHING BY YOURSELF.
RELY ON ME MORE, ALL RIGHT?
NOT JUST AFTER SOME-THING BAD GOES DOWN...
...BUT EVEN IF IT ONLY LOOKS A LITTLE BAD, CALL ME RIGHT AWAY.
DON'T THINK YOU'LL BOTHER ME OR ANYTHING.
ポン ポン
PON (PAT) PON
UHU!
!?
UHU HU HU HU!
UHU HU HU HU HU HU HU HU HU!!
NOW THAT I'M HERE, I'VE GOT FULL, UNRESTRICTED ACCESS TO ONEE-SAMA'S CLEAVAGE...

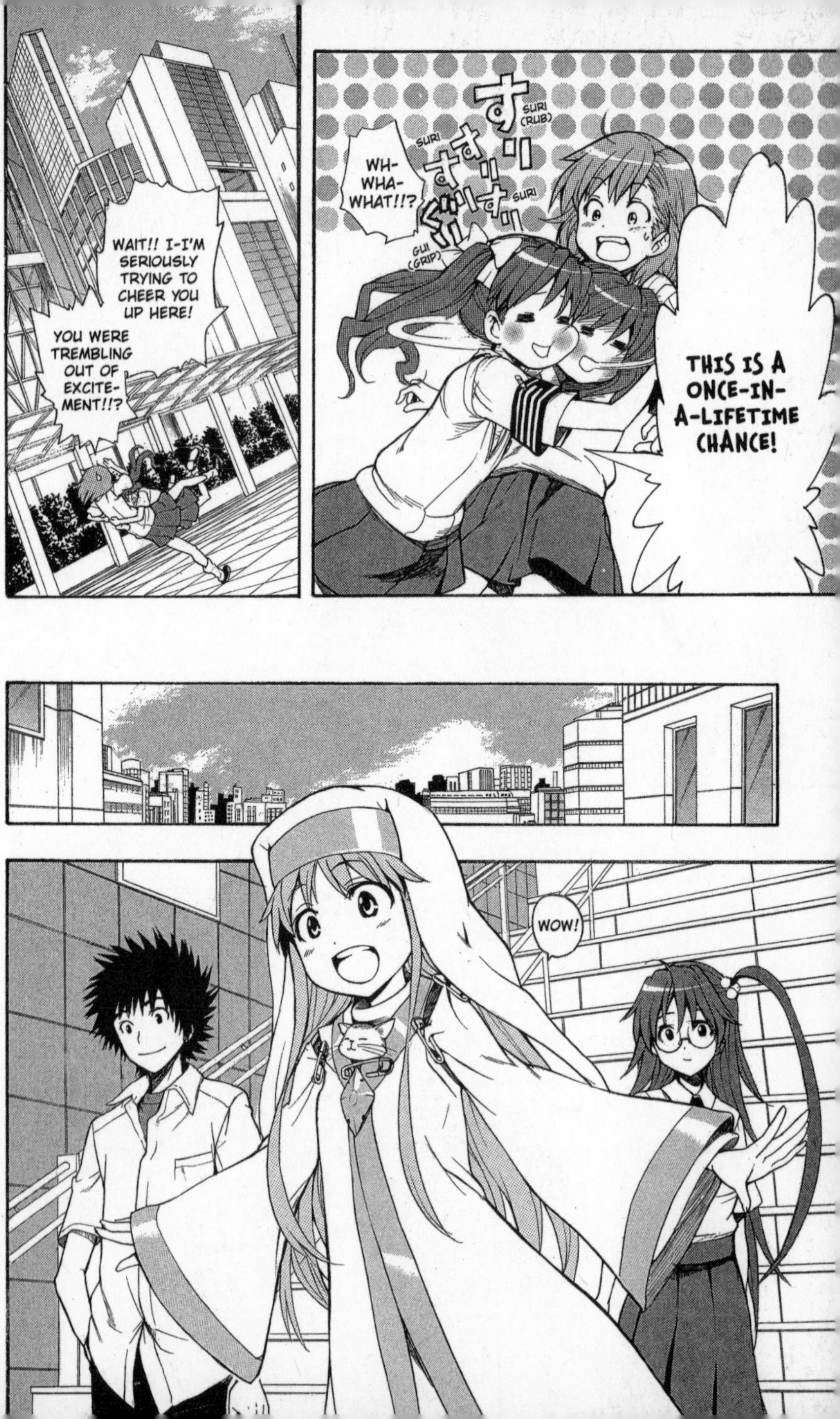
SURI (RUB)
SURI
WH- WHA- WHAT!!?
SURI
GUI (GRIP)
THIS IS A ONCE-IN-A-LIFETIME CHANCE!
WAIT!! I-I'M SERIOUSLY TRYING TO CHEER YOU UP HERE!
YOU WERE TREMBLING OUT OF EXCITE-MENT!!?
WOW!

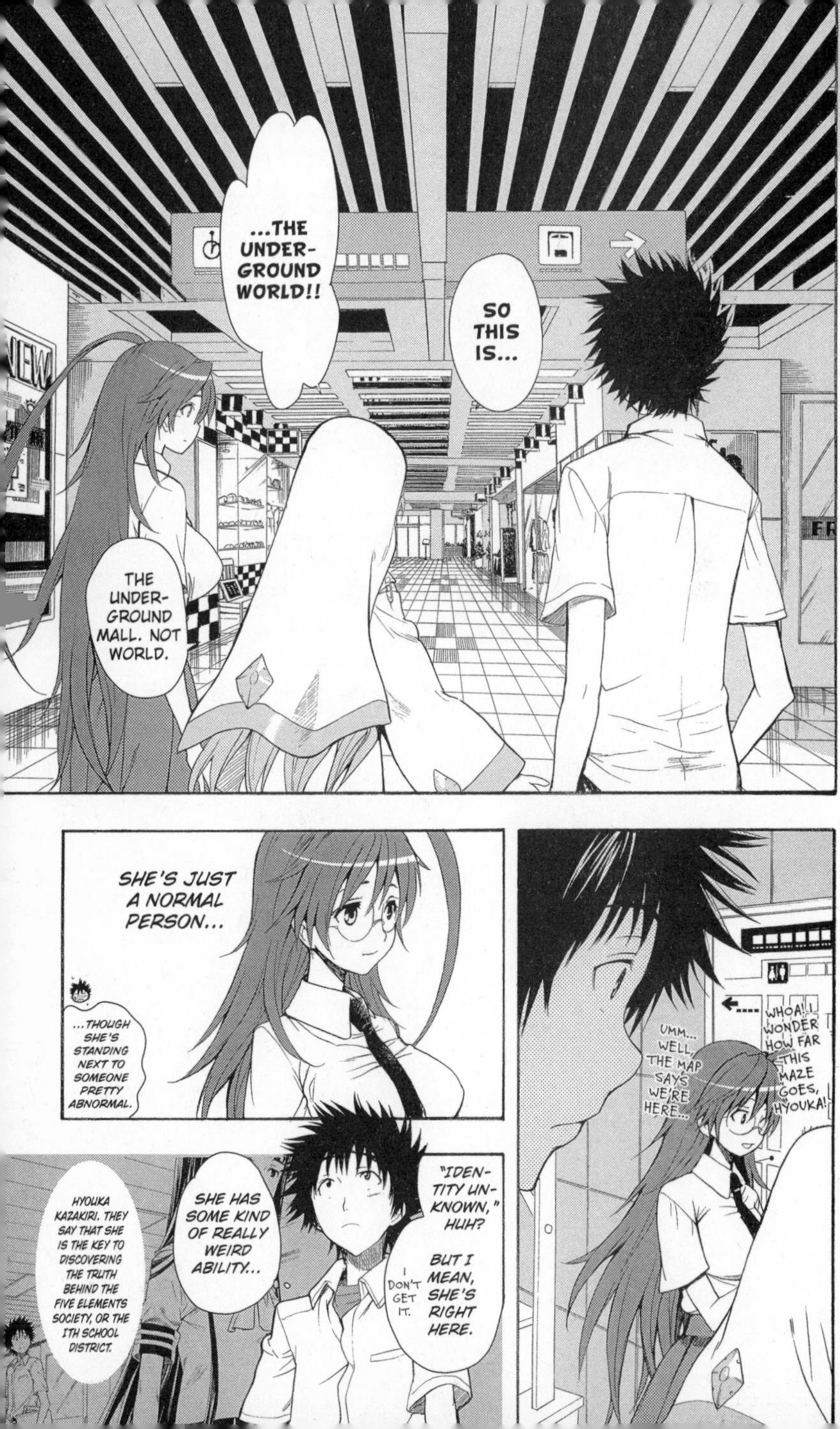
SO THIS IS...
...THE UNDER-GROUND WORLD!!
THE UNDER-GROUND MALL. NOT WORLD.
WHOA! I WONDER HOW FAR THIS MAZE GOES, HYOUKA!
UMM... WELL, THE MAP SAYS WE'RE HERE...
SHE'S JUST A NORMAL PERSON...
...THOUGH SHE'S STANDING NEXT TO SOMEONE PRETTY ABNORMAL.
"IDEN-TITY UN-KNOWN," HUH?
BUT I MEAN, SHE'S RIGHT HERE.
I DON'T GET IT.
SHE HAS SOME KIND OF REALLY WEIRD ABILITY...
HYOUKA KAZAKIRI. THEY SAY THAT SHE IS THE KEY TO DISCOVERING THE TRUTH BEHIND THE FIVE ELEMENTS SOCIETY, OR THE ITH SCHOOL DISTRICT.

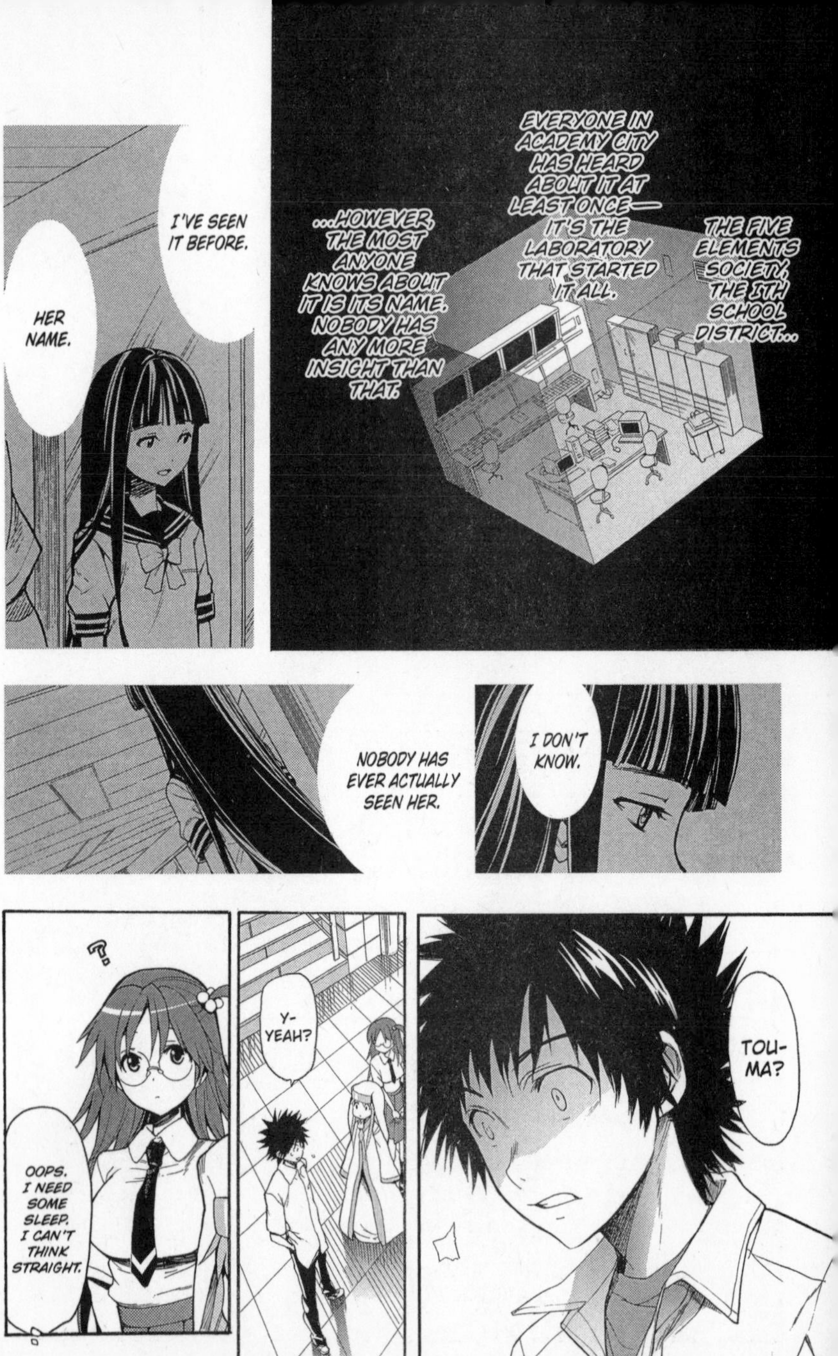
THE FIVE ELEMENTS SOCIETY, THE ITH SCHOOL DISTRICT...
EVERYONE IN ACADEMY CITY HAS HEARD ABOUT IT AT LEAST ONCE—IT'S THE LABORATORY THAT STARTED IT ALL.
...HOWEVER, THE MOST ANYONE KNOWS ABOUT IT IS ITS NAME. NOBODY HAS ANY MORE INSIGHT THAN THAT.
I'VE SEEN IT BEFORE.
HER NAME.
I DON'T KNOW.
NOBODY HAS EVER ACTUALLY SEEN HER.
TOU-MA?
Y-YEAH?
?
OOPS. I NEED SOME SLEEP. I CAN'T THINK STRAIGHT.

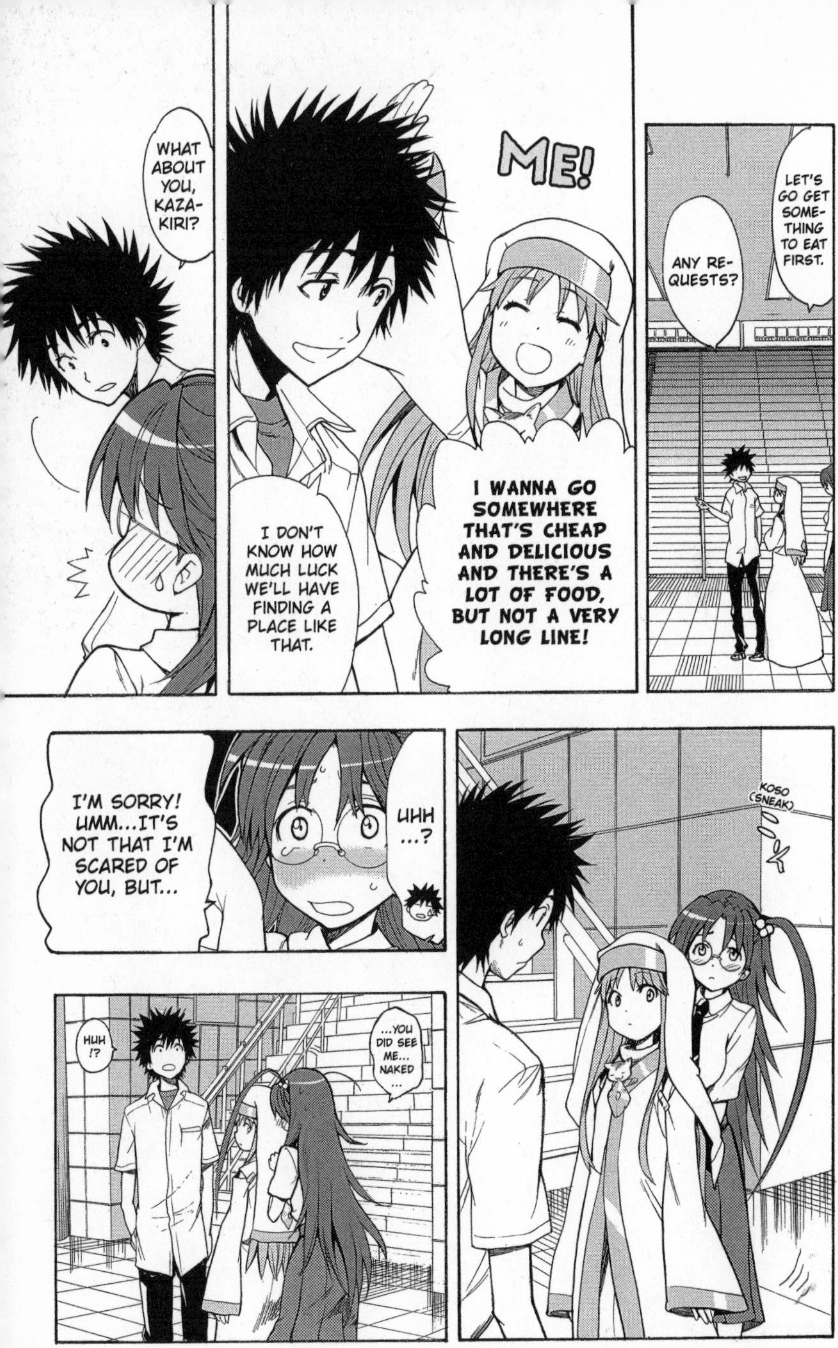
LET'S GO GET SOME-THING TO EAT FIRST.
ANY RE-QUESTS?
ME!
I WANNA GO SOMEWHERE THAT'S CHEAP AND DELICIOUS AND THERE'S A LOT OF FOOD, BUT NOT A VERY LONG LINE!
I DON'T KNOW HOW MUCH LUCK WE'LL HAVE FINDING A PLACE LIKE THAT.
WHAT ABOUT YOU, KAZA-KIRI?
KOSO (SNEAK)
UHH ...?
I'M SORRY! UMM...IT'S NOT THAT I'M SCARED OF YOU, BUT...
...YOU DID SEE ME... NAKED ...
HUH !?

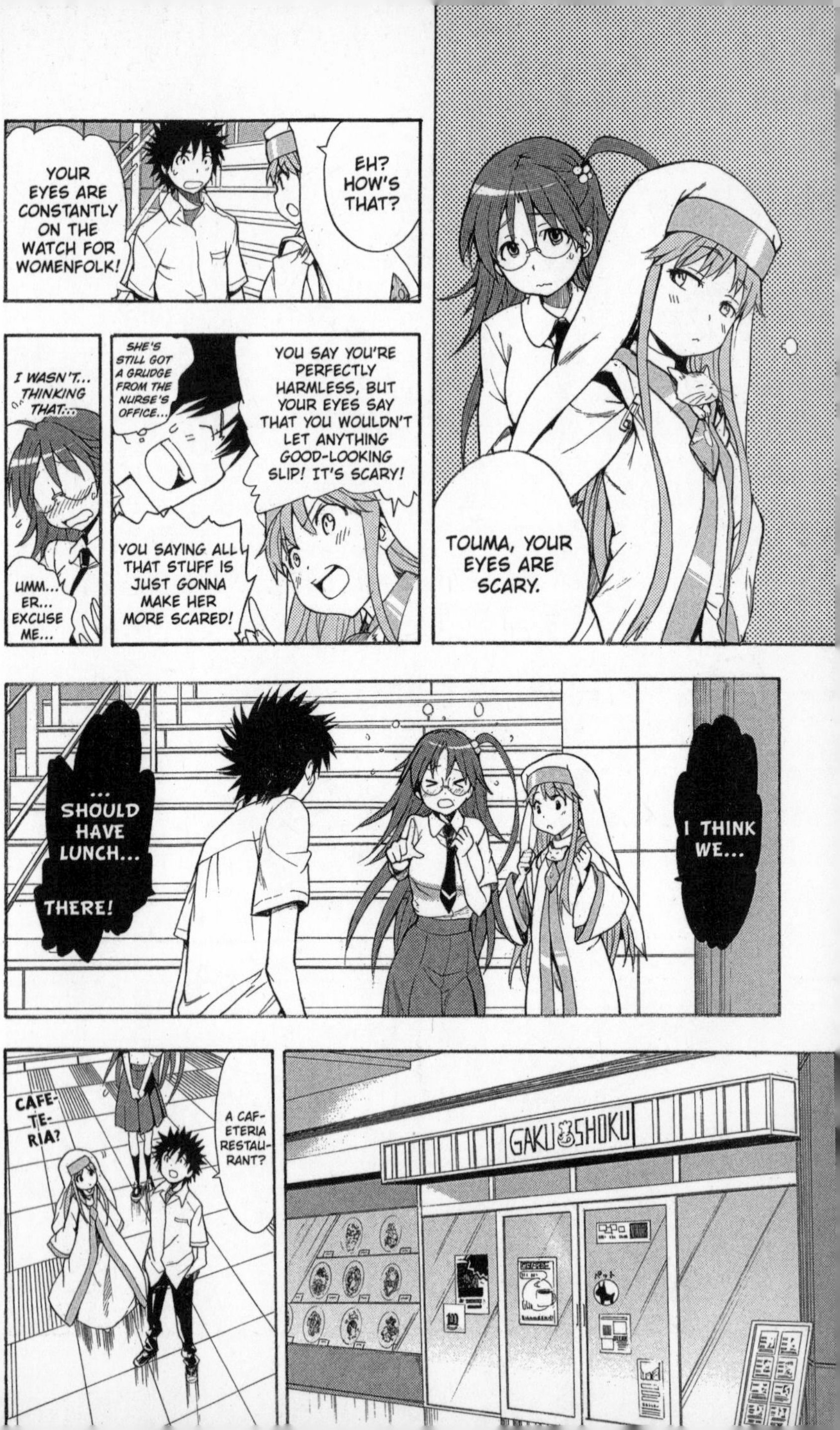
TOUMA, YOUR EYES ARE SCARY.
EH? HOW'S THAT?
YOUR EYES ARE CONSTANTLY ON THE WATCH FOR WOMENFOLK!
YOU SAY YOU'RE PERFECTLY HARMLESS, BUT YOUR EYES SAY THAT YOU WOULDN'T LET ANYTHING GOOD-LOOKING SLIP! IT'S SCARY!
SHE'S STILL GOT A GRUDGE FROM THE NURSE'S OFFICE...
YOU SAYING ALL THAT STUFF IS JUST GONNA MAKE HER MORE SCARED!
I WASN'T... THINKING THAT...
UMM... ER... EXCUSE ME...
I THINK WE...
... SHOULD HAVE LUNCH...
THERE!
GAKU SHOKU
A CAFETERIA RESTAURANT?
CAFETERIA?

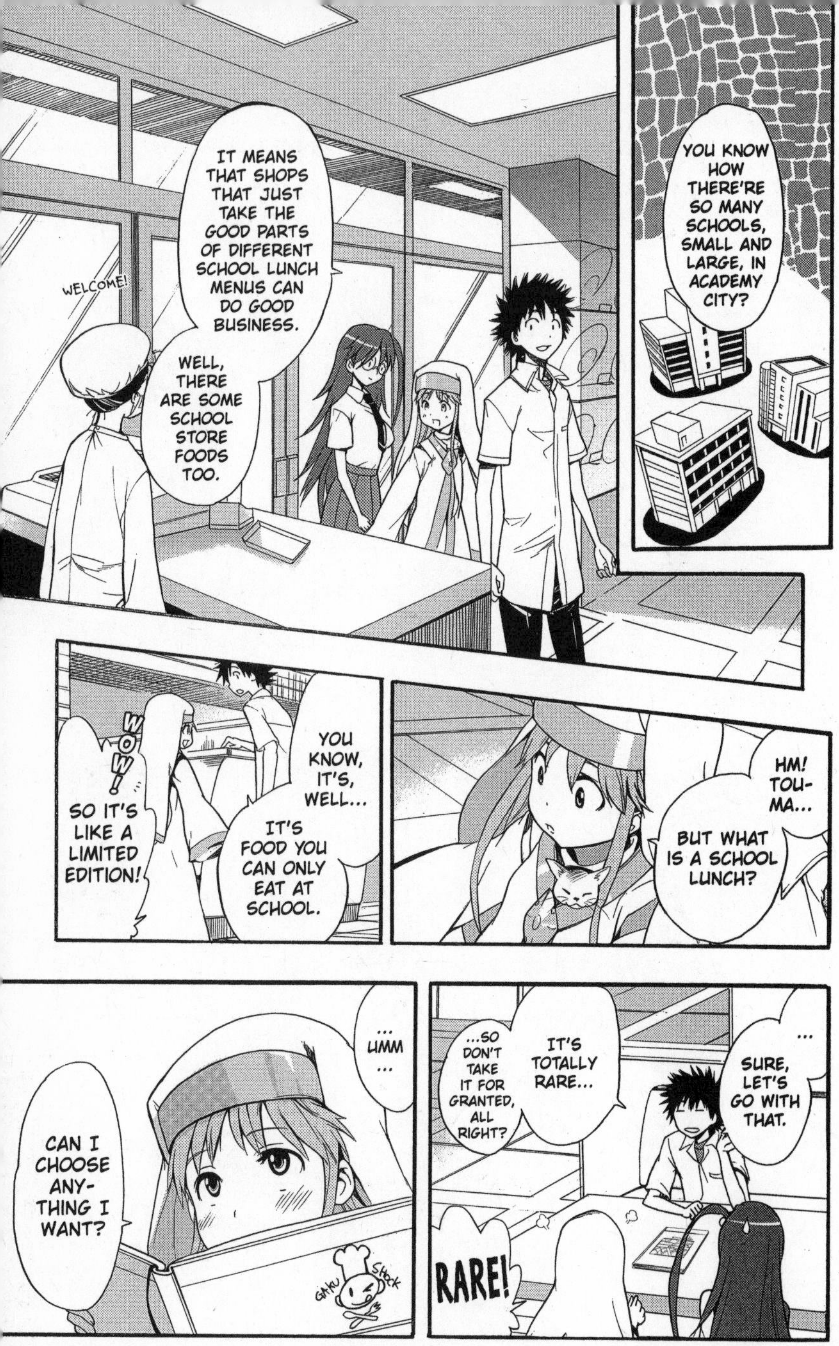
YOU KNOW HOW THERE'RE SO MANY SCHOOLS, SMALL AND LARGE, IN ACADEMY CITY?
IT MEANS THAT SHOPS THAT JUST TAKE THE GOOD PARTS OF DIFFERENT SCHOOL LUNCH MENUS CAN DO GOOD BUSINESS.
WELL, THERE ARE SOME SCHOOL STORE FOODS TOO.
WELCOME!
HM! TOUMA...
BUT WHAT IS A SCHOOL LUNCH?
YOU KNOW, IT'S, WELL...
IT'S FOOD YOU CAN ONLY EAT AT SCHOOL.
WOW!
SO IT'S LIKE A LIMITED EDITION!
...
SURE, LET'S GO WITH THAT.
IT'S TOTALLY RARE...
...SO DON'T TAKE IT FOR GRANTED, ALL RIGHT?
RARE!
... UMM ...
CAN I CHOOSE ANY-THING I WANT?
GAKU Stock

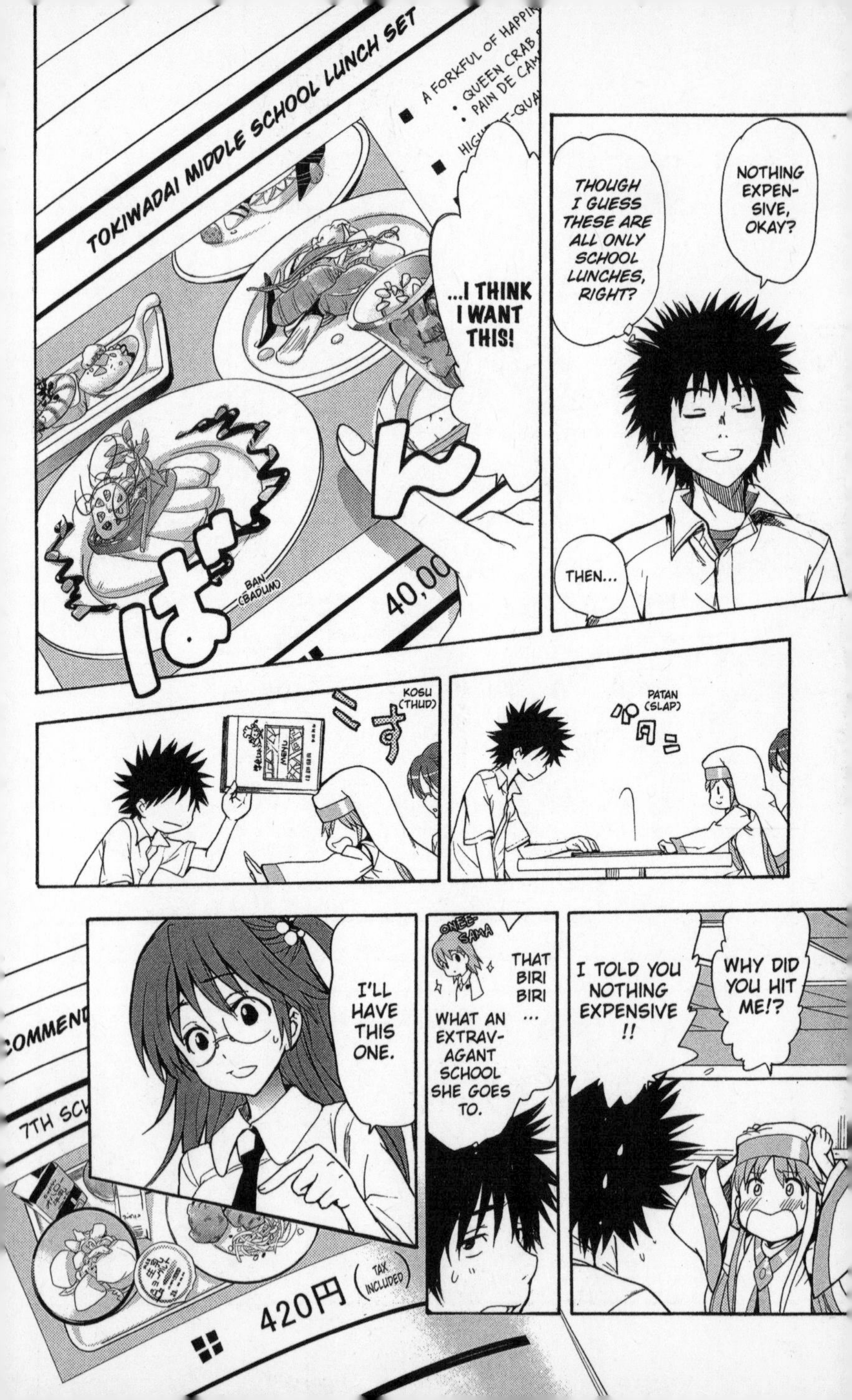
NOTHING EXPEN-SIVE, OKAY?
THOUGH I GUESS THESE ARE ALL ONLY SCHOOL LUNCHES, RIGHT?
THEN...
TOKIWADAI MIDDLE SCHOOL LUNCH SET
QUEEN CRAB
...I THINK I WANT THIS!
BAN (BADUM)
PATAN (SLAP)
KOSU (THUD)
MENU
WHY DID YOU HIT ME!?
I TOLD YOU NOTHING EXPENSIVE!!
ONEE-SAMA
THAT BIRI BIRI...
WHAT AN EXTRAV-AGANT SCHOOL SHE GOES TO.
I'LL HAVE THIS ONE.
420円 (TAX INCLUDED)

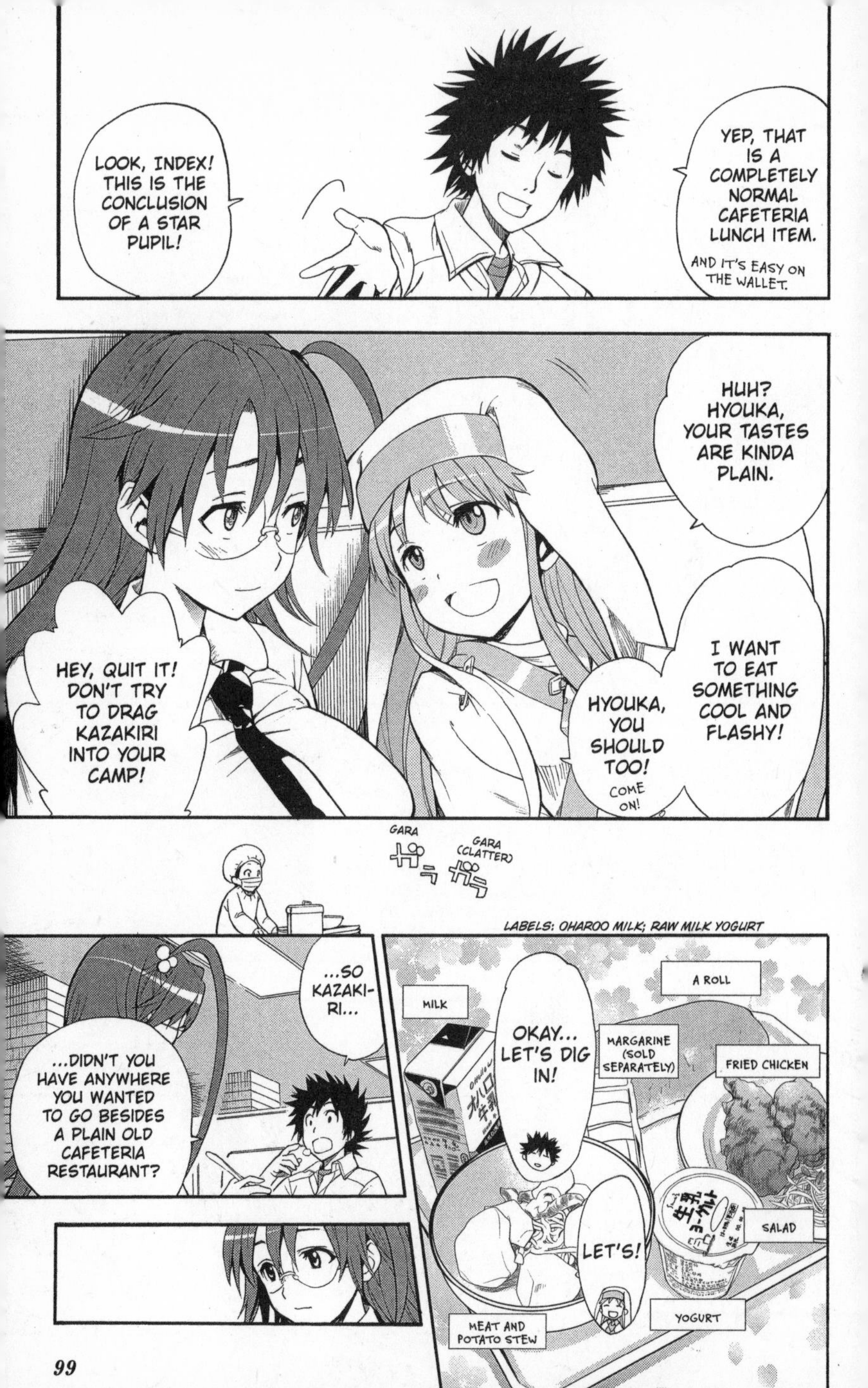
YEP, THAT IS A COMPLETELY NORMAL CAFETERIA LUNCH ITEM.
AND IT'S EASY ON THE WALLET.
LOOK, INDEX! THIS IS THE CONCLUSION OF A STAR PUPIL!
HUH? HYOUKA, YOUR TASTES ARE KINDA PLAIN.
I WANT TO EAT SOMETHING COOL AND FLASHY!
HYOUKA, YOU SHOULD TOO!
COME ON!
HEY, QUIT IT! DON'T TRY TO DRAG KAZAKIRI INTO YOUR CAMP!
GARA
GARA (CLATTER)
LABELS: OHAROO MILK; RAW MILK YOGURT
A ROLL
MILK
MARGARINE (SOLD SEPARATELY)
FRIED CHICKEN
OKAY... LET'S DIG IN!
LET'S!
SALAD
YOGURT
MEAT AND POTATO STEW
...SO KAZAKIRI...
...DIDN'T YOU HAVE ANYWHERE YOU WANTED TO GO BESIDES A PLAIN OLD CAFETERIA RESTAURANT?

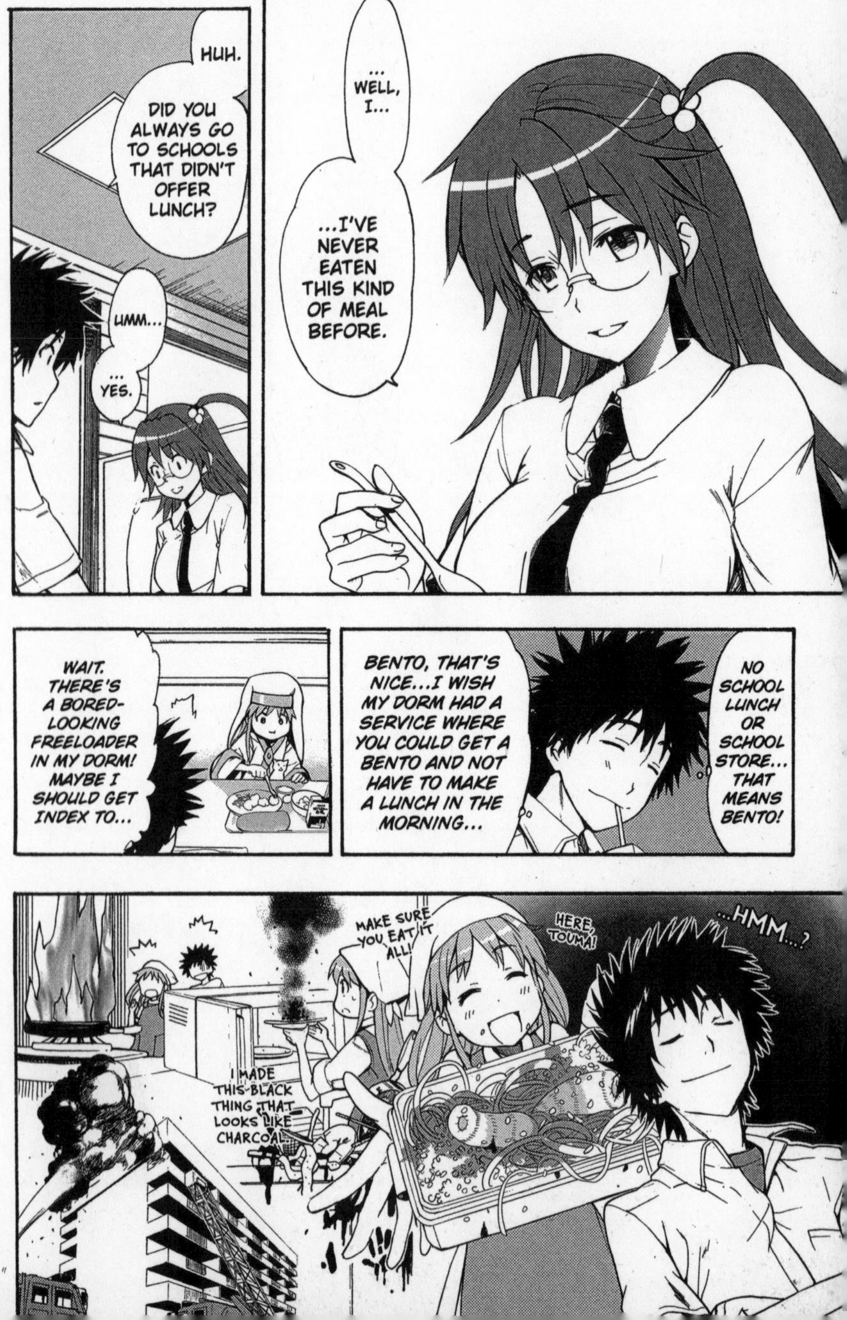
... WELL, I...
...I'VE NEVER EATEN THIS KIND OF MEAL BEFORE.
HUH.
DID YOU ALWAYS GO TO SCHOOLS THAT DIDN'T OFFER LUNCH?
UMM...
... YES.
NO SCHOOL LUNCH OR SCHOOL STORE... THAT MEANS BENTO!
BENTO, THAT'S NICE...I WISH MY DORM HAD A SERVICE WHERE YOU COULD GET A BENTO AND NOT HAVE TO MAKE A LUNCH IN THE MORNING...
WAIT. THERE'S A BORED-LOOKING FREELOADER IN MY DORM! MAYBE I SHOULD GET INDEX TO...
...HMM...?
HERE, TOUMA!
MAKE SURE YOU EAT IT ALL!
I MADE THIS BLACK THING THAT LOOKS LIKE CHARCOAL!

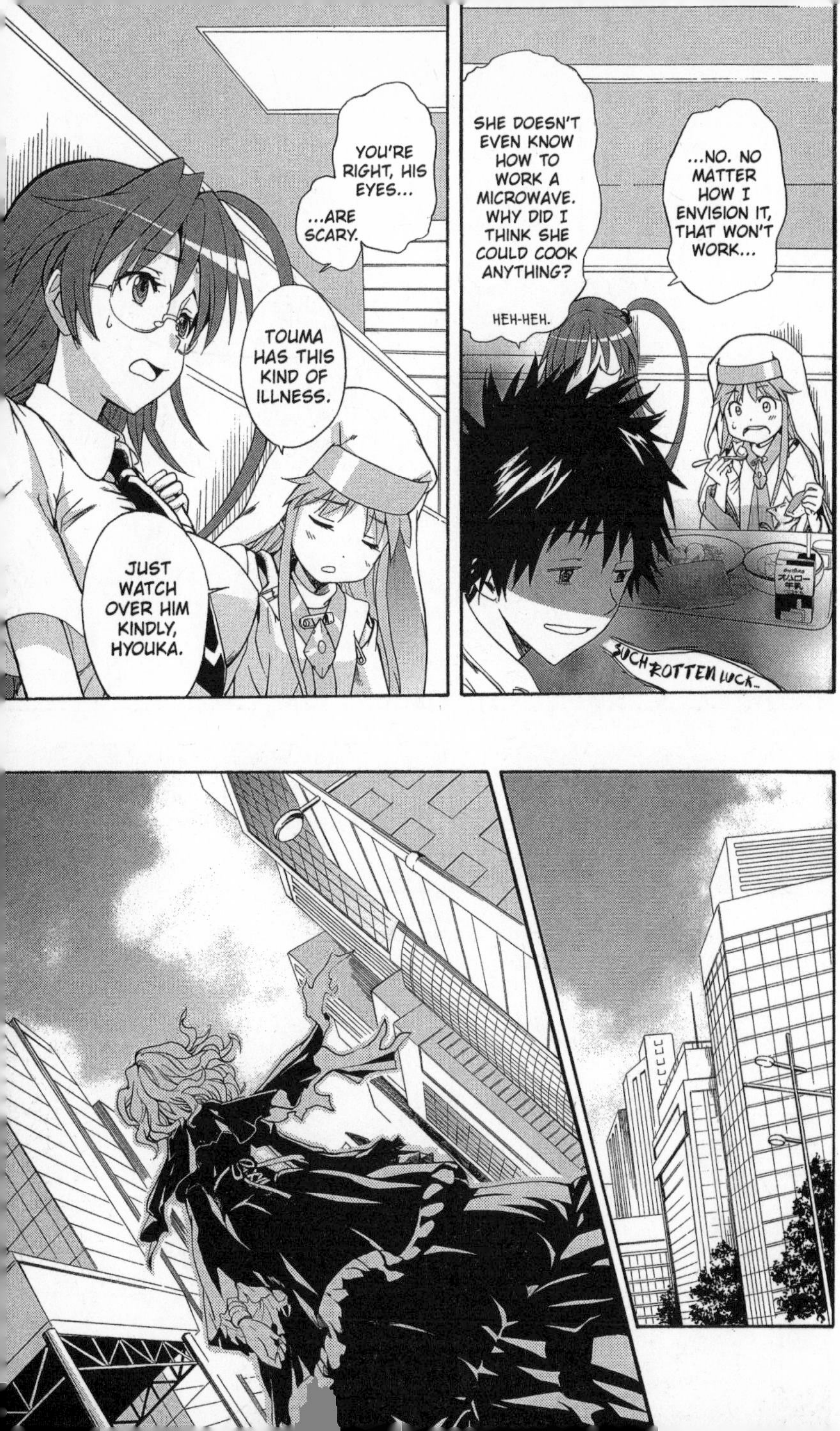
...NO. NO MATTER HOW I ENVISION IT, THAT WON'T WORK...
SHE DOESN'T EVEN KNOW HOW TO WORK A MICROWAVE. WHY DID I THINK SHE COULD COOK ANYTHING?
HEH-HEH.
SUCH ROTTEN LUCK..
YOU'RE RIGHT, HIS EYES...
...ARE SCARY.
TOUMA HAS THIS KIND OF ILLNESS.
JUST WATCH OVER HIM KINDLY, HYOUKA.

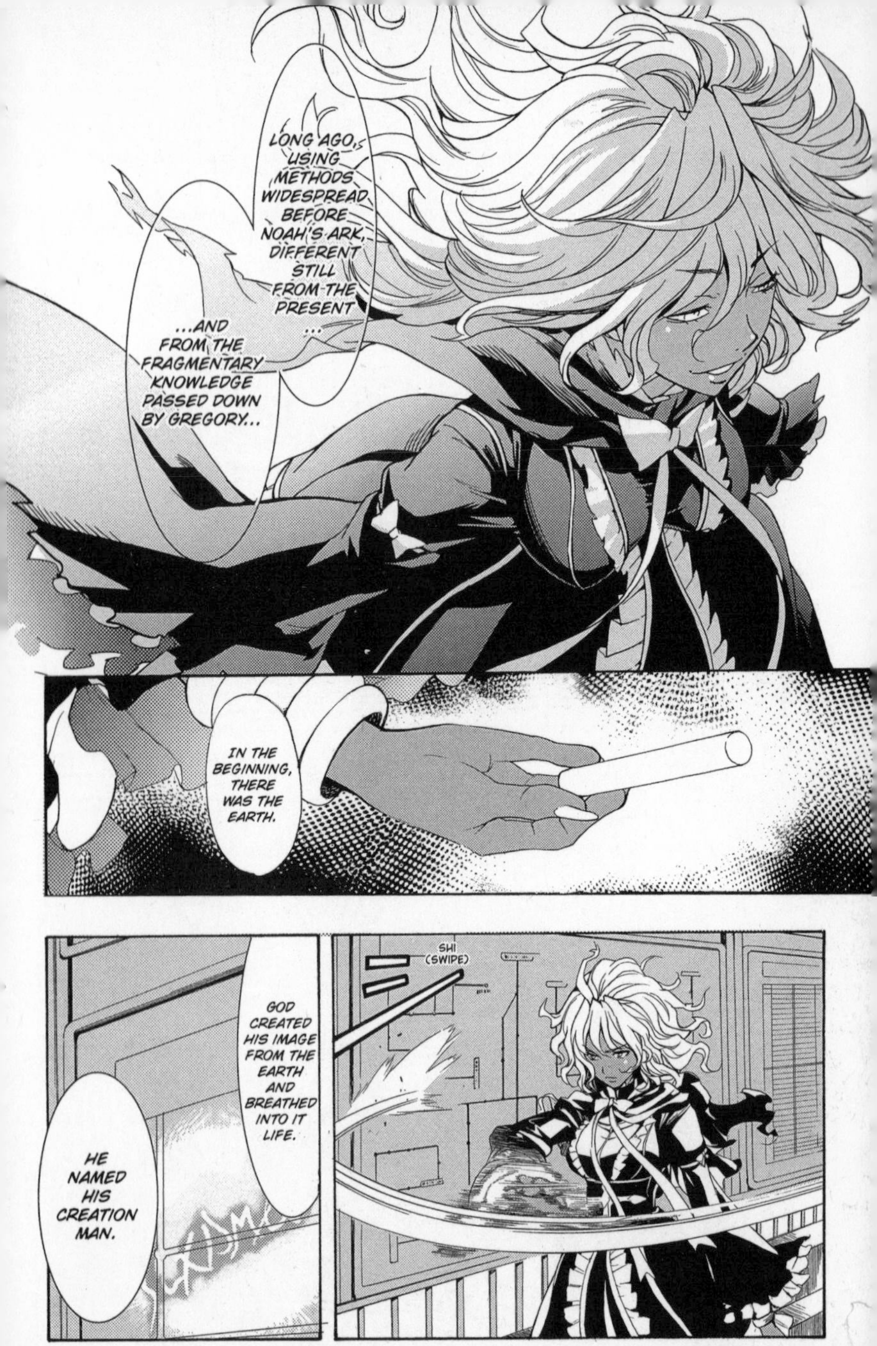
LONG AGO, USING METHODS WIDESPREAD BEFORE NOAH'S ARK, DIFFERENT STILL FROM THE PRESENT...
...AND FROM THE FRAGMENTARY KNOWLEDGE PASSED DOWN BY GREGORY...
IN THE BEGINNING, THERE WAS THE EARTH.
SHI (SWIPE)
GOD CREATED HIS IMAGE FROM THE EARTH AND BREATHED INTO IT LIFE.
HE NAMED HIS CREATION MAN.

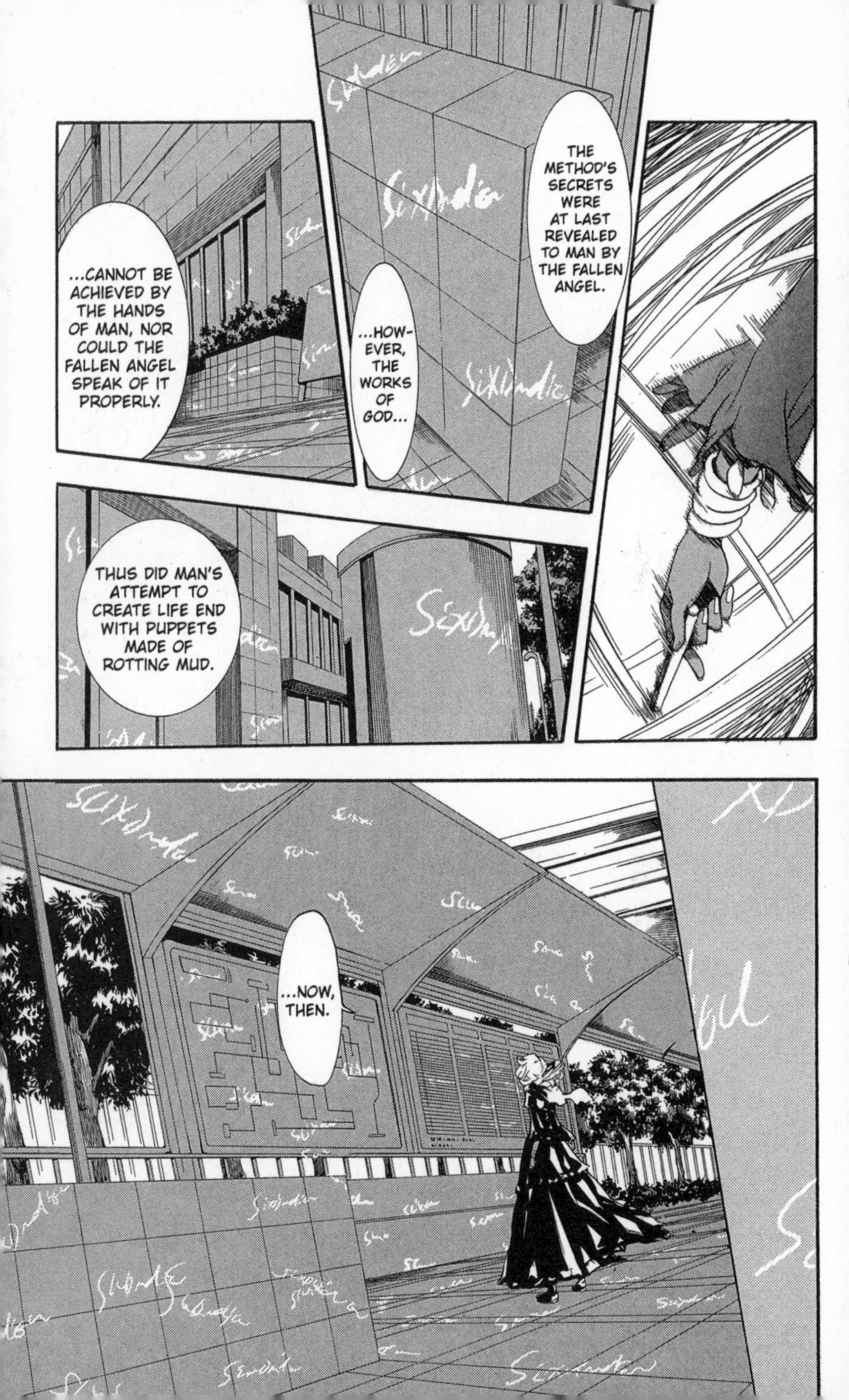
THE METHOD'S SECRETS WERE AT LAST REVEALED TO MAN BY THE FALLEN ANGEL.
...HOW-EVER, THE WORKS OF GOD...
...CANNOT BE ACHIEVED BY THE HANDS OF MAN, NOR COULD THE FALLEN ANGEL SPEAK OF IT PROPERLY.
THUS DID MAN'S ATTEMPT TO CREATE LIFE END WITH PUPPETS MADE OF ROTTING MUD.
...NOW, THEN.

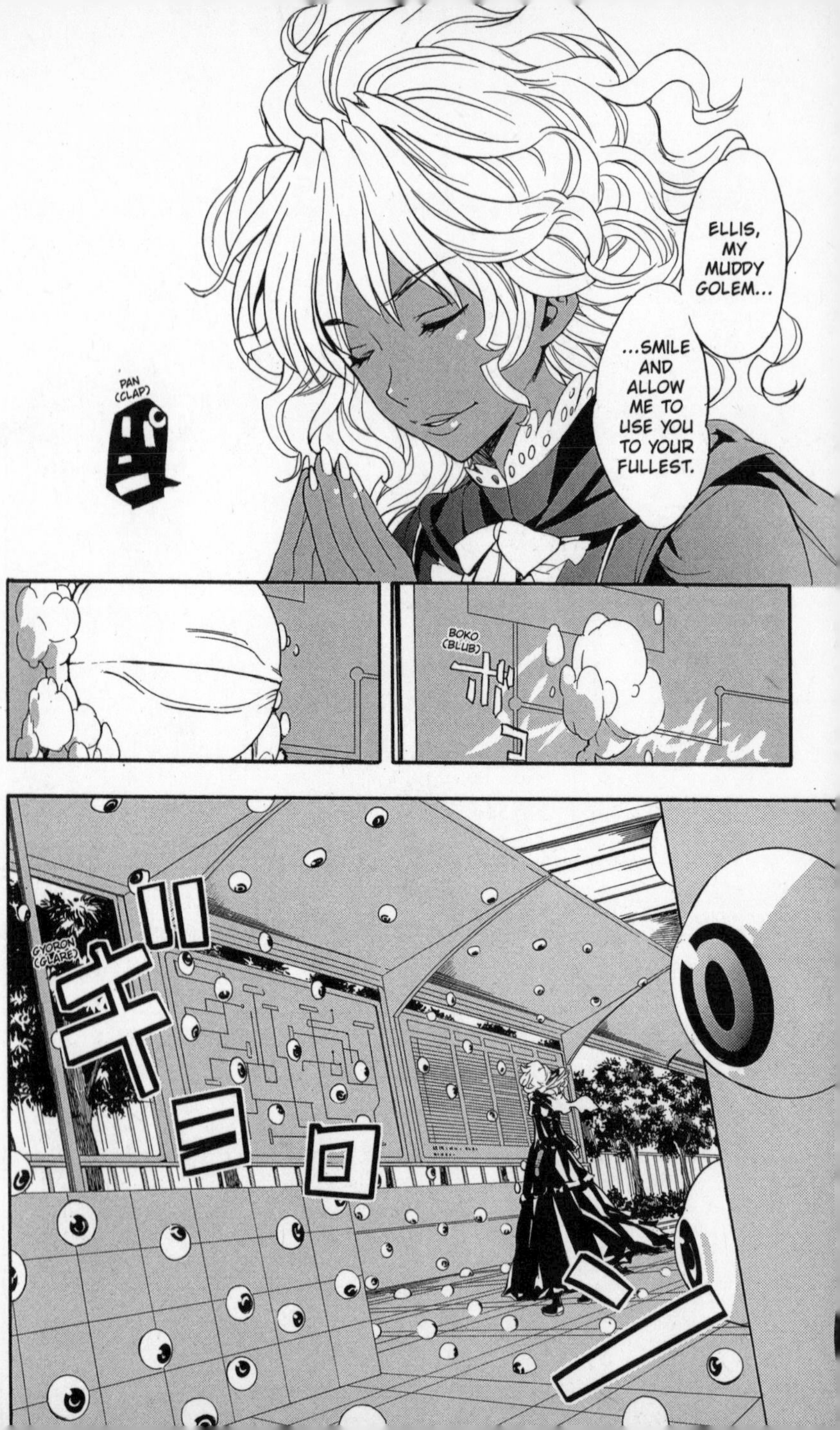
ELLIS, MY MUDDY GOLEM...
...SMILE AND ALLOW ME TO USE YOU TO YOUR FULLEST.
PAN (CLAP)
BOKO (BLUB)
GYORON (GLARE)

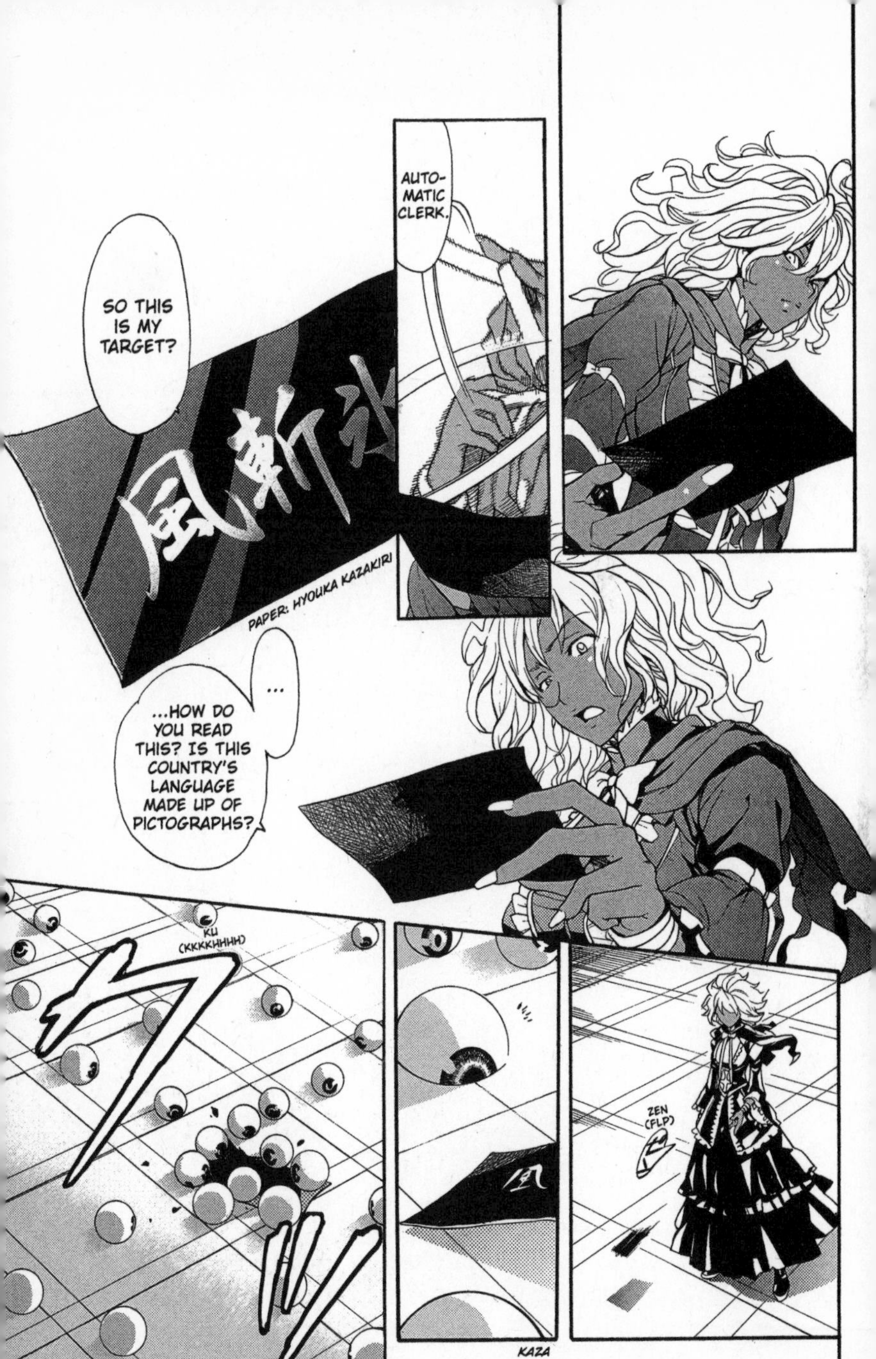
AUTO-MATIC CLERK.
SO THIS IS MY TARGET?
PAPER: HYOUKA KAZAKIRI
...
...HOW DO YOU READ THIS? IS THIS COUNTRY'S LANGUAGE MADE UP OF PICTOGRAPHS?
ZEN (FLP)
KAZA
KU (KKKKHHHH)

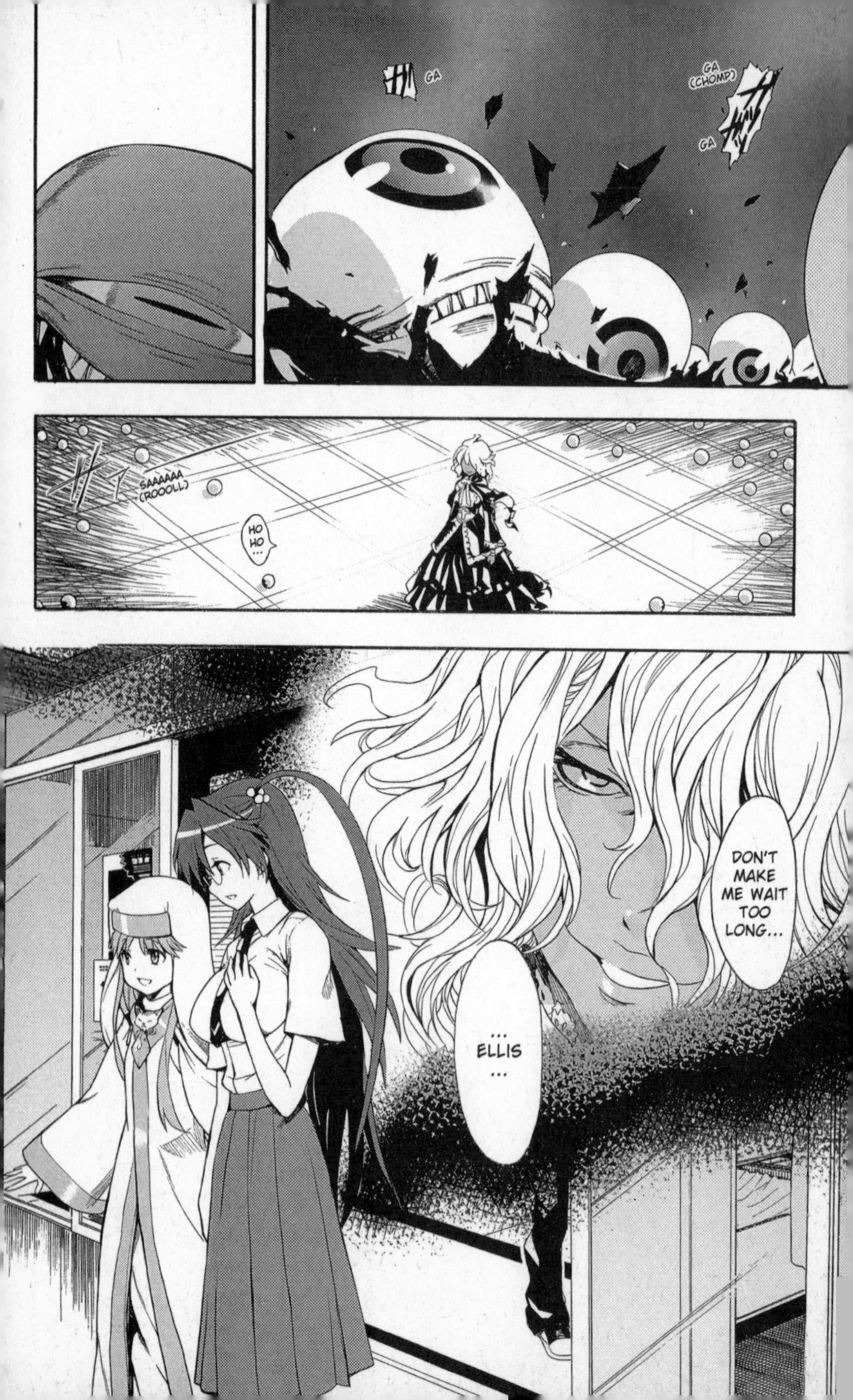
GA (CHOMP)
GA
GA
SAAAAAA (ROOOLL)
HO HO...
DON'T MAKE ME WAIT TOO LONG...
...ELLIS...

A
Certain
Magical
Index

SHE ALWAYS SEEMED SO
ADULTLIKE NEXT TO INDEX,
SO I TRIED SHRINKING HER
PROPORTIONS A BIT.

I THINK THIS IS GOOD...

KAZAKIRI

MILD MANNERED
AND MATURE, BUT HER
BLISTERING REMARKS ARE
SOMETHING I PERSONALLY
APPRECIATE. LIKE HOW SHE
CALLS INDEX "SUSPICIOUS"
AND SAYS THAT TOUMA'S
EYES ARE SCARY...

IT'S HARD TO BALANCE HER
OUT, AND FRANKLY, DIFFICULT
TO DRAW HER. I THINK SHE
MIGHT BE THE MOST
DIFFICULT CHARACTER
TO DRAW. (SORRY,
KANZAKI-NEECHIN.)

THE BIG MAN SEEMS TO LIKE
HER. HE SOUNDS SO SOFT AND
KIND WHEN HE TALKS ABOUT
HER (BREASTS)...

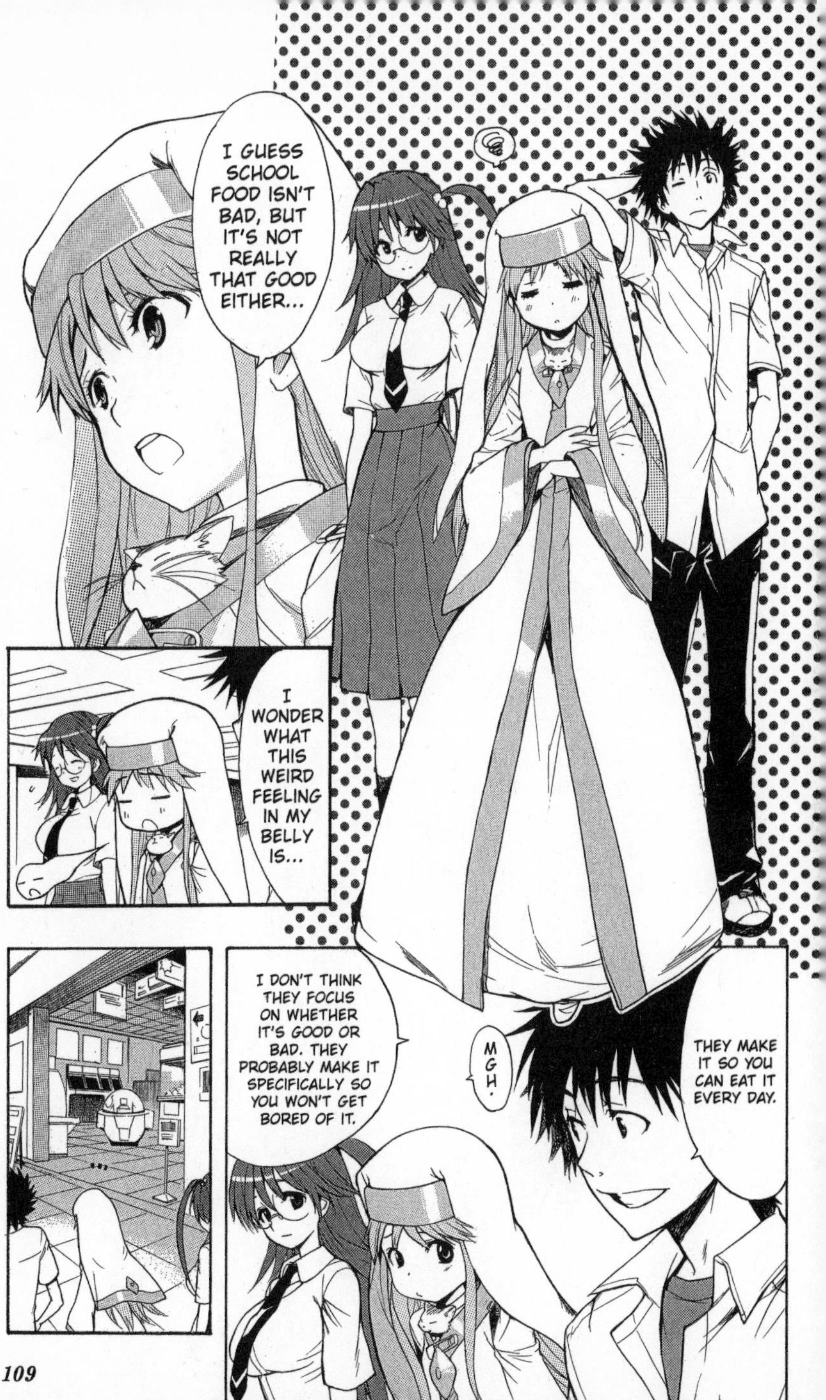
I GUESS SCHOOL FOOD ISN'T BAD, BUT IT'S NOT REALLY THAT GOOD EITHER...
I WONDER WHAT THIS WEIRD FEELING IN MY BELLY IS...
I DON'T THINK THEY FOCUS ON WHETHER IT'S GOOD OR BAD. THEY PROBABLY MAKE IT SPECIFICALLY SO YOU WON'T GET BORED OF IT.
MGH.
THEY MAKE IT SO YOU CAN EAT IT EVERY DAY.
...

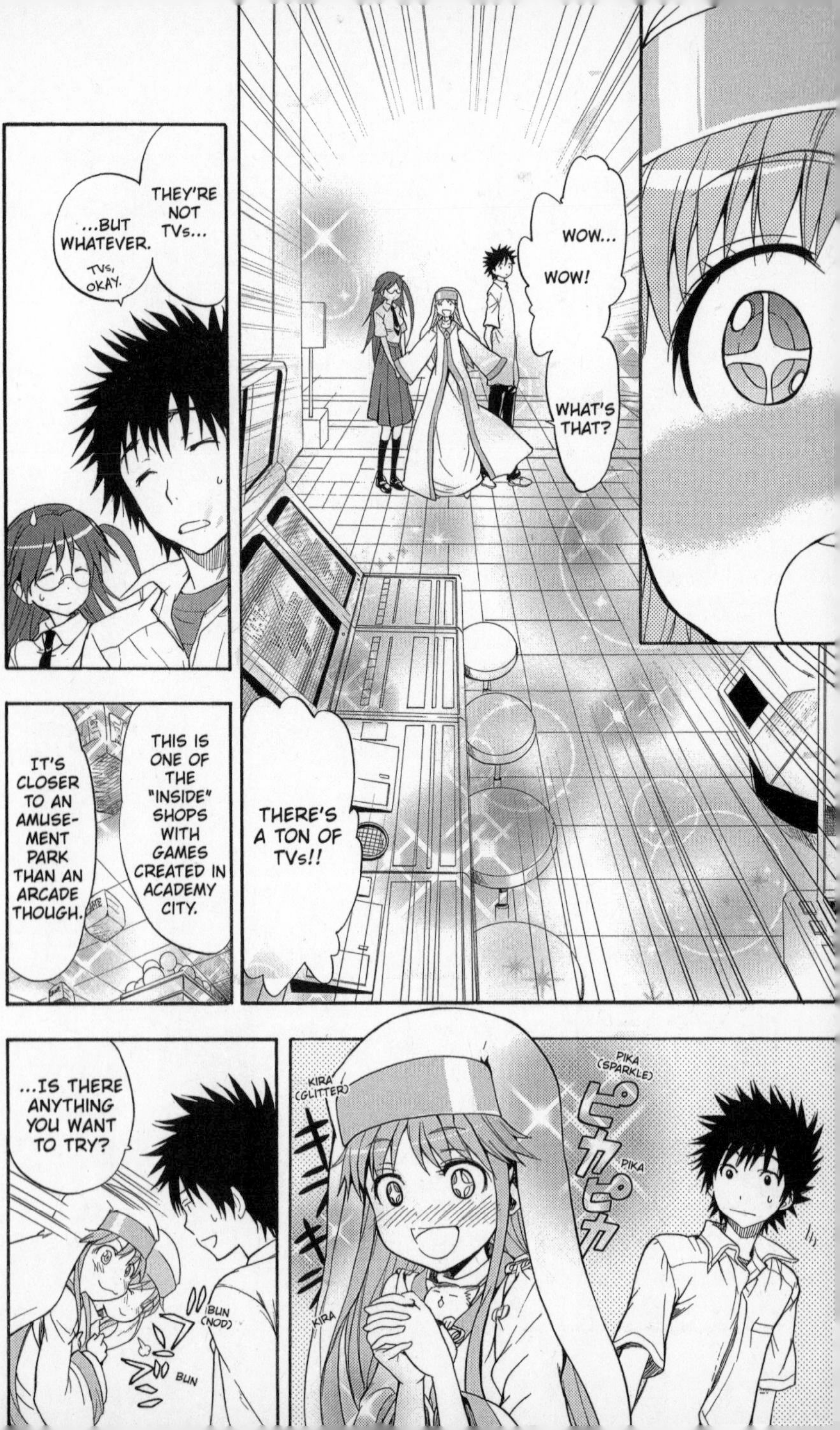
WOW...
WOW!
WHAT'S THAT?
THERE'S A TON OF TVs!!
THEY'RE NOT TVs...
...BUT WHATEVER.
TVs, OKAY.
THIS IS ONE OF THE "INSIDE" SHOPS WITH GAMES CREATED IN ACADEMY CITY.
IT'S CLOSER TO AN AMUSEMENT PARK THAN AN ARCADE THOUGH.
PIKA (SPARKLE)
PIKA
KIRA (GLITTER)
KIRA
...IS THERE ANYTHING YOU WANT TO TRY?
BUN (NOD)
BUN

#37 THE FUN SCHOOL LIFE

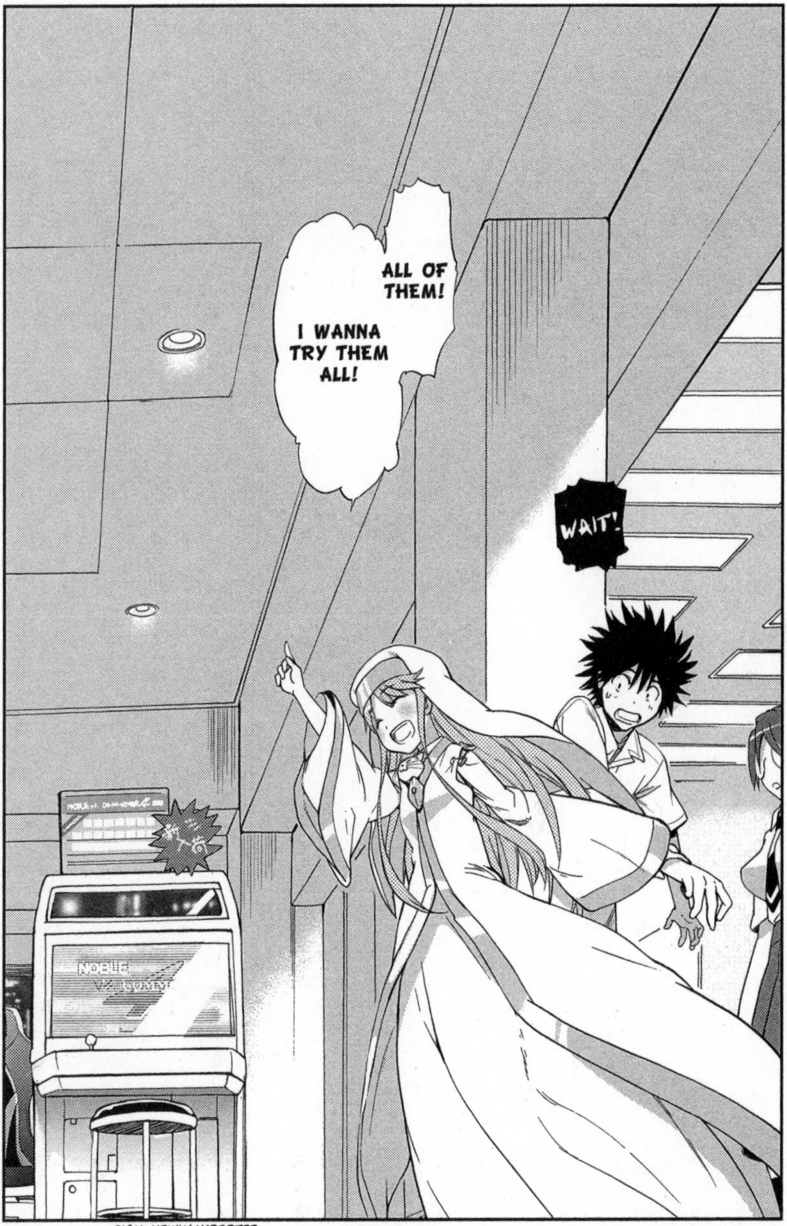
ALL OF THEM!
I WANNA TRY THEM ALL!
WAIT!

SIGN: NEWLY IMPORTED

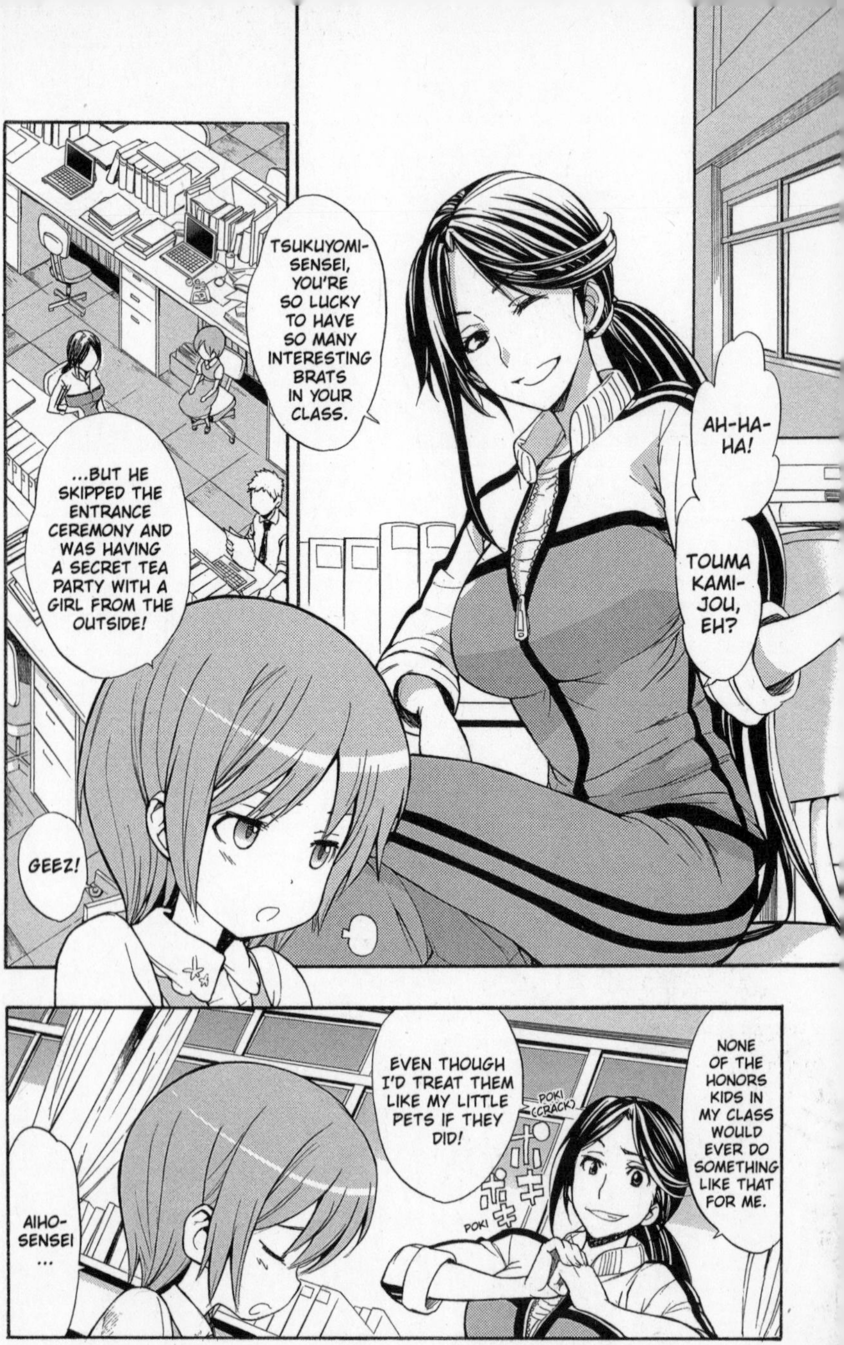
AH-HA-HA!
TOUMA KAMI-JOU, EH?
TSUKUYOMI-SENSEI, YOU'RE SO LUCKY TO HAVE SO MANY INTERESTING BRATS IN YOUR CLASS.
...BUT HE SKIPPED THE ENTRANCE CEREMONY AND WAS HAVING A SECRET TEA PARTY WITH A GIRL FROM THE OUTSIDE!
GEEZ!
NONE OF THE HONORS KIDS IN MY CLASS WOULD EVER DO SOMETHING LIKE THAT FOR ME.
POKI (CRACK)
EVEN THOUGH I'D TREAT THEM LIKE MY LITTLE PETS IF THEY DID!
POKI
AIHO-SENSEI ...

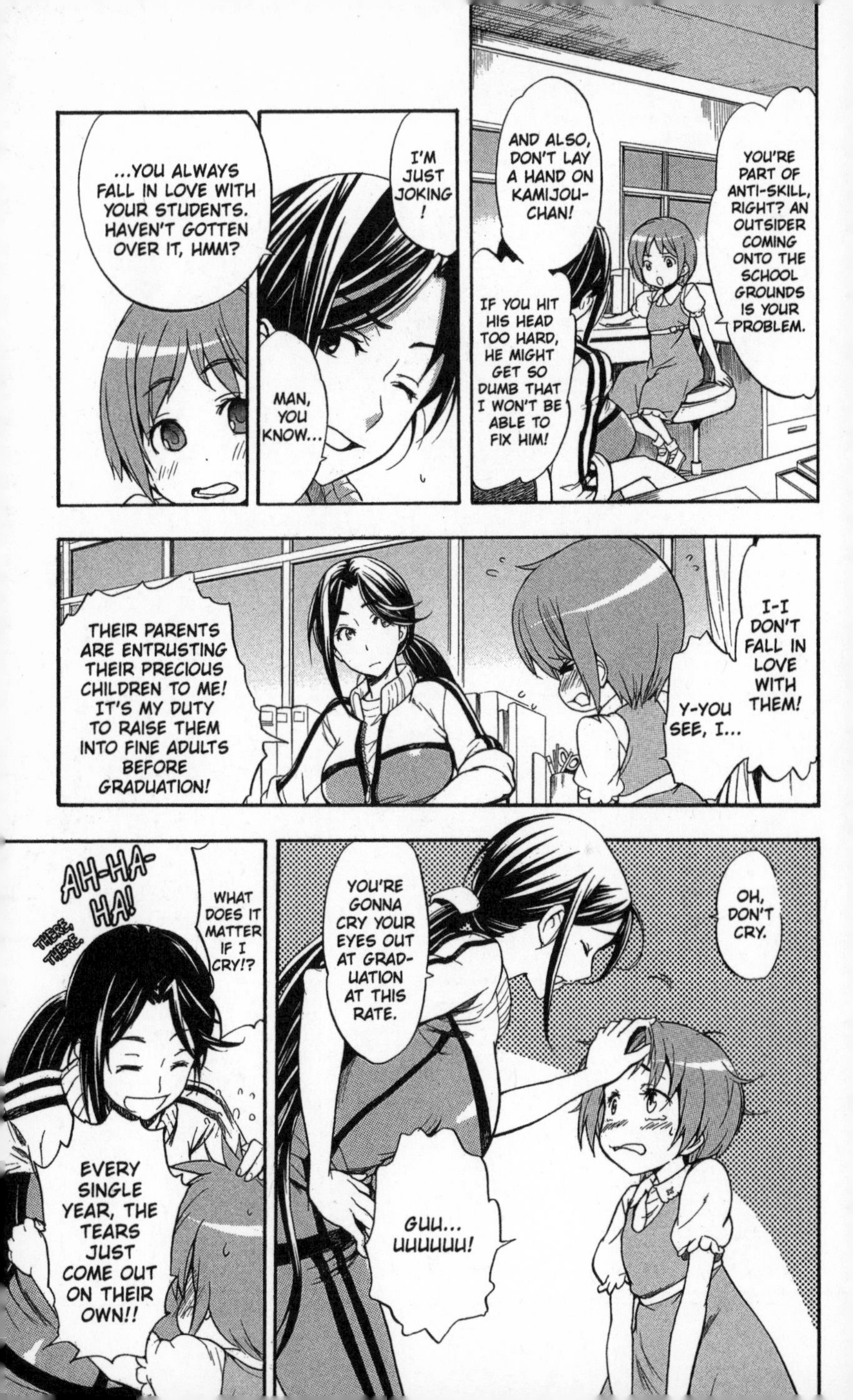
YOU'RE PART OF ANTI-SKILL, RIGHT? AN OUTSIDER COMING ONTO THE SCHOOL GROUNDS IS YOUR PROBLEM.
AND ALSO, DON'T LAY A HAND ON KAMIJOU-CHAN!
IF YOU HIT HIS HEAD TOO HARD, HE MIGHT GET SO DUMB THAT I WON'T BE ABLE TO FIX HIM!
I'M JUST JOKING!
MAN, YOU KNOW...
...YOU ALWAYS FALL IN LOVE WITH YOUR STUDENTS. HAVEN'T GOTTEN OVER IT, HMM?
I-I DON'T FALL IN LOVE WITH THEM!
Y-YOU SEE, I...
THEIR PARENTS ARE ENTRUSTING THEIR PRECIOUS CHILDREN TO ME! IT'S MY DUTY TO RAISE THEM INTO FINE ADULTS BEFORE GRADUATION!
OH, DON'T CRY.
YOU'RE GONNA CRY YOUR EYES OUT AT GRADUATION AT THIS RATE.
GUU... UUUUUU!
WHAT DOES IT MATTER IF I CRY!?
AH-HA-HA!
THERE, THERE.
EVERY SINGLE YEAR, THE TEARS JUST COME OUT ON THEIR OWN!!

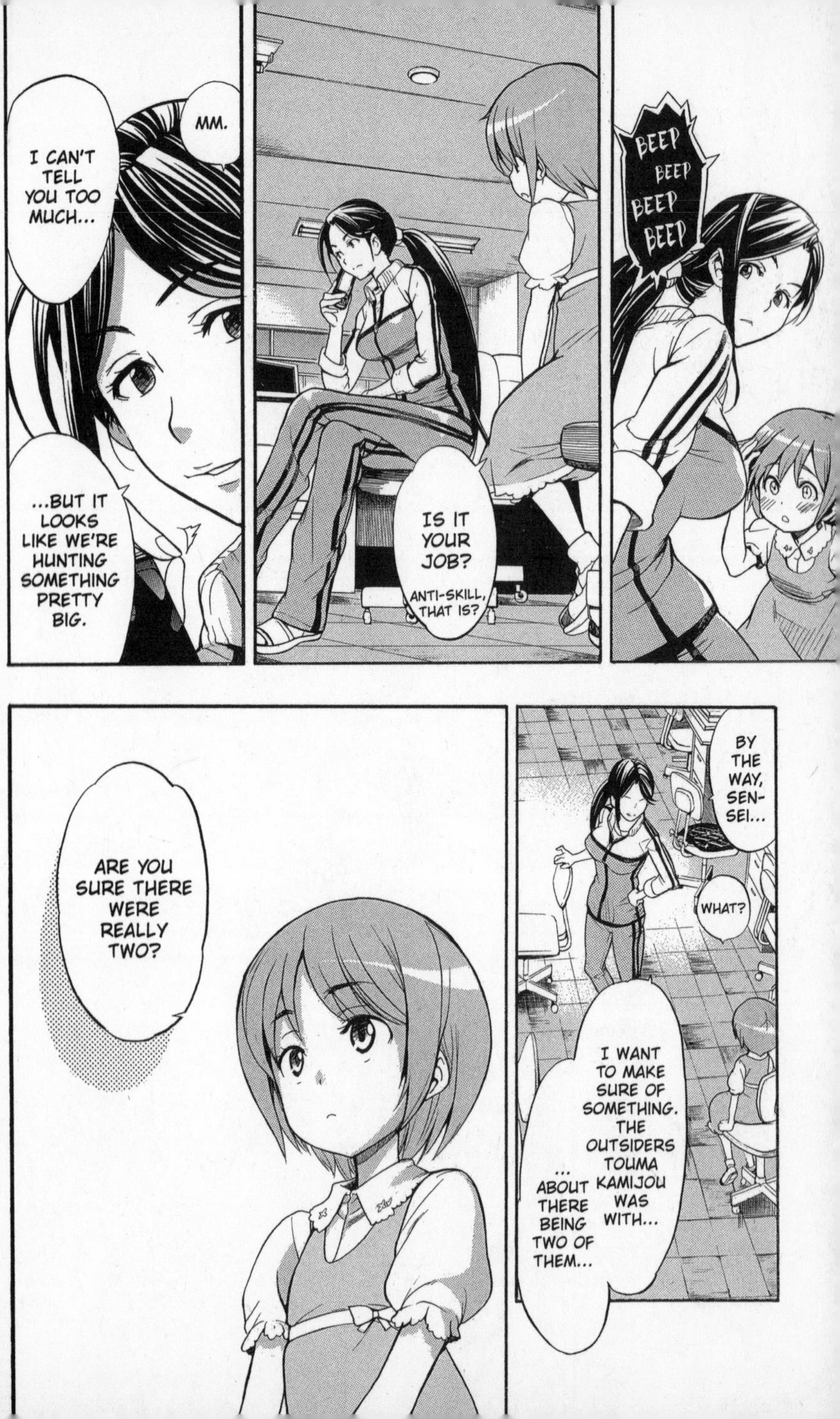
BEEP BEEP BEEP BEEP
IS IT YOUR JOB?
ANTI-SKILL, THAT IS?
MM.
I CAN'T TELL YOU TOO MUCH...
...BUT IT LOOKS LIKE WE'RE HUNTING SOMETHING PRETTY BIG.
BY THE WAY, SEN-SEI...
WHAT?
I WANT TO MAKE SURE OF SOMETHING. THE OUTSIDERS TOUMA KAMIJOU WAS WITH...
...ABOUT THERE BEING TWO OF THEM...
ARE YOU SURE THERE WERE REALLY TWO?

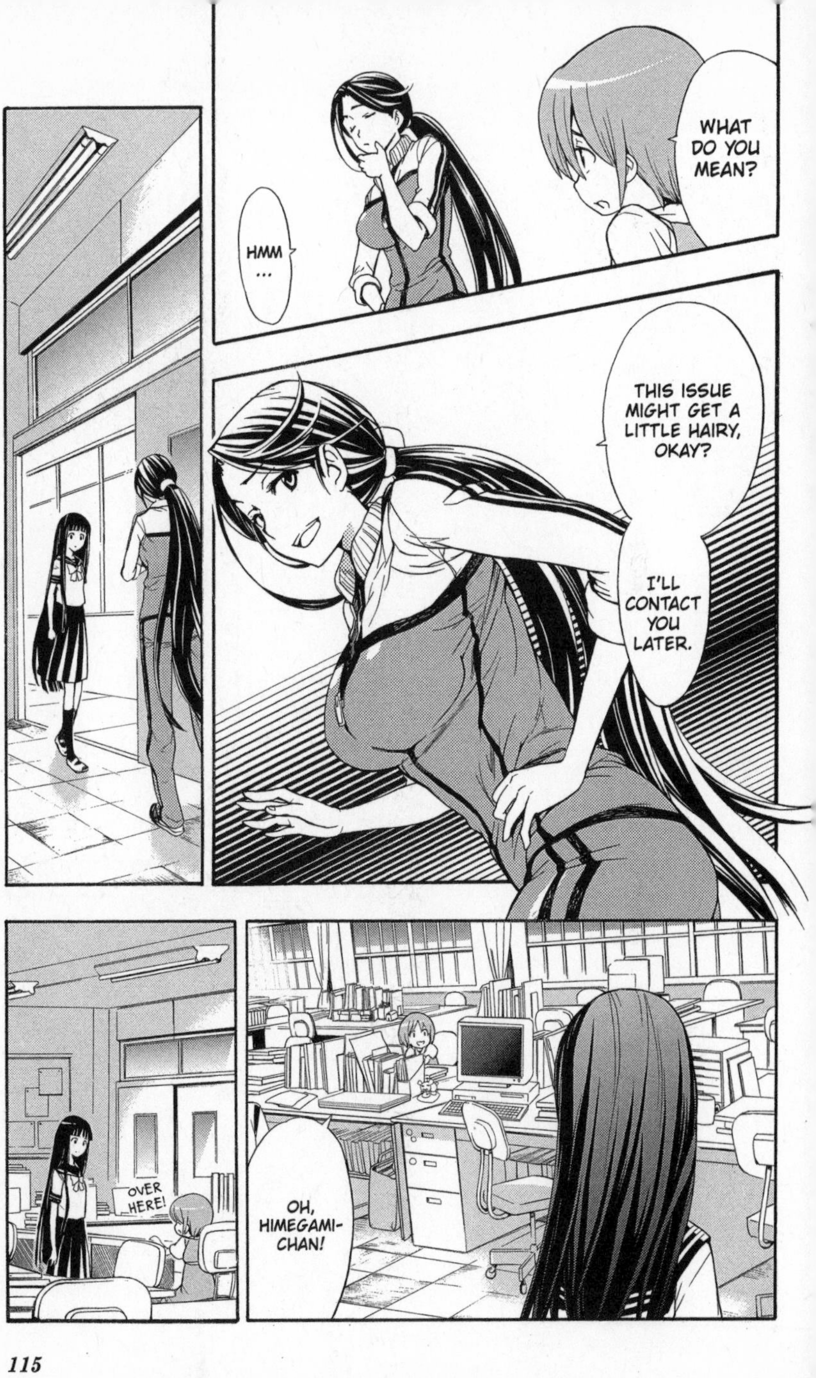
WHAT DO YOU MEAN?
HMM ...
THIS ISSUE MIGHT GET A LITTLE HAIRY, OKAY?
I'LL CONTACT YOU LATER.
OH, HIMEGAMI-CHAN!
OVER HERE!

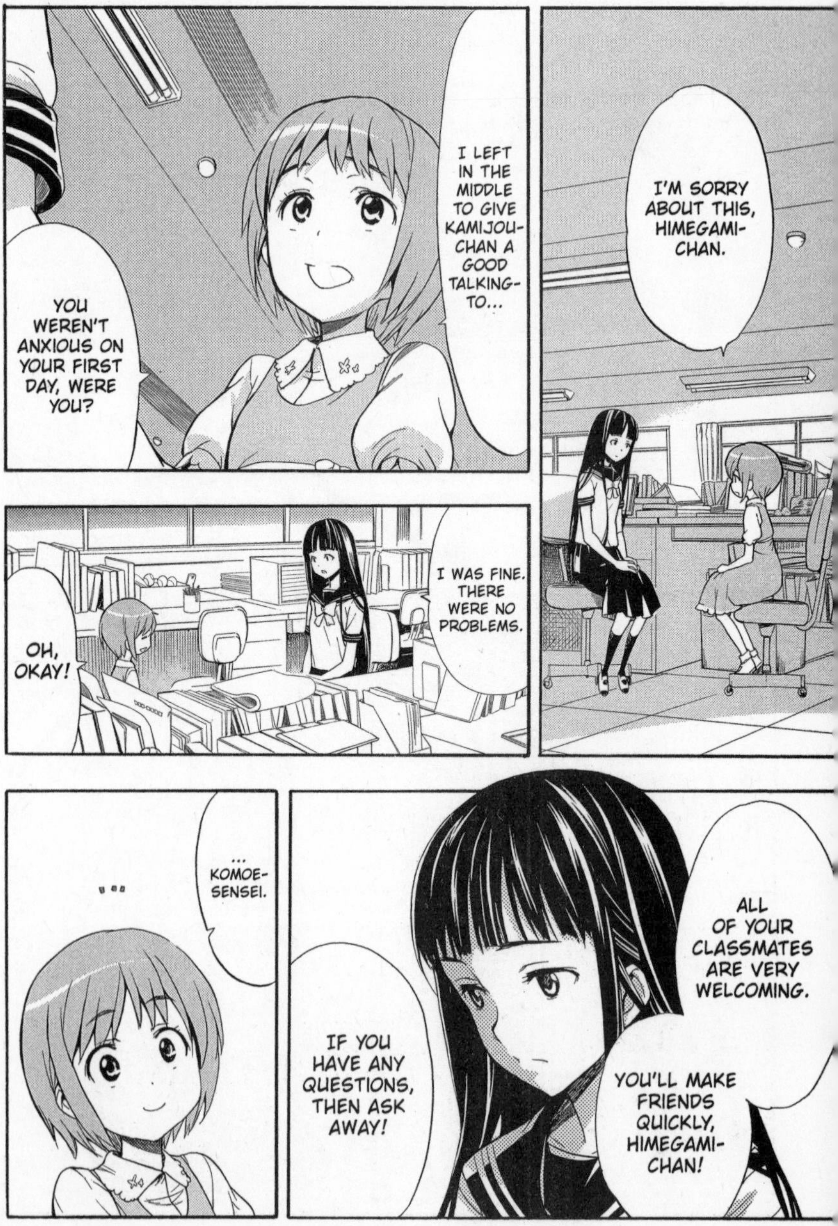
I'M SORRY ABOUT THIS, HIMEGAMI-CHAN.
I LEFT IN THE MIDDLE TO GIVE KAMIJOU-CHAN A GOOD TALKING-TO...
YOU WEREN'T ANXIOUS ON YOUR FIRST DAY, WERE YOU?
I WAS FINE. THERE WERE NO PROBLEMS.
OH, OKAY!
ALL OF YOUR CLASSMATES ARE VERY WELCOMING.
YOU'LL MAKE FRIENDS QUICKLY, HIMEGAMI-CHAN!
IF YOU HAVE ANY QUESTIONS, THEN ASK AWAY!
... KOMOE-SENSEI.
...

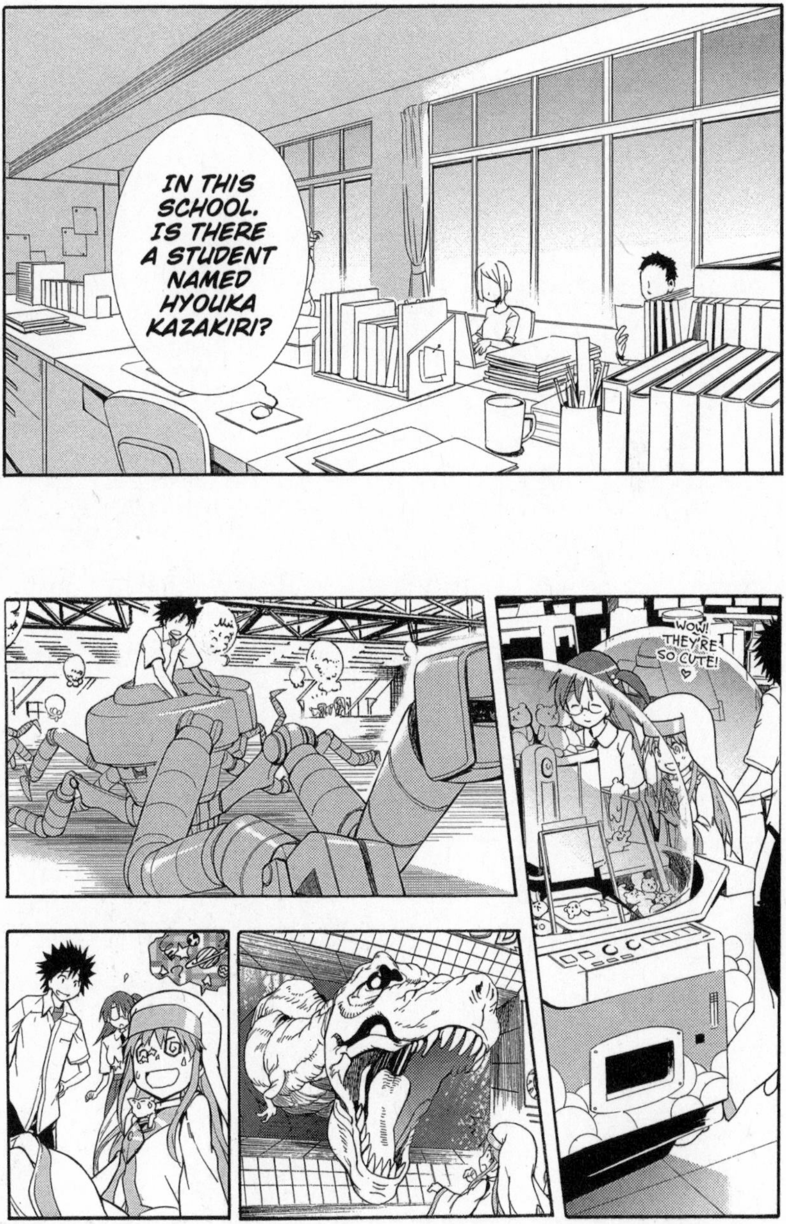
IN THIS SCHOOL. IS THERE A STUDENT NAMED HYOUKA KAZAKIRI?
WOW! THEY'RE SO CUTE!

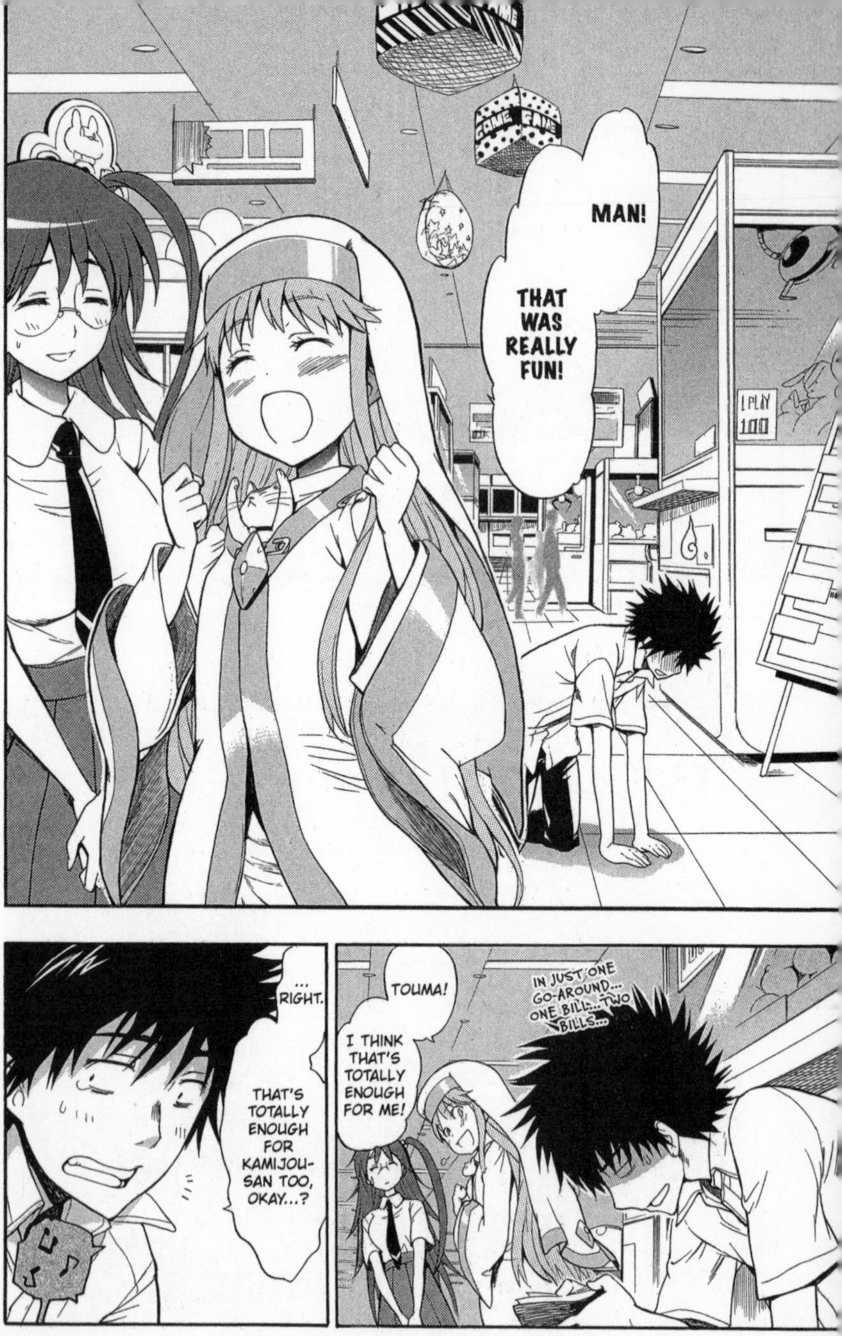
MAN!
THAT WAS REALLY FUN!
1 PLAY 100
IN JUST ONE GO-AROUND... ONE BILL... TWO BILLS...
TOUMA!
I THINK THAT'S TOTALLY ENOUGH FOR ME!
... RIGHT.
THAT'S TOTALLY ENOUGH FOR KAMIJOU-SAN TOO, OKAY...?

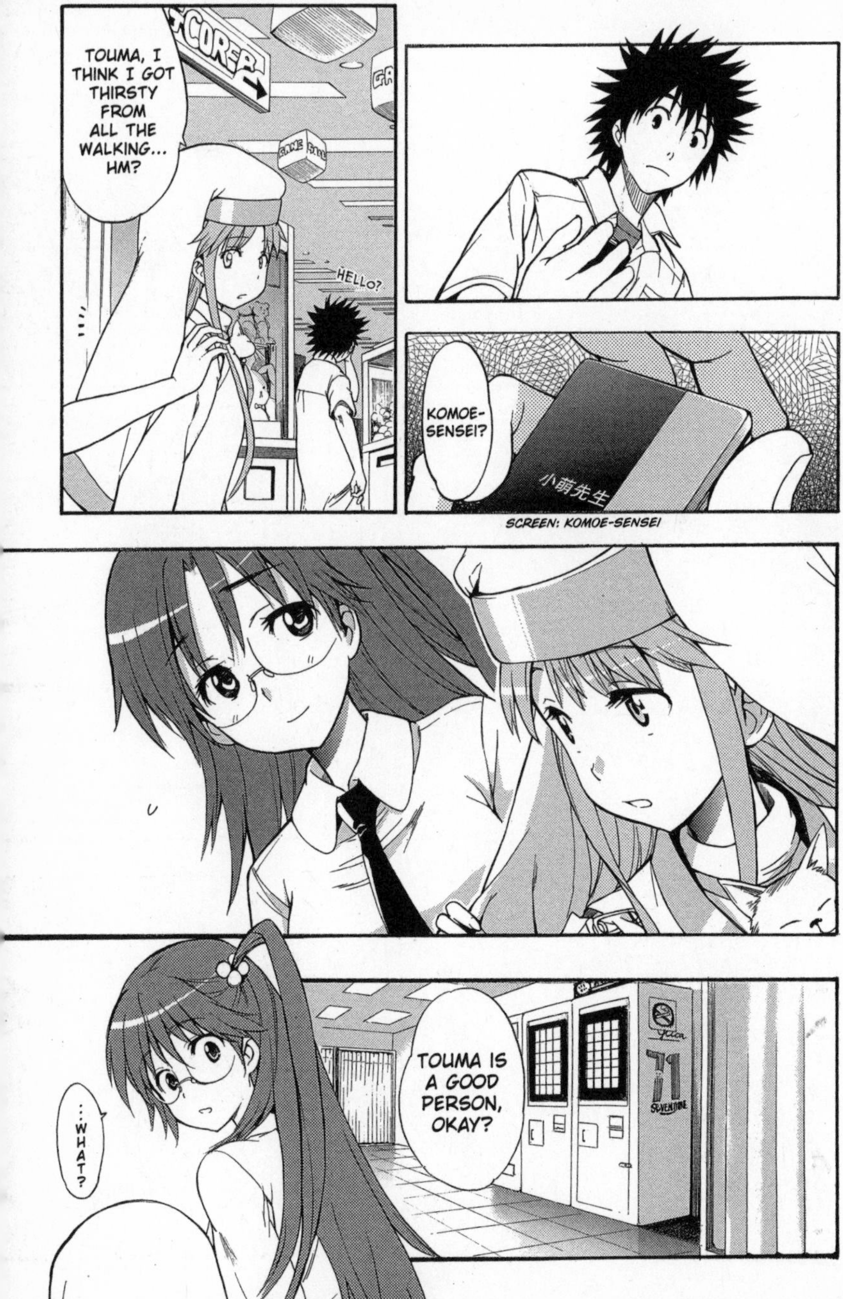
KOMOE-SENSEI?
小萌先生
SCREEN: KOMOE-SENSEI
TOUMA, I THINK I GOT THIRSTY FROM ALL THE WALKING... HM?
HELLO?
TOUMA IS A GOOD PERSON, OKAY?
...WHAT?

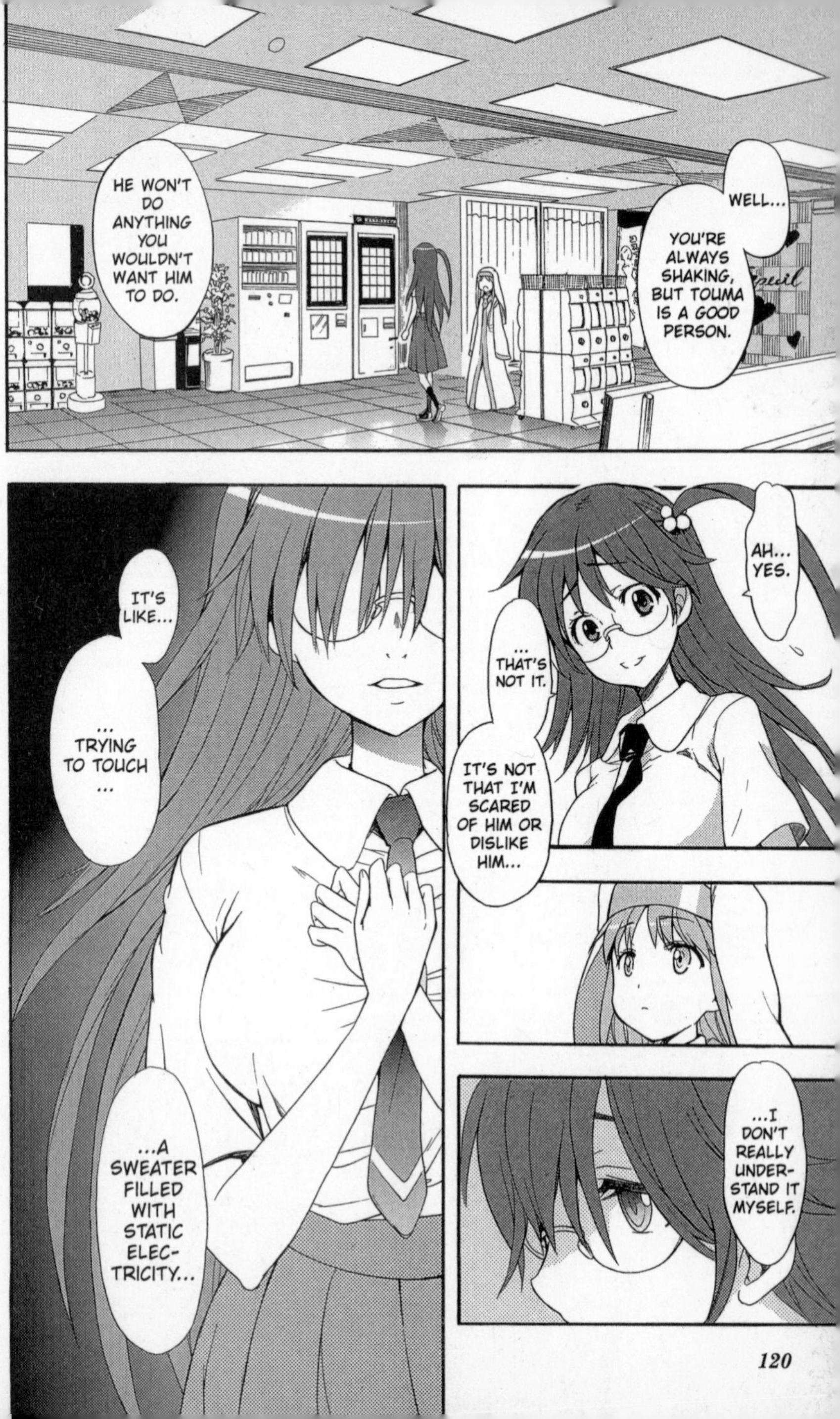
WELL...
YOU'RE ALWAYS SHAKING, BUT TOUMA IS A GOOD PERSON.
HE WON'T DO ANYTHING YOU WOULDN'T WANT HIM TO DO.
AH... YES.
...THAT'S NOT IT.
IT'S NOT THAT I'M SCARED OF HIM OR DISLIKE HIM...
...I DON'T REALLY UNDERSTAND IT MYSELF.
IT'S LIKE...
...TRYING TO TOUCH...
...A SWEATER FILLED WITH STATIC ELECTRICITY...

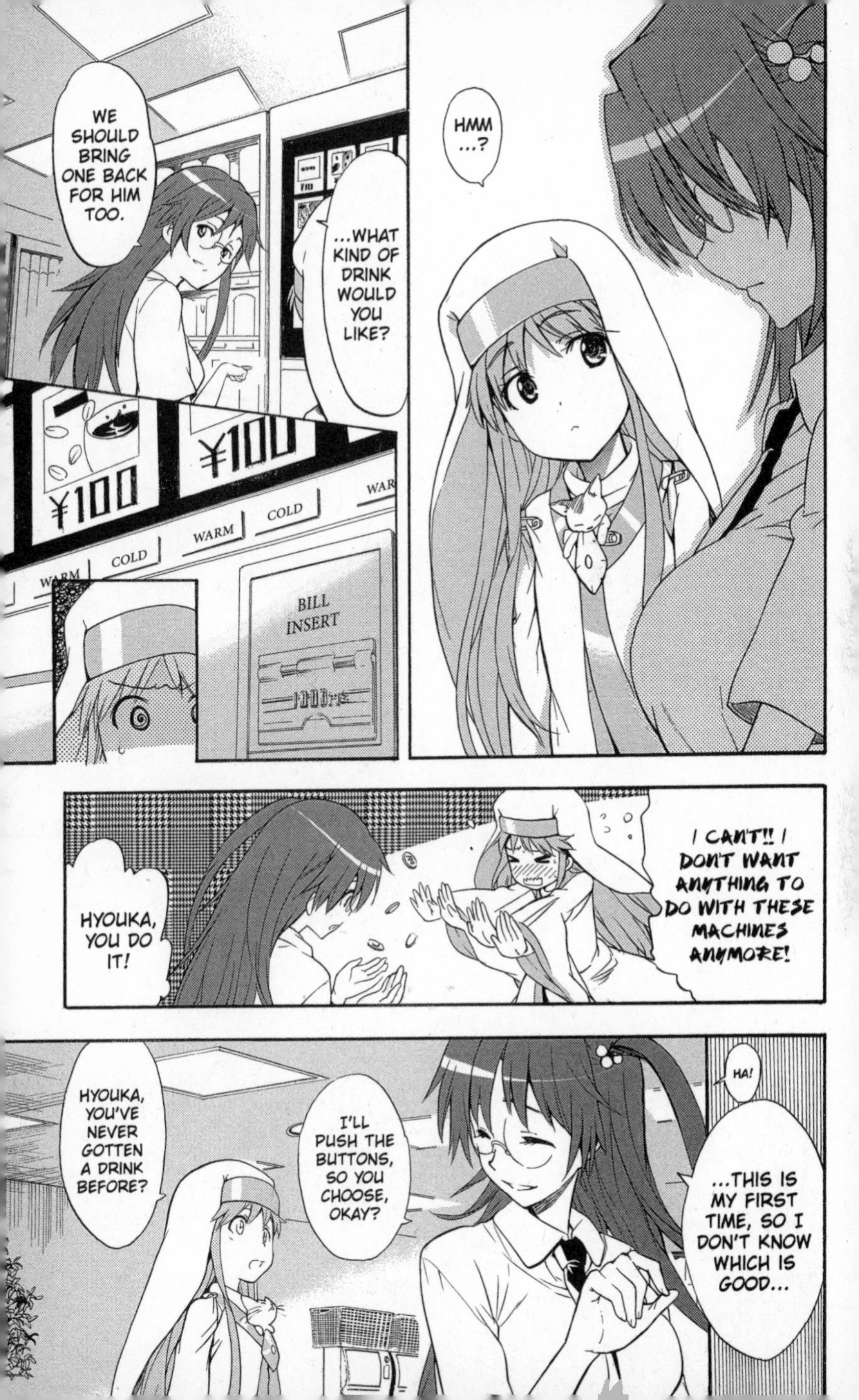
HMM ...?
...WHAT KIND OF DRINK WOULD YOU LIKE?
WE SHOULD BRING ONE BACK FOR HIM TOO.
¥100
¥100
WARM
COLD
WARM
COLD
WARM
BILL INSERT
I CAN'T!! I DON'T WANT ANYTHING TO DO WITH THESE MACHINES ANYMORE!
HYOUKA, YOU DO IT!
HA!
...THIS IS MY FIRST TIME, SO I DON'T KNOW WHICH IS GOOD...
I'LL PUSH THE BUTTONS, SO YOU CHOOSE, OKAY?
HYOUKA, YOU'VE NEVER GOTTEN A DRINK BEFORE?

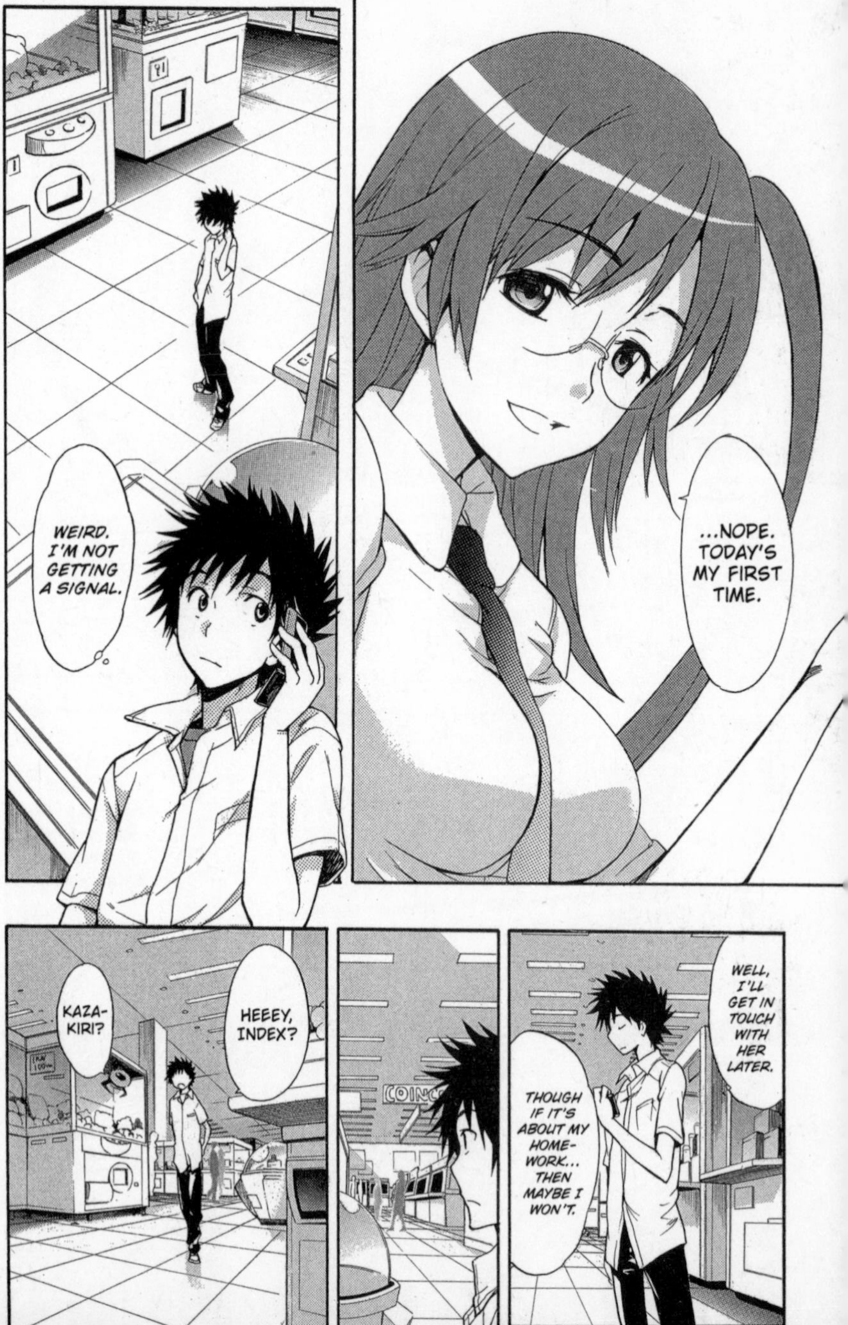
...NOPE. TODAY'S MY FIRST TIME.
WEIRD. I'M NOT GETTING A SIGNAL.
WELL, I'LL GET IN TOUCH WITH HER LATER.
THOUGH IF IT'S ABOUT MY HOME-WORK... THEN MAYBE I WON'T.
HEEEY, INDEX?
KAZA-KIRI?

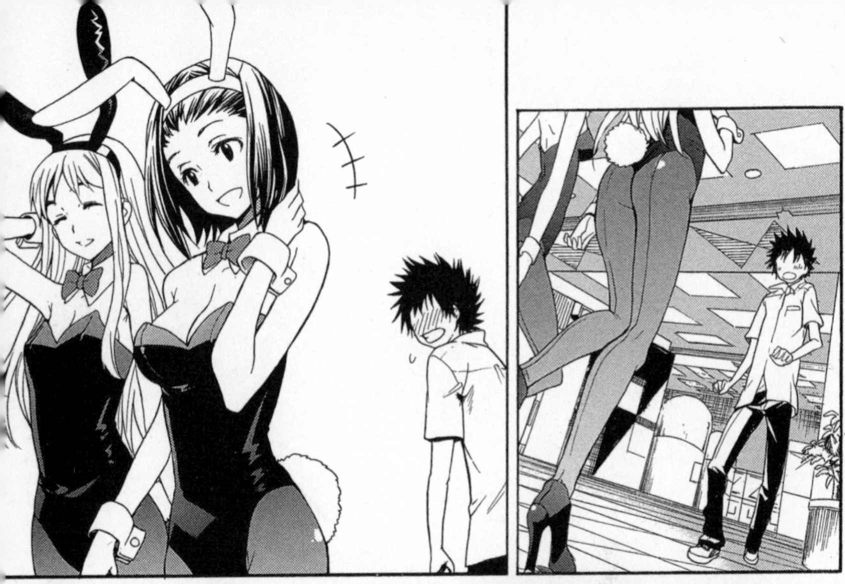

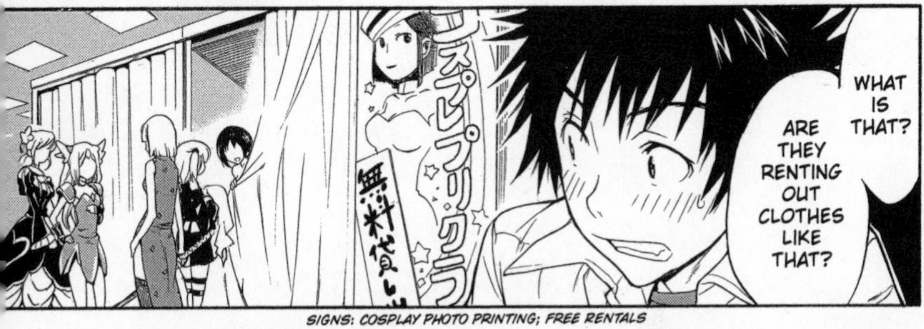
WHAT IS THAT?
ARE THEY RENTING OUT CLOTHES LIKE THAT?

SIGNS: COSPLAY PHOTO PRINTING; FREE RENTALS

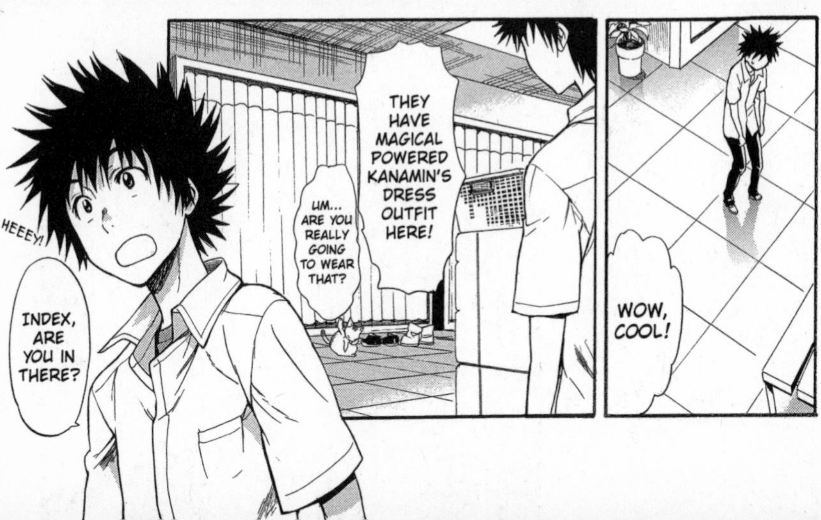
WOW, COOL!
THEY HAVE MAGICAL POWERED KANAMIN'S DRESS OUTFIT HERE!
UM... ARE YOU REALLY GOING TO WEAR THAT?
HEEEY!
INDEX, ARE YOU IN THERE?

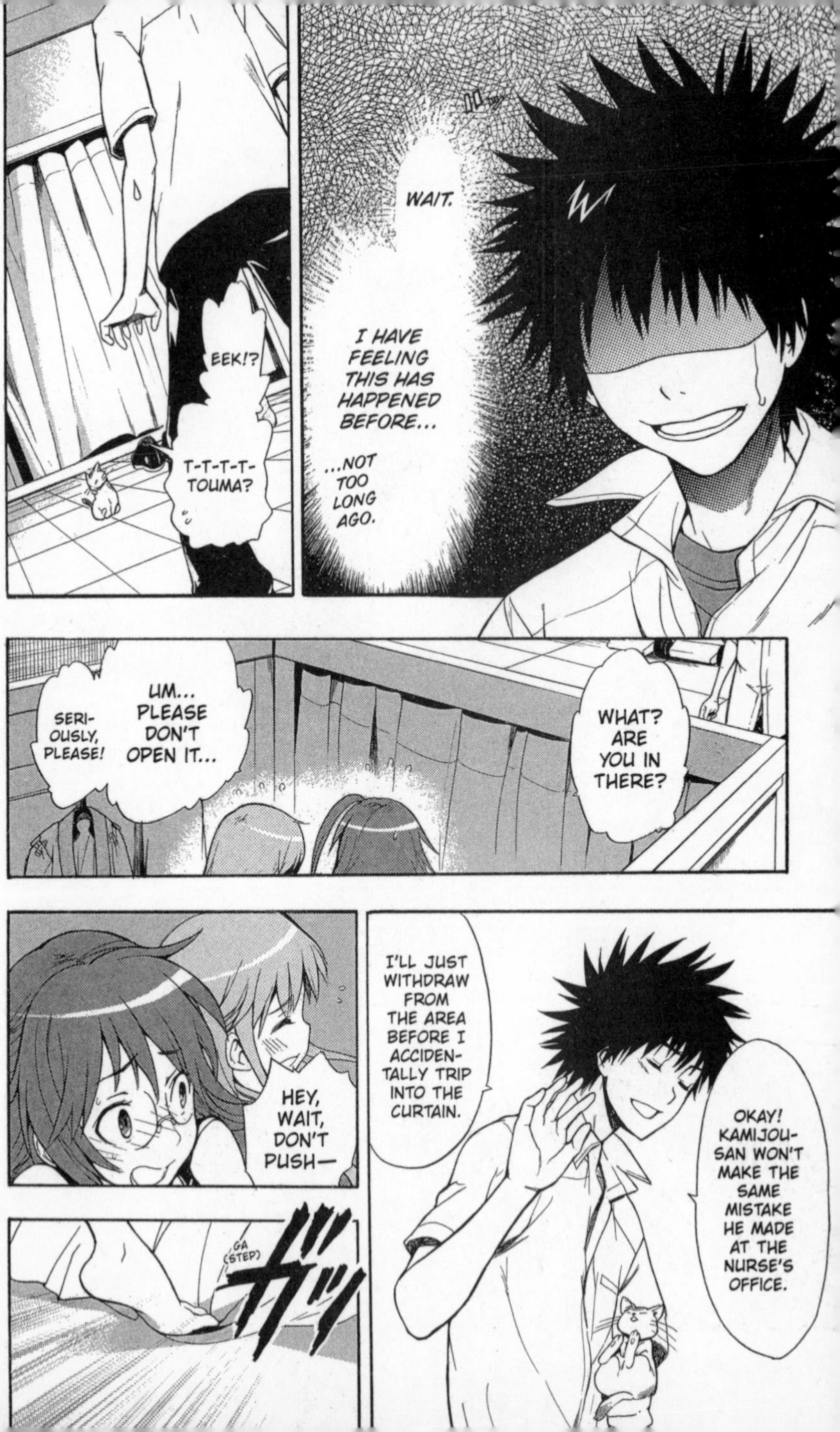
WAIT.
I HAVE FEELING THIS HAS HAPPENED BEFORE...
...NOT TOO LONG AGO.
EEK!?
T-T-T-T-TOUMA?
WHAT? ARE YOU IN THERE?
UM... PLEASE DON'T OPEN IT...
SERI-OUSLY, PLEASE!
I'LL JUST WITHDRAW FROM THE AREA BEFORE I ACCIDEN-TALLY TRIP INTO THE CURTAIN.
OKAY! KAMIJOU-SAN WON'T MAKE THE SAME MISTAKE HE MADE AT THE NURSE'S OFFICE.
HEY, WAIT, DON'T PUSH—
GA (STEP)

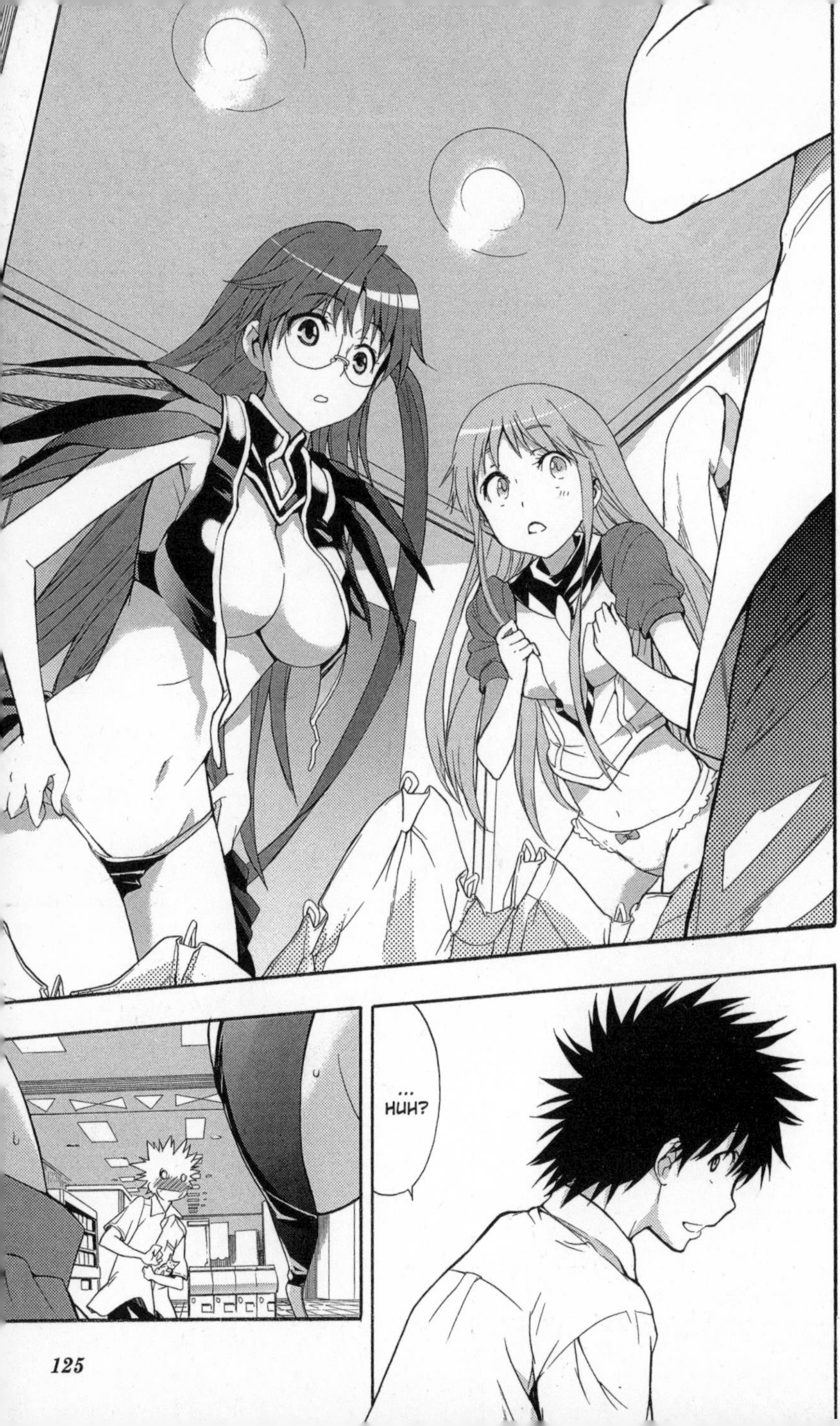
... HUH?

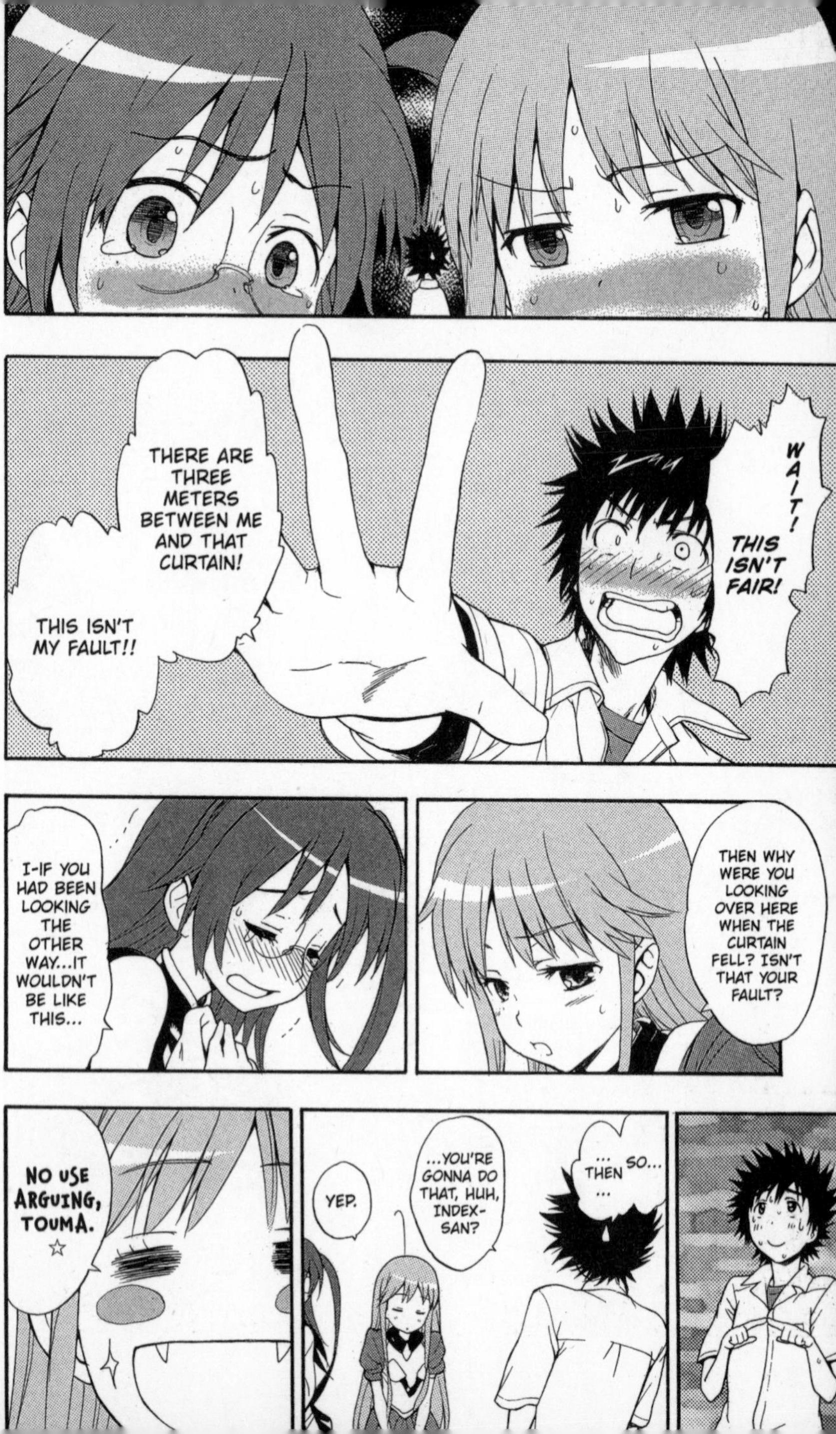
WAIT! THIS ISN'T FAIR!
THERE ARE THREE METERS BETWEEN ME AND THAT CURTAIN!
THIS ISN'T MY FAULT!!
THEN WHY WERE YOU LOOKING OVER HERE WHEN THE CURTAIN FELL? ISN'T THAT YOUR FAULT?
I-IF YOU HAD BEEN LOOKING THE OTHER WAY...IT WOULDN'T BE LIKE THIS...
SO...
... THEN ...
...YOU'RE GONNA DO THAT, HUH, INDEX-SAN?
YEP.
NO USE ARGUING, TOUMA. ☆

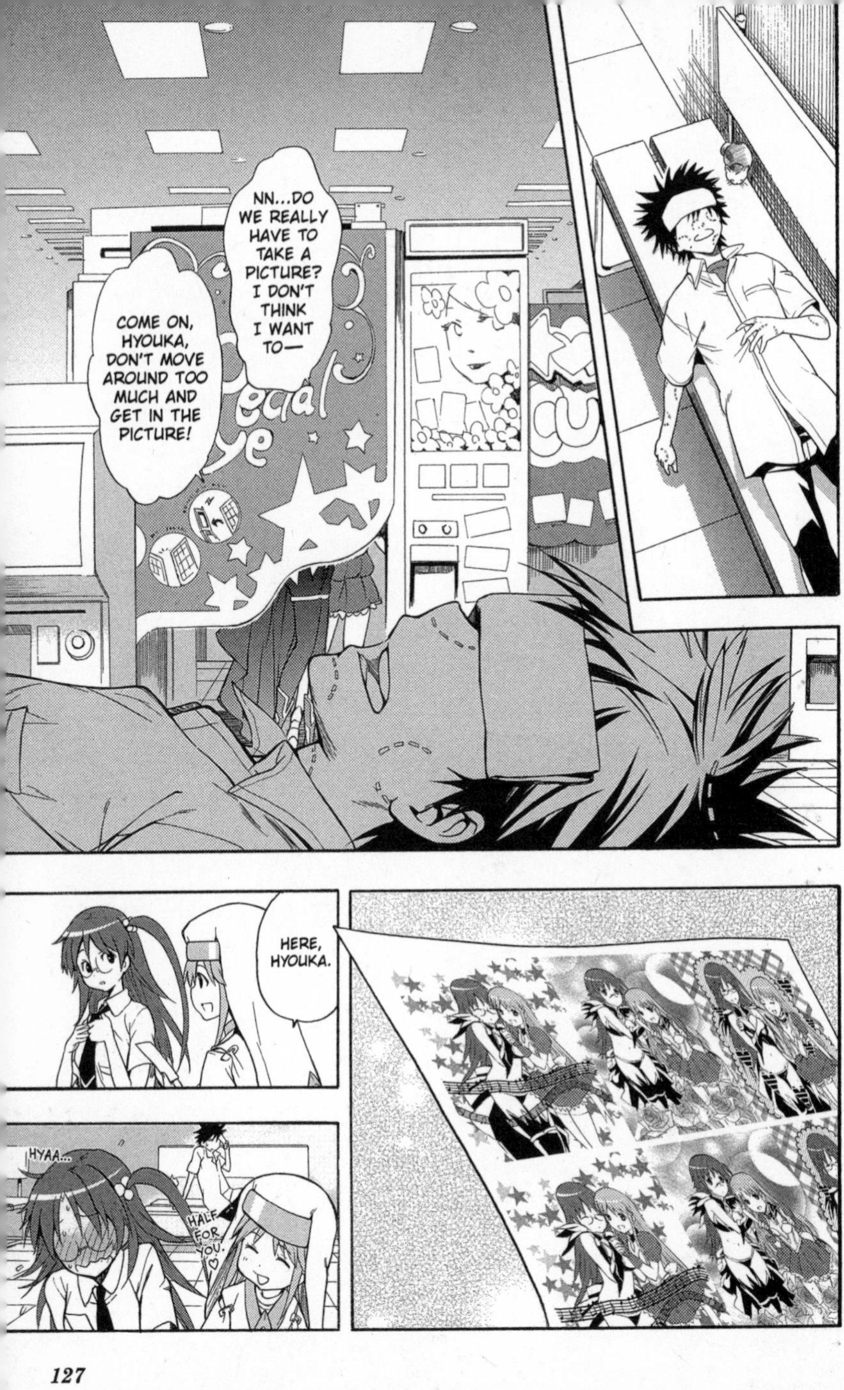
NN...DO WE REALLY HAVE TO TAKE A PICTURE? I DON'T THINK I WANT TO—
COME ON, HYOUKA, DON'T MOVE AROUND TOO MUCH AND GET IN THE PICTURE!
HERE, HYOUKA.
HALF FOR YOU. ♡
HYAA...

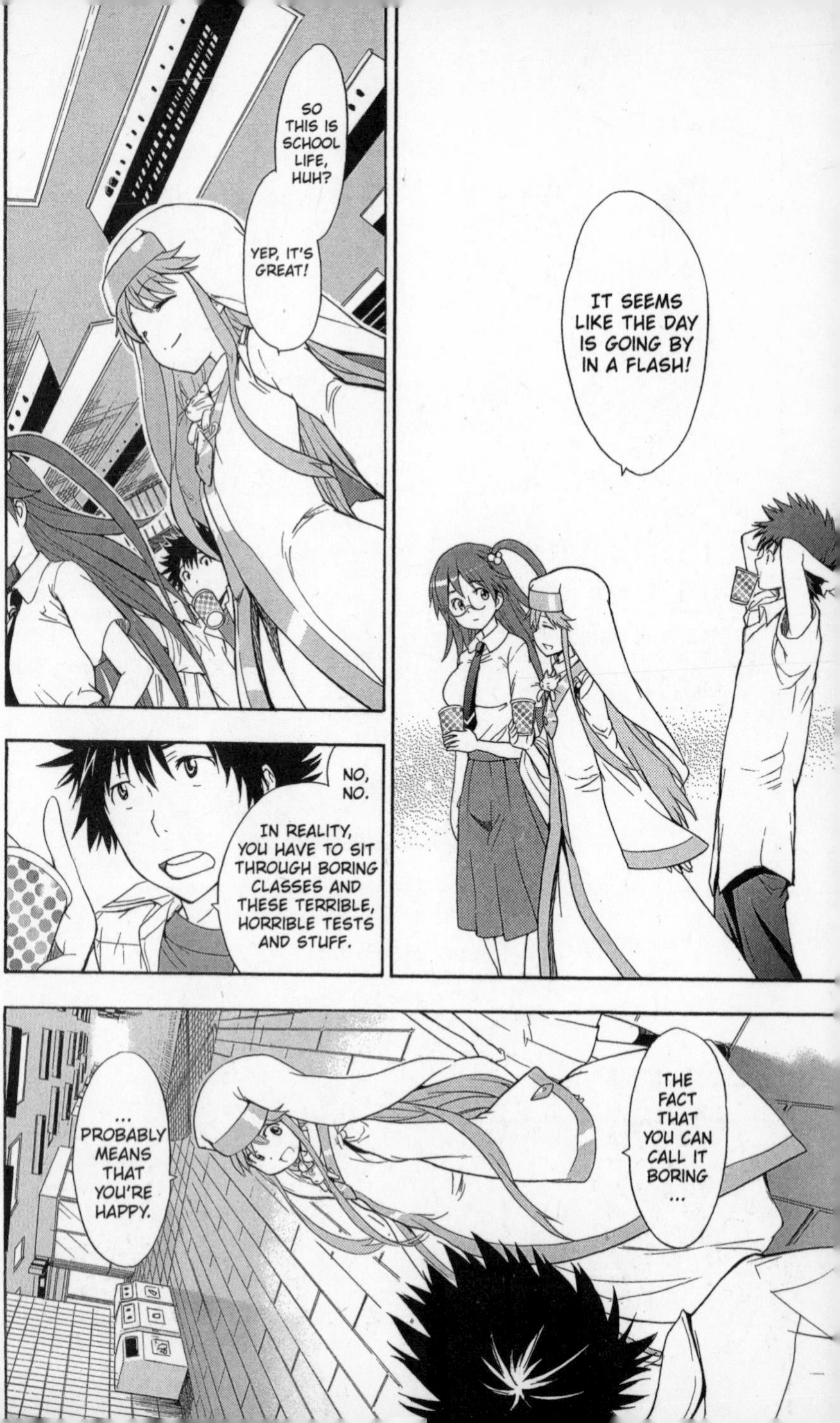
IT SEEMS LIKE THE DAY IS GOING BY IN A FLASH!
SO THIS IS SCHOOL LIFE, HUH?
YEP, IT'S GREAT!
NO, NO.
IN REALITY, YOU HAVE TO SIT THROUGH BORING CLASSES AND THESE TERRIBLE, HORRIBLE TESTS AND STUFF.
THE FACT THAT YOU CAN CALL IT BORING...
...PROBABLY MEANS THAT YOU'RE HAPPY.

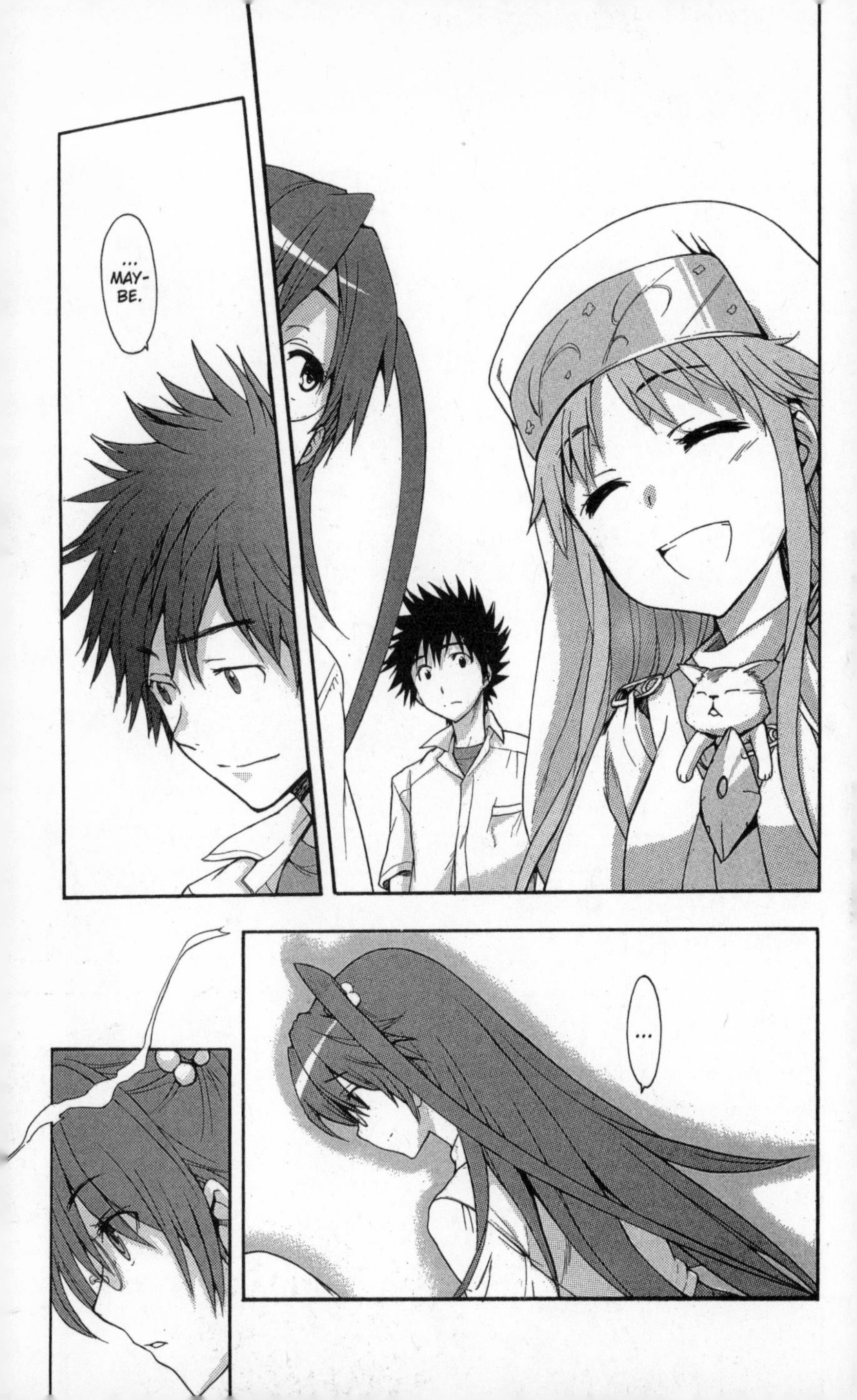

... MAY-BE.
...

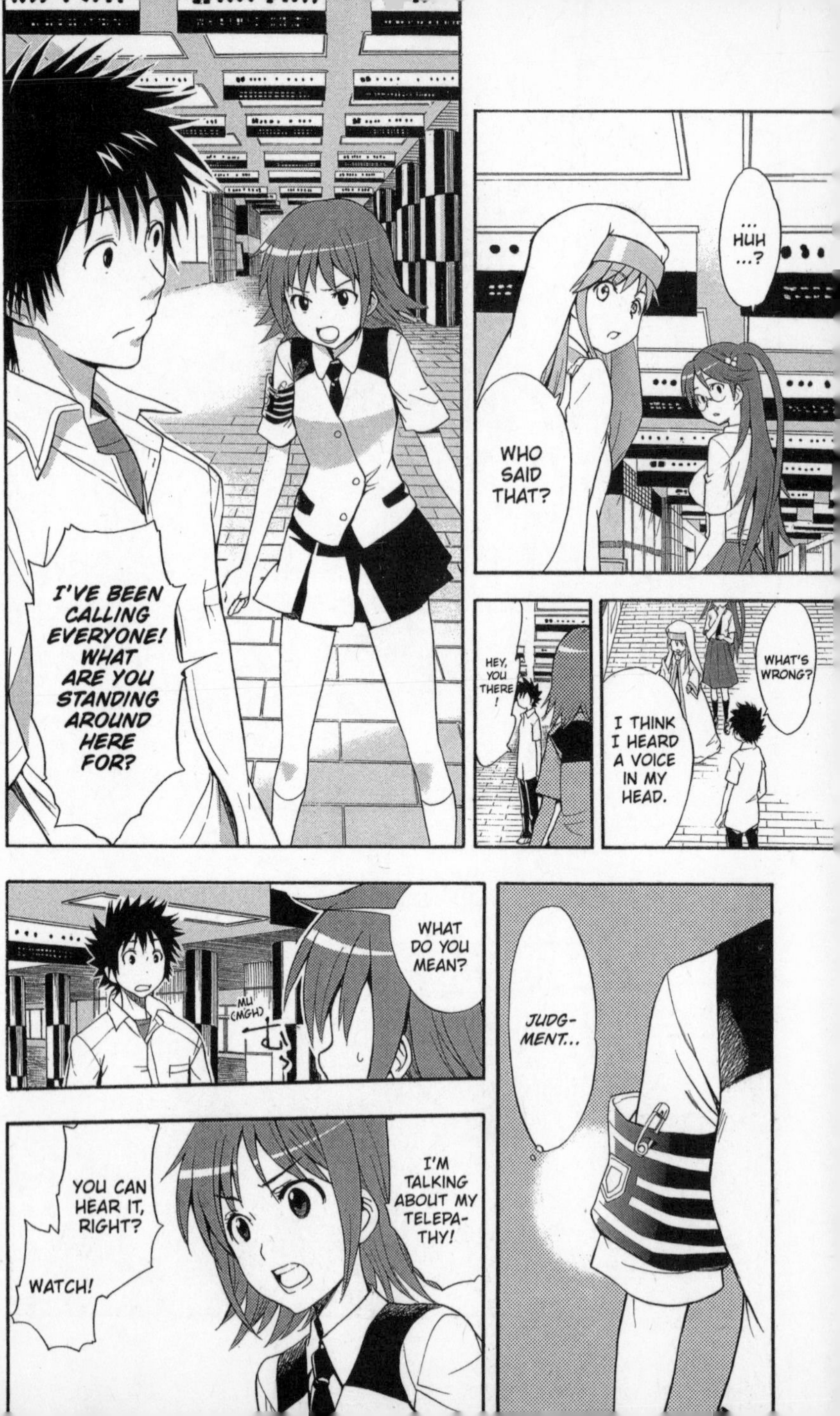
...HUH ...?
WHO SAID THAT?
WHAT'S WRONG?
I THINK I HEARD A VOICE IN MY HEAD.
HEY, YOU THERE!
I'VE BEEN CALLING EVERYONE! WHAT ARE YOU STANDING AROUND HERE FOR?
JUDG-MENT...
WHAT DO YOU MEAN?
MU (MGH)
I'M TALKING ABOUT MY TELEPA-THY!
YOU CAN HEAR IT, RIGHT?
WATCH!

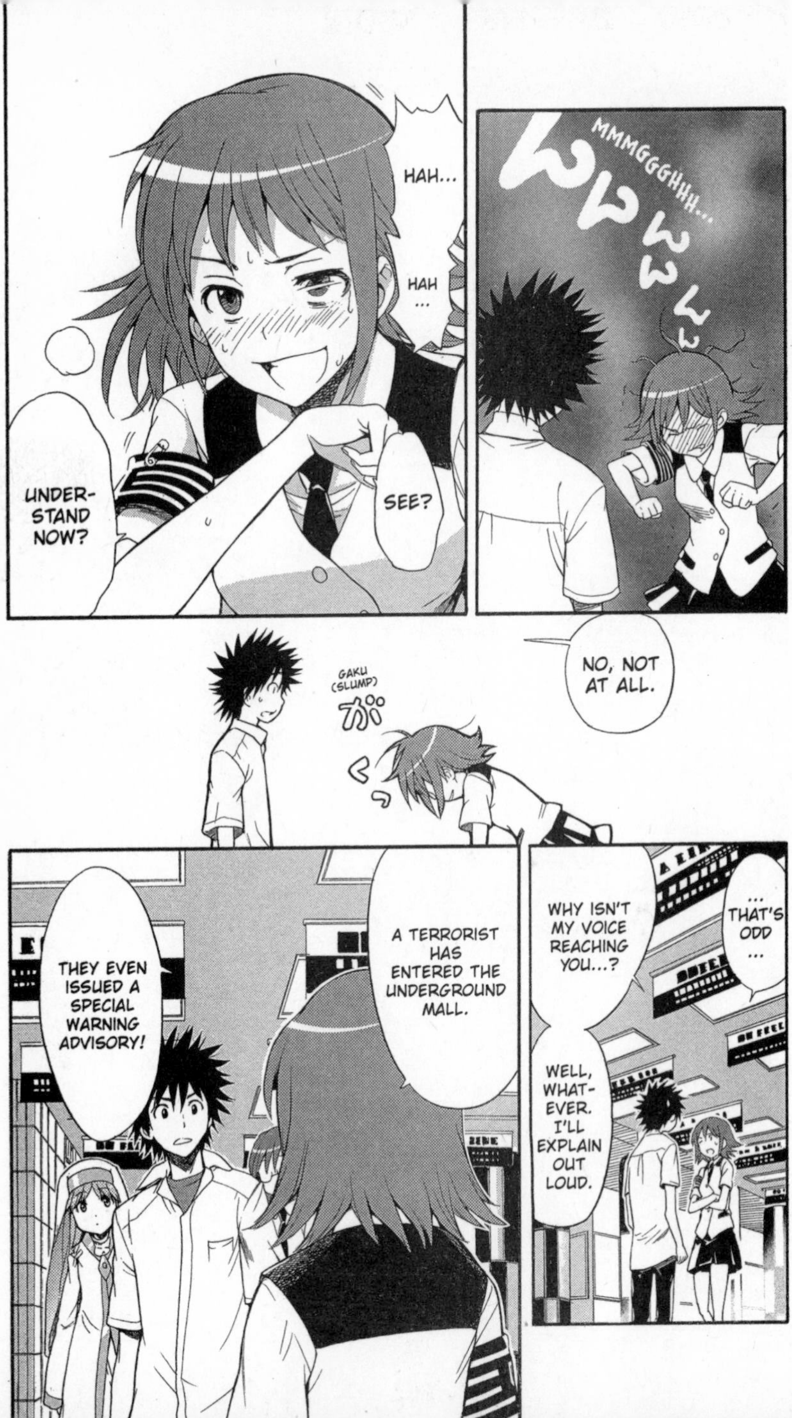
MMMGGGHHH...
HAH...
HAH ...
SEE?
UNDER-STAND NOW?
NO, NOT AT ALL.
GAKU (SLUMP)
が
... THAT'S ODD ...
WHY ISN'T MY VOICE REACHING YOU...?
WELL, WHAT-EVER. I'LL EXPLAIN OUT LOUD.
A TERRORIST HAS ENTERED THE UNDERGROUND MALL.
THEY EVEN ISSUED A SPECIAL WARNING ADVISORY!

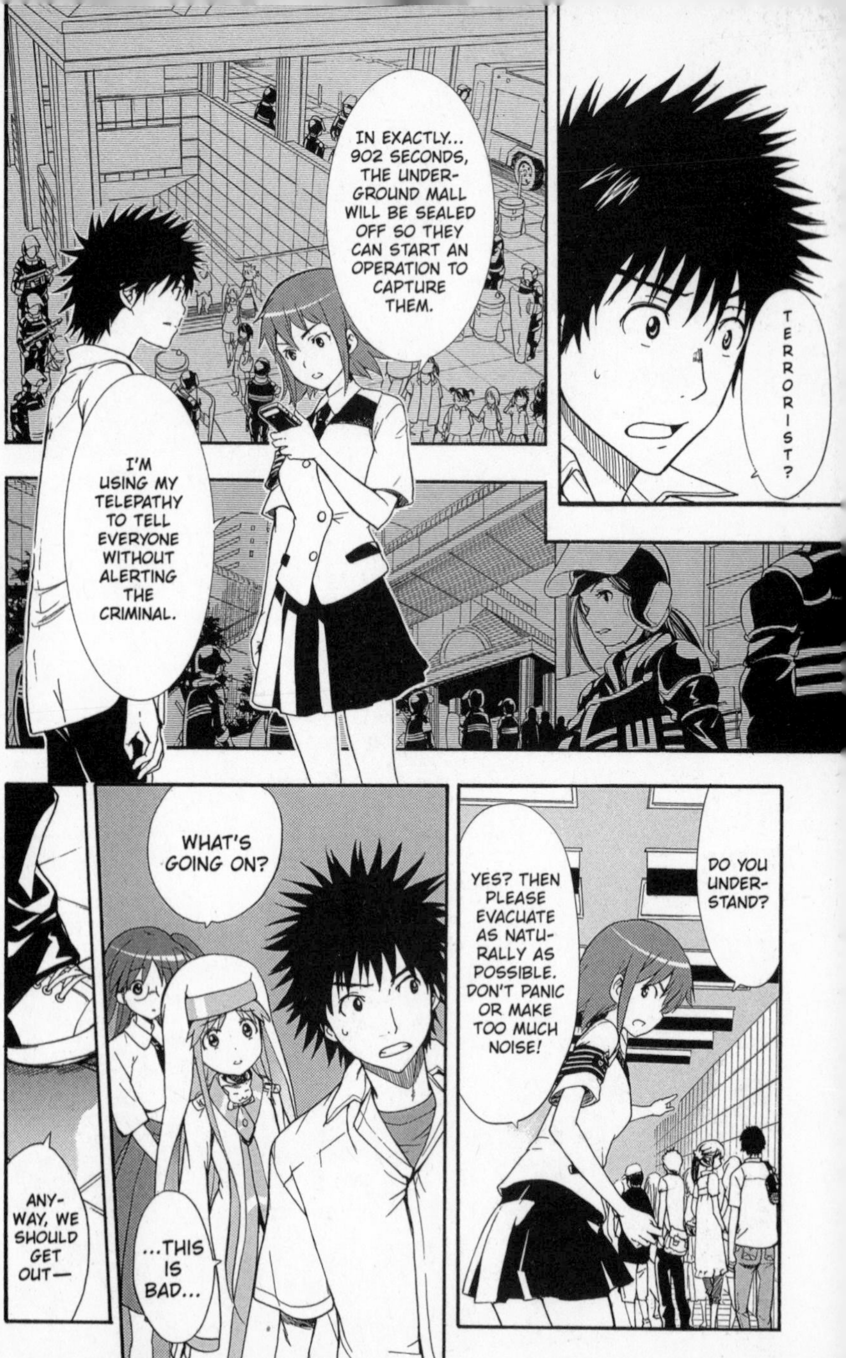
TERRORIST?
IN EXACTLY... 902 SECONDS, THE UNDER-GROUND MALL WILL BE SEALED OFF SO THEY CAN START AN OPERATION TO CAPTURE THEM.
I'M USING MY TELEPATHY TO TELL EVERYONE WITHOUT ALERTING THE CRIMINAL.
DO YOU UNDER-STAND?
YES? THEN PLEASE EVACUATE AS NATU-RALLY AS POSSIBLE. DON'T PANIC OR MAKE TOO MUCH NOISE!
WHAT'S GOING ON?
...THIS IS BAD...
ANY-WAY, WE SHOULD GET OUT—

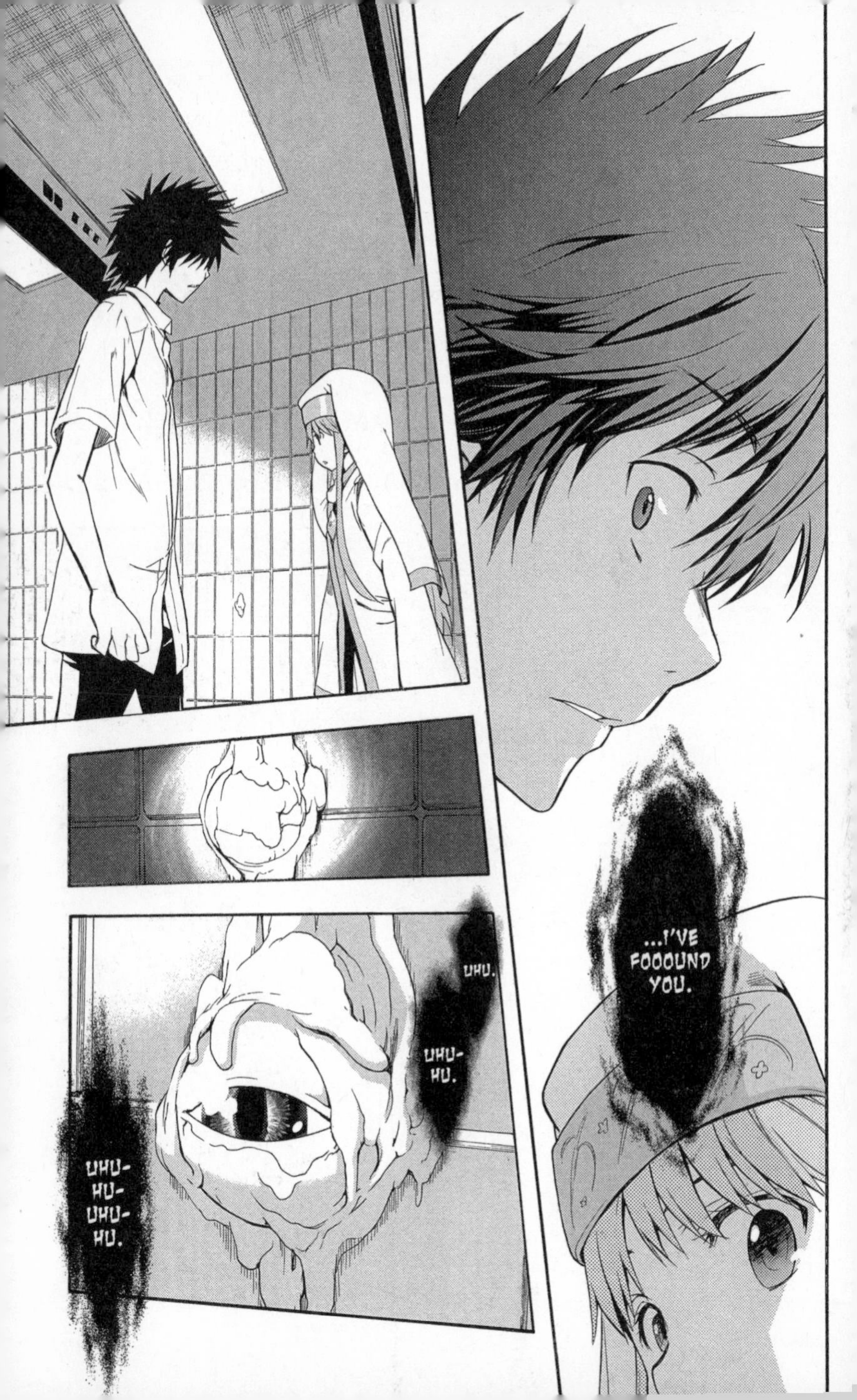
...I'VE FOOOUND YOU.
UHU.
UHU-HU.
UHU-HU-UHU-HU.

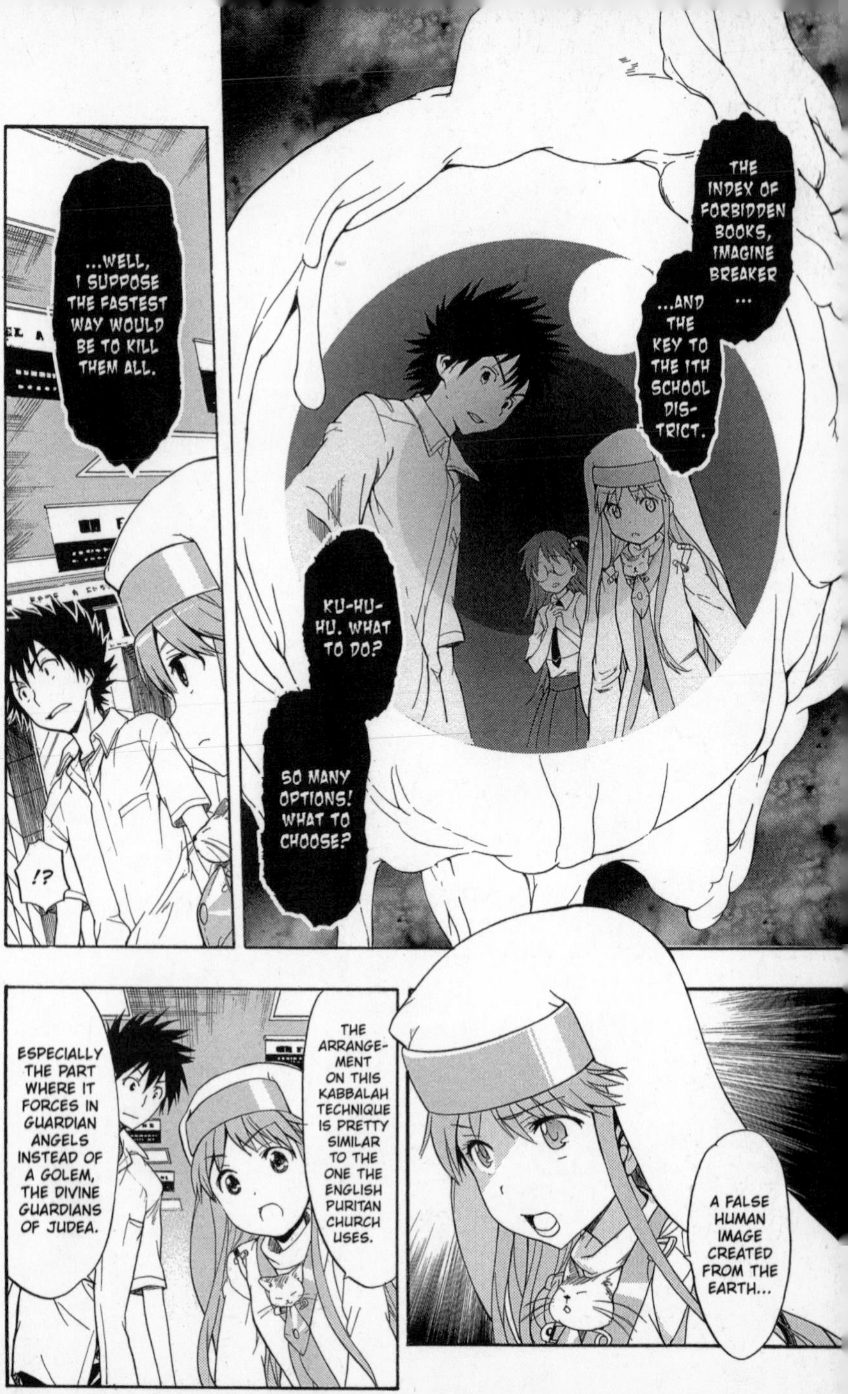
THE INDEX OF FORBIDDEN BOOKS, IMAGINE BREAKER ...
...AND THE KEY TO THE 7TH SCHOOL DIS-TRICT.
KU-HU-HU. WHAT TO DO?
SO MANY OPTIONS! WHAT TO CHOOSE?
...WELL, I SUPPOSE THE FASTEST WAY WOULD BE TO KILL THEM ALL.
!?
A FALSE HUMAN IMAGE CREATED FROM THE EARTH...
THE ARRANGE-MENT ON THIS KABBALAH TECHNIQUE IS PRETTY SIMILAR TO THE ONE THE ENGLISH PURITAN CHURCH USES.
ESPECIALLY THE PART WHERE IT FORCES IN GUARDIAN ANGELS INSTEAD OF A GOLEM, THE DIVINE GUARDIANS OF JUDEA.

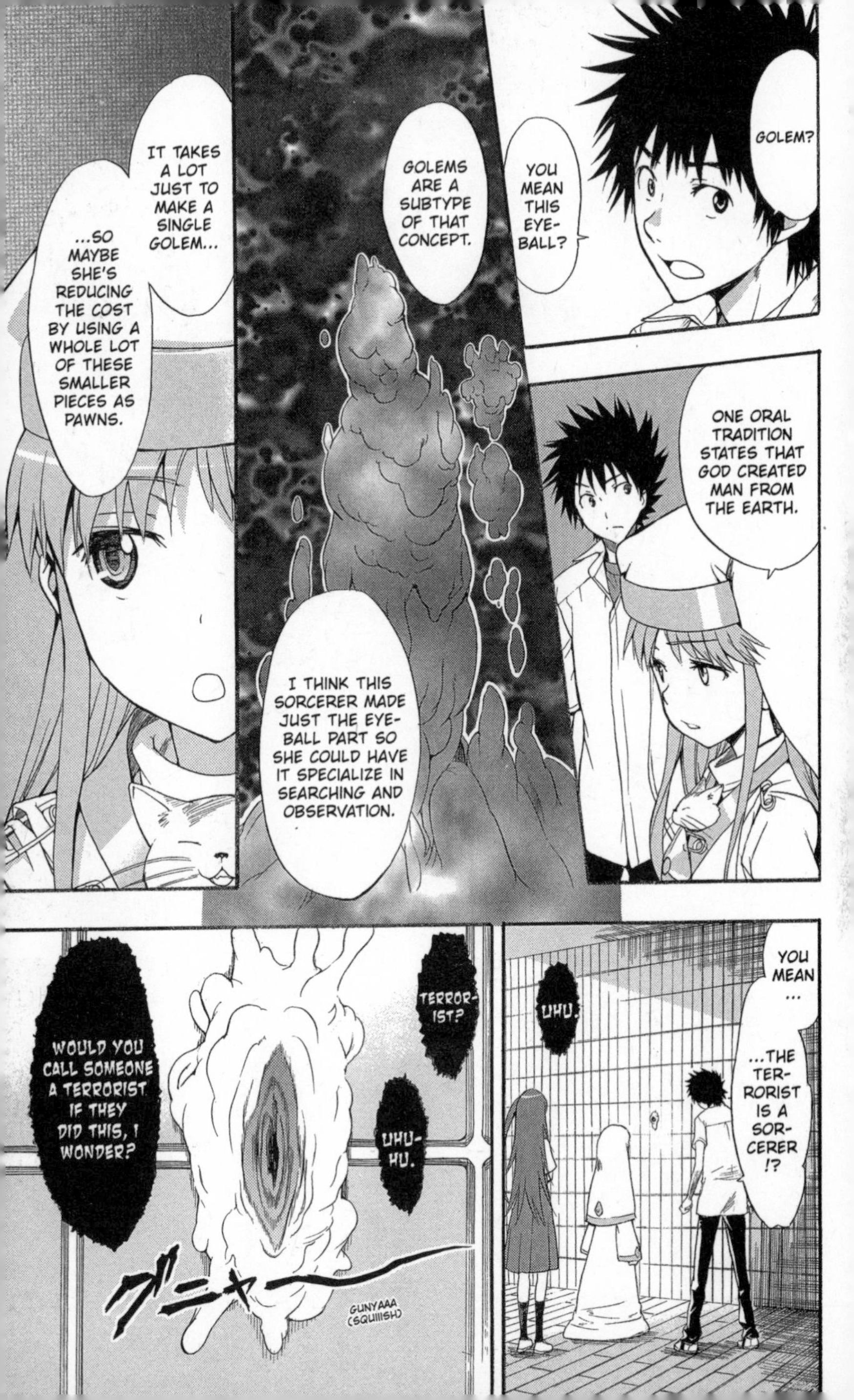
GOLEM?
YOU MEAN THIS EYE-BALL?
ONE ORAL TRADITION STATES THAT GOD CREATED MAN FROM THE EARTH.
GOLEMS ARE A SUBTYPE OF THAT CONCEPT.
I THINK THIS SORCERER MADE JUST THE EYE-BALL PART SO SHE COULD HAVE IT SPECIALIZE IN SEARCHING AND OBSERVATION.
IT TAKES A LOT JUST TO MAKE A SINGLE GOLEM...
...SO MAYBE SHE'S REDUCING THE COST BY USING A WHOLE LOT OF THESE SMALLER PIECES AS PAWNS.
YOU MEAN...
...THE TER-RORIST IS A SOR-CERER!?
UHU.
TERROR-IST?
UHU-HU.
WOULD YOU CALL SOMEONE A TERRORIST IF THEY DID THIS, I WONDER?
GUNYAAA (SQUIIISH)

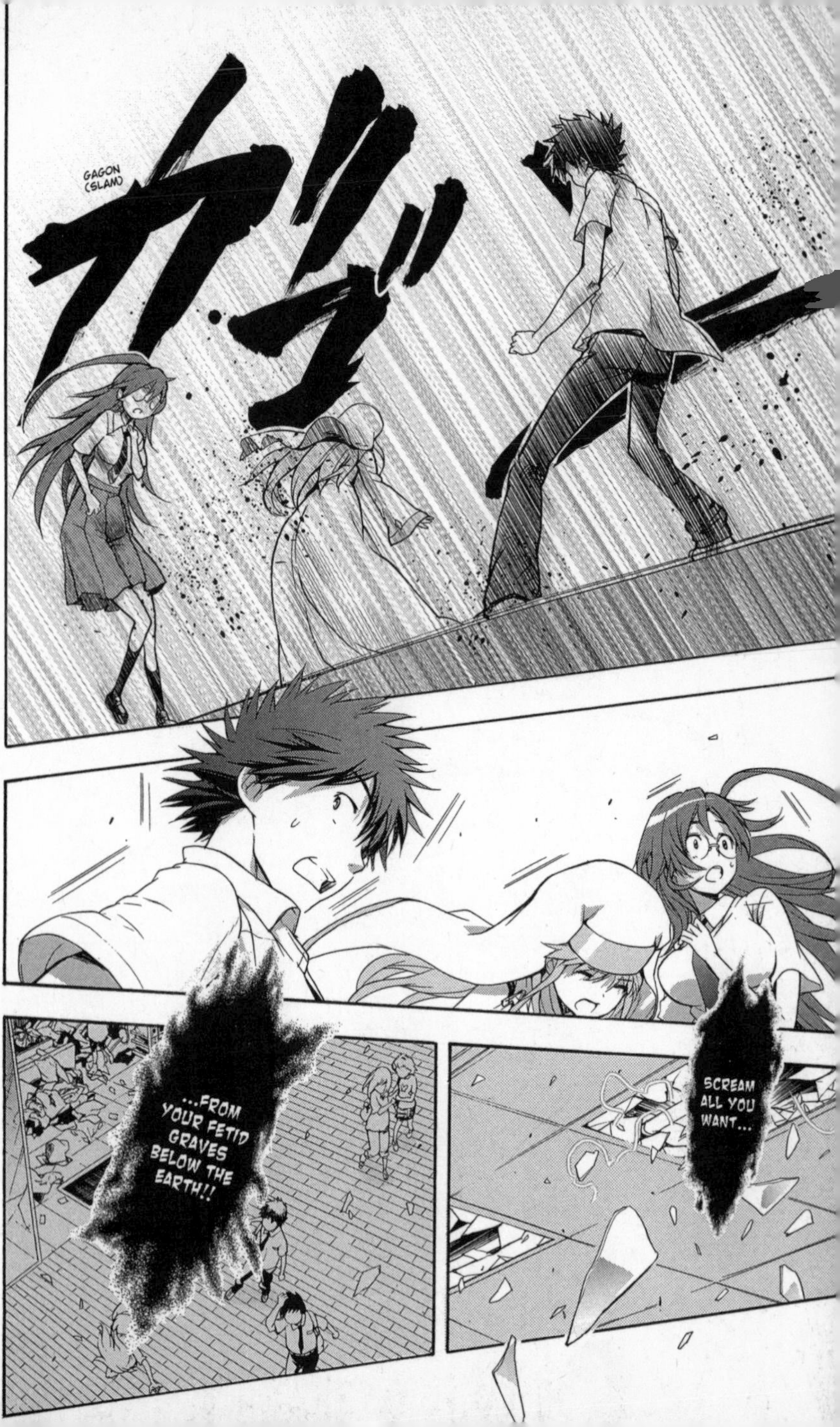
GAGON (SLAM)
SCREAM ALL YOU WANT...
...FROM YOUR FETID GRAVES BELOW THE EARTH!!

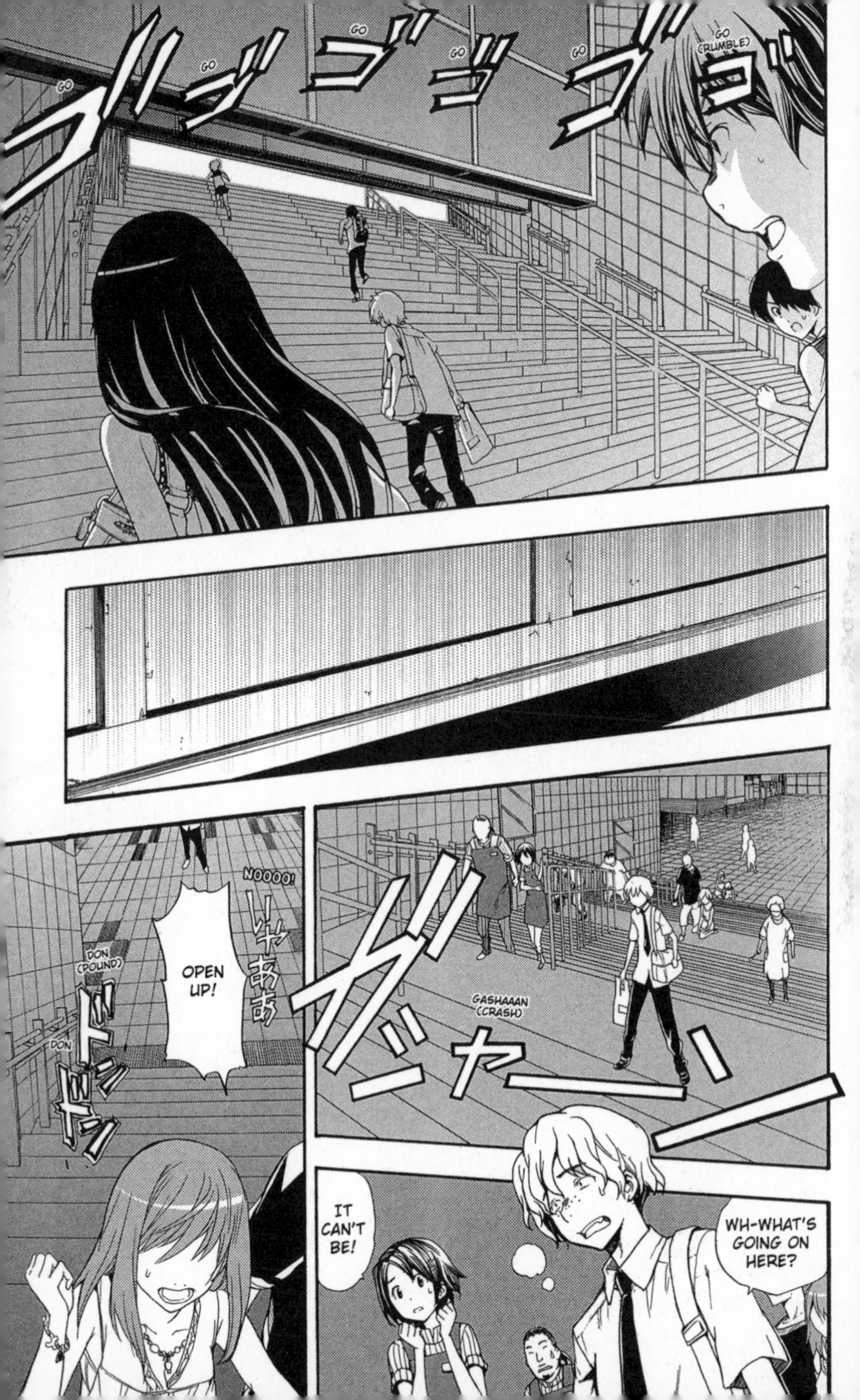
GO (RUMBLE)
GO
GO
GO
GO
GASHAAAN (CRASH)
WH-WHAT'S GOING ON HERE?
IT CAN'T BE!
NOOOO!
OPEN UP!
DON (POUND)
DON

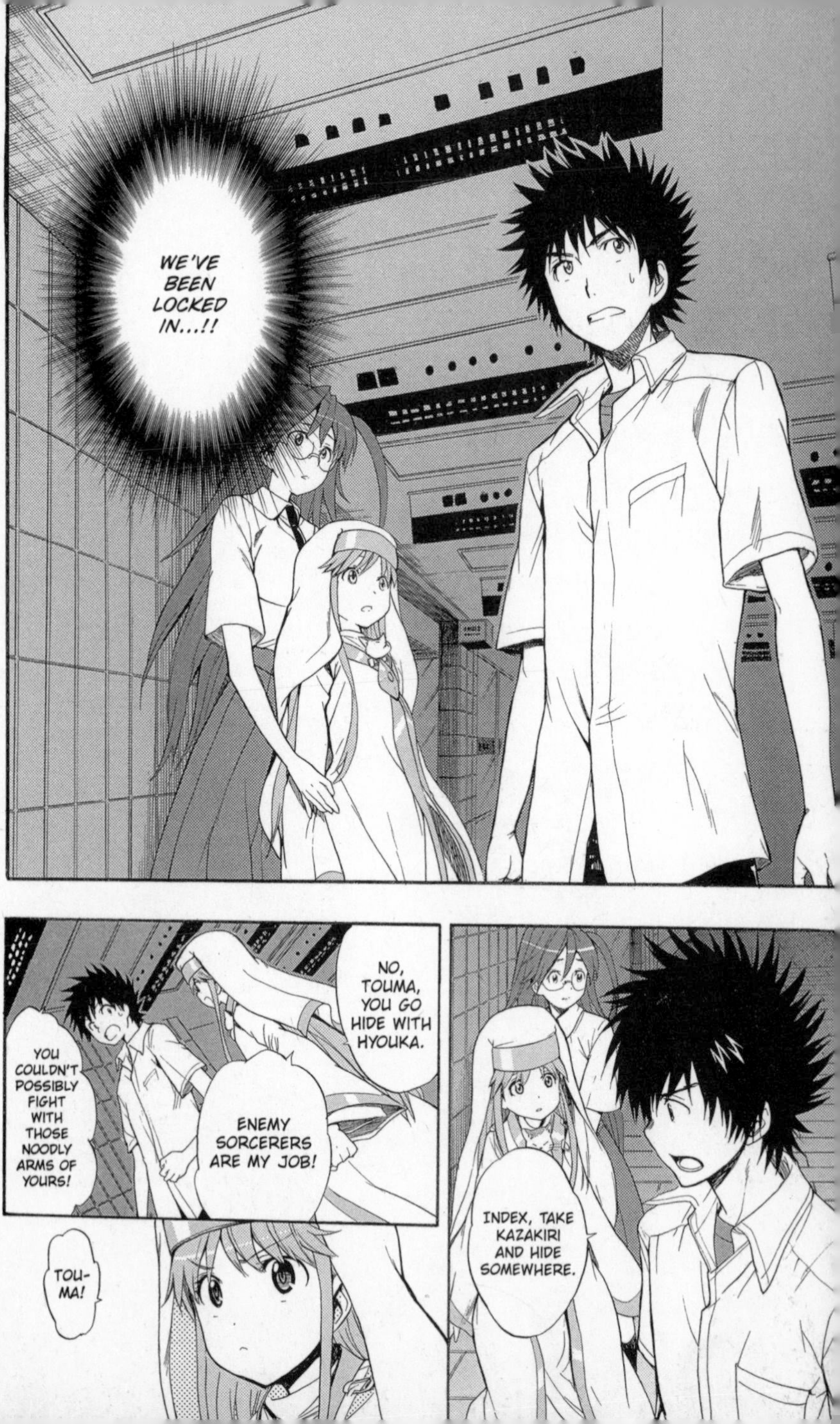
WE'VE BEEN LOCKED IN...!!
INDEX, TAKE KAZAKIRI AND HIDE SOMEWHERE.
NO, TOUMA, YOU GO HIDE WITH HYOUKA.
ENEMY SORCERERS ARE MY JOB!
YOU COULDN'T POSSIBLY FIGHT WITH THOSE NOODLY ARMS OF YOURS!
TOU-MA!

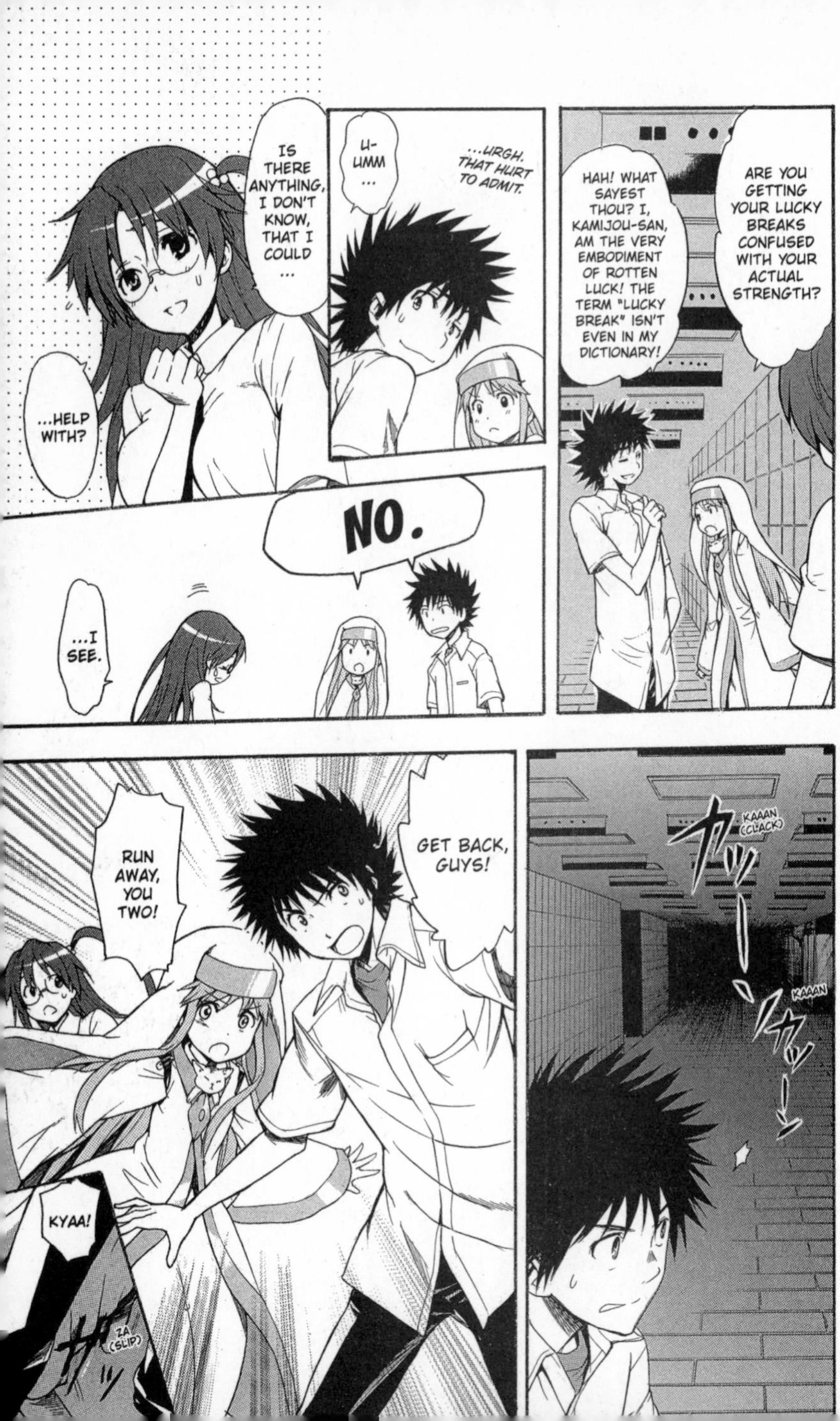
ARE YOU GETTING YOUR LUCKY BREAKS CONFUSED WITH YOUR ACTUAL STRENGTH?
HAH! WHAT SAYEST THOU? I, KAMIJOU-SAN, AM THE VERY EMBODIMENT OF ROTTEN LUCK! THE TERM "LUCKY BREAK" ISN'T EVEN IN MY DICTIONARY!
...URGH. THAT HURT TO ADMIT.
U-UMM ...
IS THERE ANYTHING, I DON'T KNOW, THAT I COULD ...
...HELP WITH?
NO.
...I SEE.
KAAAN (CLACK)
KAAAN
GET BACK, GUYS!
RUN AWAY, YOU TWO!
KYAA!
ZA (SLIP)

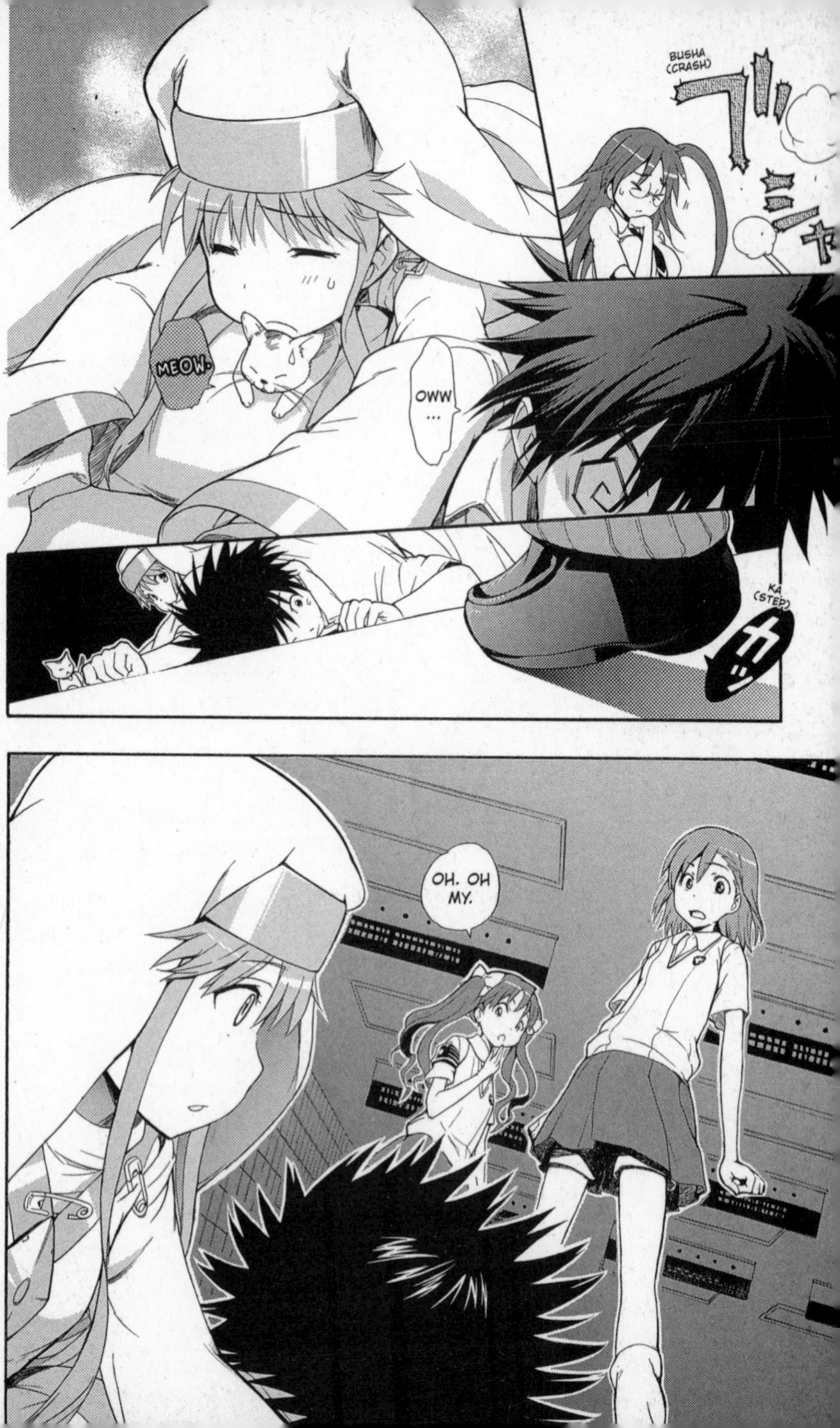
BUSHA (CRASH)
MEOW.
OWW ...
KA (STEP)
OH. OH MY.

A Certain Magical Index

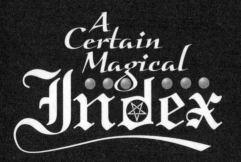

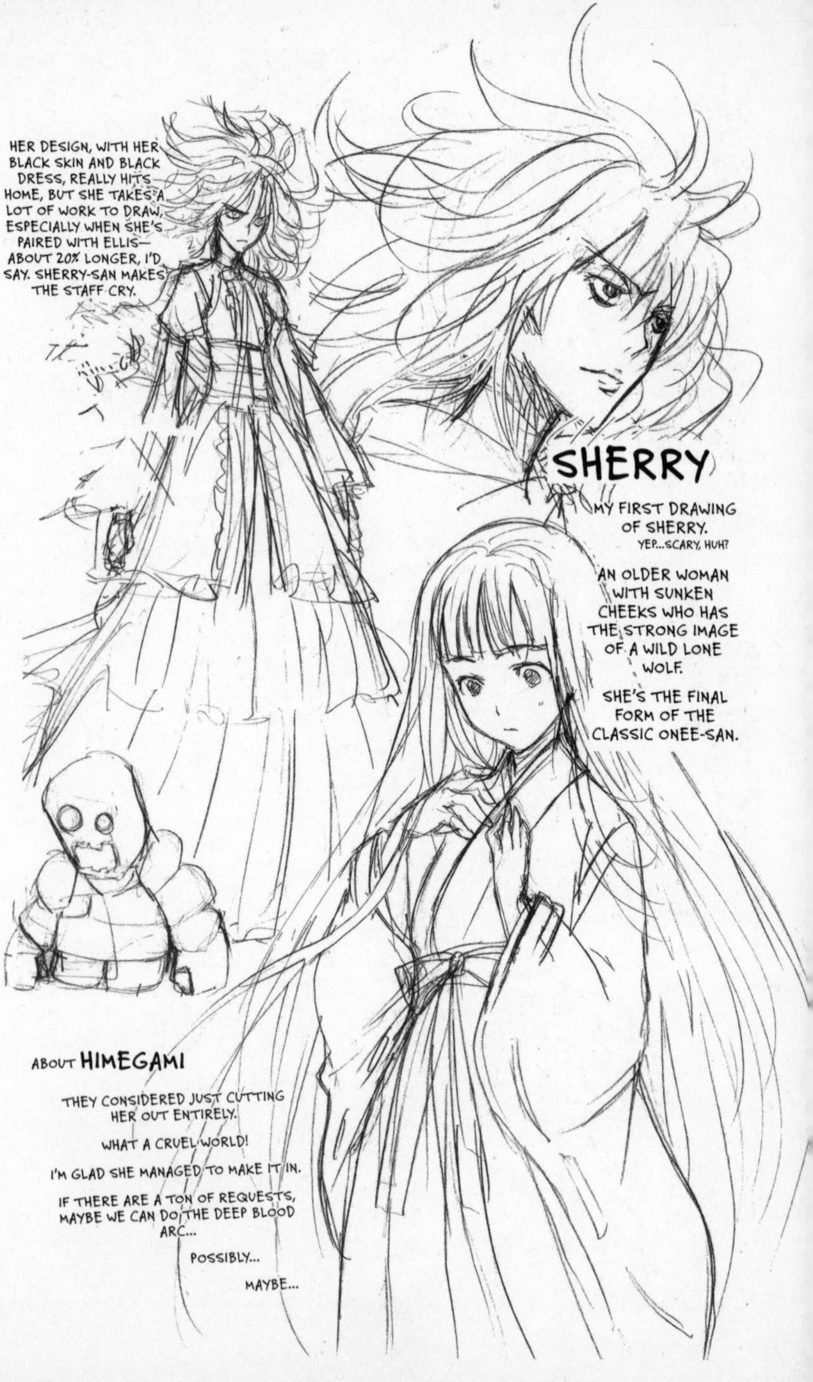
HER DESIGN, WITH HER BLACK SKIN AND BLACK DRESS, REALLY HITS HOME, BUT SHE TAKES A LOT OF WORK TO DRAW, ESPECIALLY WHEN SHE'S PAIRED WITH ELLIS—ABOUT 20% LONGER, I'D SAY. SHERRY-SAN MAKES THE STAFF CRY.
SHERRY
MY FIRST DRAWING OF SHERRY.
YEP...SCARY, HUH?
AN OLDER WOMAN WITH SUNKEN CHEEKS WHO HAS THE STRONG IMAGE OF A WILD LONE WOLF.
SHE'S THE FINAL FORM OF THE CLASSIC ONEE-SAN.
ABOUT HIMEGAMI
THEY CONSIDERED JUST CUTTING HER OUT ENTIRELY.
WHAT A CRUEL WORLD!
I'M GLAD SHE MANAGED TO MAKE IT IN.
IF THERE ARE A TON OF REQUESTS, MAYBE WE CAN DO THE DEEP BLOOD ARC...
POSSIBLY...
MAYBE...

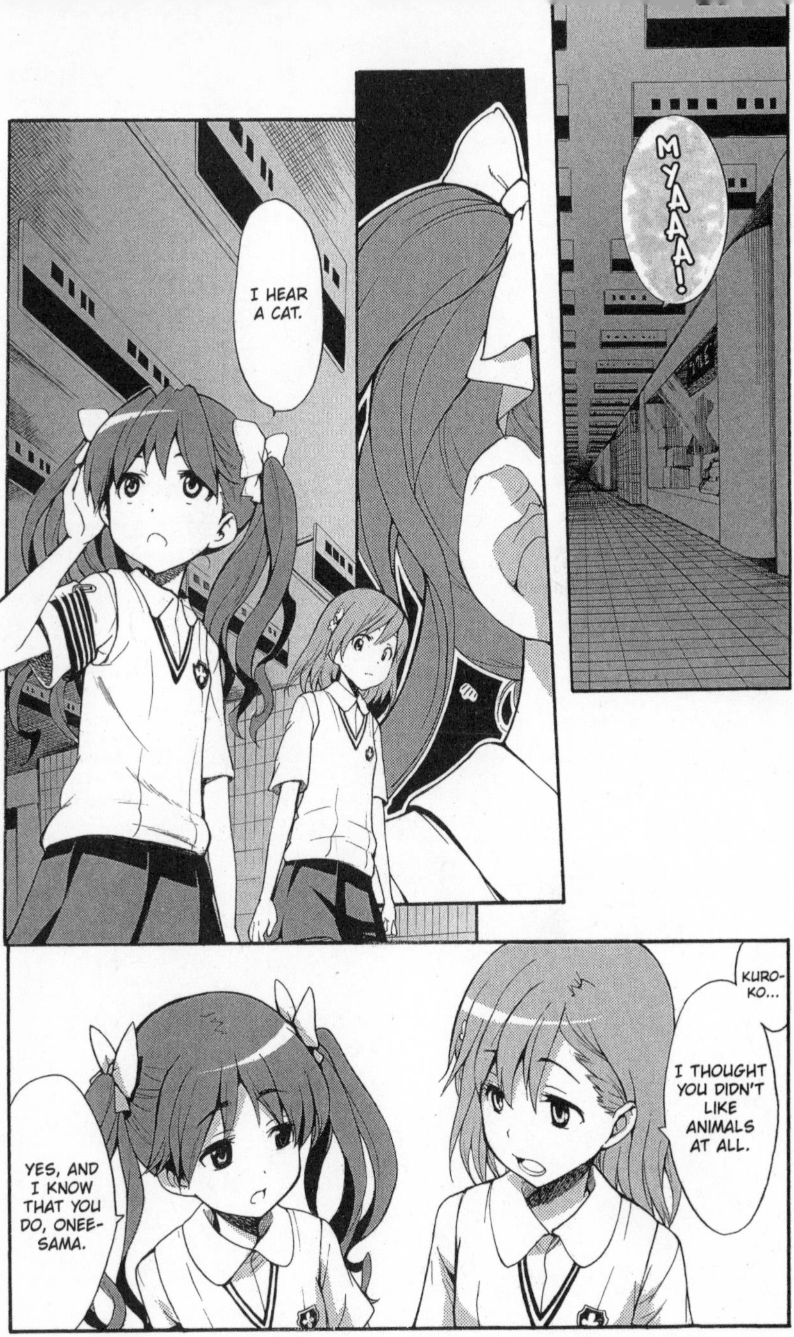
MYAAA!
I HEAR A CAT.
KURO-KO...
I THOUGHT YOU DIDN'T LIKE ANIMALS AT ALL.
YES, AND I KNOW THAT YOU DO, ONEE-SAMA.

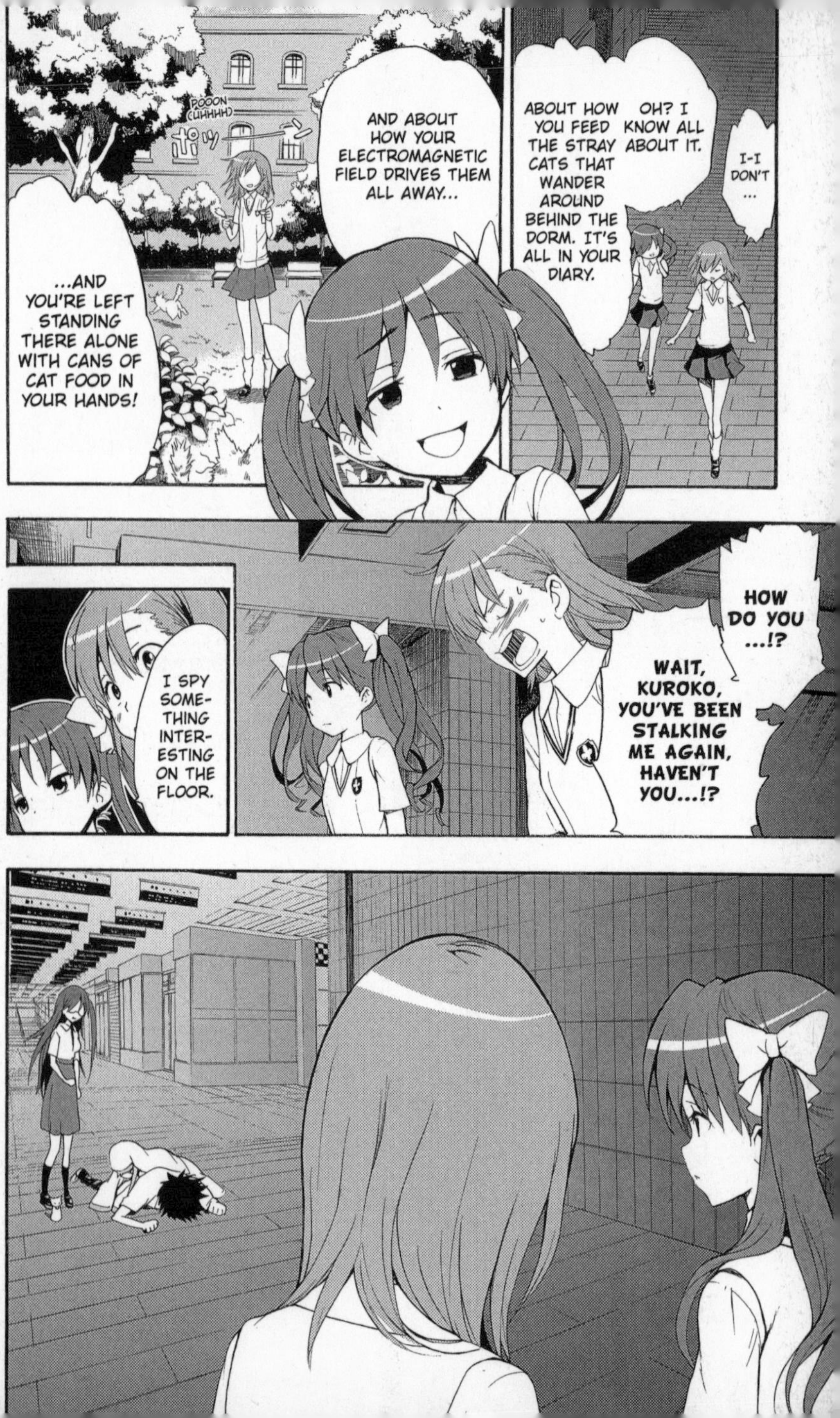
I-I DON'T ...
OH? I KNOW ALL ABOUT IT.
ABOUT HOW YOU FEED THE STRAY CATS THAT WANDER AROUND BEHIND THE DORM. IT'S ALL IN YOUR DIARY.
AND ABOUT HOW YOUR ELECTROMAGNETIC FIELD DRIVES THEM ALL AWAY...
POOON (UHHHHH)
...AND YOU'RE LEFT STANDING THERE ALONE WITH CANS OF CAT FOOD IN YOUR HANDS!
HOW DO YOU ...!?
WAIT, KUROKO, YOU'VE BEEN STALKING ME AGAIN, HAVEN'T YOU...!?
I SPY SOME-THING INTER-ESTING ON THE FLOOR.

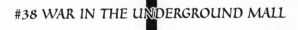

#38 WAR IN THE UNDERGROUND MALL

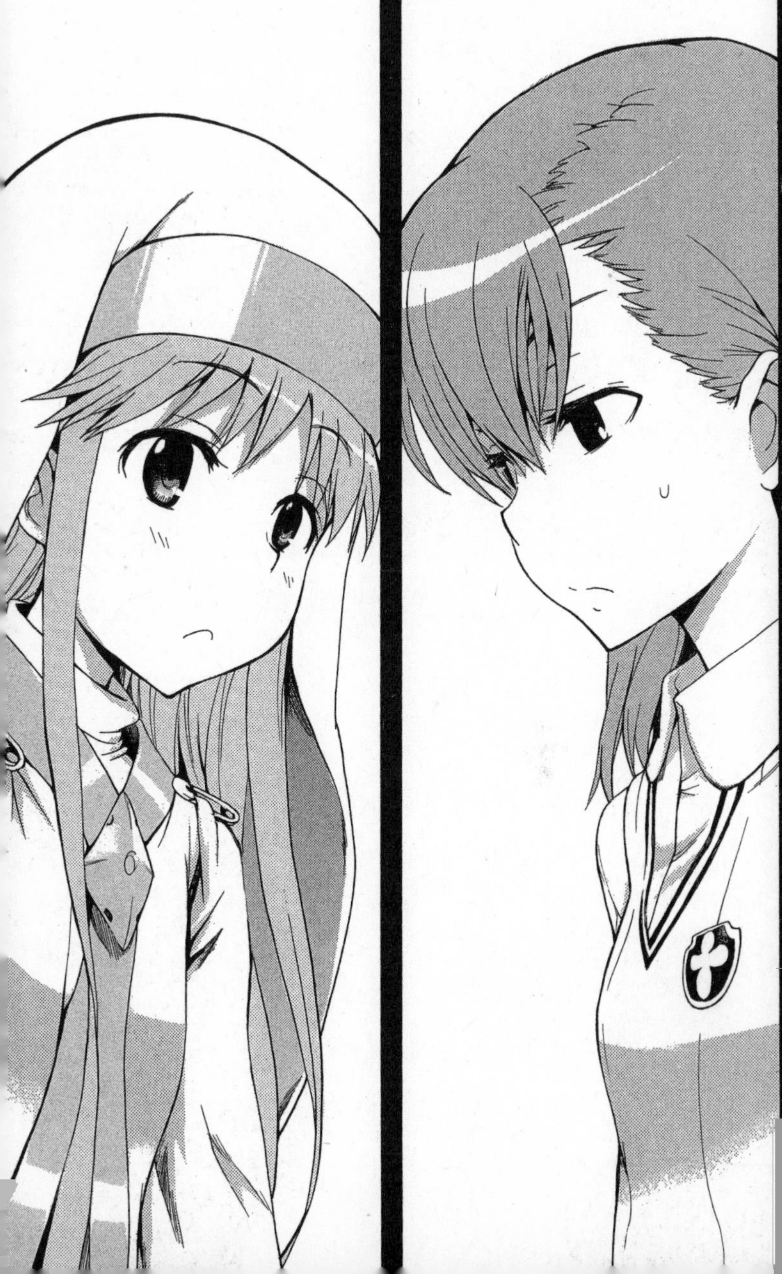

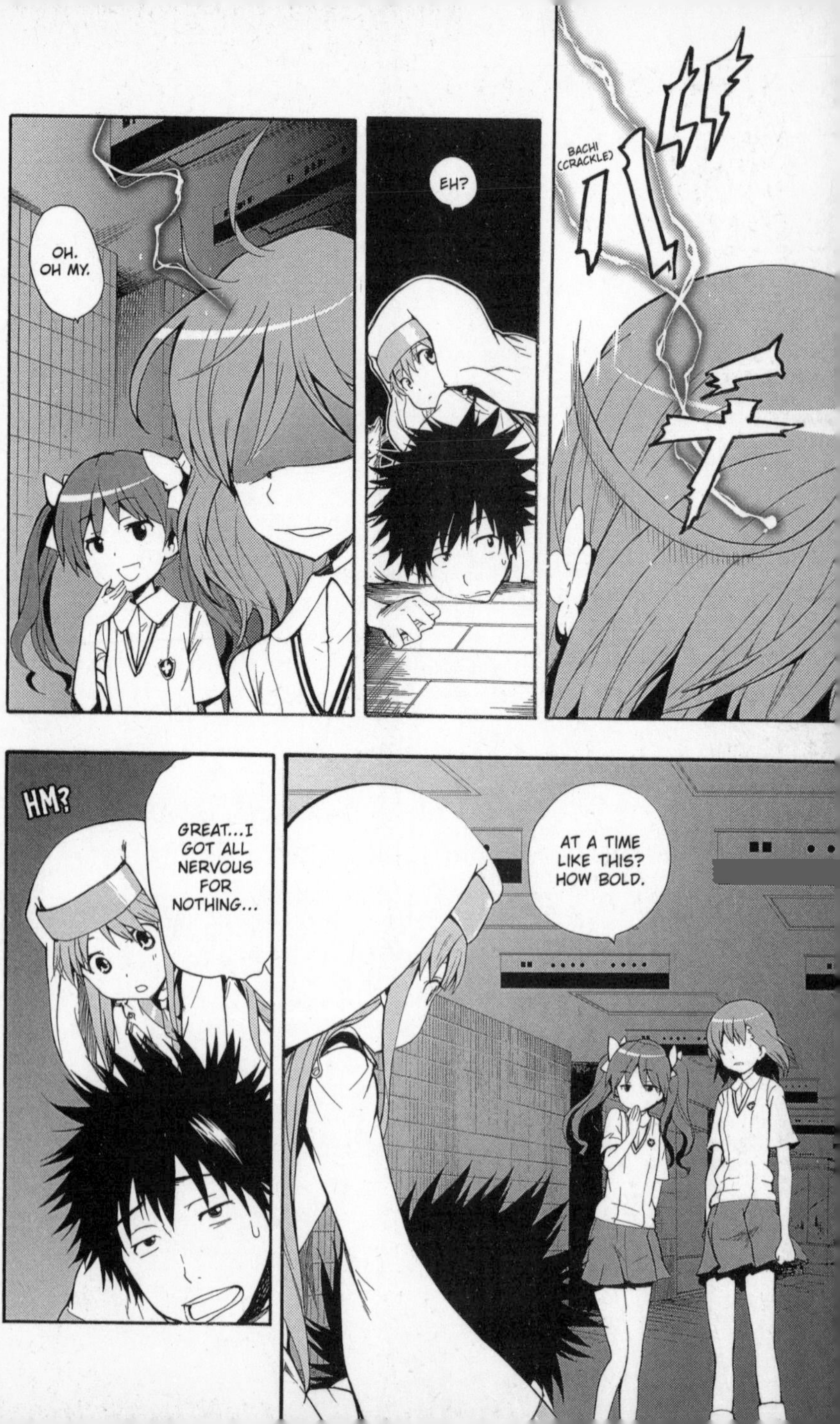
BACHI (CRACKLE)
EH?
OH. OH MY.
AT A TIME LIKE THIS? HOW BOLD.
GREAT...I GOT ALL NERVOUS FOR NOTHING...
HM?

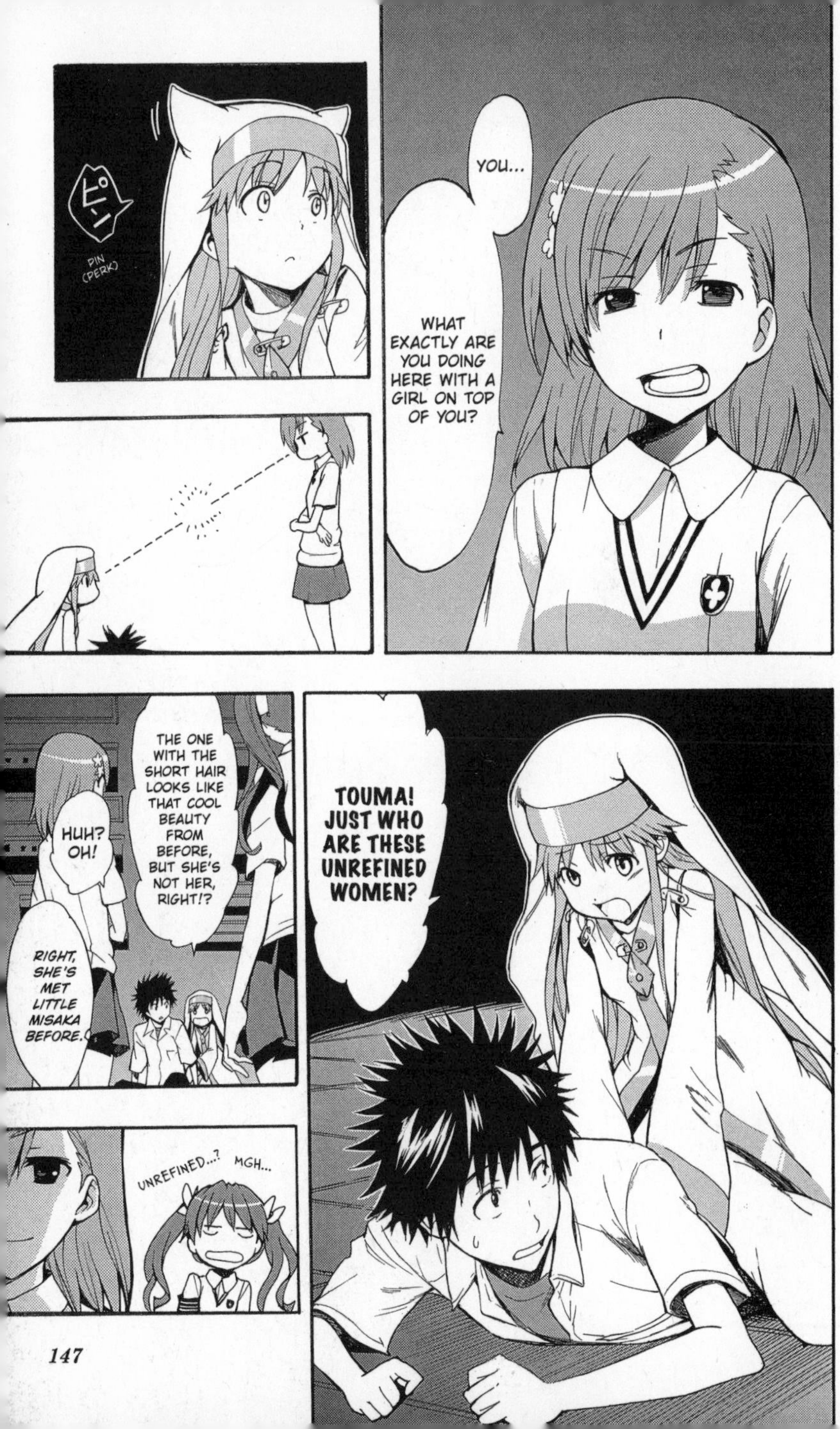
YOU...
WHAT EXACTLY ARE YOU DOING HERE WITH A GIRL ON TOP OF YOU?
PIN (PERK)
TOUMA! JUST WHO ARE THESE UNREFINED WOMEN?
THE ONE WITH THE SHORT HAIR LOOKS LIKE THAT COOL BEAUTY FROM BEFORE, BUT SHE'S NOT HER, RIGHT!?
HUH? OH!
RIGHT, SHE'S MET LITTLE MISAKA BEFORE.
UNREFINED...? MGH...

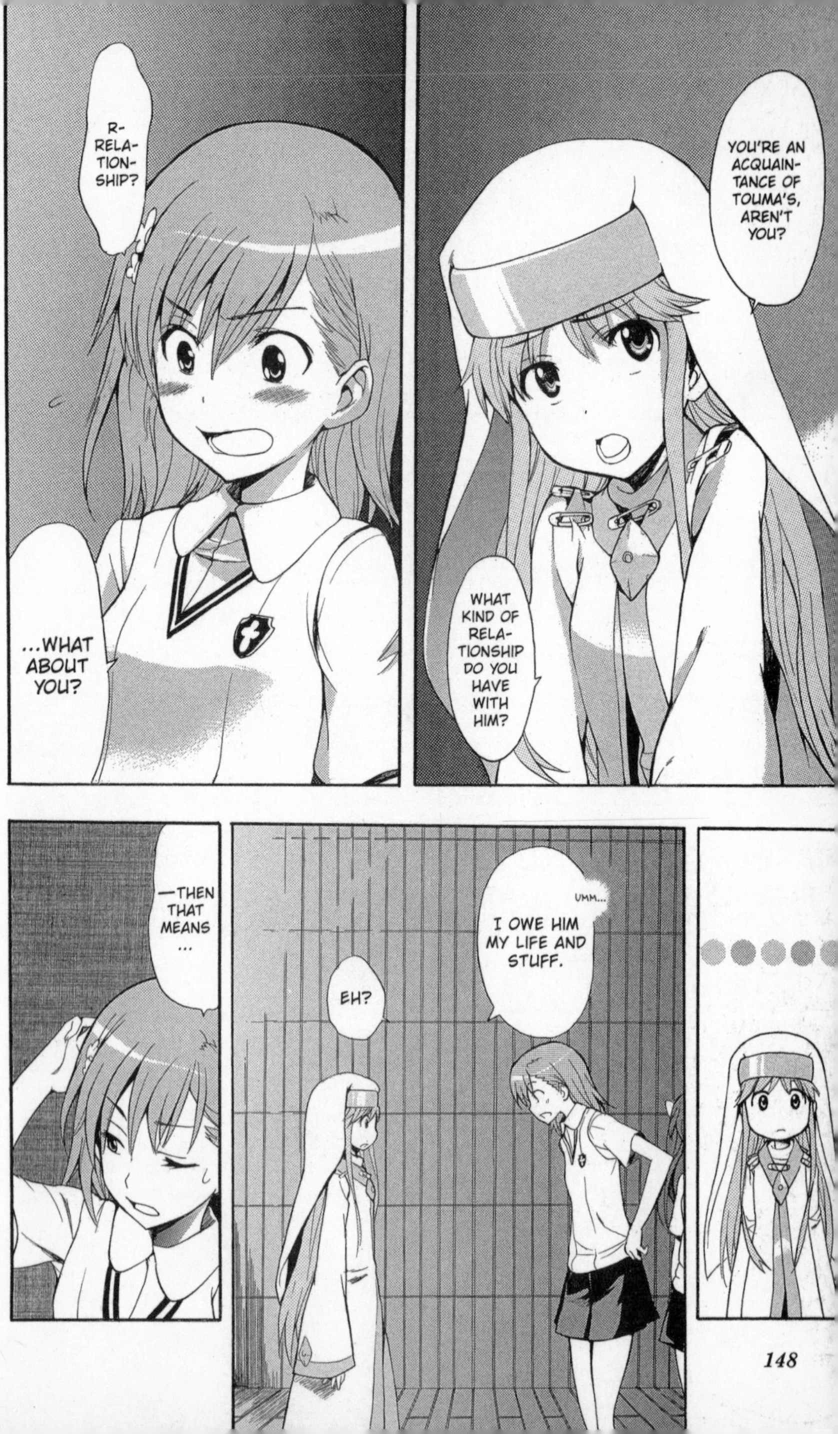
YOU'RE AN ACQUAINTANCE OF TOUMA'S, AREN'T YOU?
WHAT KIND OF RELATIONSHIP DO YOU HAVE WITH HIM?
R-RELATIONSHIP?
...WHAT ABOUT YOU?
UMM...
I OWE HIM MY LIFE AND STUFF.
EH?
—THEN THAT MEANS ...

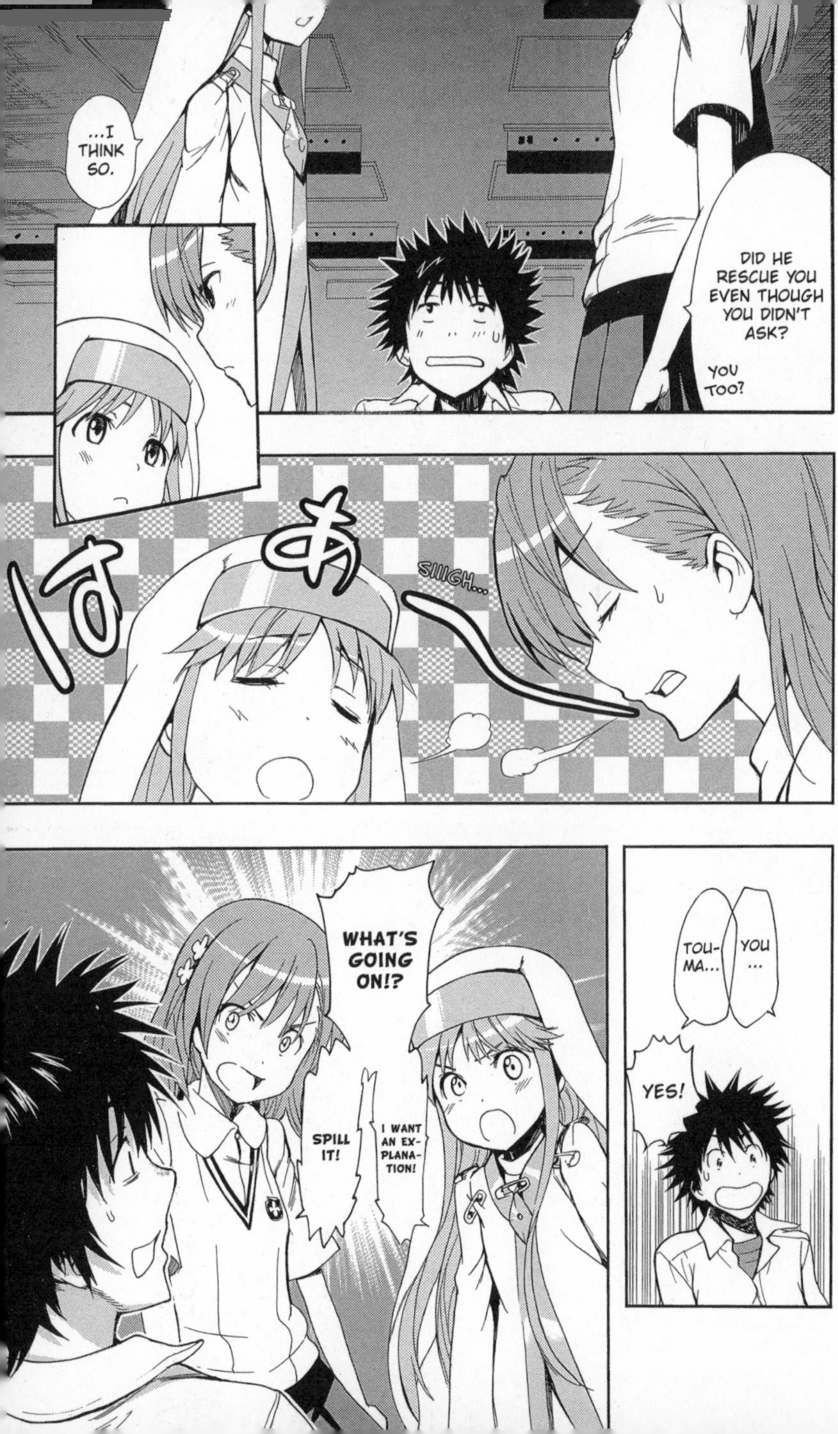
DID HE RESCUE YOU EVEN THOUGH YOU DIDN'T ASK?
YOU TOO?
...I THINK SO.
はあ〜
SIIIGH...
YOU ...
TOU-MA...
YES!
WHAT'S GOING ON!?
I WANT AN EX-PLANA-TION!
SPILL IT!

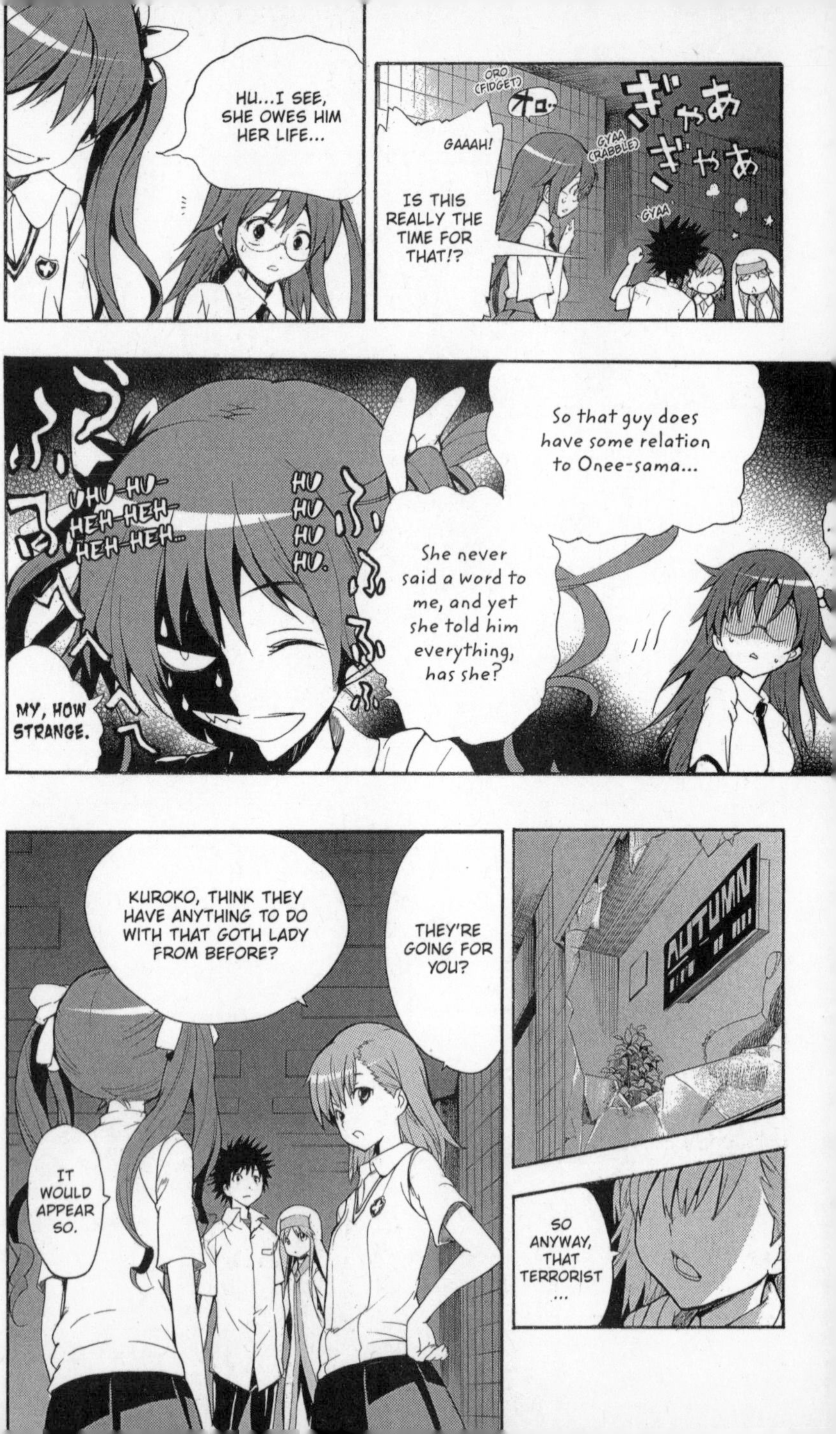
ぎゃあぎゃあ
GYAA (RABBLE)
ORO (FIDGET)
オロ…
GAAAH!
IS THIS REALLY THE TIME FOR THAT!?
GYAA
HU...I SEE, SHE OWES HIM HER LIFE...
So that guy does have some relation to Onee-sama...
She never said a word to me, and yet she told him everything, has she?
HU HU HU HU.
UHU-HU- HEH-HEH- HEH-HEH...
MY, HOW STRANGE.
AUTUMN
SO ANYWAY, THAT TERRORIST ...
THEY'RE GOING FOR YOU?
KUROKO, THINK THEY HAVE ANYTHING TO DO WITH THAT GOTH LADY FROM BEFORE?
IT WOULD APPEAR SO.

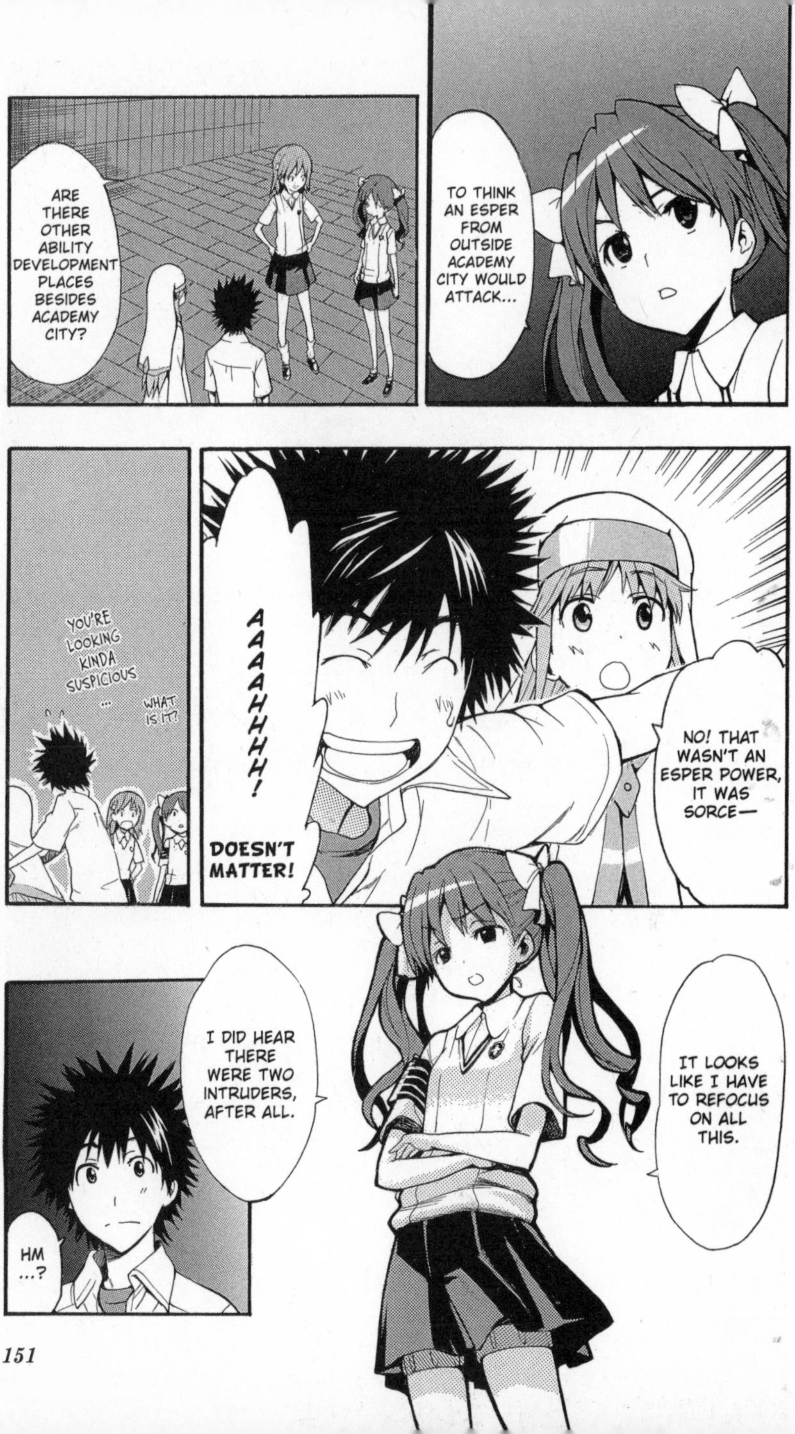
TO THINK AN ESPER FROM OUTSIDE ACADEMY CITY WOULD ATTACK...
ARE THERE OTHER ABILITY DEVELOPMENT PLACES BESIDES ACADEMY CITY?
NO! THAT WASN'T AN ESPER POWER, IT WAS SORCE—
AAAAHHHH!
DOESN'T MATTER!
YOU'RE LOOKING KINDA SUSPICIOUS ...
WHAT IS IT?
IT LOOKS LIKE I HAVE TO REFOCUS ON ALL THIS.
I DID HEAR THERE WERE TWO INTRUDERS, AFTER ALL.
HM ...?

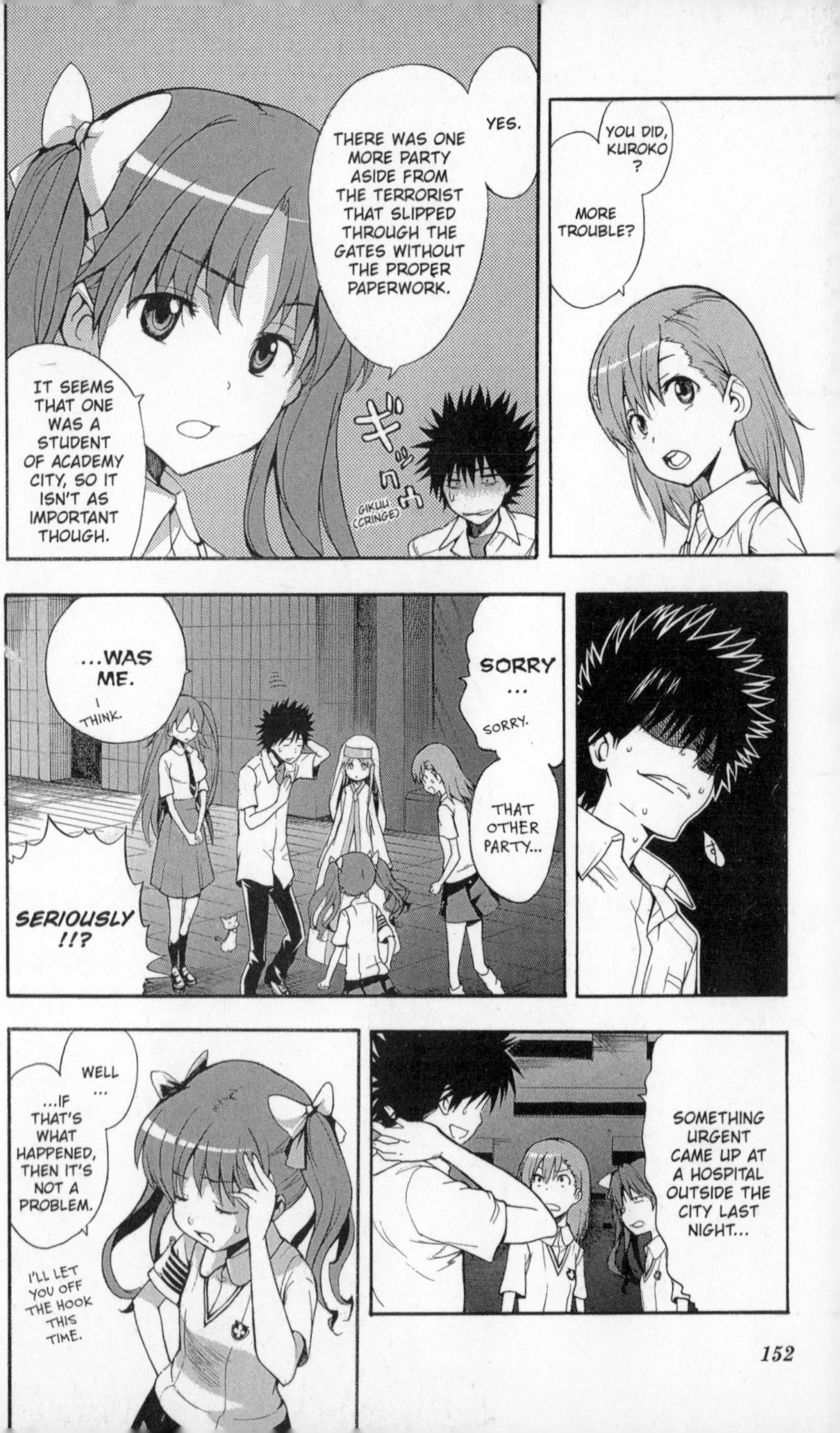
YOU DID, KUROKO?
MORE TROUBLE?
YES.
THERE WAS ONE MORE PARTY ASIDE FROM THE TERRORIST THAT SLIPPED THROUGH THE GATES WITHOUT THE PROPER PAPERWORK.
IT SEEMS THAT ONE WAS A STUDENT OF ACADEMY CITY, SO IT ISN'T AS IMPORTANT THOUGH.
GIKUU (CRINGE)
SORRY...
SORRY.
THAT OTHER PARTY...
...WAS ME.
I THINK.
SERIOUSLY!!?
SOMETHING URGENT CAME UP AT A HOSPITAL OUTSIDE THE CITY LAST NIGHT...
WELL...
...IF THAT'S WHAT HAPPENED, THEN IT'S NOT A PROBLEM.
I'LL LET YOU OFF THE HOOK THIS TIME.

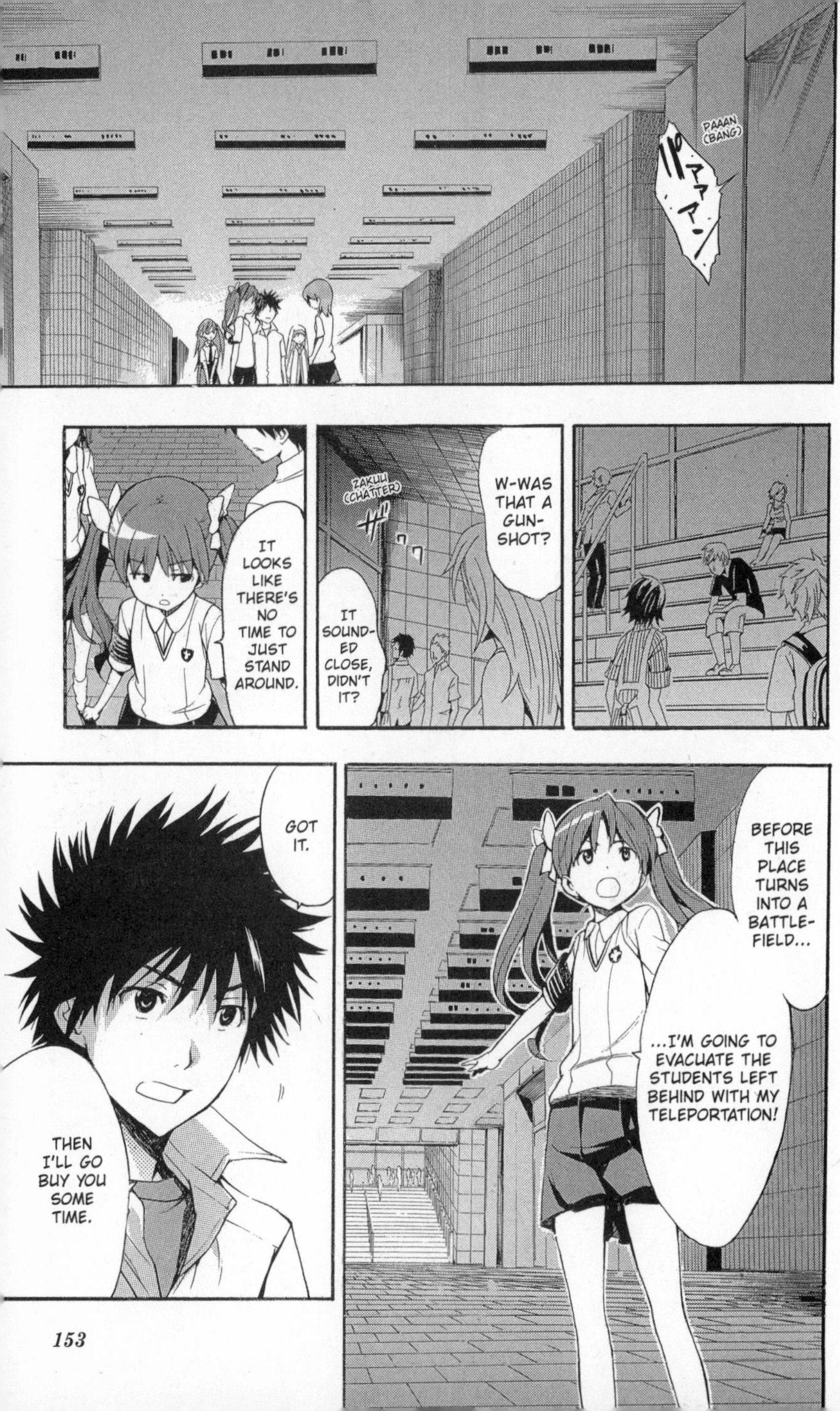
PAAAN (BANG)
ZAKUU (CHATTER)
W-WAS THAT A GUN-SHOT?
IT SOUNDED-ED CLOSE, DIDN'T IT?
IT LOOKS LIKE THERE'S NO TIME TO JUST STAND AROUND.
BEFORE THIS PLACE TURNS INTO A BATTLE-FIELD...
...I'M GOING TO EVACUATE THE STUDENTS LEFT BEHIND WITH MY TELEPORTATION!
GOT IT.
THEN I'LL GO BUY YOU SOME TIME.

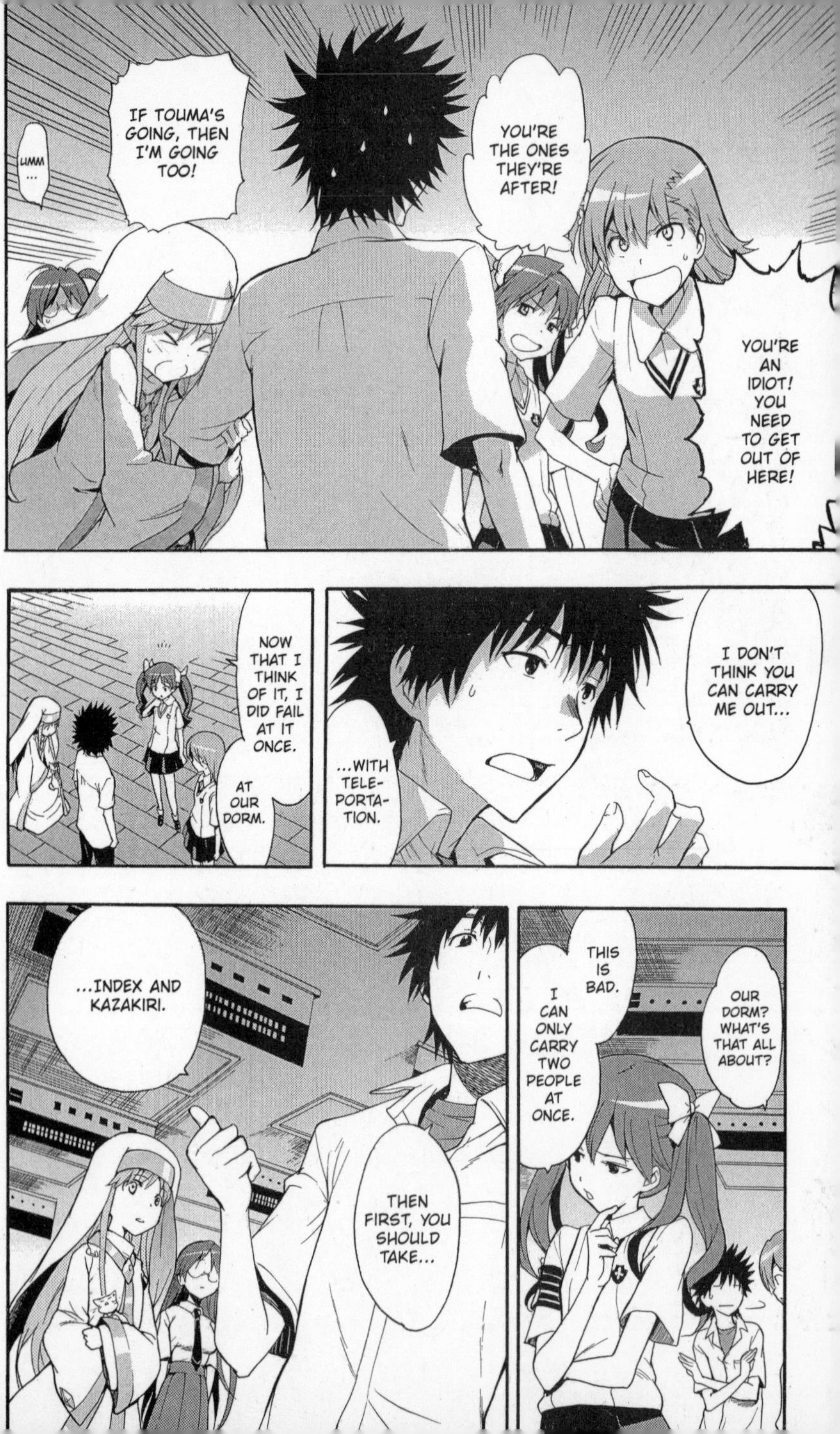
YOU'RE AN IDIOT! YOU NEED TO GET OUT OF HERE!
YOU'RE THE ONES THEY'RE AFTER!
IF TOUMA'S GOING, THEN I'M GOING TOO!
UMM ...
I DON'T THINK YOU CAN CARRY ME OUT...
...WITH TELE-PORTATION.
NOW THAT I THINK OF IT, I DID FAIL AT IT ONCE.
AT OUR DORM.
OUR DORM? WHAT'S THAT ALL ABOUT?
THIS IS BAD.
I CAN ONLY CARRY TWO PEOPLE AT ONCE.
THEN FIRST, YOU SHOULD TAKE...
...INDEX AND KAZAKIRI.

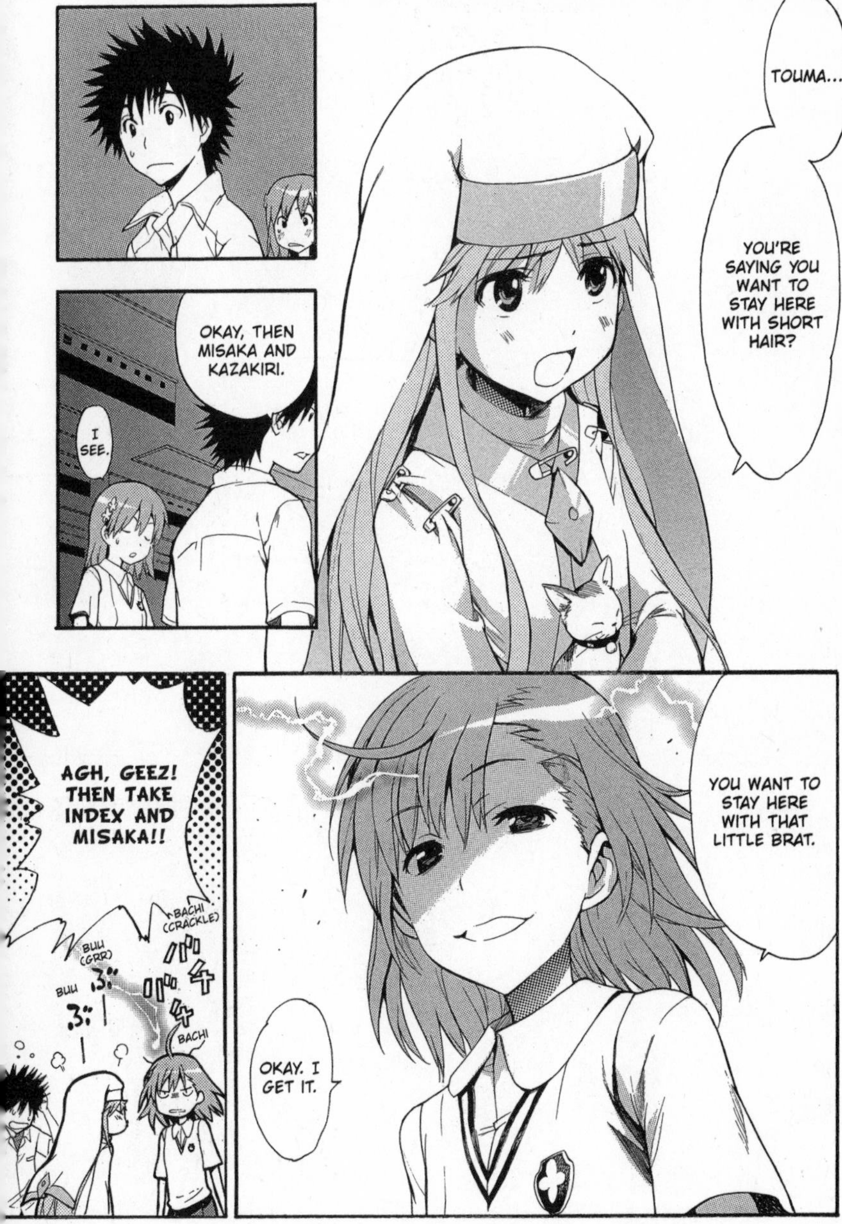
TOUMA...
YOU'RE SAYING YOU WANT TO STAY HERE WITH SHORT HAIR?
OKAY, THEN MISAKA AND KAZAKIRI.
I SEE.
YOU WANT TO STAY HERE WITH THAT LITTLE BRAT.
OKAY. I GET IT.
AGH, GEEZ! THEN TAKE INDEX AND MISAKA!!
BACHI (CRACKLE)
BUU (GRR)
BUU
BACHI

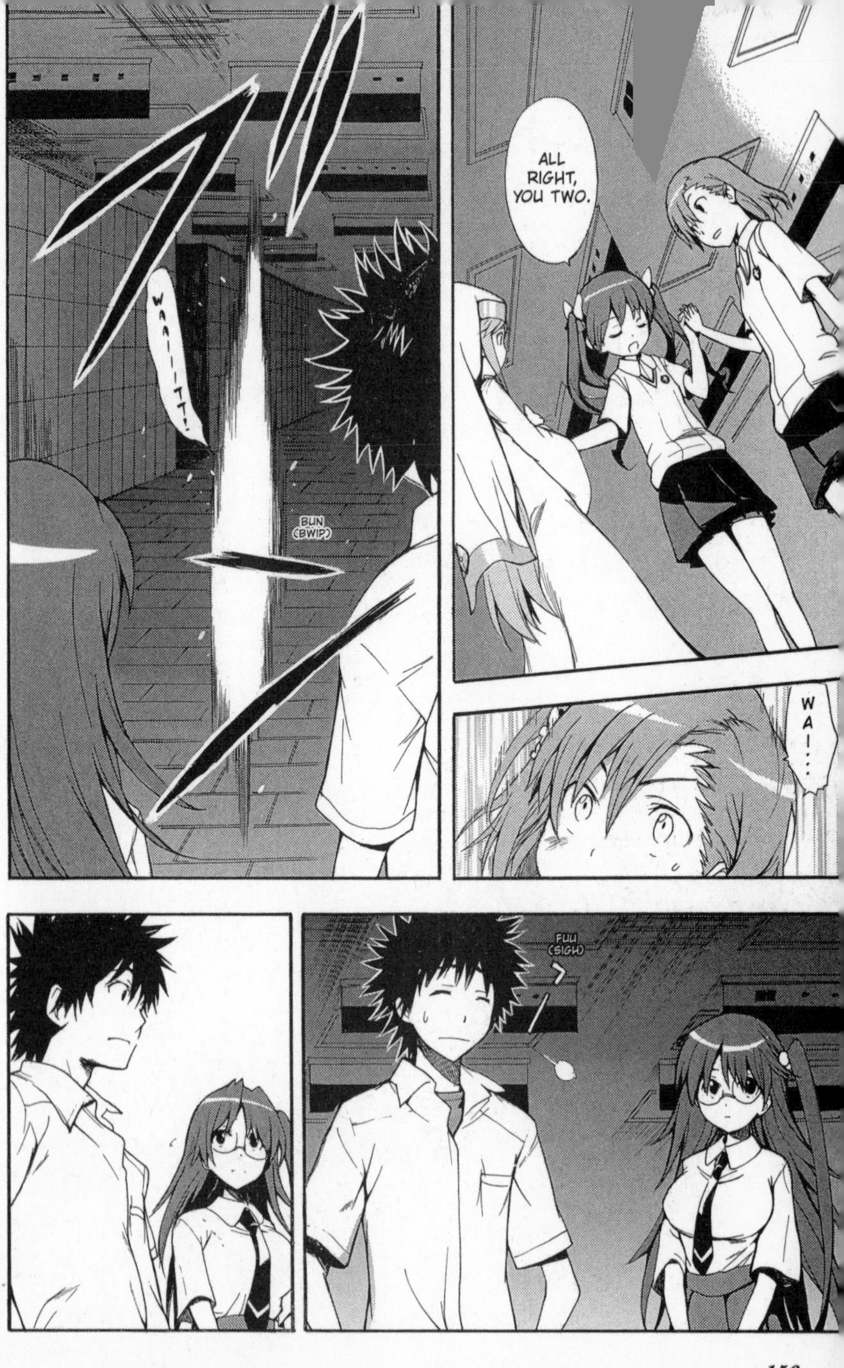
ALL RIGHT, YOU TWO.
WAI...
WAAIIITT!
BUN (BWIP)
FUU (SIGH)

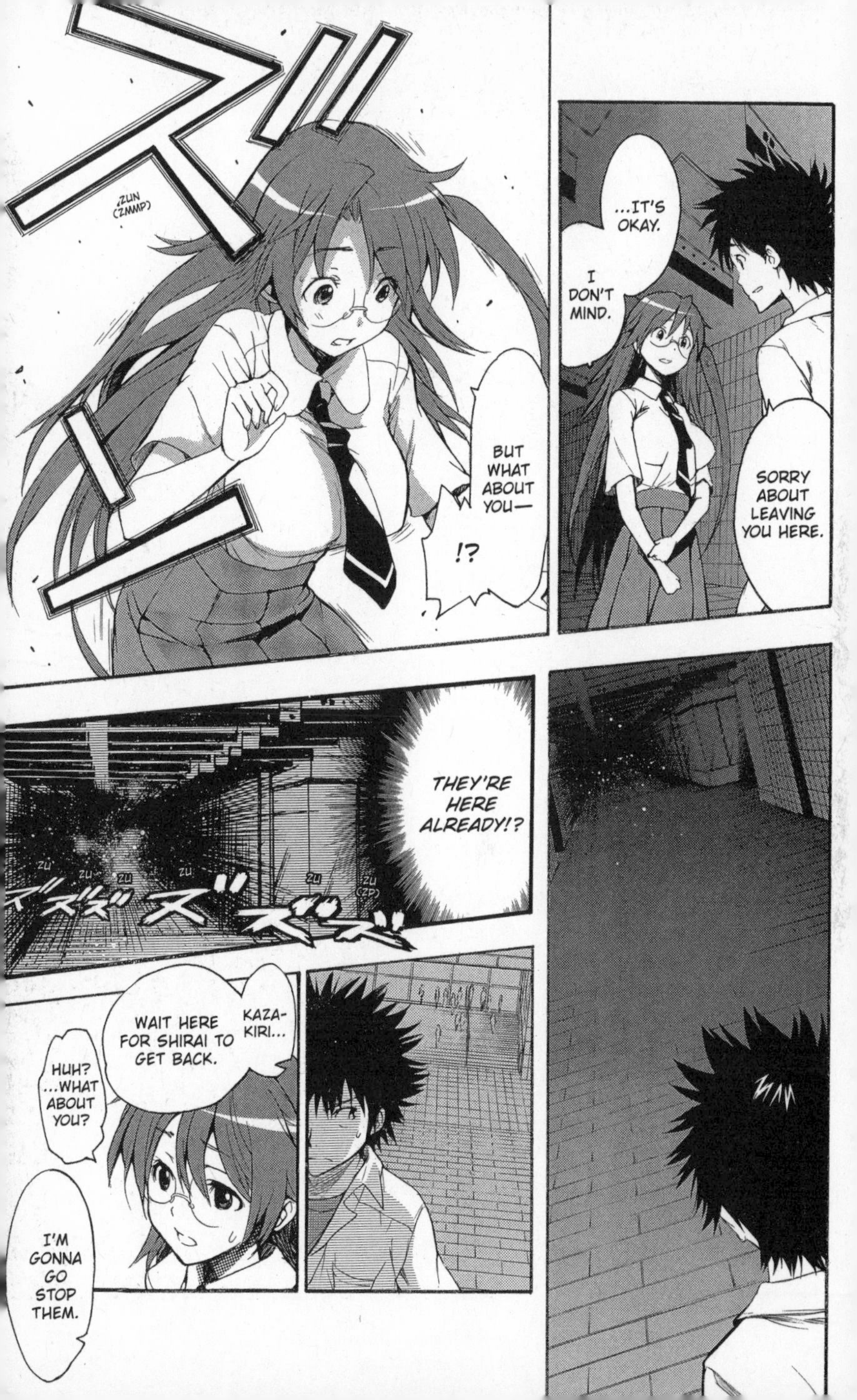
SORRY ABOUT LEAVING YOU HERE.
...IT'S OKAY.
I DON'T MIND.
BUT WHAT ABOUT YOU—
!?
ZUN (ZMMP)
THEY'RE HERE ALREADY!?
ZU ZU ZU ZU ZU ZU (ZP)
KAZA-KIRI...
WAIT HERE FOR SHIRAI TO GET BACK.
HUH? ...WHAT ABOUT YOU?
I'M GONNA GO STOP THEM.

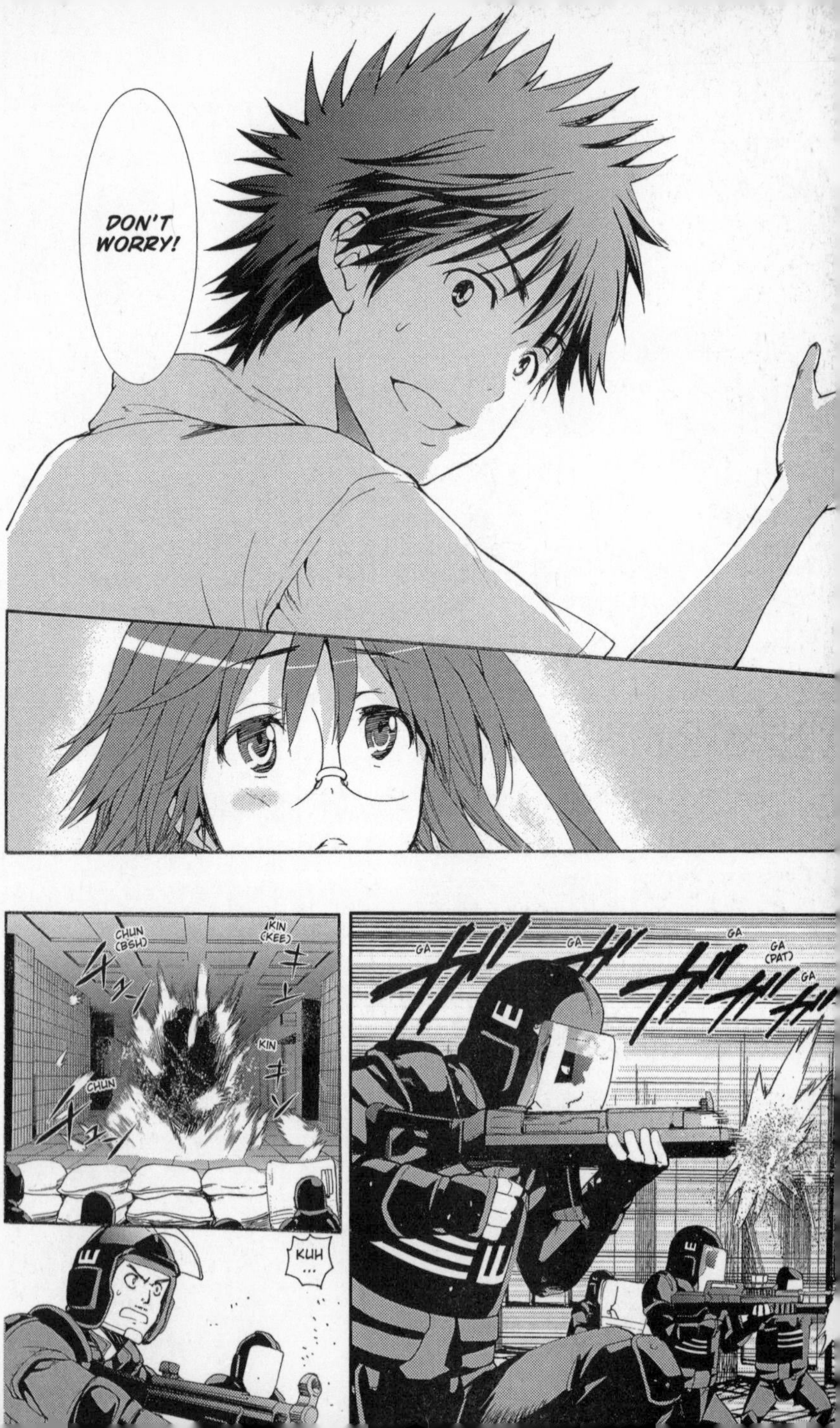
DON'T WORRY!
GA
GA
GA
GA (PAT)
GA
KIN (KEE)
KIN
CHUN (B'SH)
CHUN
KUH ...

SPIN
(CLINK)

WHAT'S
UP? WE
CAN'T EVEN
THREATEN
HER WHEN
SHE HAS
SUCH A
THICK
SHIELD!

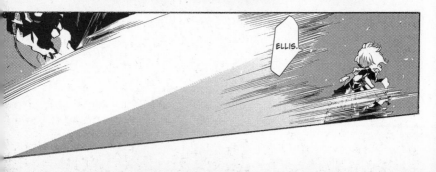

ELLIS.

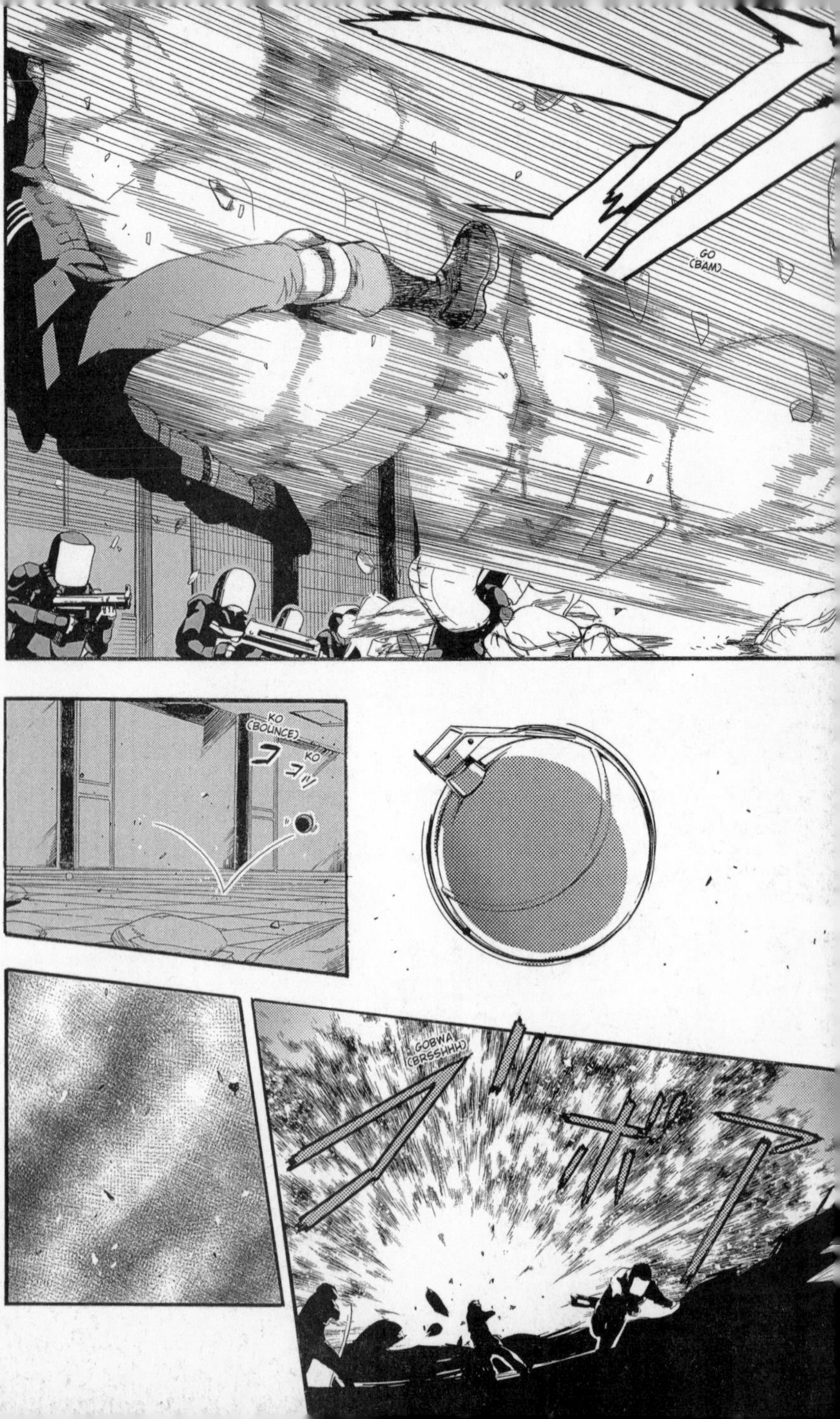
GO (BAM)
KO (BOUNCE)
KO
GOBWA (BRSSHHH)

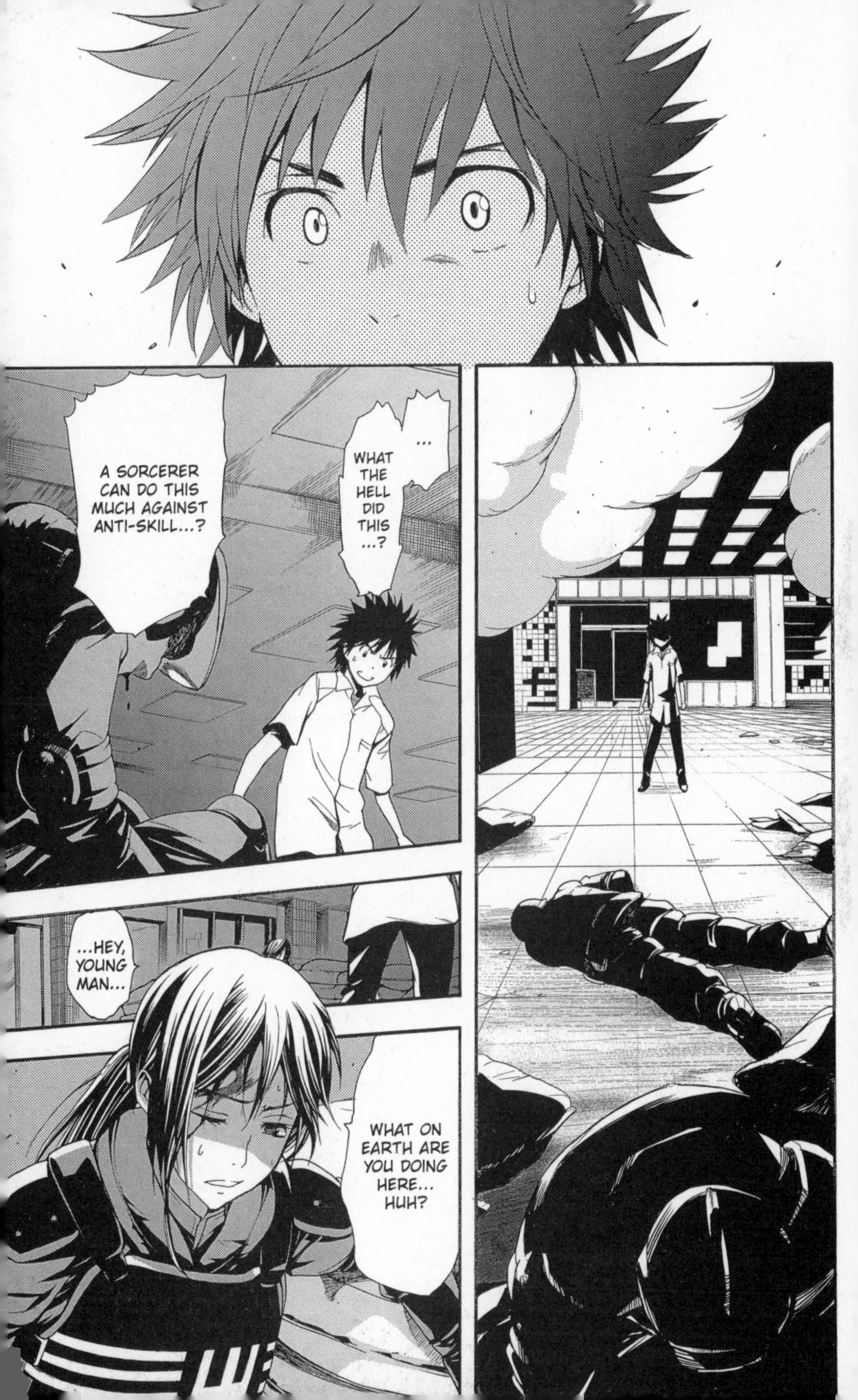
... WHAT THE HELL DID THIS ...?
A SORCERER CAN DO THIS MUCH AGAINST ANTI-SKILL...?
...HEY, YOUNG MAN...
WHAT ON EARTH ARE YOU DOING HERE... HUH?

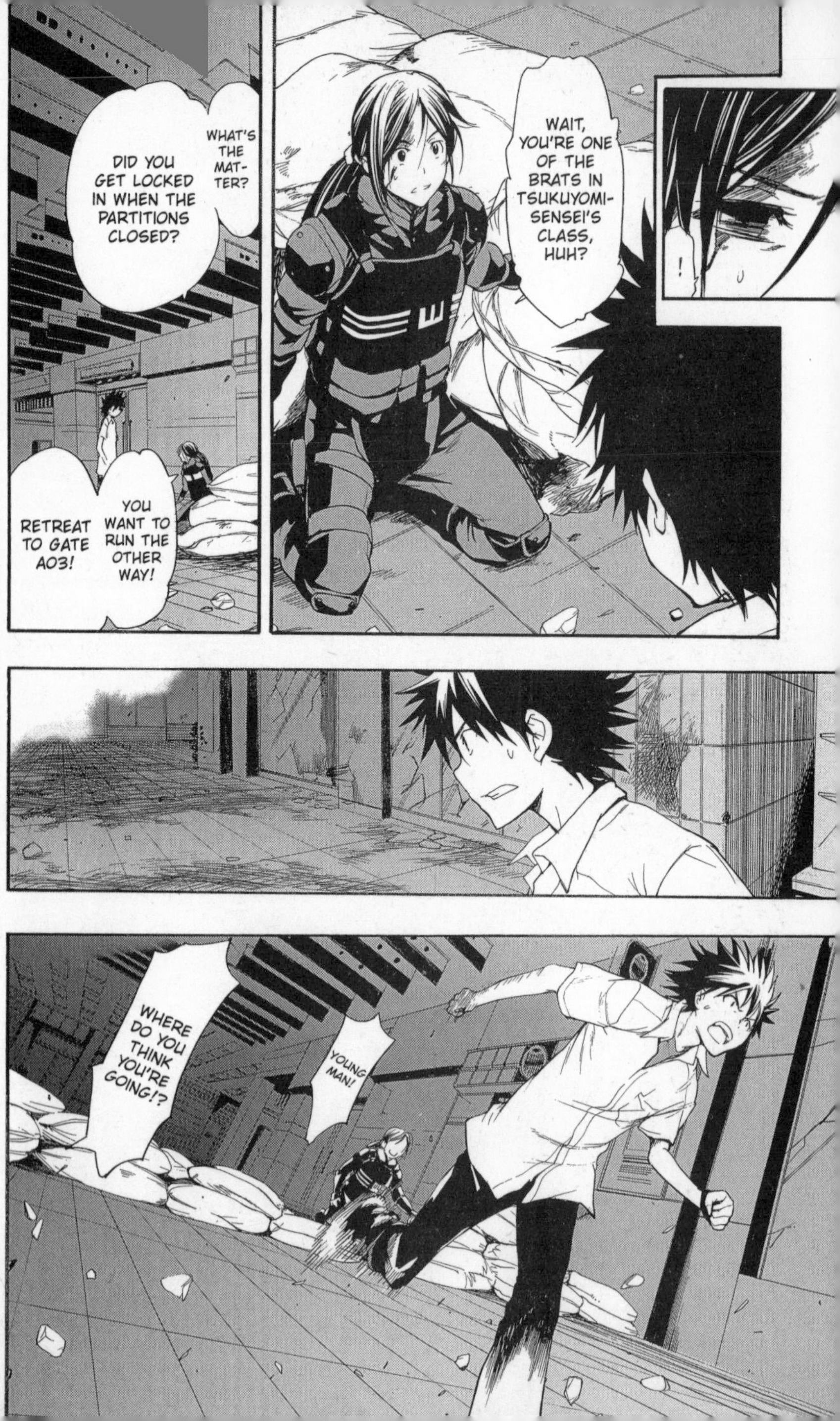
WAIT, YOU'RE ONE OF THE BRATS IN TSUKUYOMI-SENSEI'S CLASS, HUH?
WHAT'S THE MAT-TER?
DID YOU GET LOCKED IN WHEN THE PARTITIONS CLOSED?
YOU WANT TO RUN THE OTHER WAY!
RETREAT TO GATE A03!
YOUNG MAN!
WHERE DO YOU THINK YOU'RE GOING!?

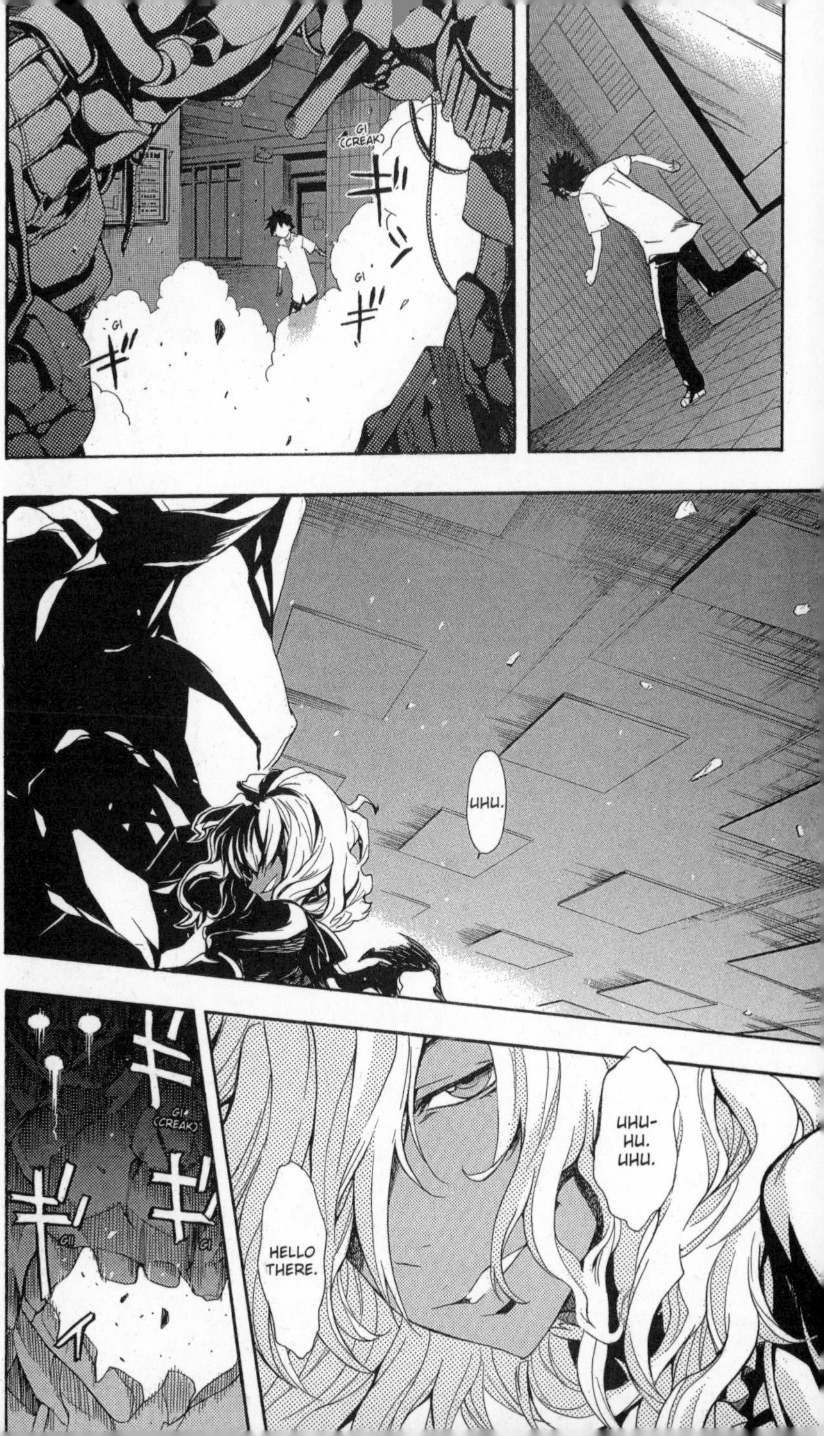
GI (CREAK)
GI
GI
UHU.
UHU-HU. UHU.
HELLO THERE.
GI (CREAK)
GI
GI

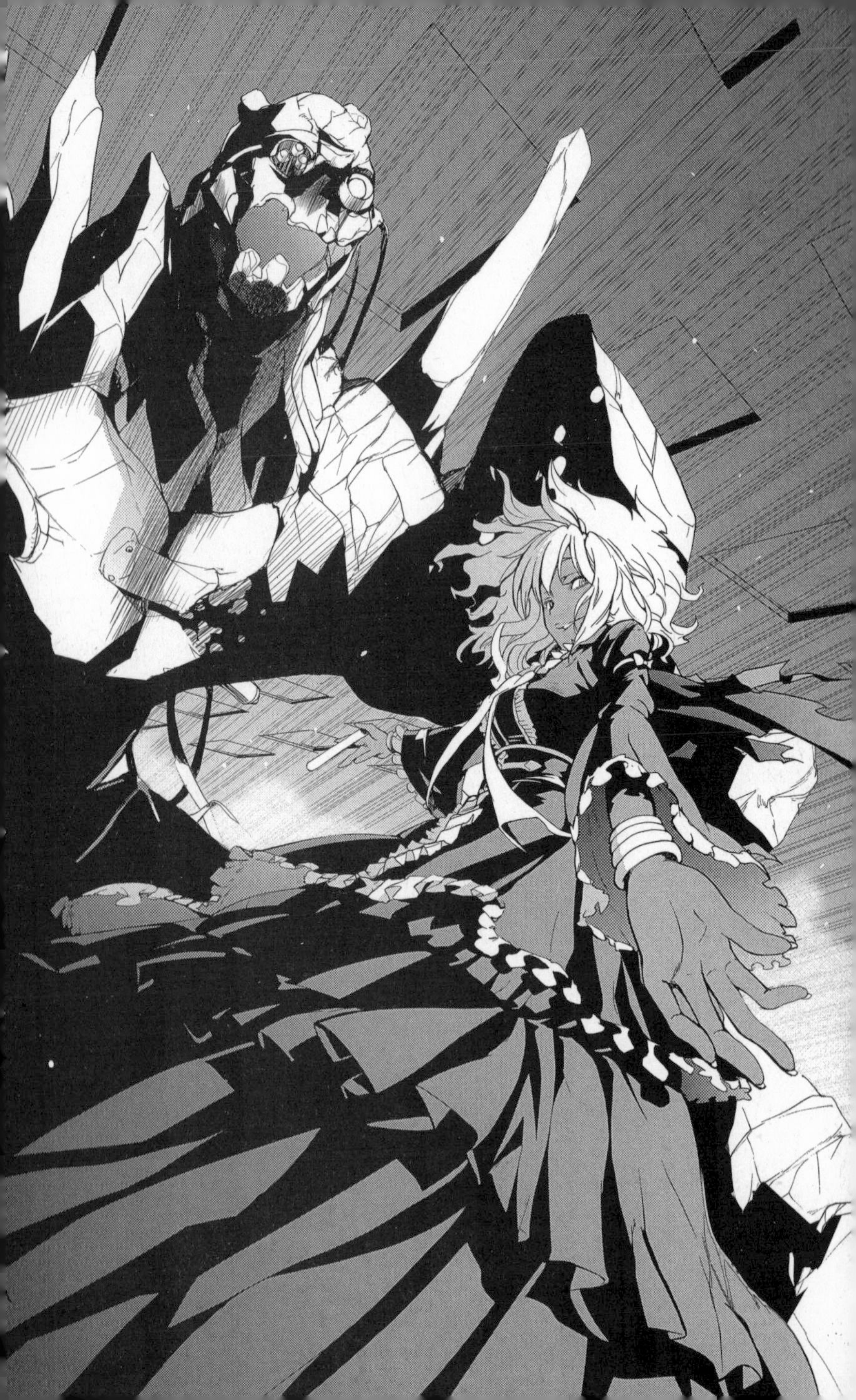

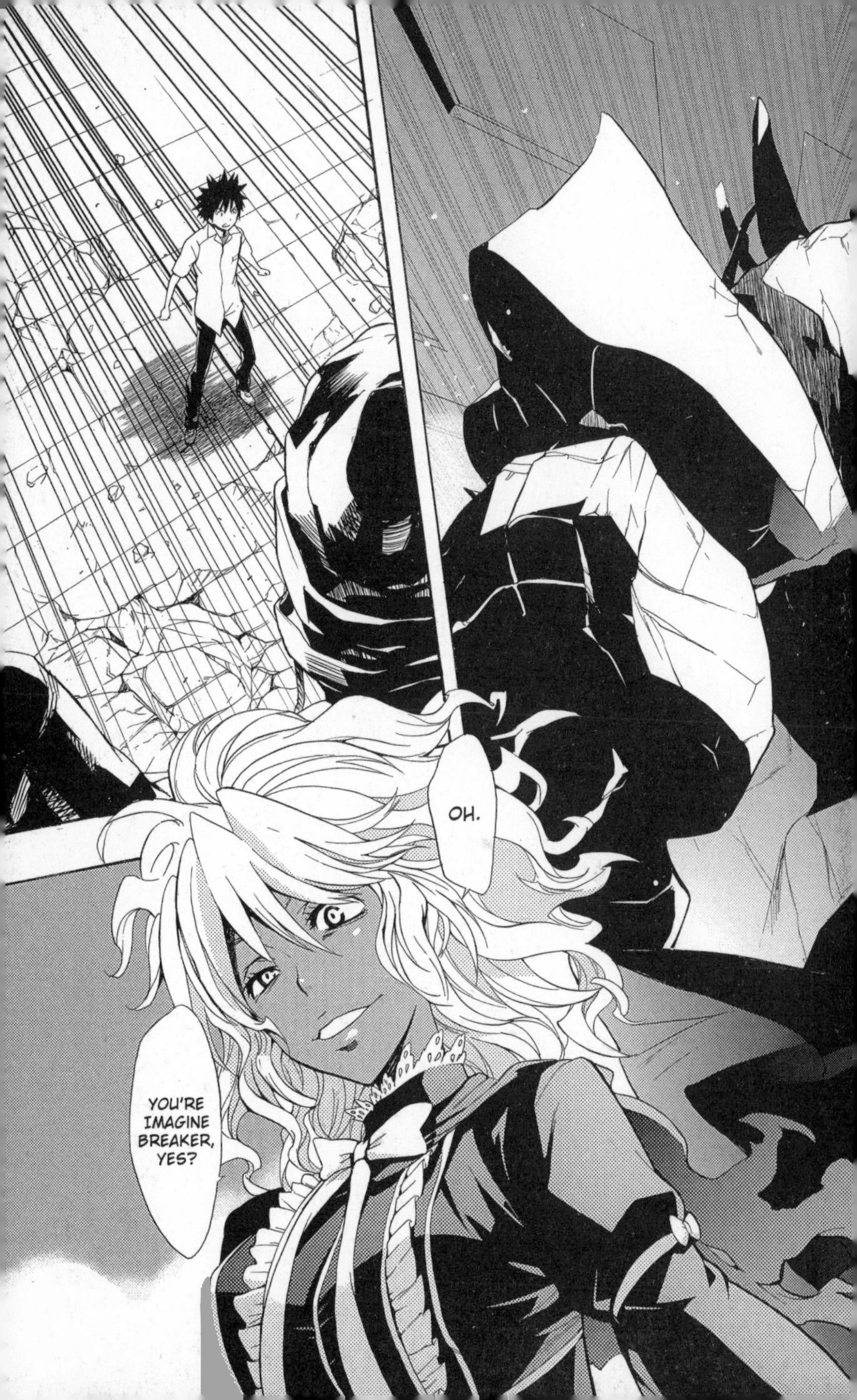
OH.
YOU'RE IMAGINE BREAKER, YES?

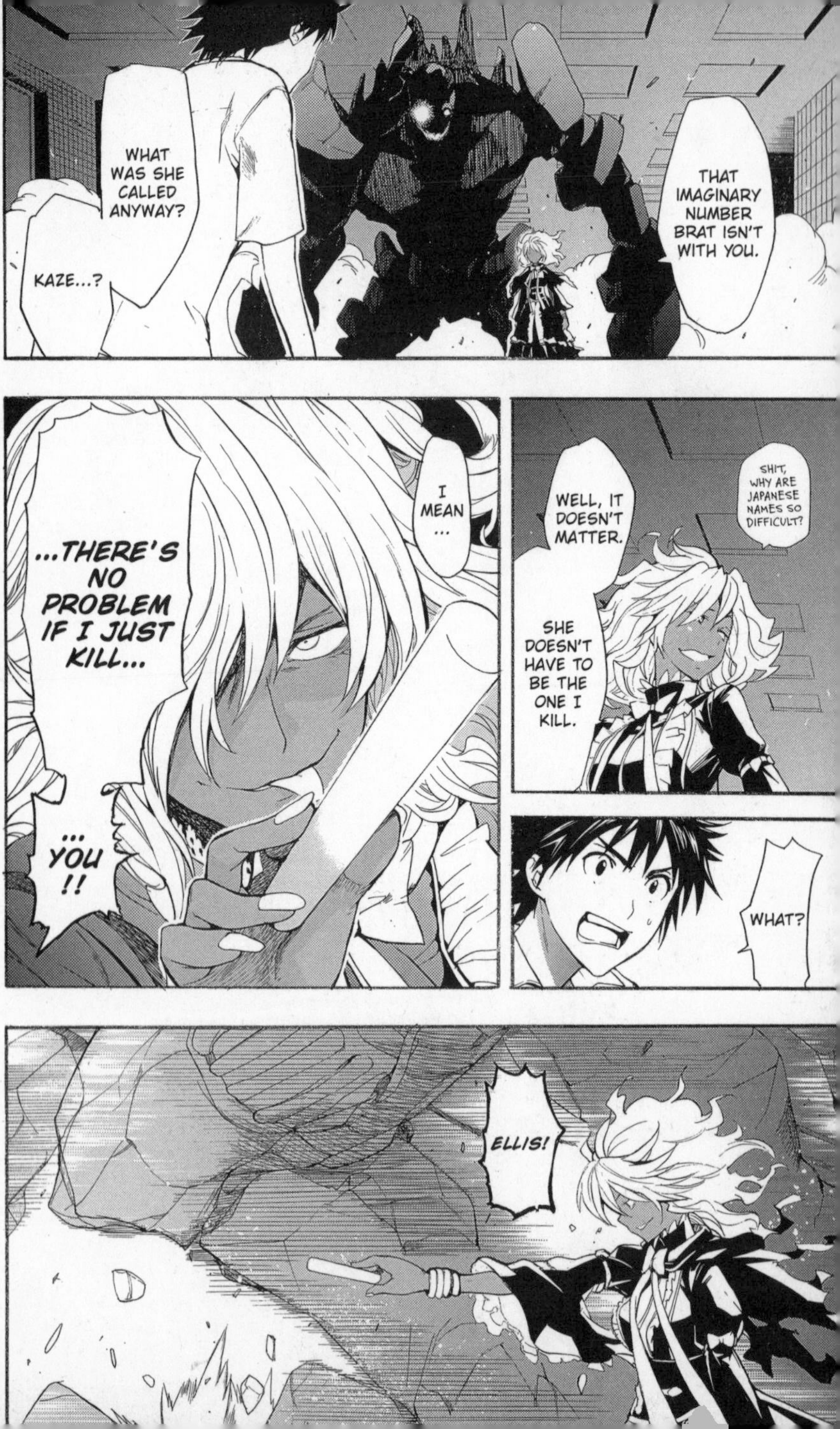
THAT IMAGINARY NUMBER BRAT ISN'T WITH YOU.
WHAT WAS SHE CALLED ANYWAY?
KAZE...?
SHIT, WHY ARE JAPANESE NAMES SO DIFFICULT?
WELL, IT DOESN'T MATTER.
SHE DOESN'T HAVE TO BE THE ONE I KILL.
WHAT?
I MEAN...
...THERE'S NO PROBLEM IF I JUST KILL...
...YOU!!
ELLIS!

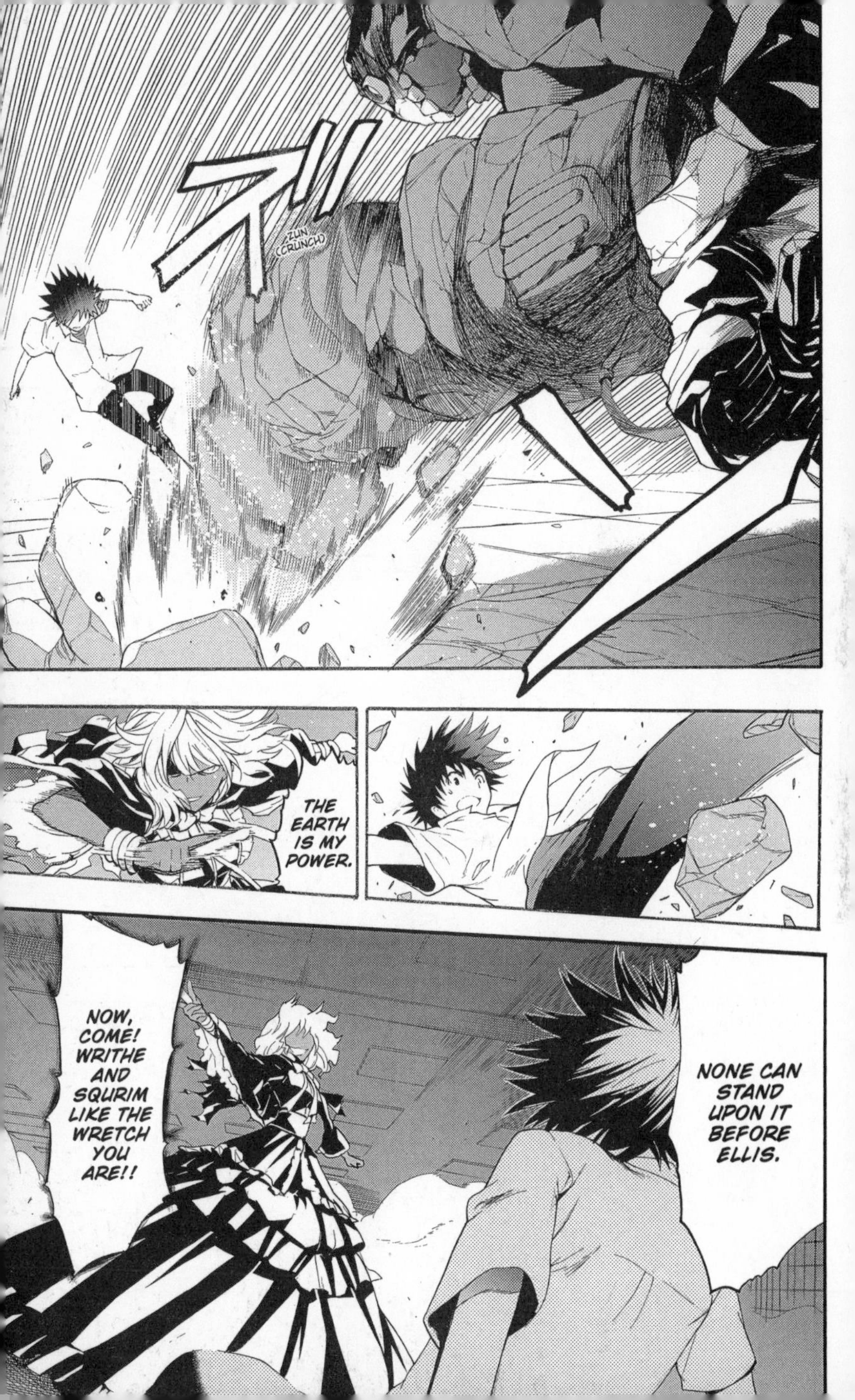
ZUN (CRUNCH)
THE EARTH IS MY POWER.
NONE CAN STAND UPON IT BEFORE ELLIS.
NOW, COME! WRITHE AND SQURIM LIKE THE WRETCH YOU ARE!!

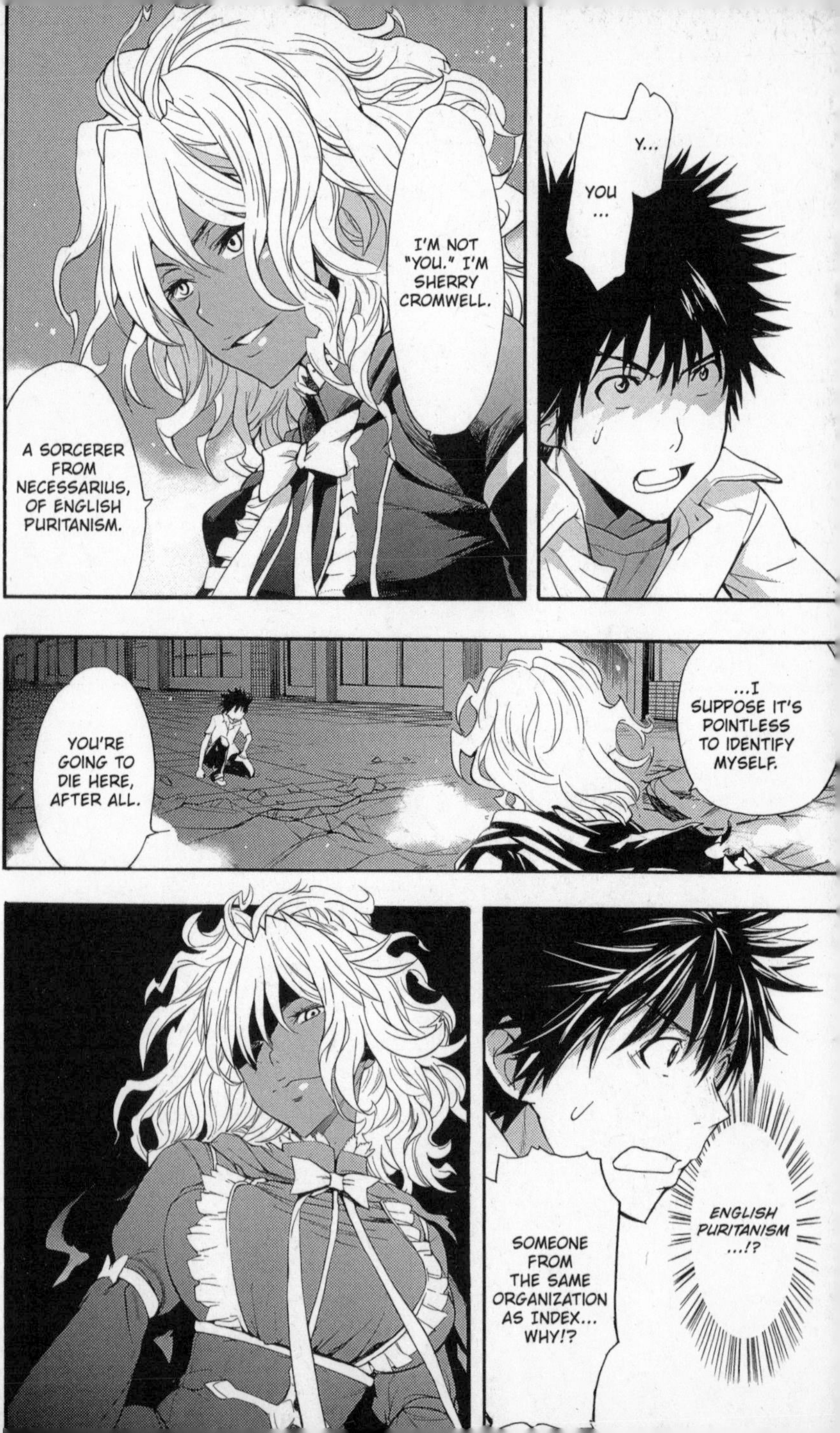
Y...
YOU ...
I'M NOT "YOU." I'M SHERRY CROMWELL.
A SORCERER FROM NECESSARIUS, OF ENGLISH PURITANISM.
...I SUPPOSE IT'S POINTLESS TO IDENTIFY MYSELF.
YOU'RE GOING TO DIE HERE, AFTER ALL.
ENGLISH PURITANISM ...!?
SOMEONE FROM THE SAME ORGANIZATION AS INDEX... WHY!?

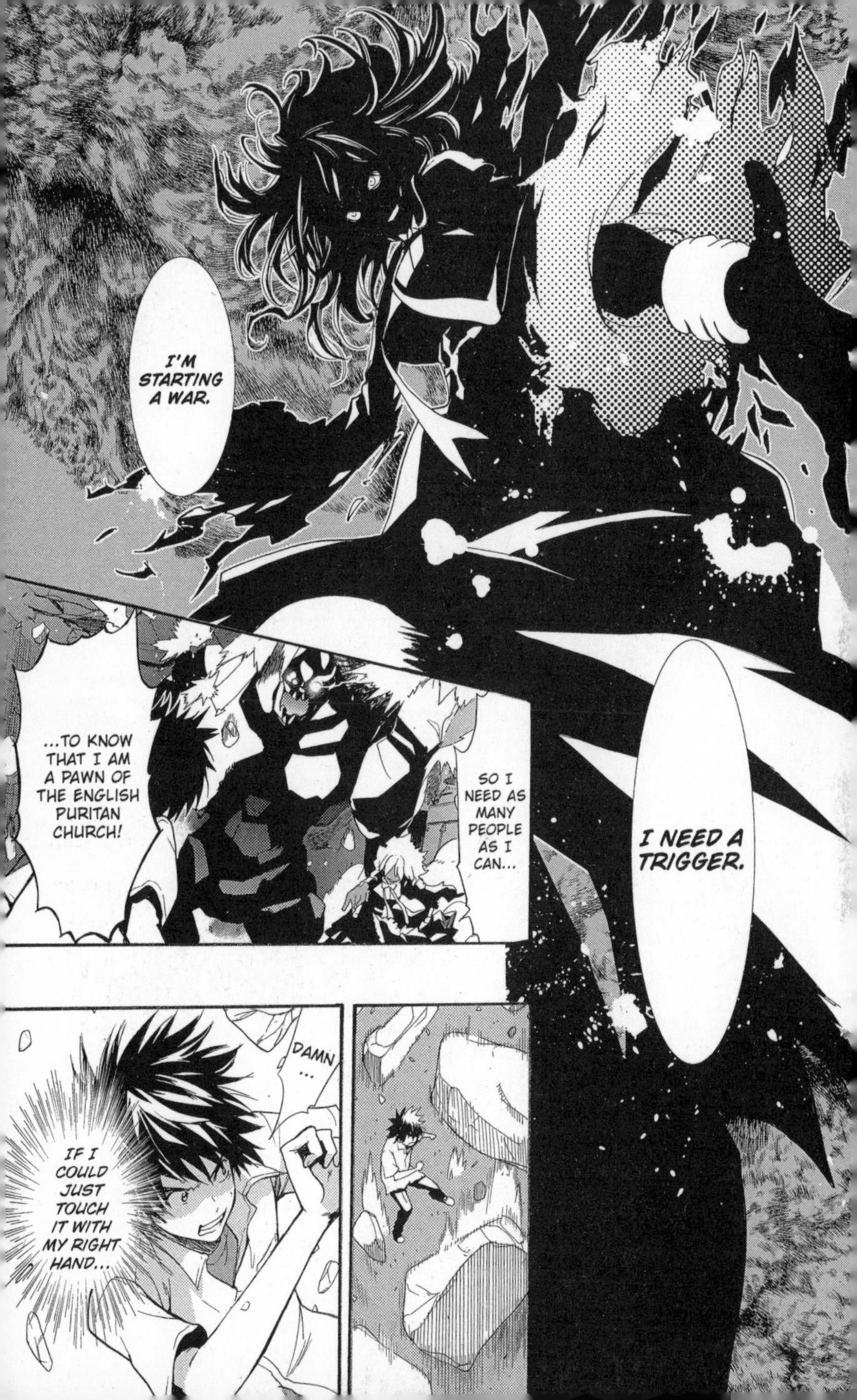
I'M STARTING A WAR.
I NEED A TRIGGER.
SO I NEED AS MANY PEOPLE AS I CAN...
...TO KNOW THAT I AM A PAWN OF THE ENGLISH PURITAN CHURCH!
DAMN...
IF I COULD JUST TOUCH IT WITH MY RIGHT HAND...

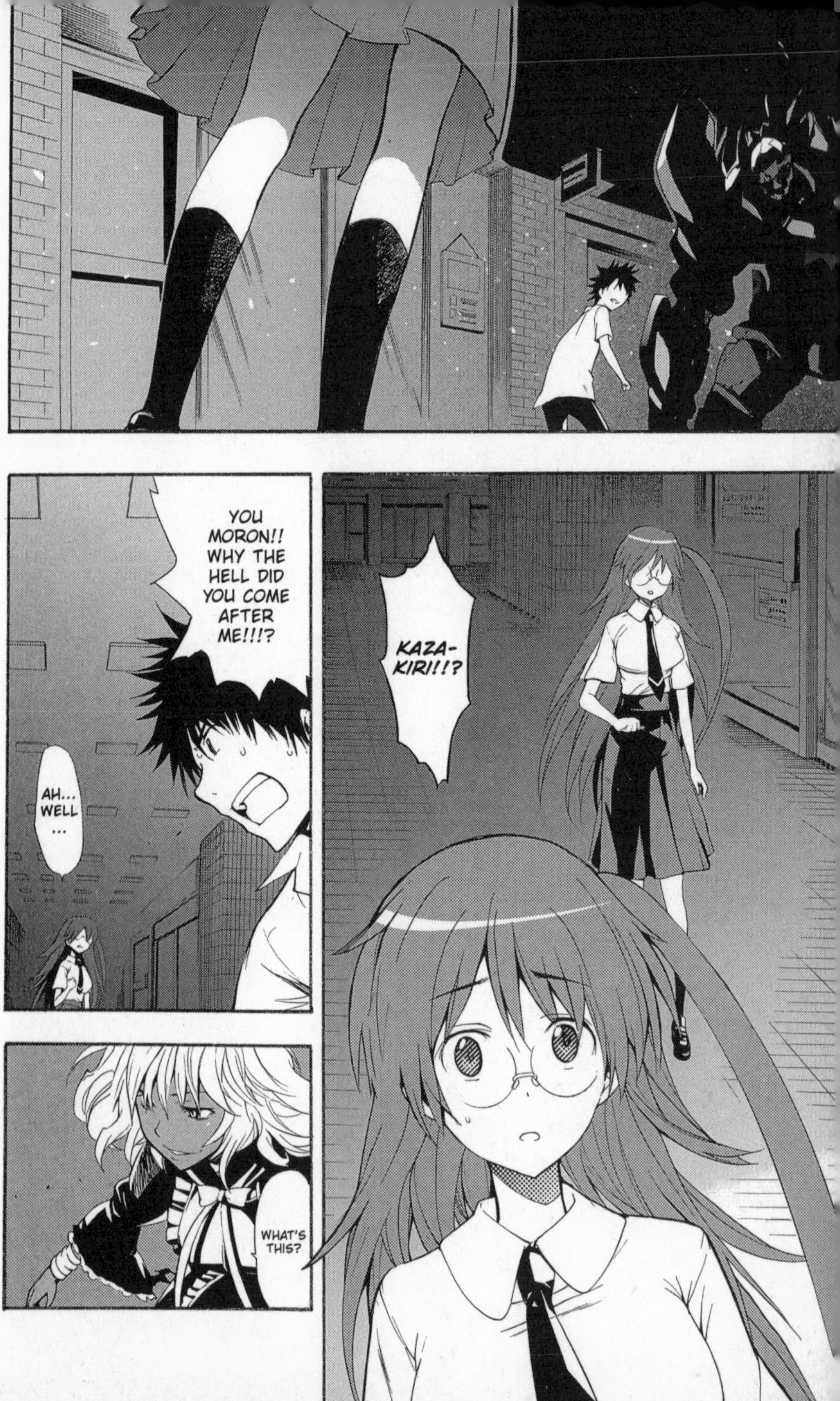
KAZA-KIRI!!?
YOU MORON!! WHY THE HELL DID YOU COME AFTER ME!!!?
AH... WELL ...
WHAT'S THIS?

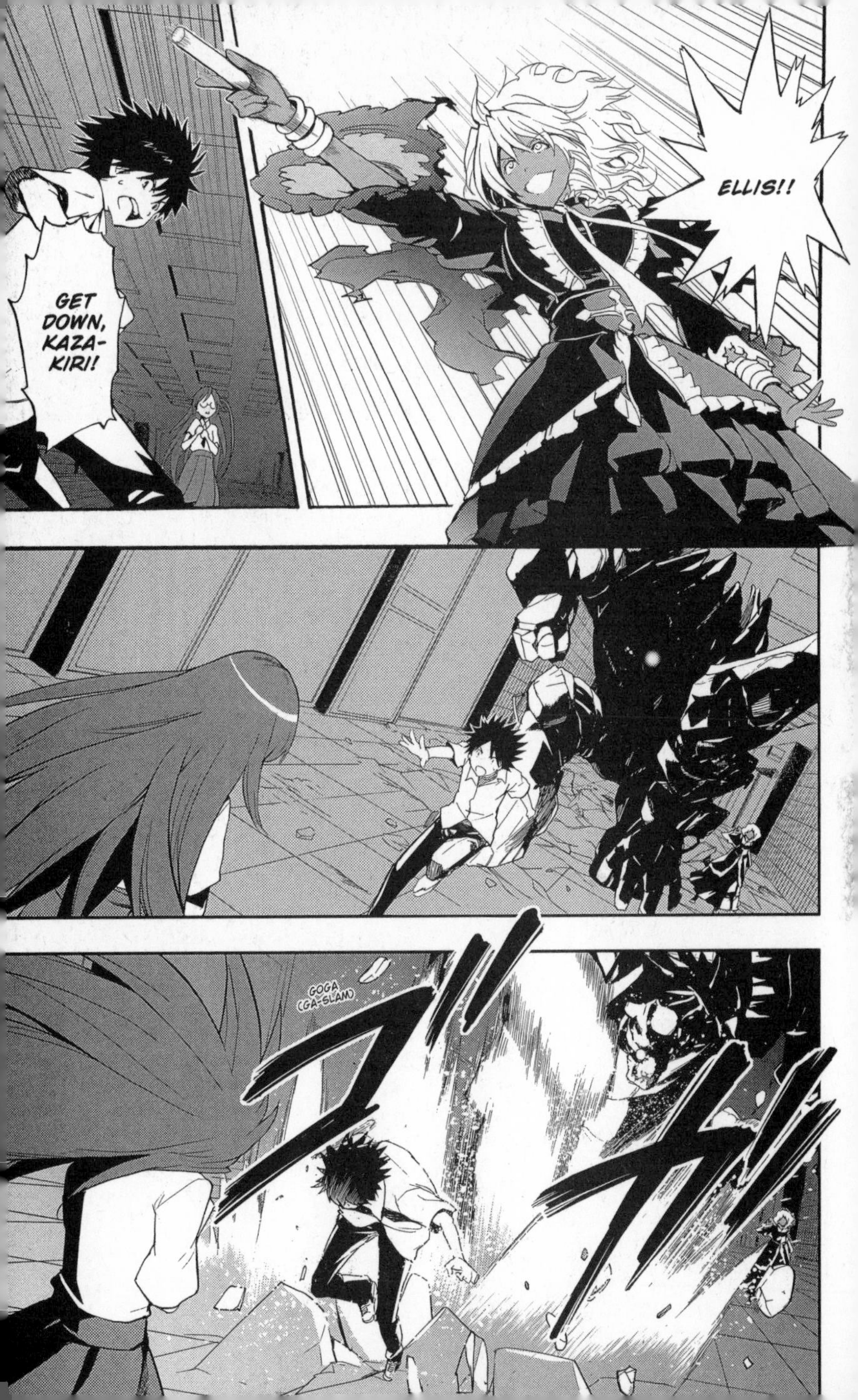
ELLIS!!
GET DOWN, KAZA-KIRI!
GOGA (GA-SLAM)

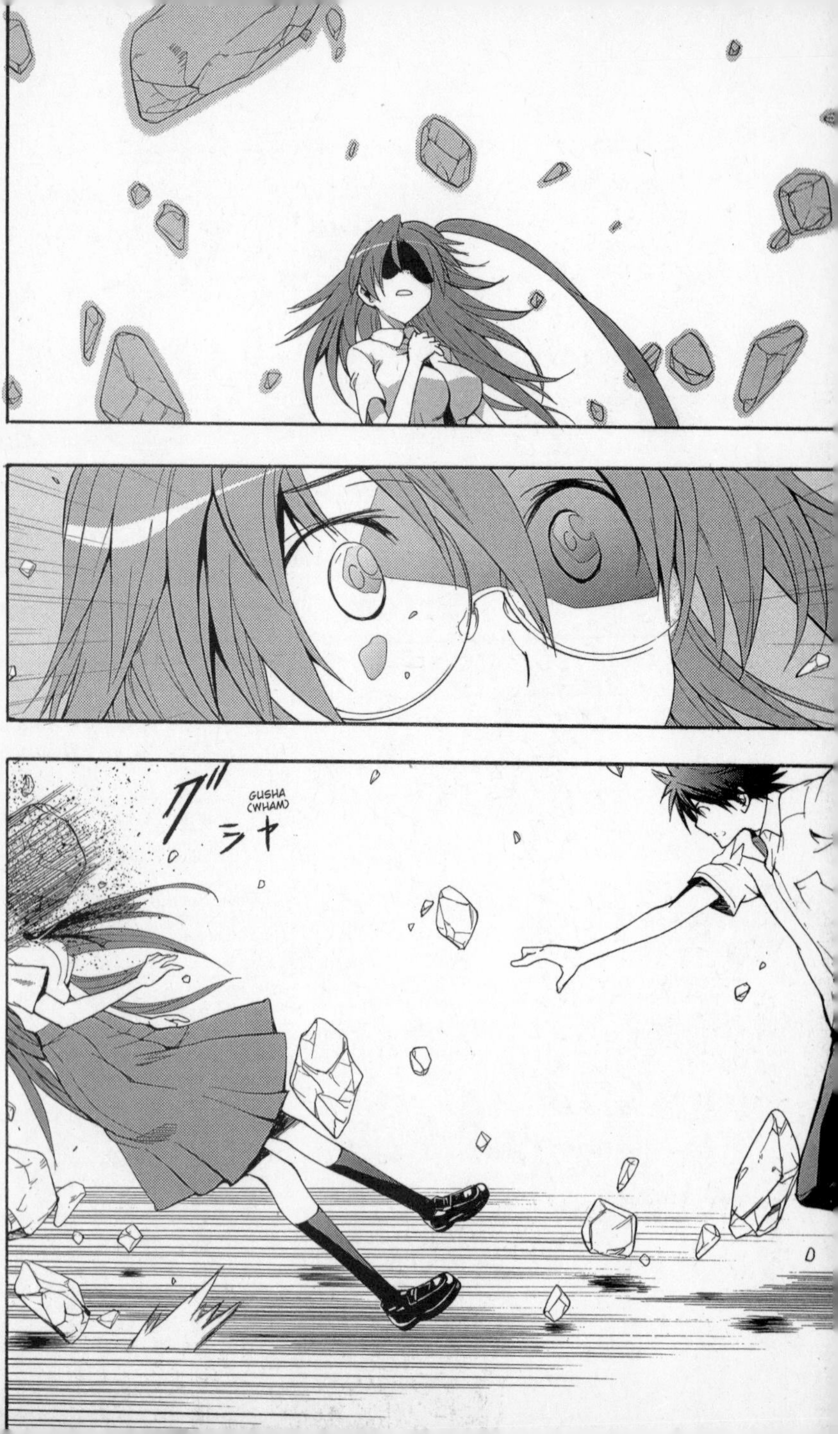

グシャ
GUSHA
(WHAM)

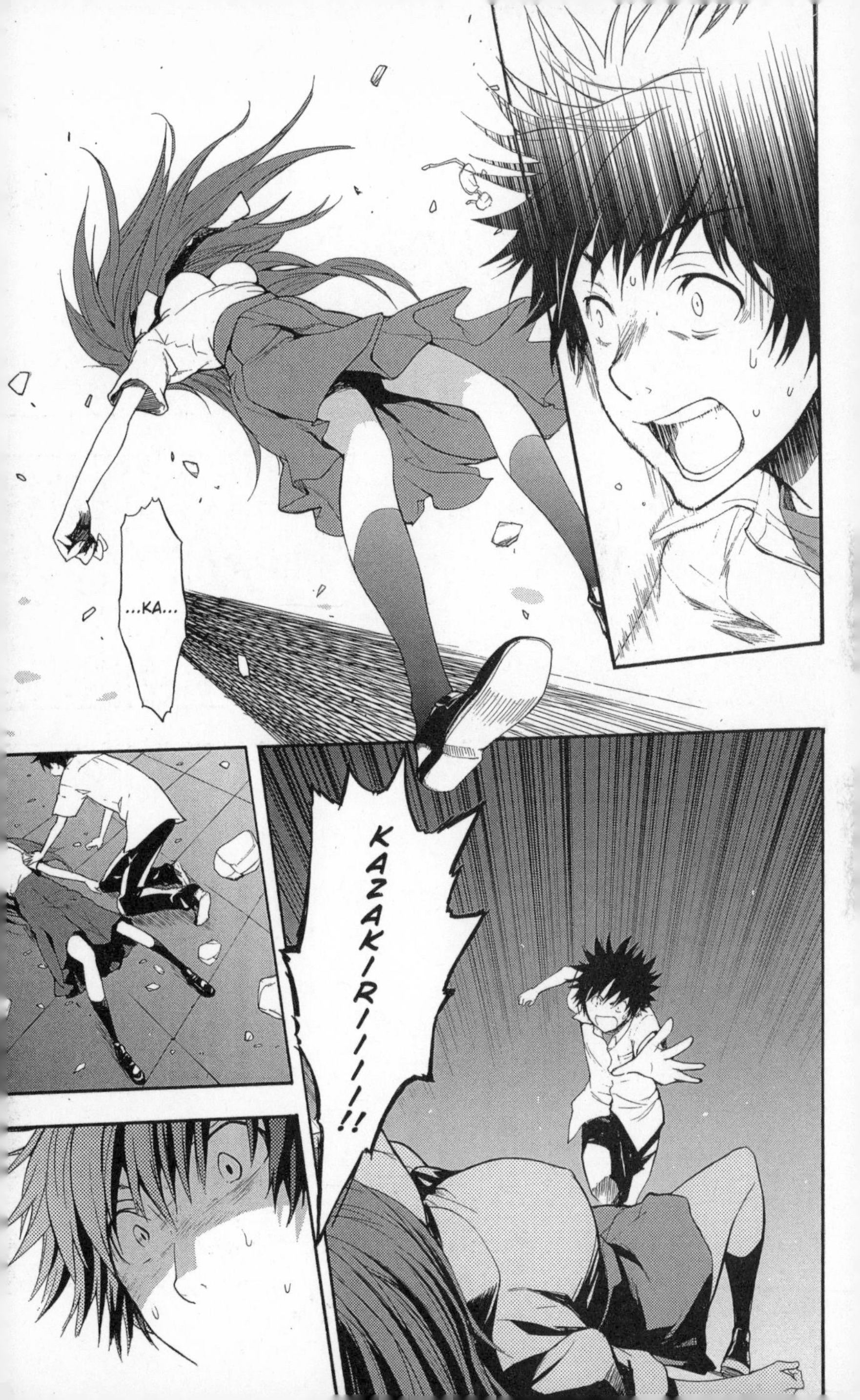
...KA...
KAZAKIRI-I-I-I-I-!!

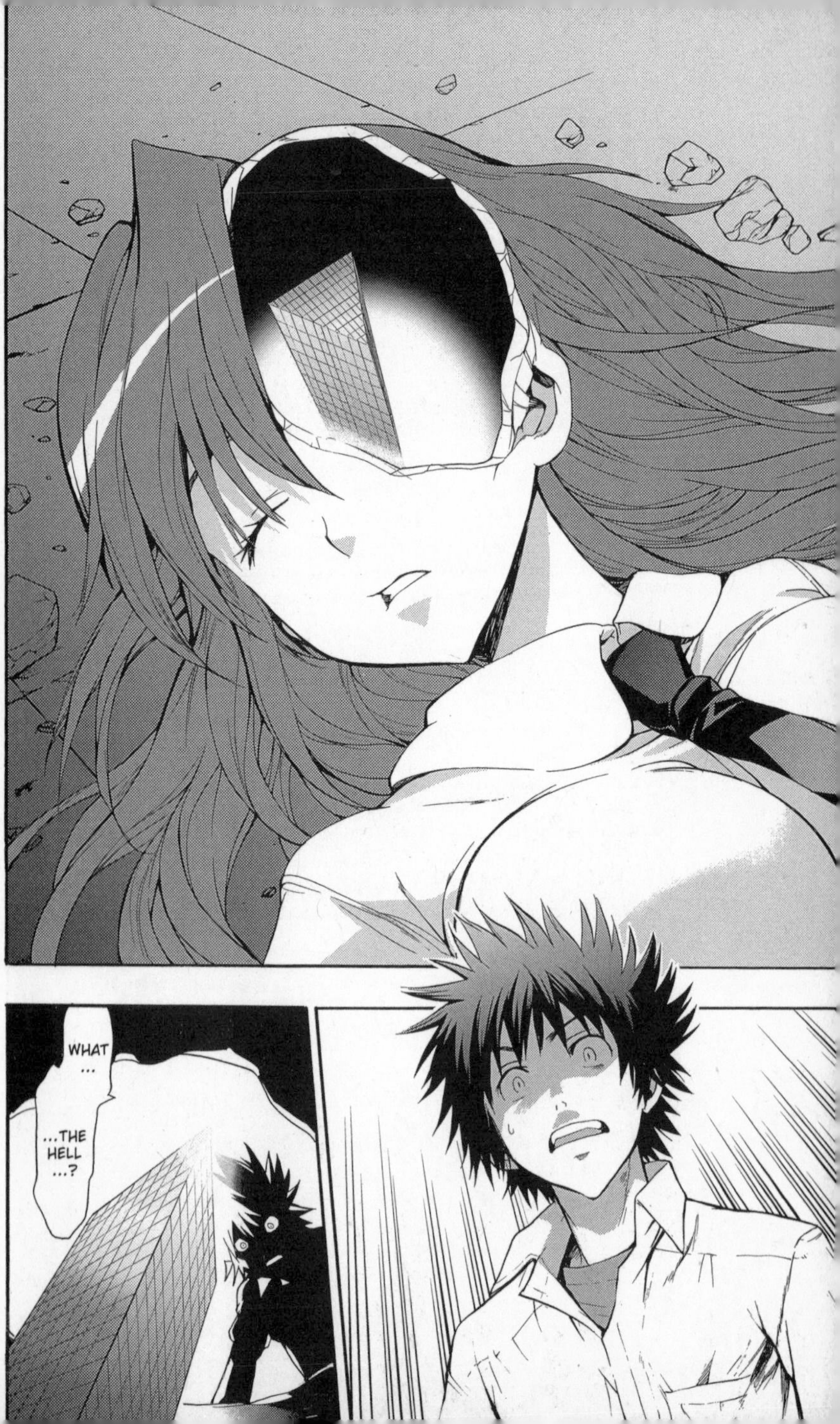
WHAT ... ...THE HELL ...?

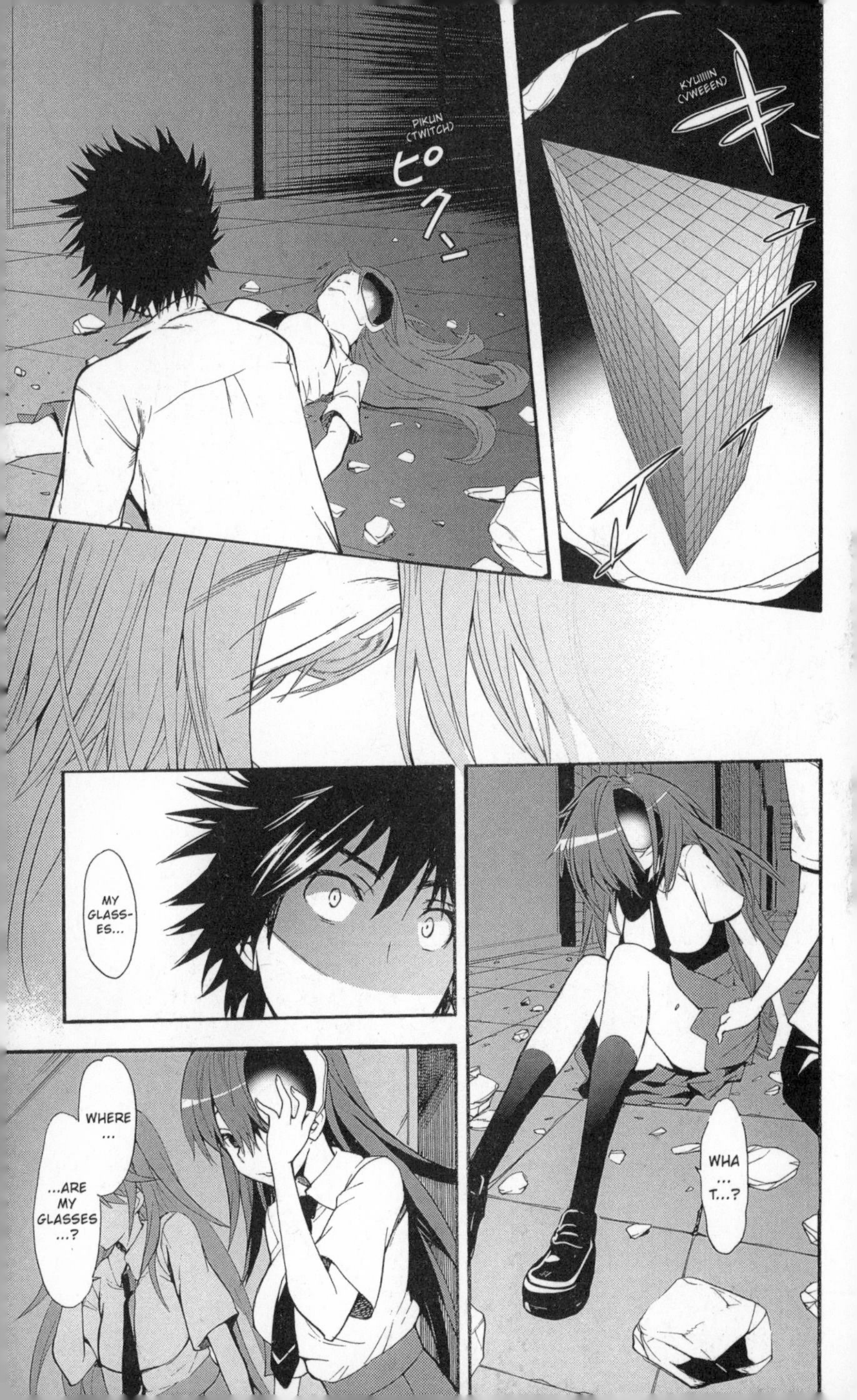
KYUIIIIN (VWEEEN)
PIKUN (TWITCH)
WHA... T...?
MY GLASSES...
WHERE ...
...ARE MY GLASSES ...?

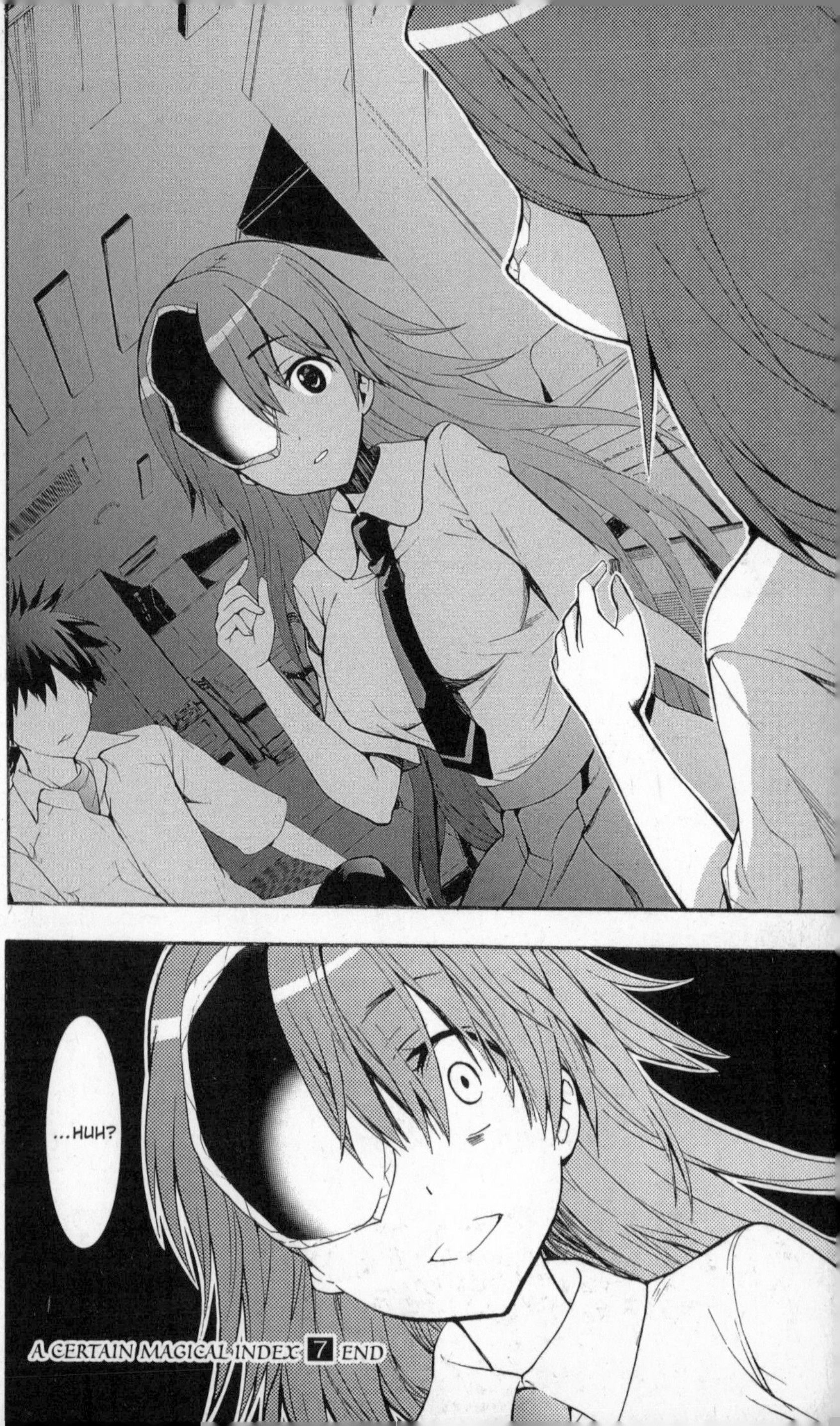
...HUH?
A CERTAIN MAGICAL INDEX 7 END

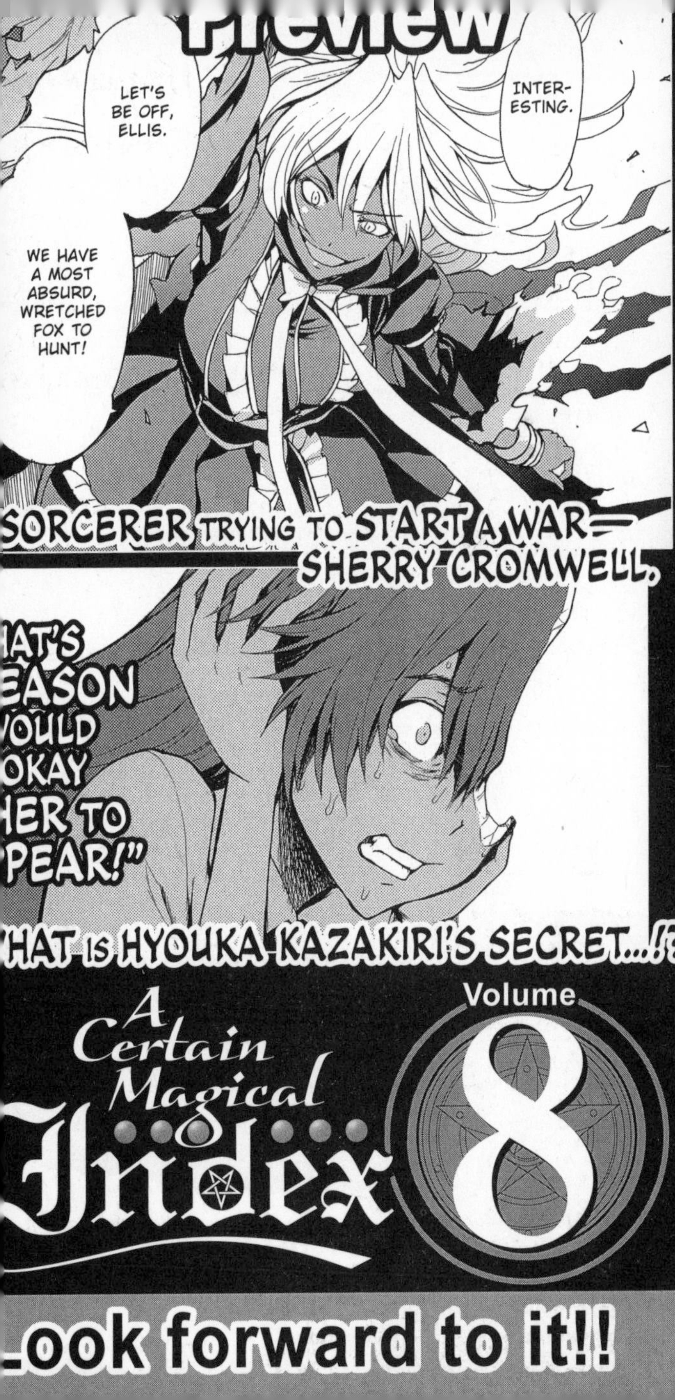
Preview
INTER-ESTING.
LET'S BE OFF, ELLIS.
WE HAVE A MOST ABSURD, WRETCHED FOX TO HUNT!
SORCERER TRYING TO START A WAR— SHERRY CROMWELL.
HAT'S EASON OULD OKAY HER TO PEAR!"
HAT IS HYOUKA KAZAKIRI'S SECRET...!?
A Certain Magical Index
Volume 8
ook forward to it!!

A CERTAIN MAGICAL INDEX ❼

KAZUMA KAMACHI
KIYOTAKA HAIMURA
CHUYA KOGINO

Translation: Andrew Prowse

Lettering: Brndn Blakeslee

This book is a work of fiction. Names, characters, places, and incidents are the product of the author's imagination or are used fictitiously. Any resemblance to actual events, locales, or persons, living or dead, is coincidental.

TOARU MAJYUTSU NO INDEX Vol. 7
© 2010 Kazuma Kamachi
© 2010 Chuya Kogino / SQUARE ENIX. CO. LTD.
Licensed by KADOKAWA CORPORATION ASCII MEDIA WORKS
First published in Japan in 2010 by SQUARE ENIX CO., LTD.
English translation rights arranged with SQUARE ENIX CO., LTD.
and Yen Press, LLC through Tuttle-Mori Agency, Inc.

English translation © 2016 by SQUARE ENIX CO., LTD.

Yen Press
1290 Avenue of the Americas
New York, NY 10104

Visit us at yenpress.com
facebook.com/yenpress
twitter.com/yenpress
yenpress.tumblr.com
instagram.com/yenpress

First Yen Press Edition: October 2016

Yen Press is an imprint of Yen Press, LLC.
The Yen Press name and logo are trademarks of Yen Press, LLC.

The publisher is not responsible for websites (or their content) that are not owned by the publisher.

Library of Congress Control Number: 2015373809

ISBN: 978-0-316-34601-6

10 9 8 7 6 5 4 3 2 1

BVG

Printed in the United States o